Y0-AFJ-956

Sociological research

Philosophy and methods

The Dorsey Series in Sociology

Editor ROBIN M. WILLIAMS, JR. *Cornell University*

Sociological research

Philosophy and methods

HENRY L. MANHEIM, Ph.D.
Professor of Sociology
Arizona State University

with a chapter by

Bradley A. Simon
City Librarian, Pomona Public Library
California

1977

THE DORSEY PRESS Homewood, Illinois 60430
Irwin-Dorsey Limited Georgetown, Ontario L7G 4B3

The selection from E. E. Cummings on page 322 is reprinted with permission from George J. Firmage, literary agent for E. E. Cummings.

First Printing, February 1977

ISBN 0-256-01943-8
Library of Congress Catalog Card No. 76-47739

Printed in the United States of America

For my sons and daughter,
Mike, Tom, and Ratri—
who make it all worthwhile

Preface

This book is designed to present a unique combination of the philosophical assumptions underlying any research activity and the practical methods of doing research in the social sciences.

As is true of the frame of reference of any activity, the philosophical assumptions that are fundamental to research serve as criteria for decision-making and guides for the practical steps that must be taken in doing research. To do first-rate research it is not sufficient to be skilled in the many techniques and methods of forming hypotheses, designing research, and collecting and manipulating the resulting data. Also needed are sound, consistent criteria for choosing among these alternatives and using them effectively. These criteria are supplied by the frame of reference, here referred to as the philosophy of research.

Because the most important—indeed essential—parts of the philosophy of research in today's world come from science, a thorough examination of science, especially the philosophy of science, becomes mandatory. Surprisingly, there exists a widespread lack of real understanding and appreciation of the requirements, restrictions, limitations, potentialities, and general attributes which characterize a field *merely* because that field is a science.

The philosophy of research must also take into account the closely related matter of the relationship between theory and research. The nature of their relationship forms an essential part of the philosophy of research, and is important in the actual doing of research. The lack of recognition of the closeness of this relationship has been an impediment in the training of sociologists in the United States.[1] Similarly, the place of values,

[1] Sibley, 1963, chap. 2.

policymaking, applications of research findings, and social and political activism must be dealt with in order for research to make maximum contributions.

Understanding of the above points is fundamental to engaging in research activity of real significance. For this reason, the first portion of this book is devoted to the philosophy of research, which includes an examination of the place of sociology in the larger scientific framework, the nature of science and scientific research, and the place of values and policymaking.

The remaining part of the book consists of a thorough investigation of the methods of doing sociological research: the formulation of a research problem, research design, data collection, data processing, data analysis, and report writing and dissemination of results. The objective is for the student to acquire a comprehensive overview of all research techniques and procedures, and sufficient competence in some so that he or she could successfully undertake a limited independent project. Furthermore, the attentive student will, I hope, acquire a greater familiarity with the use of the scientific approach to problem solving.

However, it is important to understand that this does not purport to be a complete, detailed presentation of all current research techniques in sociology. Additional reading and training will be needed before the student can undertake significant independent research. But this second portion of the book (and, to a lesser extent, the first portion) is planned to serve as a guide, a key, or a map which will point the way to other sources of information that go into far more detail than is possible or necessary here. Some techniques or procedures will be covered only briefly here—perhaps because they are not suited for beginning researchers, or because they are relatively uncommon, or because they are relatively unimportant—but the attempt has been made to provide references for more detailed information in every case. Especially in the sections on designing research and data collection, the footnotes contain many references which will enable the student to pursue any particular interest as far as it will be useful for him or her.

Thus it is seen that this book is designed for the advanced undergraduate or beginning graduate student who has not had previous training in research methods, with the possible exception of statistics. A course in statistics is not a prerequisite for this book, although it is assumed that sociology majors will have such a course as part of their undergraduate training.

I have used the materials contained in this work regularly in teaching an upper division one-semester course required of all sociology majors. I believe that the book could also be used in a two-semester course, in which the first semester would go beyond the philosophy of research and include a more detailed examination of current sociological theory and construction of axiomatic theories, while the second semester could provide a more intensive study of specific research techniques, including statistics.

The following points may assist the reader in using the book more effectively. The organization of this book is planned in part to assist the reader in becoming a skilled "consumer" of research. This is because most undergraduates while still in college, and subsequently as jobholders with a Bachelor's degree in sociology, are more likely to find themselves reading, evaluating, and reacting to research done by others than they are to be engaged in doing independent research. Those who continue into graduate training will usually study research methods at a more advanced level, and then the practical details and techniques of being a "doer" of independent research become more crucial.

The methods of research are discussed here from a problem-solving point of view, with particular attention to the many practical decisions that must be made and the sequence of making them in the design and execution of research. The specific methods of data collection are discussed in the framework provided by a new classification of types of sociological data. At the end of each chapter in Part II, exercises are provided which are designed to encourage creative thinking on the part of the student in applying the subject matter to practical research topics. These should provide valuable experience in doing research—especially useful when an entire research project cannot be carried out as part of the class activities.

Definitions have been used consistently throughout the book so there should be no misunderstanding, even though they are not always the customary definitions. In general, I have used *Dictionary of Modern Sociology* as a standard for terms which I have not defined.[2] Footnotes are numbered sequentially within each chapter. Footnote references to items in the bibliography are in abbreviated form, consisting only of the author's name and the year of publication (followed by a letter if needed to distin-

[2] Hoult, 1969.

guish among two or more items). Full publication information appears in the bibliography. Rather extensive use has been made of footnotes even though some readers may regard them as annoying interferences with the flow of the text. Footnotes are especially important here because they will refer the reader with an inquiring mind to sources of further information, details, discussions, and elaboration about the various topics, in addition to the usual function of identifying sources. Whenever I have used the masculine pronouns "he," "his," or "him," or other similar constructions, they should be understood to refer to both males and females. I fully agree with the current efforts to eliminate sexual discrimination in writing (as well as other areas) but I also deplore the awkwardness of using "he/she," "his or her," and so on.

Throughout, an attempt has been made to prevent this textbook from becoming a book on "American" or "Western" sociological research methods—whatever those terms may mean. Undoubtedly as a result of my rewarding two years of affiliation with sociologists—students, teachers, and researchers—as a Senior Fulbright Lecturer in India, I have been led to even greater efforts to eliminate any statement or point of view that would seem narrow or provincial to non-Western eyes. Consequently, all that is said (unless explicitly noted to the contrary) is intended to apply to sociology in any society, and is aimed at students of sociology wherever they may be. Among other things, the references include some older works which may be more widely available than recent ones, the discussion of techniques and tools has avoided undue emphasis upon procedures which may be expensive or require hard-to-get materials, and I hope that the examples given will not appear culture-bound.

January 1977 HENRY L. MANHEIM

Acknowledgments

I want to acknowledge the many debts, both academic and personal, which I recognize in the writing of this book. It was Harvey J. Locke who introduced me to sociological research methods and guided me throughout my doctoral work at the University of Southern California; it is hard to find words adequate to express my appreciation to him. My work has benefited from the advice and suggestions of Thomas Ford Hoult, Frederick B. Lindstrom, John W. Hudson, and Marilyn L. Bidnick, in the Sociology Department at Arizona State University. Similarly, James D. Carney and Robert L. Rein'l of the Philosophy Department, and G. C. Helmstadter of the College of Education, rendered very helpful assistance. I owe an especial debt of gratitude to Morris J. Starsky, also then of the Philosophy Department, who stimulated my interest in symbolic logic and steered me to many important sources of information.

I appreciate the prompt and helpful responses to my requests for information from Richard C. Rockwell, Carol H. Weiss, and Marcello Truzzi. Special thanks for the ingenious and challenging exercises in Part II are extended to Ronald D. Loague, sociology doctoral candidate at A.S.U. Thanks are also due to former student assistant, Claudia Glenn, former graduate assistant, Reba Touw, and former student, Philip S. Koch. Norma Fisher, late secretary of the Sociology Department, was a gold mine of information, a worker of administrative magic, and a valued friend. Patti-Sue Stanton made many valued suggestions, and provided aid in many other ways.

In the summer of 1963 I was a participant in the Social Science Research Council Institute on Mathematical Models of Social Structure. James M. Beshers, the director, and the 11 other participants, made an enormous contribution to my intellectual growth, and I suspect that the seeds of this book were planted that summer. I hope they find their ideas recognizable and not unduly distorted, and it pleases me to be able publicly to express my appreciation to them and to the SSRC. Robin M. Williams, Jr., consulting editor, provided assistance on all fronts, and made many valued suggestions on both substantive issues and the organization and style. It is difficult to find a page which isn't improved because of his comments. Thanks are due too, to the reviewers, among whom are Marshall J. Graney and Stephen Bahr, who read the entire manuscript.

There are many other teachers, colleagues, and students (all of whom have been, in reality, my teachers), who have contributed in so many ways and I express my thanks to them.

To my wife, Bhavani Banerjee Manheim, I owe the deepest debt of all—for her emotional support, her unfailing encouragement, her willing acceptance of considerable interference with her own professional anthropological work, and for her indispensable contributions toward providing the environment in which I could complete this work.

H.L.M.

Contents

PART I

SCIENCE AND THE PHILOSOPHY OF RESEARCH

Objectives. The objectives of Part I are to assist the reader in becoming better able to understand, evaluate, interpret, and appreciate sociological research. Therefore the first five chapters are intended to facilitate an understanding of the assumptions underlying research, of the relationships between research and theory, and of the theoretical and philosophical aspects of research. They also seek to extend recognition and acceptance of the idea that research can be done on people and their interrelationships. The reader should strive to keep these objectives in mind when reading the following pages.

Chapter 1

Science and research: Initial considerations

RESEARCH

Research is an absorbing, exciting, enjoyable, and, hopefully, enormously productive activity. Many men and women have devoted the greatest parts of their lives to this kind of extremely rewarding pursuit, and have made great contributions to the knowledge, welfare, and progress of the human race. The names of Einstein, Curie, Darwin, Pasteur, and Newton are outstanding. Countless others, perhaps less famous, have just as devotedly made their contributions to mankind. Without research, our world would be vastly different from the one we know. Yet there are many misconceptions regarding research, particularly what its relationships are with other forms of activity. For example, much is heard about research "versus" theory, especially in the social sciences; many things are labelled research which, in fact, are not research; research on certain kinds of subject matter is said to be impossible, and so on. These and many other misconceptions and negative views about research will be examined in the pages which follow; more important, the positive characteristics of research will be studied in detail.

To understand what research is and how it is done, we must gain an understanding of the relationship between research and other intellectual activities. Just as one cannot fully understand and appreciate the meaning and significance of a bit of observed behavior without a knowledge of the norms and values of the society in which the behavior takes place, so must the sociologist engaged in research have an understanding of the philosophical assumptions upon which research is based.

The professional sociologist certainly deals with the products of research constantly in the course of his career, and most sociologists engage in some form of research activity themselves. The doing of research is the most exciting and challenging part of sociology—it is here that the frontiers of knowledge are pushed back, it is here that new discoveries are made, it is here that the knowledge is acquired by means of which we make predictions.

Research is defined as *the careful, diligent, and exhaustive investigation of a specific subject matter, having as its aim the advancement of mankind's knowledge*. Thus it includes a wide variety of activities—the physical scientist in his laboratory, the artist studying in the museum, the archeologist digging in the ruins, the sociologist observing patterns of marital interaction, management teams competing through computerized business "games," the physician devising new surgical procedures, the historian or litterateur searching in the library, and the philosopher meditating in his study, to name a few. According to this definition, it is doubtful whether the ordinary undergraduate term paper is properly referred to as a research paper, except insofar as it provides *training* in doing research. Similarly, an activity undertaken solely for the purpose of personal learning, or growth, or enlightenment, is not research, nor is any casual or perfunctory investigation, regardless of how rewarding and beneficial it may be. But one thing which is definitely implied in this definition, and which is, in fact, a basic assumption of any research, is that knowledge is desirable and is preferable to ignorance.

There are several sub-types of research among which it is important to distinguish. In the first place there is the research associated with a specific class of subject matter or academic discipline—astronomical research, biological research, sociological research, and so on. Our main interest here is, of course, the last named.

A more crucial distinction is that between scientific and nonscientific research. Scientific research is research that utilizes the scientific method, while nonscientific research denotes all other research. In the modern world, when research is spoken of in connection with sociology and related fields, almost invariably scientific research is what is meant. Indeed, this book will be concerned only with scientific research. The alert reader will raise an important question here: We have defined research as a certain kind of activity aimed at *advancing knowledge.* Since it is reasonable to assume that our aim is, ultimately, to advance knowledge, why are we limiting ourselves to only one kind of research, namely, scientific research? Why are we not concerned with *all* means of contributing to the advancement of knowledge? Why are we categorically eliminating nonscientific research? The nature of the scientific methods, and the reasons for this seeming limitation will be made clear, in some detail, in the pages which follow. The sociologist must answer this question to his own satisfaction. The answer to this query and to many similar questions to be considered later will have a vital bearing upon the many practical decisions which much be made in the course of any research activity. These decisions can only be made, ultimately, by reference to a basic frame of reference; this frame of reference consists of answers to many questions similar to the above—why do we limit ourselves to scientific research?

Sometimes the term "empirical research" is used, meaning that kind of research which starts with empirical or factual observations. Close analysis of the context usually reveals that what is actually meant is scientific research, as the term is here being used.

Another distinction which is frequently made is between library research and empirical or scientific research. This, too, is usually a misleading and an artificial distinction. Library research (meaning research done in a library situation as distinguished from research involving observation of, or interaction with, people) may be just as empirical or factual or scientific as any other kind of research. Furthermore, the use of the library is a necessary part of virtually any sociological research. Usually, when people make the distinction between library and scientific research, they have a specific kind of library research in mind, namely, historical or biographical research. While historical research (e.g., a study of the history of the treatment of criminals), or biographical research (e.g., research into the life and times of Georg Simmel, or research on the influence of Sumner upon the thinking of W. I. Thomas) are legitimate research activities for the sociologist, they should probably be regarded as special cases, since rigorously they are not subsumed under the heading of scientific research. They are historical research, and the sociologist engaged in this kind of research is actually functioning as a historian, in this one context.

By way of summary, we have seen here something of the general nature of research, and have noted that our interest will be confined to scientific research. In the following sections a closer examination of the nature of scientific research will be undertaken, along with the reasons for confining our interest to scientific research.

SOCIOLOGY

In the previous section we have said that our interest will be confined to scientific research. In this section we will take the first steps toward explaining this limitation. We will look at the field of sociology—what it is, the variety of definitions—in order to make some preliminary statements about the place of sociology in the general field of science. We will select one definition that is most tenable, and look at some of the results or implications of this definition.

The advanced student has long ago encountered the seemingly bewildering variety of definitions (or descriptions) of sociology. They cluster around various concepts such as society, institutions, groups, interaction, human relationships, systems, and social order. But this variety should not be bothersome to the student; instead, it should be regarded as an indication of the changing and dynamic qualities which characterize this field. It is, in fact, a healthy sign. One expert has attempted to define sociology through an examination and discussion of three kinds of information: the views of the founding fathers, what type of work contemporary sociologists actually do, and an approach based on reason and analysis.[1] His conclusions are consistent with our definition: *that science which studies human interaction.* However, it should be noted that the substantive content of this definition is not crucial to what follows. Regardless of how various writers define the field, almost all are in agreement that it is a science or branch of science. What is important is that we note that the field is defined as a science—regardless of the specific description of the area of investigation of that science, which follows in the definition. There are certain important *consequences* of this definition of sociology as a sci-

[1] Inkeles, 1964, chap. 1.

ence, as well as some *problems* that are raised by it. First we will examine some of the problems. (One obvious problem is that we have not yet attempted a definition of "science," nor will this be done until the next section. However, we must start somewhere, and for the moment we will have to proceed, fully recognizing the handicap thus created.)

The discerning reader will note that defining sociology as a science is actually an assumption, because of the above disagreement as to exactly *what* sociology is. (The complexities of "proving" or determining the truth of a definition will be discussed later.) In this context we can neither prove nor disprove such an assumption. We accept such a definition as a foundation, upon which to build a complex structure. Because it is the starting point, it is a *fundamental* statement for all that follows. In the pages which follow we try to show that it is a *reasonable* assumption.

For many years there has been disagreement about whether sociology is a science, or can be a science, or should be a science (i.e., disagreement as to the definition of sociology). While this controversy is not so pronounced now as it has been in the past, the dispute is still far from having been settled to the satisfaction of all concerned. While the great majority of contemporary sociologists do subscribe to the view that it is properly a science, strongly dissenting voices are still heard from within and without the field. One prominent philosopher of science takes the view that such debates as to whether or not a given discipline is really a science characterizes what he calls a "pre-paradigm" period of the development of that discipline.[2] By this he means that the discipline has not yet produced achievements of such magnitude that they set the course of the discipline for its future development, the discipline does not yet have agreement on rules for scientific practice, and consensus about the accomplishments of the discipline has not yet appeared. It is only when the discipline reaches the paradigm period that it becomes what he calls a "normal science."[3] Despite the fact that this description seems to fit sociology at this time, it is profitable further to examine the issue.

Those who take the position that sociology *is not*, or *cannot be*, or *should not be*, a science, offer a wide variety of reasons to

---

[2] Kuhn, 1962, pp. 47–48.

[3] Ibid., pp. 10–11.

support their stand. Some of these reasons are readily vulnerable to serious examination, but others are more complex and less easily counterattacked. The major reasons offered in support of the "anti-science" views of sociology can be divided into three categories: assumptions about human behavior, assumptions about society and social events, and assumptions about science in general, social science in particular. The first group of assumptions typically center around the view that for some reasons human behavior is not amenable to rigorous investigation—it is too changeable, too subtle, too subjective, too unpredictable, and so on. The assumptions about social events usually make reference to the familiar concept of cultural relativism to illustrate the view that social events do not occur regularly nor do they obey any laws. The third group of assumptions are more varied, but frequently include the following views: that mathematics and statistics are necessary to science but incompatible with the study of human behavior, that scientific objectivity is impossible to attain when studying human behavior, that Heisenberg's "principle of uncertainty" from physics indicates that social phenomena cannot be known with certainty, and that science is incompatible with religion.[4] We will briefly return to these objections in a later section (Chapter 5) when we will be in a better position to assess their merits. For the moment we will simply make the statement (which should be no surprise) that the view here is that *none* of these "anti-science" arguments holds water. If the reader can tentatively accept this then we can proceed on the assumption that our categorization of sociology as a science is at least, a reasonable assumption.

The question of whether or not sociology is a science is extremely important because *if* we accept the view that sociology is a science, this means that as a consequence we *must* accept the whole body of procedures, assumptions, methods, restrictions, and points of view which characterize science. These things have immense practical importance in terms of designing and executing a research project. Knowing whether or not sociology is a science will influence us in every step of doing research. The reader will probably not be surprised to note that

[4] For a variety of views on these issues, see the following: Inkeles, 1964, pp. 92–98; Nagel, 1961, chap. 13; Skinner, 1965; Feigl, 1953-b, pp. 14–18; Mazur, 1968; Goode & Hatt, 1952, p. 2; Louch, 1966; Schlesinger, 1962, p. 770.

we are moving in the direction of being able to say that science *is better than* non-science for gaining knowledge, and thus this issue of whether sociology is a science assumes greater significance.

Thus it becomes clear that it is necessary to examine, in considerable detail, the whole field of science. This will be done in the following pages.

To sum up, then, we have in this section defined sociology as a science, and have taken note of some of the objections to this view. Since we have said that it is at least a reasonable view (that sociology is a science), we now find it necessary to turn to an examination of what science is.

CHARACTERISTICS OF SCIENCE

We have stated that our interest is confined to scientific research. Furthermore, we have defined sociology as a science, that is, we have *assumed* that it is a science. We now say that *if* we grant that assumption for the time being (regardless of whether we "really believe" it), then it follows that whatever is true of the sciences in general must be true of our field of sociology. Therefore, we now turn to a detailed examination of the question: Just what do we mean when we refer to something as a "science?" What are the implications and ramifications of this? What are the limitations? What difference does it make whether or not sociology is a science? Science has long since become a familiar term to all of us. As children we were exposed to courses in science, and as adults we are well aware of the impact of science upon our lives—indeed, some have even referred to science as a religion. Yet despite its pervasive presence in our lives, relatively few people have a clear understanding of what science is and what it's all about.

In order to answer these questions we will consider five topics in the following pages. First we will explore the characteristics of science, especially its definition, functions, and aims. In the next chapter we will examine axiomatic systems and their place in science. In Chapter 3 we will consider the place of inductive reasoning and retroduction in scientific activity. Finally, in Chapter 4, we will recapitulate the whole subject with a discussion of the scientific method. We have all been hearing about the scientific method ever since we took our first course in science, and so we know all about it. Or do we? A new look at this familiar old concept may help us a long way in our research activities.

Definition

As is the case with so many subjects, we encounter with "science" a great variety of descriptions and definitions. Not only do scientists themselves espouse differing views, but the same is true of philosophers specializing in the philosophy of science. Yet there are two central themes around which most views cluster. On the one hand many descriptions say that science is basically a *method* of inquiry, while on the other hand many other descriptions indicate that science refers to the *results* of that inquiry into a given area. In other words, some definitions emphasize the method of gathering knowledge, while others focus upon the knowledge which is gathered by this method. At this point we need to agree upon a definition—not because we must resolve the differing viewpoints as to the "best" definition, but rather because we must have a specific concept as the basis for the ensuing discussion. What is vital is not that all are agreed as to the precise wording of the definition, but rather that all are able to *communicate* about the subject matter, with reasonable agreement as to the *nature* of the subject matter. Our definition of a science is: *an objective, accurate, systematic analysis of a determinate body of empirical data, in order to discover recurring relationships among phenomena.* This is suggested not as the only definition, nor even necessarily the best, but as a useful and meaningful definition, and one which is clear and easily understood.

To derive full benefit from this definition, a brief examination of the meanings of the various terms contained in it will be useful. Our concern here is not with words themselves, needless to say, but with the fact that these words give us information about "science."

"Objective," of course means unbiased, unprejudiced, detached, impersonal, the characteristic of viewing things as they "really" are. One writer has suggested that a statement is objective "if its subject matter is something other than an event in somebody's mind."[5] The implication is that such a statement is

[5] L. Gross, 1967, p. 59.

capable, at least in principle, of being tested by any person possessing the necessary intelligence, skills, and facilities. Furthermore, since any statements made or conclusions reached are done independently of any individual factors or characteristics which are not shared by all competent investigators, all such observers substantially would agree in their observations. This is what the philosopher of science means by "intersubjectivity," and it is the mark of objectivity:

> Science aims at knowledge that is *objective* in the sense of being intersubjectively certifiable, independently of individual opinion or preference, on the basis of data obtainable by suitable experiments or observations.[6]

In addition, objectivity carries with it the clear understanding that the scientist does not become so ego-involved in his research activities that he is not willing to modify or abandon his ideas, when the evidence so indicates. Objectivity, thus, is the hallmark of the scientific endeavor, implying, as it does, that scientists deal with their subject matter in such a manner that all can agree as to just what's "out there" and that, therefore, their findings will not be merely a result of personal biases or idiosyncrasies.

"Accurate" means that the scientist strives to be definite, precise, and exact. Great care and fidelity to truth are exercised.

"Systematic" carries with it the implications that science is methodical, thorough, and regular in its procedures, that it involves some kind of classificatory scheme. Further, it is characterized by interrelatedness of its various parts, and these parts form a coherent whole—it is *not* merely a collection of facts, like an encyclopedia.

"Analysis" means that the scientist is concerned with the identification and study of the component parts or elements which make up the things which he studies. He is concerned, for example, not only with the social interaction which he observes, but also with the elementary behavior of which the interaction is composed.

"Determinate" means that each science has relatively agreed-upon, defined, limits or boundaries which specify what kind of things that science studies. The sociologist does not

---

[6] Hempel, 1965, p. 141. For further discussions of objectivity in social science: Kaplan, 1964, p. 128; Popper, 1961, p. 44; and Scheffler, 1967.

study the structure or distribution of rocks on the earth's surface; the biologist is not concerned with the composition and motion of the planets. Yet the scientist clearly recognizes that, in the aggregate, scientific knowledge is comprehensive, and all areas of investigation are ultimately related to one another.

Empirical data and facts. We pay special attention to the phrase "empirical data" in the definition of science, because much confusion often surrounds these terms. "Empirical" refers to knowledge or beliefs acquired through observation or experience. (Sometimes it carries the additional implication that adequate regard for theory and system are omitted. We do not use it in that sense here.) Thus, empirical means, simply, observable or verifiable, and carries with it the distinct implication that all competent observers would be in agreement as to the characteristics of this experience or event or object.

It has been pointed out that there are at least three levels of *data* in scientific research—and there may be more.[7] In the first place, "data" may refer to the *phenomena* which we seek to study—the actual object or event itself, "out there" in the "real world." The other levels roughly correspond to the number of minds through which the original information passes. At the second level, "data" may refer to the *observations* of these phenomena by first-hand observers. That is, at this level, the perceptual processes of those observers must be taken into account, or at least the existence of the processes must be recognized as a possible source of distortion or modification of the original data. At the third level, "data" may refer to the *recorded descriptions* of these observations. These descriptions may be recorded directly by the first-hand observer of the original phenomena, or they may be passed orally by the observer to a second person who, in turn, records them. Thus the data may also be modified by the communicative characteristics and abilities of the persons involved. Obviously, there may be several other intermediaries through whom the data pass from the original observer until they are finally recorded in a laboratory report, an ethnographic monograph, a journal article, or the like, and at each one of these additional levels distortion may enter. The scientist must ever be alert to the existence of these three levels of data, and, more importantly, of the possibility of dis-

[7] Martel and McCall, 1963; this is considerably modified from their version.

crepancies between actual phenomena themselves and the recorded descriptions of them. It is these recorded descriptions, of course, which largely comprise the effective data, or "public fact-pool" of the various sciences, since, strictly speaking, observations are personal, private matters which exist only inside the observer and are not directly accessible to anyone else.

To illustrate, it is common in anthropological literature to encounter descriptions written by the trained field worker of rituals or events as reported to him by an informant whose own source of information may be stories or other oral descriptions of actual phenomena which took place long ago. Or, to use another example, the phenomena may consist of the interaction occurring among three people discussing some topic. The observations made by the researcher ("They are enjoying themselves," "There is a distinct status hierarchy within the group," "They agree upon a conservative political view,") are necessarily products of his perception of the situation. Then the researcher's recorded description of his observations must be a product of his own communication skills, and therefore these skills affect the information that the "consumer" actually receives about the original discussion taking place among the members of the triad.

The term "fact" is commonly used as being synonynous with "event" or "phenomenon," and it is sometimes used interchangeably with "data." However, there is more to it than that. "Fact" carries with it the additional idea of *truth*—a fact is a statement about some aspect of reality that is believed to be true. Thus completely to discuss it involves an excursion into epistemology, which is beyond the scope of this book. However, we can note two key ideas. First, we cannot equate facts with direct sensory impressions.[8] The fallibility of sensory impressions is well known. A good illustration is the simple demonstration which many have encountered in high-school science classes. Take a bowl of hot water, a bowl of water at room temperature, and a bowl of ice water. Put one hand in the hot water and the other in the ice water, for a minute or two. Then take both hands out and plunge them into the room-temperature water. The hand that has been in the hot water feels cold, while the hand that has been in the ice water feels hot, yet both hands are experiencing water of the same temperature. We can gen-

[8] Cohen and Nagel, 1934, pp. 217–18, 391–92.

eralize from such examples and see that our sensory impressions or judgments in many ways may turn out to be misleading or erroneous.

Second, the evaluation of the truth or falsity of a statement, i.e., whether or not it is a fact, depends upon the evidence offered to support it. What is accepted as sufficient evidence is a function of the culture of the particular society at a particular time. It is a fact that the solar system is composed of nine planets rotating around the sun. It is a fact that communication among humans takes place only through the media of the five senses. It is a fact that the earth is round. It was a fact, in medieval Europe, that the earth was flat. It is a fact, in some societies, that ingesting the flesh and blood of the elders of one's tribe will result in one's acquiring that elder's great qualities. It is a fact, for some, that diligent prayer and observance of rituals will result in one's going to heaven after death. All of these statements are, or have been, regarded as true, that is, as *facts*, by some peoples, and all have been regarded as false by others. Of course one needs to consider that there are different "kinds" of facts, for example: commonsense facts, religious facts, scientific facts, and so on. *Whether* or not a given statement is a scientific fact depends upon the kinds of evidence offered to support it. Much of this book is about the criteria of acceptability of evidence, particularly the "rules" which science provides for identifying facts and their interrelationships, i.e., "proof." In the meantime we note that for *any* statement of truth, i.e., for any fact, the evidence is *always* incomplete. There is always the possibility that tomorrow we will have new evidence which will show today's fact to be false. Another authority may show up tomorrow to disprove a fact of today, just as Magellan's circumnavigation of the world showed it to be round, rather than flat. All we can say of facts is that there is *considerable evidence* to support them and that they are *probably* true, but we do not speak of facts as being *certainly* true. The scientist does, however, constantly strive for new facts, and for increasing the confidence with which we regard already-known facts as being statements of truth.

"Recurring relationships among phenomena" is the final phrase in the definition of science. It implies, first, that we deal with events which are repetitive or repeatable—things which happen over and over again, or which would happen again given the same identical circumstances. Thus we are assuming some regularity in the events which science deals with, and, in fact, this assumption of the *uniformity of nature* is one of the most important assumptions of science. "Relationships among phenomena" means, of course, that the scientist's concern is not merely with the phenomena or facts themselves, but with how these are related to one another—the *relationship* between the mass of an object and the force which it exerts, the *relationship* between the amount of nitrogen in the soil and the rate of plant growth, the *relationship* between status differences in a group and the characteristics of emergent leadership. Of course, it is entirely possible that two phenomena will have no discernible relationship, but that, too, is a contribution to knowledge.

This emphasis upon interrelationships, and the resulting comprehensiveness of science, is one of the features which distinguishes science from common sense. Science attempts to relate things which often seem to be unrelated. For example, it is now a commonplace fact that visible light, radio and television waves, infrared (heat) waves, ultraviolet, X rays, and gamma rays, all of which superficially seem to be very different from one another, are basically the same. They are all propagated by electromagnetic waves, and differ from one another only in that they occur in different wavelengths and frequencies. And what a remarkable advance in knowledge when we can take two things which seem to be very different, and totally unrelated, and see that they are really the same thing! Thus, all that is known about one is suddenly seen to be applicable to the other. In sociology, for example, two long-time, noteworthy, and popular areas of specialization are studies of the family and of small groups. But when it was recognized that a family is merely a specific instance of a more general class of objects known as small groups, the insight immediately opened up the way for great strides in our knowledge of both. All the accumulated knowledge about small groups was seen to be pertinent to families, and vice versa. This convergence of two or more bodies of knowledge is one of the most exciting aspects of the scientific endeavor, and is an important means of advancing scientific knowledge.

As mentioned before, our definition of science is not presented as the only one or the absolutely correct one or anything like that—it is presented just as a very useful one which tells us a lot about science. And so it does. (It also tells us that the often-heard statement to the effect that "if it isn't quantitative it isn't scientific" has no basis, although, to be sure, mathematics is an important and widely-used tool in many types of scientific activity.) But there are still more questions to be asked—and answered—about science. And these we examine in the following section.

Functions of science

In the previous section we examined what science *is*. But we must now face the questions: What is science *for?* What does it *do?* What are the functions of science? As a start we can say, simply enough, that science studies nature. Nature here refers to the entire physical universe—not the universe in the astronomical sense, nor in the specialized sense as used by the physicist, but rather all phenomena existing in space and time. Science studies *all* these phenomena. This statement points to the important fact that the *separate* sciences are not characteristics of nature. They are devices *made by man* in order to study and to teach. Nature, itself—the world we live in—is not "chopped up" into geology and biology and zoology and sociology and chemistry and physics and psychology and so on. Nature is just *there*, all around us (and, of course, nature includes us). It is *we*, people, and our universities, who have chopped nature up into these various sciences, purely as a pedagogical device, as a practical means to enable us to study and to teach. The necessity of this is simply because our world—or at least our knowledge about our world—is so complex that it is impossible for one person to master it all, or even to grasp the salient points. We cannot study all of nature at once. We must, in some manner, divide it up into manageable portions, in order to cope with it.

This has not always been the case. Aristotle, for instance, wrote on every subject from animals to physics. This was possible at that point in history, even aside from the fact that he was a remarkable man. He was able to write on, and give serious thought to, many different subjects—things that even a man of his caliber today would be unlikely to embrace simply because of this great complexity and proliferation of ideas and knowledge. We live in an age of specialists, and those individuals who are able to bridge the gaps, to use materials from various fields, and to bring together and coordinate these materials are very rare and sought after. But the specialization is necessary—one can't earn a Ph.D. in "knowledge," it must be a Ph.D. in sociology or anthropology or botany, and, what's more, in one particular *branch* of that field.

Each one of the sciences has its own particular view of nature—its own "determinate body of empirical data" with which it is concerned. Each science is concerned with a particular aspect of nature, and thus it is only when they are all combined that we get a relatively complete picture of nature. What the sociologists can contribute is just one view which must be supplemented by what the psychologists, the anthropologists, the biologists, and everyone else can contribute. Any part of nature can be studied and dealt with from a multitude of viewpoints. The old fable of the blind men "looking at" the elephant is too obvious and tempting an analogy to omit. Each perceived the elephant from his own point of view; each was correct, but only partially so. So with the several sciences—it is only the *aggregate* of all these individual views that provides a relatively complete and accurate picture. A race riot, for example, might be legitimately and productively studied by sociologists, psychologists, anthropologists, political scientists, biologists, and economists, to name a few. Each of these would study that particular natural phenomenon from its own peculiar viewpoint. Only the combination of all these findings would present a relatively complete description of what the riot was really like. Every scientist must constantly bear in mind that while his own field can make significant contributions to the understanding of nature, it can never completely understand it.

Discussion of this sort necessarily touches upon the question of what "reality" is, although again, this is more properly considered by the epistemologist. When research is undertaken on a specific aspect of nature, the researcher frequently is saying, essentially, that he wants to learn *all about* that particular phenomenon, but that for practical reasons he is limiting his investigation to some specific part of it. Perhaps he is interested in status relationships within a group, or in the question of why people perceive colors differently, or in the problem of how one can cut through a piece of steel with a laser beam. Whatever the researcher's interest, he would need to be a specialist in more than one field if he would learn "all about" a specific topic. To learn about reality, to learn what is *really out there*, requires this aggregation of the contributions of the various sciences. No single field can tell us what reality is.

What does science do? What are the advantages of science? Why do we prefer science? These and similar questions must be answered now, although they have already partially been answered. We have seen that science is a method of gaining knowledge, but note that we do not say that science is *the only* way of gaining knowledge. There are other means of gaining knowledge, and, perhaps, other *good* means. It may even be that the best means of acquiring knowledge is through the method of divine inspiration, or by some kind of psychic or spiritual experience, or through common sense, or by ESP (extrasensory perception), or some other similar method. We should not, and we do not, say that these methods cannot exist, and do not exist.[9] We *do* say that we don't have any objective evidence that these things do exist—at least not any evidence which meets commonly accepted standards. ESP, for example, has been the subject of considerable experimental research, by reputable psychologists and other scientists. So far, however, none of the experimental results conclusively demonstrate, within a reasonable degree of probability, that ESP really exists. (Note that the mere fact that it has not been shown to *exist* does not mean that it does *not* exist. It simply means that we don't know for sure, at this time, *whether* it exists or not). Perhaps these methods of gaining knowledge do exist, even though we do not have any satisfactory evidence to say so now, or we will find out next year, or next century, that they do. And perhaps they will be much better methods of gaining knowledge than science is.

But what we do believe is that, today, science is the *best* method we have of acquiring knowledge. None of the other methods which are now known to exist is as dependable as science is. No other method now known to man can come as close to providing us with what are the distinguishing characteristics of knowledge: truth, proof, and certitude.[10] It is for this reason that science has become an honorific term in contemporary American society. It is the ultimate authority in television

[9] For an interesting comparison of scientific and nonscientific methods of inquiry, see TenHouten and Kaplan, 1973.

[10] Perry, 1954, p. 304.

advertising—all one needs to sell something is to have a TV ad with a scientist (usually a man in a white coat!) saying that this product is better than that product. Science has acquired an aura, a mystique, about itself, and many people, including many who should know better, have come to regard science as being inherently better than non-science. This is hardly a tenable viewpoint for the educated person, especially the academician. We accept the more limited statement, that science is a better way *of gaining knowledge* than is non-science, but we do not enlarge upon that and say that therefore science is better than non-science in *every respect*.

The most obvious example of non-science which is often seen as being opposed to science is so-called common sense. In an excellent (and highly recommended) comparison of these two kinds of knowledge it is pointed out that despite the fact that science has grown, in part, out of practical and commonsense concerns, the explanation of these practical concerns is generally far more complex and elaborate than what we have in mind when we talk about common sense.[11] Science introduces refinements which are not found in commonsense thinking, and conflicts of judgment occur in commonsense thinking which are, hopefully, eliminated in scientific thinking. The language of science permits more precise and accurate statements than does commonsense language, and, furthermore, the procedures of thinking and reasoning and examining evidence are made explicit in science, whereas they usually are not in commonsense thinking. Finally, as indicated earlier, there are many misconceptions and erroneous beliefs about science, and, further, many well-known writers and others subscribe to them. For some it is simply a matter of misunderstanding, but for others there is a definite *anti-science* attitude, for whatever reason.

Aims of science

The last of the characteristics of science to be examined is its aims. Regardless of the definition or approach taken, there is considerable agreement that there are three aims of science.

The first is *description*. This is the basic step, and must precede the others. The first thing that science does is to answer the

[11] Nagel, 1961, chap. 1.

questions, What are the facts? What is the case? What is out there? What is on the other side of the moon? What is the rate of juvenile delinquency in Phoenix? What happens when you mix this chemical with that chemical? What is the composition of the earth's crust three miles down? How does the per capita income of Sweden compare with that of the United States? What is it like at the bottom of the ocean? How thick is the ice in the Arctic Ocean? Description answers the question, "What?" At this level, science describes nature, or that portion of nature with which the particular science is concerned. Description, obviously, must come first—before one can make any intelligent statements about anything else. We must first know what we are talking about.

Explanation is the second aim of science. Explanation answers the question, "Why?" *Why* is a man's weight on the moon only one sixth of what it is on earth? *Why* is there a higher rate of suicide in Phoenix, Arizona, than there is in Syracuse, New York? *Why* does a mixture of these two chemicals turn litmus paper red? *Why* is textile weaving a man's art among the Hopis and a woman's art among the Navajo? *Why* is the rate of sediment deposition on the ocean floor about twice as fast in the Atlantic as in the Pacific? *Why* does this drug cure these people? Explanation tells us how things and events come about, what causes them, what are the laws which determine their occurrence. Explanation brings *meaning* to the description. First the scientist *describes* the situation and then he *explains* it.

The question naturally arises: just what is an explanation? To explain means to make something more clear or plain. An explanation must always be considered in terms of the background information which one possesses. That is, *what* is accepted as an explanation is related to how much and what kind of information one already has. For instance, the *description* of a certain social characteristic might be that a given community has a high divorce rate. What constitutes a satisfactory *explanation* of this high rate will depend upon whether one is talking to a child, an adult layman, or a trained marriage counselor. However, in general, an explanation consists of a series of statements which lead up to a final statement, this final statement being the thing to be explained, (i.e., the description). The statement being explained is known as the *explicandum*, while the statements which lead up to the explicandum, and which do the explaining, are known as the *explicans*. The statements in the explicans offer evidence for the explicandum; the explicandum may be understood or intelligible when one encounters the explicans.

There are at least two types of explanation which are important for scientific purposes.[12] The first of these is the *deductive* explanation. In this kind of explanation, the explicandum is a *logically necessary* consequence of the explicans; it follows absolutely, necessarily, without any question or doubt, from the explicans. (The very important terms, "deduction" and "logic," will be defined and discussed in detail later in this chapter.) This is commonly regarded as being the ideal form of explanation, the highest, most dependable and fruitful type, and the type toward which all scientific activity should strive, although most do not attain this.

Two examples, as suggested by Nagel, are as follows:

1. The description is: a smaller percentage of Catholics committed suicide than did Protestants in European countries during the last quarter of the 19th century. This is the explicandum, the thing to be explained. In this case it is a single historical phenomenon. One widely accepted answer to the question of *why* this was the case consists of the following statements (i.e., the explicans):

a. The social organization under which Catholics lived made for a greater degree of social cohesion than did the social organization of Protestants.
b. The existence of strongly knit social bonds (social cohesion) among members of a community helps to sustain human beings during periods of personal stress.

If these statements are accepted, along with some additional trivial statements, the explicandum follows as a necessary consequence, and we have a satisfactory explanation.

2. Why does ice float on water? Here the explicandum is a universal law. The explicans contains statements such as these:

a. The density of ice is less than that of water.
b. The Archimedean law that a fluid buoys up a body with a force equal to the weight of the displaced fluid.
c. Other similar physical laws of equilibrium.

---

[12] The following discussion draws heavily upon Nagel, 1961, chap. 2. See also: Hempel, 1968; Hempel, 1965; Smart, 1968, chap. 3; Scheffler, 1963, chaps. 1–9; and Brown, 1963. Additional useful works are: Kaplan, 1964, chap. 9, and Carney and Scheer, 1964, chap. 18.

Again, the explicandum is the logical consequence of the explicans.

The second form of explanation is the *probabilistic* explanation. Here the explicans does not lead *necessarily* to the explicandum, but instead it makes the explicandum *likely* or *probable*. Frequently, in this kind of explanation, the explicans contains one or more statistical assumptions about a whole class of elements, and the explicandum is a statement about a single member of that class. Nagel suggests the following illustration:

> Why did Cassius plot the death of Caesar? One explanation is to be found in the inbred hatred which Cassius bore toward tyrants. However, this is not a complete explanation. The explicans must also include statements such as some assumptions about the way in which hatred is manifested in a given culture by persons of a certain social class. These statements would be unlikely to be universally true, but would instead take the form: a certain percentage of men of a certain sort, in a certain kind of society, will behave in a certain manner.

In this case, the explicans simply make the explicandum probable. It is important to note that the distinction between this type of explanation and the preceding type has nothing to do with how sure we are that the statements in the explicans are true statements, or how much confidence we have in their truth. The "probabilistic" part of the explanation does not refer to the idea that the explicans statements are only probably true. Rather, the distinction refers to the way in which the explicans is related to the explicandum.

It should also be noted that there is some merit to the view that probabilistic explanations are "only temporary halfway stations on the road to the deductive ideal" [13] and that when additional knowledge becomes available these statistical assumptions may be replaced by statements asserting universally true relationships. However, given the present state of knowledge, especially in the social sciences, probabilistic explanations must be regarded as occupying an important place in scientific endeavor.

Two additional types of explanations which are frequently discussed are the *functional*, or *teleological*, and the *genetic*, or *historical*. These, however, have been shown to be essen-

[13] Nagel, 1961, p. 23.

tially the same as the deductive and probabilistic kinds respectively.[14]

The third aim of science is *prediction*. This is the ultimate step, and has been referred to as one of "the most desirable fruits of scientific labors."[15] Prediction means making inferences from facts or laws. When the scientist predicts, he says that such and such will happen, or if *these* conditions prevail then so and so will occur. For example,

> If I take this child out of this home and place him in a foster home, then his juvenile delinquent activities will be reduced.
>
> If the rocket engines fail to ignite at the predetermined time, the rocket will go into permanent orbit around the moon.
>
> Under these precise conditions, nuclear fission will take place.
>
> This couple has a much lower likelihood of having a successful marriage than that couple.

As will be seen in more detail later, the scientist rarely makes absolute predictions, but instead speaks in terms of probabilities. But to be able to make statements of this kind is indeed one of the most desirable fruits of our labors. Furthermore, whatever contributions science may make to the practical world come about primarily as a result of the successful achievement of this aim of prediction.

The concept of cause is often confused with prediction, and sometimes with explanation. Indeed, some would say that the aim of science is to determine *causes* of phenomena. However, the concept of cause is extremely complex, and it is one about which considerable disagreement marks the philosophical world. One rather widely held view is that "cause" refers to an invariable relationship between specified characteristics of events, or between various kinds of elements. This invariable relationship is regarded as usually involving a temporal span, with the cause preceding the effect in time. Furthermore, the relationship is asymmetrical, in the sense that, if "A" causes "B," it would *not* be the case that "B" causes "A". A detailed

---

[14] Hempel, 1968, p. 79; and Nagel, 1961, chaps. 12, and 15. For an alternative view of explanations, which rejects the idea of deductive explanations, see Meehan, 1968.

[15] Feigl, 1953-b, p. 11.

analysis of this traditional view of cause (which analysis is beyond the scope of this book) would show it to have great similarities to the concept of prediction. However, because of the considerable amount of controversy surrounding "cause" we will here avoid its use and speak, instead, in terms of explanation and prediction. It should also be noted that the late Bertrand Russell, one of the greatest contemporary philosophers, has stated that "the word 'cause' is so inextricably bound up with misleading associations as to make its complete extrusion from the philosophical vocabulary desirable. . ."[16]

According to some viewpoints control is a fourth aim of science, or it is substituted for prediction, or it is equated with prediction. If "control" is taken to refer to the influencing of the inanimate, material part of nature (e.g., control of weather through cloud-seeding) then it is essentially the same as prediction. On the other hand, "control" may carry with it the implication of regulation or manipulation of people, and these ideas are foreign to what is usually regarded as the scientific framework, or scientific thinking. Take hydrogen bombs, for example. We are at the prediction stage. The processes involved can be described, explained, and predicted. We can say that if we take these ingredients and combine them under certain conditions the result will be a big, fat, mushroom-shaped cloud, and obviously this knowledge and these devices can be used for purposes of manipulation or regulation. One nation can control the activities of another by the threat, or actual use, of such a bomb. Thus we see that control, when used in this sense, involves policymaking. The relationship between science and policymaking will be discussed in Chapter 5, but for the moment we merely state that it is not properly a part of science. For these reasons we do not consider control to be one of the aims of science, although it is recognized that it can become an outcome of the scientific endeavor.

It was stated above that description must precede explanation or prediction. However it is important to note that explanation does not necessarily precede prediction. In some cases it is possible to predict without being able to explain. Many times we know *that* an event will occur, without knowing *why* it will

---

[16] Russell, 1953, p. 387. Additional pertinent discussions of cause are to be found in Feigl, 1953-a; Cohen and Nagel, 1934, pp. 245–49; Hanson, 1965, chap. 3; and Walker, 1963, chap. 6.

occur. For example, some intrauterine devices provide an effective and widely-accepted method of birth control, and yet the reason for their effectiveness is not known. We can predict that if this device is inserted the probability of conception is greatly reduced but we do not know the reason for this. We have prediction without explanation. But it is also important to note that this kind of prediction may be a limited kind of prediction simply *because* of the lack of explanation. That is, the prediction may be quite limited in the number or kinds of situations to which it is applicable, or in the extent to which the prediction can serve as an effective means of adding to our knowledge. To continue the same example, if the explanation of the effectiveness of the intrauterine device were known, it might be possible to modify their manufacture and use in such a way that they could serve as a practical means of slowing the world's birth rate. (Ordinary aspirin serves as another illustration. Its successful use as an analgesic can be predicted despite the fact that we do not have an explanation as to why it is effective. Were the explanation available it might be possible to modify the formula so as to eliminate its undesirable side effects and to increase its usefulness. Similarly, current knowledge of acupuncture apparently permits prediction without explanation.) Thus it can be seen that while prediction can occur without prior explanation, it may be a much poorer prediction than it would be if the explanation were available.

A careful examination of the above discussion implies that, of the three aims of science, description, explanation, and prediction, the paramount one is explanation. And this implication is intentional. We have seen that description is a basic step, but that it is only through explanation that any significance or meaning can be attached to the description.[17] And we have also seen that prediction without explanation is relatively unfruitful. In addition, the deductive form of explanation, as described above, really embraces the concept of prediction, since a deductive system may be likened to an "If . . . then . . ." statement, and

---

[17] A case can be made for the view that the distinction between description and explanation is, at best, hazy, and that ultimately every explanation may be regarded as a more sophisticated description. Zetterberg, for example, in discussing scientific theories, says, "On the one hand, it is a system of information-packed descriptions of what we know; on the other hand, it is a system of general explanations." (1965, p. 11) Nevertheless, for the purposes of our exposition here, it introduces no error to continue to make the distinction.

this in turn is really a predictive statement. In the next chapter we will elaborate on the relationship between explanation and prediction. What we are saying here is that explanation is really the central aim of science. This is what science is all about—answering the question, "Why?" The very subtitle of Nagel's volume on the philosophy of science, "Problems in the Logic of Scientific Explanation," illustrates this.[18]

In this section we have, first, defined science and seen some important ramifications and implications of that definition. Then we took note of the fact that science is the best method we have of studying nature. And finally, we have examined the aims of scientific activity, with especial attention to a discussion of explanations—what they are and what their significance is.

---

[18] Nagel, 1961.

Chapter 2

Axiomatic systems

INTRODUCTION

In order to describe, explain, and predict (which is what science does) it is necessary to make statements about things. Indeed, all knowledge can be formulated in statements, or declarative sentences. Examples are:

The leaves have turned yellow.
Patti got a B in Research Methods.
The dentist pulled my wisdom tooth last week.
The pressure is 5 kilograms per square centimeter and dropping.
God is not dead.
That question warrants careful research.
Tom is handsome.
The court declared the movie obscene.
My friend feels the movie is not obscene.
Status differences appear in every group.
Some groups do not have status differences.

We define a *proposition* as "the meaning of a declarative sentence." The meaning of the sentence is distinguished from the sentence itself, because sentences in different languages may all have the same meaning while nevertheless being quite different sentences. For example,

That is a book.
Este es un libro.
C'est un livre.

Woh ek kitab hai.

Das ist ein Buch.

Adu ondu pustaka.

all have the same meaning, although the sentences are quite different in appearance. It is, of course, the *meaning* in which we are interested, not the sentence itself. Note also that there is no implication that a proposition is factual or that it is true. *Propositions may be either true or false.*

But science is not content with merely formulating propositions, as important as that may be. As we have seen, a far more important concern—indeed, the central concern—is formulating explanations, that is, showing relationships among propositions, discovering some systematic organization of propositions. Therefore, the question arises, how do we go about organizing propositions into some kind of system? To do this it is necessary to consider *arguments.* An argument is a group of two or more propositions, one of which is claimed to follow from (be affirmed by) the other(s). The proposition which is affirmed is known as the *conclusion.* The proposition(s) which supply the reason or evidence for affirming the conclusion are known as *premises.* (Note the similarity between the premises and conclusions, on one hand, and the explicans and explicandum, on the other. This similarity will assume some importance later.)

Consider the following common (although misguided) argument: "We should stay together for the sake of our children, because broken homes are associated with juvenile delinquency." The premise is "broken homes are associated with juvenile delinquency," while the conclusion is "We should stay together." Or consider this familiar example of an argument:

All graduate students are poor.

Mike is a graduate student.

Therefore, Mike is poor.

Here the first two propositions are the premises, and the third is the conclusion. That is, the first two propositions offer evidence for affirming the conclusion.

And as another, and more complex, example, here is an argument excerpted from a newspaper editorial:

A local business man told us, the other day, that he would not run for the school board because "It takes too much time, and there is no money in it." School board members must be willing and able to put in long hours if they are to know what is going on and render intelligent decisions. Traditionally, school board members throughout the country serve without pay, although in contrast, legislators and councilmen do get paid. Therefore we think that school board members should be paid, too.

The premises of this argument are:

1. School board members must put in long hours.
2. Businessmen cannot afford to devote the time without getting paid.
3. Other similar public officials do get paid.

And the conclusion is: School board members should be paid.

Or still another argument: "Every Slobovian I've ever known has been lazy and undependable and so I'm convinced they all are!" The premise, of course, is "Every Slobovian I've ever known has been lazy and undependable," and the conclusion is "they all are (lazy and undependable)."

Countless other illustrations of arguments could be given, and they form a common part of our everyday lives. Note again that the propositions may be true or false, and further, note that there is no implication, in what has been said so far, that the argument "makes sense," or is "right," or "correct," or "true." For example, the following, despite its absurdity, *is* an argument: Since the earth is flat, ships should stay close to land lest they fall off the edge.

There is no difference between a proposition which serves as a premise and one which serves as the conclusion of an argument. In fact, a given proposition may be a premise in one argument and the conclusion in another. In the fictitious argument, "Sixty percent of the inmates in schools for delinquents come from broken homes, while only 30 percent of the general high school population come from broken homes. Therefore broken homes are associated with juvenile delinquency," the proposition "broken homes are associated with juvenile delinquency" is the conclusion, whereas in the earlier example the same proposition served as premise.

In all arguments the claim is made that the premises supply evidence for the truth of the conclusions. However, in *some* kinds of arguments the premises provide *absolutely conclusive* evidence, while in other kinds, the premises supply only *some* evidence. The former are known as *deductive* arguments while the latter are *inductive* arguments. This is a very important distinction, and much will be found to hinge upon it as we go on to examine these two kinds of arguments. (The commonly heard distinction that deductive arguments consist of reasoning from the general to the particular, while inductive arguments are reasoning from the particular to the general, is misleading and should not be used.)

As would be expected, some arguments are better than others. That is, there are such things as correct and incorrect arguments, or good and bad arguments (although other terms will shortly be substituted for "correct," "incorrect," "good," and "bad"). The study of these is known as logic. Logic is "the study of the methods and principles used in distinguishing correct (good) from incorrect (bad) arguments."[1] To put it another way, logic is concerned with the evaluation of the adequacy of the evidence to affirm a conclusion. Thus when one is presented with an argument it is necessary in some manner to analyze the argument to determine whether it is correct or incorrect. This involves not only examining the propositions themselves but also the way in which they are related to one another, in order to determine whether or not they really do supply adequate evidence to support the conclusion. This examination of the evidence for an argument is extremely important, and much of the practical aspect of studying research methods consists of learning how to weigh the evidence for a conclusion. In current usage, "logic" is generally used to refer to only the study of *deductive* arguments. *Formal* logic is a subcategory of deductive logic, dealing with arguments in terms of their *form* as distinguished from their content. Most of what follows in the next section is logic, including a few small excursions into formal logic.

DEDUCTIVE ARGUMENTS

Deductive arguments are those arguments in which the premises are believed to supply absolutely conclusive evidence for the truth of the conclusions. What this means is that *given* that the premises are true, the conclusion *must* be true. Or, if the premises are true, then the conclusion *must* be true—absolutely, conclusively, without any doubt. Another way of saying this is

[1] Copi, 1954, p. 1.

that the premises *entail* (or *imply*) the conclusion. A simple example of a deductive argument is:

Premise: Pat is a mother.

Conclusion: Therefore, Pat is female.

The premise here supplies absolutely conclusive evidence for the truth of the conclusion. This is very obvious in this example, but in more complicated arguments (which are very common) it is sometimes not clear whether the premises do, in fact, entail the conclusion. And, of course, sometimes a very careful, rigorous, examination of an argument will show that the conclusion is not entailed by the premises even though a superficial examination seems to indicate that it is. It is the task of logic to enable one to distinguish between such arguments, and so the distinction is made between *valid* and *invalid* deductive arguments. A deductive argument is said to be *valid* "when its premises and conclusion are so related that it is absolutely impossible for the premises to be true unless the conclusion is true also."[2] Another way of saying this is that in a valid argument, if the premises are true and the conclusion is false, the result is a contradiction. Notice that we are not saying that the premises or conclusion *are* true or false, we are merely considering a *relationship* among them. Furthermore, it should be noted that the terms "true" and "false" are not applied to arguments, but only to propositions, just as the terms "valid" and "invalid" are not applied to propositions, but only to arguments.

A common form of deductive argument (although by no means the only form) is the syllogism, and it serves as a good illustration of many of the characteristics of deductive arguments in general. Syllogisms are arguments which, typically, are composed of two premises and a conclusion. Following are several examples of syllogisms, all of which are valid deductive arguments.

1. All bats are mammals.
   All mammals have lungs.
   Therefore, all bats have lungs.

2. All potatoes are vegetables.
   All vegetables are edible.
   Therefore, all potatoes are edible.

[2] Ibid., p. 4.

3. All diamonds sparkle.
   This stone is a diamond.
   Therefore, this stone sparkles.

4. All men are mortal.
   Socrates is a man.
   Therefore, Socrates is mortal.

5. All dogs have four legs.
   Simone is a dog.
   Therefore, Simone has four legs.

In each of these, the first two propositions are the premises and the third is the conclusion. And in each case these propositions are so related that it is absolutely impossible for the premises to be true without the conclusion also being true. Thus they are all valid arguments.

It will also be noted that the first two syllogisms are of the same *form*, namely,

All As are Bs.
All Bs are (have the quality of) C.
Therefore, all As are (have the quality of) C.

And the last three are also of the same form:

All As are (have the quality of) B.
C is an A.
Therefore, C is (has the quality of) B.

These are but two of the many different examples of *formal* arguments. It is easy to see that *any* argument which has the same form will also be valid. That is, *regardless* of what terms one may wish to substitute for A, B, and C, the above arguments will be valid as long as the substitutions are made consistently. This is of considerable importance in analyzing arguments, because we can have information about a vast number of different specific arguments once we have established that they have the same form as some other arguments which we already know about.

Thus far we have been considering only valid arguments. However, there are certain common forms of arguments which are invalid. Here are two examples of invalid syllogisms:

6. If I were the president I would be famous.
   I am not the president
   Therefore, I am not famous.

7. All scholars are educated.
   All leaders are educated.
   Therefore, all scholars are leaders.

There are, of course, countless numbers of other invalid arguments. These two are easily shown to be invalid because it is perfectly possible for the premises to be true and the conclusion false. All one need do is to substitute "Neil Armstrong" for "I" in syllogism 6, above, and it is clear that the premises may be true while the conclusion is false. Or, substitute the following for syllogism 7:

8. All dogs are animals.
   All cats are animals.
   Therefore, all dogs are cats.

Both 7 and 8, it will be noted, are of the same form:

All As are Bs.
All Cs are Bs.
Therefore, all As are Cs.

And thus we see that *any* argument of that same form will, similarly, be invalid.

Lest there be any confusion in the reader's mind it should be stated here that we have not considered—nor will we—the methods whereby one can distinguish between a valid argument and an invalid one. That is left to the logician. Here we have merely been using some easily understood examples. Furthermore, the reader is again reminded that in all of the above discussion of syllogisms and deductive arguments, nothing has been said about the actual truth or falsity of the premises nor the conclusions. We have only considered *whether* the premises *entail* the conclusions. That is, we have been concerned only with the *form* of the arguments, and whether they are valid or invalid, but we have not been concerned with the truth or falsity of the propositions which are the components of the various arguments. In actual practice, of course, we are very much concerned with questions of truth or falsity, and shortly we will see how we deal with these. But in considering validity of arguments, we set aside these questions. We may or may not believe the premises to be actually true, but for the moment we set those beliefs aside and merely assume that they are true.

Now let us consider some additional characteristics of valid arguments, again using syllogisms as illustrations. And here we do take note of truth and falsity. A little reflection will show that there are, in fact, various possible combinations of truth and falsity of the premises and conclusions of valid arguments. Thus a valid argument may contain all true propositions. Examples 1 through 5 above illustrate this. A valid argument may also contain one or more true premises, one or more false premises, and a true conclusion:

9. All whales are fish. (False)
   All fish live in water. (True)
   Therefore, all whales live in water. (True)

Again, a valid argument may contain one or more true premises, one or more false premises, and a false conclusion:

10. All trout are mammals. (False)
    All mammals have lungs. (True)
    Therefore, all trout have lungs. (False)

Or a valid argument may contain all false premises and a true conclusion:

11. All trout are mammals. (False)
    All mammals have scales. (False)
    Therefore, all trout have scales. (True)

Finally, a valid argument may have all false premises and a false conclusion:

12. All trout are mammals. (False)
    All mammals have wings. (False)
    Therefore, all trout have wings. (False)

It will be noted that these last four examples (9, 10, 11, and 12) are all of the same *form* as the first two examples.

The above syllogisms were used as illustrations of deductive arguments in general. And so it can be seen that a valid argument can have *any* combination of true and false premises and conclusions, with the single exception that it cannot have true premises and a false conclusion. This is, of course, the definition of a valid argument. Our "common sense," or "intuition" might leads us to make certain assumptions about the relationships among some of these (for example, a valid argument might be thought to lead to a true conclusion), but an examination of the following 12 statements which summarize the above discussion will show that such assumptions may not be accurate.

1. True premises do not ensure a true conclusion (see examples 7 and 8).
2. True premises do not ensure a valid argument (6).
3. One (or more) false premises do not ensure a false conclusion (9, 11).
4. One (or more) false premises do not ensure an invalid argument (9, 10, 11, 12).
5. A true conclusion does not ensure all true premises (9, 11).
6. A true conclusion does not ensure a valid argument (6).
7. A false conclusion does not ensure one or more false premises (7, 8).
8. A false conclusion does not ensure an invalid argument (10, 12).
9. A valid argument does not ensure all true premises (9, 10, 11, 12).
10. A valid argument does not ensure a true conclusion (10, 12).
11. An invalid argument does not ensure one or more false premises (6, 8).
12. An invalid argument does not ensure a false conclusion (6).

This can be further summarized as follows. For *all* combinations of true and false premises, valid and invalid arguments, and true and false conclusions, there are only *three* useful statements which can be made with certainty:

1. If all the premises are true and the argument is valid, the conclusion *must* be true.
2. If the conclusion is false and all the premises are true, the argument *must* be invalid.
3. If the conclusion is false and the argument is valid, at least one premise *must* be false.

These statements are particularly important, because they are the basis of advancing our knowledge of any subject, and they also provide the groundwork for scientific research activity.

When we are presented with an argument, as occurs regularly in reports of research activity, we must be able to evaluate it. If we find the first statement above to be applicable, then of course we have established the truth of something—this is exactly *how* scientific truths are established. If the second or third statements are found to be applicable, that is, the knowledge that the conclusion of an argument is false, then we have clues as to where and how to undertake corrective measures. These ideas will be elaborated upon in Chapter 3 (in the section on "reality testing").

Returning to a point emphasized above, we recall that in *no* case have we said that the premises of any argument *are,* in fact, true. We have either ignored this point or perhaps, for the sake of discussion, we have implicitly assumed that they were true or might be true—regardless of whether in fact we *believe* them to be true. The discerning reader will have already noted that all of the above syllogisms and deductive arguments, in general, are better thought of in terms of "if . . . then . . ." statements. Even elaborate deductive arguments may be thought of as giant "If . . . then . . ." statements. That is, we may think of these as being phrased, "*If* the premises are true, *then* the conclusions are true." *If* all trout are mammals, and *if* all mammals have wings, *then* all trout *must* have wings. *If* all dogs have four legs, and *if* Simone is a dog, *then* Simone *must* have four legs. We do not say *that* all trout are mammals, or *that* mammals have wings, nor do we even say *that* all dogs have four legs or *that* Simone is a dog. All we have been saying in our examples so far is, "In the event that certain things are true then certain other things are true." In other words, we have been concerned thus far only with the *forms* of arguments, with validity and invalidity, and not with the actual truth or falsity of the propositions. As a matter of fact, *establishing the truth or falsity of propositions is definitely excluded from the province of deductive logic.*

Yet it must be recognized that we, as practicing scientists, *are* concerned with precisely that: the truth or falsity of propositions. Therefore we must come to grips with a question of utmost importance. *Why are deductive arguments important to science?*

To answer this question, we now return to our discussion of explanations. It was pointed out that an explanation consists of a series of propositions, the explicans, which offers the reasons leading up to a final proposition, the explicandum. And further, it was noted that a deductive explanation is considered the ideal form of a scientific explanation. A deductive explanation, of course, is one which utilizes a deductive form of reasoning. Thus we see now that a deductive explanation is simply a (valid) deductive argument, in which the premises are the explicans and the conclusion is the explicandum. So if one has a series of propositions, linked together in such a fashion that the final one follows necessarily from the preceding ones (i.e., a valid deductive argument), then this series of propositions (the explicans) *is* an answer to the question, "Why?" and *is* an *explanation* of the explicandum or conclusion. Thus, a deductive argument *is* an explanation, with the premises constituting the explicans and the conclusion being the explicandum.

It is interesting to note that in such an explanation one starts with the explicandum, the thing to be explained, the thing about which we ask the question, "Why?" and then, in a sense, works back toward a deductive argument and premises which will result in that conclusion.[3] On the other hand, if one starts with the premises and the deductive argument, then the resulting conclusion is what we know as a *prediction*. Therefore we see that in a deductive argument the premises explain the conclusion, while the conclusion is a prediction derived from the premises. Thus explanations and predictions are so closely related that it is difficult to separate them.

Now we expand our discussion and inquire as to how deductive arguments fit into the larger scientific framework, and especially how they fit into the research activity. How do we obtain deductive arguments? How do we use them in such a manner as to enable us to make contributions to scientific knowledge, to explain phenomena? To answer such questions we now turn to an examination of axiomatic theories.

AXIOMATIC THEORIES

Traditionally, the most common usage of the word "theory" in sociology has been to refer to a basic frame of reference which serves as a starting point for sociology, or as a way of organizing or viewing the subject matter of sociology. However, in contemporary usage, theory is regarded as an "array of logically

[3] See chapter 3, section on "retroduction."

interrelated propositions which purport to explain a set of phenomena. . ."[4] Here we use the terms "theory" and "axiomatic theory" as being equivalent. ("Axiomatic system," "deductive theory," and "deductive system" are also widely used in the literature as synonymous to "axiomatic theory," although philosophers of science occasionally make distinctions among them.) An axiomatic theory can be regarded as a vast and complex deductive argument. Thus all that has already been said about deductive arguments in the preceding section applies to axiomatic theories as well. However, at this level not only is different terminology customarily used, but some additional relationships and implications are found to exist which are of great significance for scientific research.

Elements of an axiomatic theory

An axiomatic theory is composed of a relatively small number of different kinds of elements or components. Every such theory must contain four specific components and may also contain two others. These will now be considered in turn. Throughout the following discussion, ordinary plane (Euclidean) geometry will be used as an illustration. One reason for this is the assumption that most of the readers of this book have been exposed to geometry at some time during their academic careers, and perhaps some of it will sound at least vaguely familiar. But a far more important reason for using geometry as an example is that it is without doubt one of the most beautiful examples of an axiomatic theory that exists.[5]

The first element, which is a necessary part of any axiomatic theory, is *undefined terms,* also known as *primitive terms.* These are terms whose meaning is not specified or defined. The meaning or interpretation of these may be given implicitly, through their use in other parts of the theory, or examples may be used to illustrate their meaning (i.e., a denotative definition[6]), or it may be that it is merely assumed that the meaning is clear and agreed upon. Perhaps there may be no assump-

[4] Hoult, 1969, p. 331.

[5] It should be noted that while the ancient Egyptians knew many of the geometrical propositions, and utilized them in practical matters, it was the Greeks who introduced *system* to geometry by showing relationships and deducibility. Euclid, particularly, is credited with making geometry into an axiomatic theory.

[6] See the following discussion of definitions.

tions at all about their meaning. Sometimes it is the case that the term has such an obvious or fundamental meaning that it is difficult to define it in a way which would make the meaning any clearer. However, that is not necessarily the case. It should be noted that these terms are *undefined*, and not *undefinable*. Without primitive terms, one would be involved in the kind of circularity which is frequently found in a pocket dictionary, where, for example, "big" is defined as "large," and when one looks up "large" it is found to be defined as "big." The meaning of *one* of these terms must be known for the other to have any meaning. Examples of primitive terms in geometry are "point" and "line." It is common to define "line" as "the path of a moving point," and point is commonly defined as "the intersection of two lines." Thus the meaning of either one of these must be assumed, in order for the definition of the other to be meaningful.

The second kind of element of an axiomatic theory is *definitions*. Definitions, or defined terms, are not necessary parts of such a theory, but are, rather, used as a matter of convenience. When a term is defined, this definition ultimately can be reduced to a statement containing only primitive terms. Thus the definition could be eliminated, but it is simpler to use a definition than to substitute for it a statement containing only primitive terms. For example, in the geometry illustration, let us assume that "point" is a primitive term. Then "line" may be defined as "the path of a moving point," and "triangle" may be defined as "a figure bounded by three straight lines." We *could* use the phrase "a figure bounded by three straight paths of moving points" every time we wanted to discuss such objects, but this would be unwieldy and unnecessarily complicated. And in more complex definitions or propositions we can merely substitute the word "triangle" for this much more elaborate statement.

Since primitive terms must be present, the ideal cannot be to have a system in which *all* terms are defined, but rather the ideal is to have a system in which a *minimum* number of primitive terms suffice for the definitions of all the others. This is an expression of the well-known and widely accepted "law of parsimony" which has come to be interpreted as meaning that it is scientifically unsound to use more than the least possible number of assumptions to explain something. This "law" is taken as a guideline throughout all scientific endeavor. We constantly strive to do things in the *simplest* possible way.

In actuality, a considerable number of different kinds of definitions can be identified, and here, as in other cases we have examined, there is less than complete agreement among the experts as to the precise characteristics of these types of definitions, and the factors which distinguish among them.[7] Only a few of these need concern us here, namely, nominal, denotative, real, and operational.

A *nominal* definition (also sometimes known as a syntactical or verbal definition) is

> an agreement or resolution concerning the use of verbal symbols. A new symbol called the *definiendum* is to be used for an already known group of words or symbols *(the definiens)*. The definiendum is thus to have no meaning other than the definiens.[8]

In other words, this is merely a verbal convention—an agreement to use a certain verbal symbol in a certain way. For example, Comte's use of the term "sociology" to refer to the science of human social relationships was a nominal definition. Similarly, Walfred A. Anderson's suggestion of the term "hurelure" to refer to human relationship structures is also a nominal definition.[9] As will be seen from the above illustrations, it is meaningless to talk about the truth or falsity of such a definition, and indeed it is a necessary characteristic of nominal definitions that they can be neither true nor false, and thus a nominal definition cannot be a proposition. Therefore, a nominal definition cannot serve as a premise. Its advantage is that it is a convenience or a shorthand term which is substituted for the definiens, but it has no meaning other than the definiens. When a definition appears as one of the six possible elements of an axiomatic theory, it will be a nominal definition.

Definition by *enumeration*, that is, by naming or specifying the components or factors of a term, is a form of nominal definition.[10] For example, Zetterberg defines military morale as: "confidence in officers, confidence in training, confidence in

[7] For example, see: Kaplan, 1964, pp. 71–78; Carney and Scheer, 1964, pp. 97–105; DiRenzo, 1966, pp. 3–18; Zetterberg, 1965, pp. 34–43.

[8] Cohen and Nagel, 1934, p. 228.

[9] Bierstedt, 1959, p. 127.

[10] Zetterberg, 1965, p. 40.

equipment, confidence in rear echelons, identification with the war effort, hatred of the enemy, satisfaction with the task assigned, . . . and so forth."[11] While definitions by enumeration have the advantage of lending themselves readily to empirical investigation, they have the disadvantage that the various factors may be unrelated to one another, and furthermore there may well be other, and more important, factors which are not enumerated.

A *denotative* definition is a definition by giving examples. We may point to an object, or otherwise physically indicate it, or give verbal examples, when asked to define it. A *nonverbal* denotative definition is frequently called an *ostensive* definition. When a child asks, "What is a painting?" the parent may reply by showing the child several examples of paintings ("This is a painting, this is a painting, and so is that. But this one is not a painting—it is a photograph.") Or when asked to define the sociological term, "position," we may reply that occupations such as professor, lawyer, newspaper reporter, policeman, clerk, accountant, and kinship terms such as mother, daughter, son, cousin, uncle, grandfather, and other terms such as group leader, follower, expediter, recorder, tension-reliever, and so on, are all examples of positions. These are both denotative definitions. Obviously these definitions do not really tell us the essence, or the distinguishing characteristics, of "painting," or of "position," but they do convey a fairly good idea of what these things are. The main advantage of denotative definitions is that they are easily understood and readily used. The more "typical" the examples used, the better usually will be the understanding conveyed by such a definition. However, a denotative definition, while having practical everyday value, will never have the rigor necessary for use in a scientific context.

In a *real* definition (also sometimes known as an *analytic* definition),

> the definiens is an *analysis* of the idea, form, type, or universal *symbolized* by . . . [the definiendum]. Both the definiens and the definiendum refer to the same thing or character. They each possess a meaning independently of the process of definition which equates them. The definiens, however, indicates the *structure* of that to which both refer.

[11] Ibid.

> A *real definition,* therefore, is a genuine proposition, which may be either true or false. Since the definiendum and the definiens must symbolize the same universal, and since the definiens must express the structure of that universal, a real definition can be true only if the two sides of the definition are equivalent in meaning and the right-hand side represents a correct analysis of it.[12]

Since a real definition is a proposition, it may appear in an axiomatic theory. When it does, however, it will be as an axiom or as a derived proposition (see below), and not as a definitional element, as discussed above. It will be seen from the above definition of "real definitions" that a real definition, as distinguished from the previous types, does tell something about the essential qualities of the definiendum. It should be noted, however, that here the emphasis is upon the referent (i.e., the thing, object, event, or phenomenon denoted by the definiendum) rather than the definiendum itself. Most of the definitions given in this book (e.g., "research," "sociology," "science") are real definitions. Similarly, a dictionary contains real definitions.

Customarily, four rules for constructing real definitions are observed, in order to ensure that they will be precise and lucid.[13] The first is that a definition must give the essence of that which is being defined; the definiens must be equivalent to the definiendum, and only to the definiendum. In other words, the definition must enable the user to determine clearly whether or not a given referent is an example of the definiendum. According to the second rule, a definition must not be circular—it must not contain, either directly or indirectly, the subject being defined. We can distinguish between the logical and psychological purposes of a definition. If a circular definition is used (for example, defining "courage" through its synonym, "bravery") it may contribute to the psychological purpose of a definition but no logical gain is achieved. If one does not know the "essence" of "courage," one will not be any further ahead for knowing that it means the same as "bravery." A less obvious example of a circular definition is defining "sun" as "the star which shines by day," since in order to define day we must refer to the shining of the sun. The third rule—not as stringently applied as the others—is that, if possible, definitions should be couched in

[12] Cohen and Nagel, 1934, p. 230.

[13] The following is based upon Cohen and Nagel, 1934, pp. 238–41.

positive rather than negative terms. Generally it is clearer and simpler to state what a thing is, rather than what it is not. Sometimes, however, negative definitions may be unavoidable or preferable—e.g., defining an orphan as a child with no parents. Finally, the fourth rule states that definitions should not be expressed in obscure or figurative language. The importance of this is almost self-evident, since a definition should clarify matters and add to understanding. A problem may arise if the definition includes a term which has different meanings in various contexts, since a term which appears quite straightforward and obvious to one person may be obscure or ambiguous to another.

It is very important fully to recognize the distinction between nominal and real definitions. In a significant article, Bierstedt sees this distinction as being basic to a very serious theoretical problem in sociology, namely, the gap between methodological and substantive theory.[14] He likens nominal definitions to mathematical models (see below) and says that empirical knowledge is necessary to construct a real definition. Nominal definitions lead to methodological theory, while real definitions lead to substantive theory. Since substantive theory is the ultimate goal of sociological inquiry, the important thing for research purposes is to recognize that the "logical danger . . . is that when nominal definitions become familiar, as they tend of course to do, we sometimes forget they are nominal and begin to treat them as real."[15]

While some would subsume *operational* definitions under nominal definitions[16] and a good case can be made to subsume them under real definitions, they are important enough to be treated separately.

> An operational definition of a term is conceived as a rule to the effect that the term is to apply to a particular case if the performance of specified operations in that case yields a certain characteristic result.[17]

The operations to be performed, in order to operationally define a term, may be physical operations (such as reading a meter), or symbolic operations (e.g., writing, verbal operations, or mental

[14] Bierstedt, 1959.

[15] Ibid., p. 128.

[16] DiRenzo, 1966, pp. 14, 270.

[17] Hempel, 1965, p. 123.

experiments) or they may consist simply of observation. The classic sociological example of an operational definition is Lundberg's statement that "a recipe for a chocolate cake may be regarded as an *operational definition* of such a cake."[18] That is, the specific operations involved in baking a cake (measuring ingredients, mixing, heating at a certain temperature, etc.) *constitute* the operational definition of such a cake. Similarly, we commonly hear IQ defined (operationally) as that which is measured by a certain test. That is, by so defining it, the problems involved in constructing a real definition of IQ are avoided, and recognition is taken of the fact that there is considerable disagreement and ambiguity in the concept of IQ. "Leader" might be operationally defined as "one who has been elected to office." For all of the above terms, other types of definitions could be given, of course (e.g., "A leader is one who effectively controls the behavior of others, this control being based upon prestige, persuasion, or skill"—this being a real definition, of course).

Operational definitions have been the subject of continuing discussion and debate ever since P. W. Bridgman, the noted physicist, first proposed the idea in 1927.[19] These issues need not be of concern here, however, other than to point out two which are of particular importance for practical research. A strict application of the principles of operationalism implies that "every scientific term should be defined by means of one unique operational criterion."[20] This means that if two different sets of operations are used to define the same term, in reality there are two *different* terms, or referents, involved. Therefore, it would be important to recognize in doing research that if, say, some measurement is made using these two operational definitions, there are really two different referents which are being measured. Another problem is that ad hoc operational definitions may become "institutionalized," and widely used and accepted without ever being subject to careful scrutiny as to their adequacy and validity.[21] Despite these and other objections to oper-

[18] Lundberg, 1942, p. 89.

[19] Bridgman, 1927. For an account of the controversies surrounding this concept, with particular reference to sociological research, see Sjoberg, 1959. See also Hempel, 1965.

[20] Hempel, 1965, p. 124.

[21] Hadden, 1969, p. 277.

ational definitions, they have become almost universally regarded as being not only acceptable but, in fact, necessary for empirical research. Certainly in any research which calls for counting or measuring something, there must be a specific definition, or set of rules, whereby the researcher can recognize or identify the referent with which he is dealing. The practical use of operational definitions in research will be more fully discussed below, in Chapter 6.

At this point there is no necessity to try to choose among these four kinds of definitions. However, it is necessary to recognize the differences among them as well as their appropriateness for different purposes and situations, and their relative advantages and disadvantages. To repeat, nominal definitions may serve as elements of axiomatic theories; real definitions may also appear in axiomatic theories, as axioms or derived propositions; denotative definitions are very useful in everyday situations; and finally, operational definitions play a crucial role in research.

Axioms are the third element of an axiomatic theory. Axioms are defined as "propositions which are accepted as being true without proof." (Sometimes the term "postulates" is used instead of "axioms," although in some of the older mathematical writing different meanings were attached to these terms. Now they are regarded as synonymous, and "axiom" is the preferred term.) Axioms state properties of the primitive terms, or relationships among them, or are related to the primitive terms in some other way. We explicitly do *not* say that axioms are self-evidently true, nor do we say that they *cannot* be proven. *Any* proposition of a system can be an axiom if its truth is assumed rather than proved. There are *no* propositions which are *intrinsically* undemonstrable or unprovable, in a system. It may be that there is available a considerable amount of evidence for the truth of an axiom, or it may be that no such evidence is available. In either case, this evidence (or lack of it) is definitely outside the system, and we are not concerned with it at this point. Axioms may be regarded as the real starting points of the theory. We have to start somewhere, and so we select some propositions as axioms. There *must* be some axioms in an axiomatic theory; otherwise the system would be circular, as in the above example of the pocket dictionary. Thus the axioms are among the premises, the "if . . ." part of the argument. Indeed, in an axiomatic theory we speak of axioms rather than premises.

Here, too, the parsimony principle applies, and the goal in constructing an axiomatic theory is to have a *minimum* number of independent axioms. Two axioms are independent if neither one of them can be logically derived from the other. If one *could* be derived from the other, one of them would, of course, be superfluous. Another important characteristic of the axioms in a theory is that they be consistent with one another. This means that they should not lead to *contradictory* propositions. Such contradiction would render the theory useless, at best. Hopefully, also, the axioms should be fertile, that is, they should entail or imply many other propositions. This characteristic, however, may well be less a characteristic of the axioms than of the persons utilizing the theory.

The question of what propositions are to be selected to serve as axioms is far from a trivial question. When it is recognized that the axioms do function as the premises of a deductive argument, it becomes clear that the entire development of the axiomatic theory must depend upon the axioms. Whatever conclusions are derived from the theory will depend, obviously, upon what axioms (i.e., premises) it contains. Again we see an excellent example from geometry. One of the axioms is "Through a given point one and only one straight line can be drawn parallel to a given line." It was the substitution of another axiom for this one (by the Russian, Lobachevsky, and the Hungarian, Bolyai, working independently) which resulted in the development of so-called non-Euclidean geometry—an important and significantly different branch of mathematics. We may also suggest an illustration from the behavioral sciences. One might select as an axiom a statement such as "People basically love one another" or some similar proposition of human behavior, and use that axiom as a building block for a theory of human behavior. Conversely, one might instead select as an axiom a paraphrase of the common expression, "People are no damn good," and use *that* axiom as a base for a theory of human behavior. Either one of these propositions, that people love one another or don't love one another, sounds "reasonable" as a fundamental statement, or axiom, upon which to build a theory of human behavior. There are those who would feel more inclined to adopt the first as an axiom, while others would prefer the second. Clearly, the resulting theories would differ in very crucial ways, as a result of the two different axioms. At an informal and personal level, this is of course what each one of us does—we have acquired some sort of basic "attitude" toward people, such as one of the above two, or perhaps others, and this basic point of view colors or affects all of our dealings with people. Ordinarily this is not a sufficiently formal or thought-out system to be called a theory, but it nevertheless illustrates the point.

The fourth element of an axiomatic theory is some kind of *logic.* That is, all the rules, laws, terminology, and procedures of logic are specifically included as part of the axiomatic theory. Logic is included on an equal basis with the primitive terms and axioms of the theory. This is necessary, because logic constitutes the set of rules which tell how to relate the primitive terms, definitions, and axioms to one another in a meaningful and productive manner. Just as in the game of football, not only must one have players, a field, a ball, and other equipment, but must also have a set of rules, so, in an axiomatic theory, one *must* have the rules of logic in addition to the other elements. (The phrase "some kind of logic" was used above to emphasize that there are various kinds of logic. However, these are of more interest to the philosopher than to the practicing scientist, and we are concerned almost exclusively with the traditional form of logic already discussed.) In addition to, or as part of, the logic which is included in the theory, it is quite common to include mathematics as another set of rules which are utilized in theory construction, thus permitting all the procedures of mathematics to be used upon the components and results of the theory.

The fifth element which may appear in some axiomatic theories is propositions which are derived from the axioms through the use of logic. These *derived propositions* will appear in the more complex theories, and are intermediate steps leading up to the theorems.

The final element of any axiomatic theory is *theorems.* A theorem is the last in a series of propositions, each of which is an axiom, or a definition, or a derived proposition. Such a series of propositions is known as a *proof.* The theorem is said to be proved, or deduced, or derived, or established, on the basis of the proof. That is, theorems are the elements which are equivalent to the conclusions of a deductive argument, while the axioms, definitions, and other derived propositions are equivalent to the premises. Thus the theorem is deduced from the axioms by logic alone, and therefore in whatever circumstances the axioms are accepted as being true the theorem must necessarily also be accepted as true. Again, *if* the axioms are true, *then* the theorem is true. And again, the question of the truth or falsity of the axioms and theorems is not of concern to the axiomatic theory, but only to the practical *user* of the theory. In general, theorems are universal statements, or generalizations, about a broad class of objects.

A theorem from one theory may, of course, also appear as a derived proposition in the proof of a theorem in another axiomatic theory.

Any axiomatic theory is composed of at least these elements: primitive terms, axioms, logic, and theorems. It may also contain definitions and derived propositions. As was pointed out before, axiomatic theories are vast and complex deductive arguments. Therefore it follows that an axiomatic theory is an explanation or series of explanations, or predictions, or both. Axiomatic theories are, in fact, the ideal explanations and predictions. They are the systems toward which all scientific activity strives as an ultimate goal.

Mathematical models

Regardless of how rigorous one attempts to be in establishing an axiomatic theory, the very language used may carry implications and meanings which are difficult or impossible to set aside, and these may interfere with the deductive processes. Furthermore, the implications of propositions in such a theory may be obscured. Even Euclid made such errors in his geometry, and thus it turns out that some of his proofs are not completely correct because the theorems do not follow from the axioms and primitive terms on the basis of logic alone. Some meanings, or implications, resulting from the choice of particular terms were included and did interfere with the logical implications.

To avoid this kind of error, the scientist frequently makes use of models. Models of ships, aircraft, automobiles, implements, and buildings are the most familiar examples of models, and are more precisely known as material or physical models. In these, the physical appearance of the model, and perhaps its functioning, resemble that of the original. Aside from their use as toys, such models may serve a more serious purpose as in their use in wind-tunnel testing of models of experimental aircraft. In addition to physical models there are many other kinds of models which fill various functions. The essential characteristic of a model is that there be some correspondence between part of the model and the original. In the case of physical models it is the physical shape and configuration which is important. In other models this correspondence may be in the assumptions made about the object, or in the functioning of it (as a hydraulic model of an electric circuit), or in the nature of the material used, and so on.

The kind of model of most interest to us here is the symbolic model, especially the *mathematical model.* In a mathematical model the correspondence is between selected characteristics of the original, and mathematical statements and equations which describe those selected characteristics. As indicated above, our concern here is to construct mathematical models of axiomatic theories in order to eliminate the problems which may arise because of the use of ordinary language. In such a model, all the significant terms of the axiomatic theory—and perhaps even *all* the terms—are replaced by symbols, and their relationships are expressed as equations, as in algebra. Since we are then concerned only with the *form* of the statements as distinguished from their substantive content, such a mathematical model is also known as a *formalization* of the theory. These terms ("mathematical model" and "formalization") are used interchangeably. We have already encountered simple examples of this in the syllogisms which were discussed earlier—"All As are Bs," etc.—and what we are discussing now is a further example of the use of formal logic. A mathematical model of an axiomatic theory is completely expressed in symbolic terms. Since the statements which the formalization contains are not really propositions (since it is nonsensical to speak of them as being either true or false) but are, instead, formal symbolic expressions of propositions, the formalization of the theory is completely devoid of substantive meaning. A formalization is thus also known as an *uninterpreted* axiomatic theory. Once it has been formalized, a theory is more easily analyzed for all of its logical implications and consequences, and the theorems are more rigorously identified.

Such mathematical models are of considerable importance to the potential advancement of the social sciences. It should be recognized that mathematics is a language—it is a system whereby complex ideas can be expressed with great precision, succinctness, lack of ambiguity, and freedom from emotional overtones. Thus when a theoretical statement in sociology (or any other field) can be expressed in mathematical terms, the result is a statement of greater precision, succinctness, lack of ambiguity, and freedom from emotional overtones. This is sorely needed, given the present state of theoretical writing in the social sciences! Not only does the expression of such a statement in mathematical terms have these advantages, but more importantly, it makes it possible to apply the entire body of mathematics and logic to these statements. It thus becomes far easier to identify all the consequences and implications of a particular theory or theoretical statement as well as to detect possible contradictions. Not incidentally, it also becomes possible to utilize computers and other sophisticated devices in the manipulation of theoretical statements. Thus it is clear that, to the extent that sociological theories or theoretical statements can be expressed as mathematical models, they become far more fertile and originative.

An important aspect of formalization and model building is that a given formal axiomatic theory may have several, or many, interpretations, or concrete representations. These representations may be vastly different in superficial appearance, and yet be identical in logical structure. In this connection the term *isomorphism* is used, which means that two or more systems have a one-to-one correspondence. That is, the elements or components of one correspond to the elements of the other, and furthermore, for every relationship which exists among the elements of the first system there is a similar relationship among the elements of the second system. An ordinary scale model of a ship is isomorphic with the ship itself. For every mast on the ship, there is a mast on the model which corresponds to it, and the proportionate heights of the actual masts are preserved in the masts of the model. Similarly, for every other portion of the ship's structure there is a like structure on the model. Any other scale model of a larger thing is isomorphic with the original. A map, too, is isomorphic with the actual terrain. For every indentation on the real coastline, there appears a similar indentation on the map. And if Cleveland, Ohio, is due north of the westernmost part of South America (which it is), then on the map Cleveland is shown directly north of that same portion of Peru. A less obvious example is that the same set of principles applies to the motion of the planets in the solar system, the motion of a pendulum, and the motion of a falling body, and thus these three kinds of phenomena are also seen to be isomorphic. A further example of the use of isomorphism in axiomatic theories follows. Let us say that there is a given concrete axiomatic theory, designated by "A," and a formalization of this theory, "B." Then A and B would be said to be isomorphic with one another. Furthermore, there might well be a second, different, concrete axiomatic theory, "C," which is also an isomorph of B. Then A and C would also be said to be isomorphic. (It should also be noted that while two whole systems or theories might be incompatible, it is possible that they would, nevertheless, have isomorphic *sub*-systems.)

Examples of axiomatic theory in sociology

To illustrate much of the above, let us say that we have developed a small theory about group membership in organizations.[22] We axiomatize the theory, and have the following:

P–1 *Primitive term:* "person."

D–1 *Definition:* "Group" is defined as "class of persons."

Axioms:

A–1 Every group contains at least two persons.

A–2 There are at least two groups.

A–3 Two groups do not have two persons in common.

A–4 For any two persons there is a group which contains them both.

At this point it is possible, through the use of logic, to deduce various theorems directly from the above. However, in this case the decision is made to formalize the theory first, as follows:

Substitute the symbol *E* for "person," and *F* for "group." Then the above primitive term, definition, and axioms become:

P–1′ *Primitive term: E.*

D–1′ *Definition: F* is defined as "class of *E*s."

Axioms:

A–1′ Every *F* contains at least two *E*s.

A–2′ There are at least two *F*s.

---

[22] This is adapted from an illustration appearing in Hochberg, 1959, p. 422 ff.

A–3′ Two Fs do not have two Es in common.

A–4′ For any two Es there is an F which contains them both.

It is now possible to deduce various theorems from these symbolic expressions, using only logic, and without any reference whatsoever to real meaning. For example:

Step 1	There are two Fs—call them M and N.	By A–2′
Step 2	M has two Es, m_1 and m_2, and N has two Es, n_1, and n_2.	By Step 1 and A–1′
Step 3	At most, one E of M can be identical with one E of N. Hence there are three Es.	By Step 2 and A–3′

Therefore,

T–1 *Theorem:* There are at least three Es.

Another theorem may be constructed as follows:

Step 1	There are three Es, x, y, and z.	By *T*–1
Step 2	There is an F, M, that contains x and y; There is an F, N, that contains y and z; There is an F, Q, that contains x and z.	By Step 1 and A–4′
Step 3	M, N, and Q are distinct.	By Step 2 and A–3′

Therefore,

T–2 *Theorem:* There are at least three Fs.

Note that Steps 1, 2, and 3, in both of the above proofs, are *derived propositions.*

Thus we have deduced these two theorems, *T*–1 and *T*–2, which apply *regardless* of what the meanings of the various symbols may be. When we return to the original concrete theory the two theorems are interpreted to mean "There are at least three persons," and "There are at least three groups," respectively. These propositions are not contained in the original theory. Thus, new knowledge has been added to the system—

the theory has provided us with these hitherto unknown facts, namely, that there are at least three persons and three groups. These theorems are known to be true, provided, of course, that the axioms are known to be true. The above formalized theory, or model, is isomorphic with the original interpreted theory.

It should be noted that this interpretation is only one of many which could be made of this same formalized theory. For example, if E is taken to symbolize "point," and F is "line," then the theory, including the theorems, has a geometrical interpretation and does, in fact, express some fundamental geometrical truths. Thus, this geometrical axiomatic theory and the above sociological one are isomorphic.

The significance of isomorphism becomes clearer when we find that two (or more) hitherto apparently unrelated theories are, in fact, isomorphic. This *may* indicate some closer connection between the two theories. Just *because* isomorphism exists, of course, does not mean that there is any necessary connection between the two theories, as in the above examples, but it certainly behooves the scientist to search closely for such connection. This is another example of the great benefit which comes to knowledge by showing relationships among phenomena. As Cohen and Nagel point out:

> Science has been characterized as a search for system (order, constancy) amidst diversity and change. The idea of isomorphism is the clearest expression of what such a system means.[23]

Despite the great potential for advancement of sociological knowledge through axiomatization of theories, the literature shows a disturbingly small number of attempts to do so. Possible reasons for this are the small number of theories of any kind which exist in contemporary sociology, and the relatively small number of sociologists with adequate training in logic and mathematics. It is to be hoped that both of these situations will change in the near future.[24]

---

[23] Cohen and Nagel, 1934, p. 139.

[24] The name of Hans Zetterberg is most frequently associated with axiomatization in sociology (1965). See Costner and Leik, 1964, and Movahedi and Ogles, 1973, for critical views of Zetterberg's work. For a discussion of the place of formalization in sociology, see Land, 1971. For constructing theories, see Blalock, 1969.

For specific examples of axiomatization of theories, see the following: Catton, 1960–61; Hage, 1965; Kinch, 1963; Maris, 1970 (see also several comments and reply in *American Sociological Review*, vol. 36 [August 1971], pp. 706–15); Quinney, 1970, chap. 1; Schwirian and Prehn, 1962 (see also comments and response in *American Sociological Review*, vol. 28 (June 1963), pp. 452–53); H. Simon, 1952; and Nagasawa and von Bretzel, 1974. See also Bailey, 1970.

CONCLUSION

We have seen that deductive arguments constitute the ideal form of explanations, which are the ultimate goal of scientific activity. Furthermore, we have seen that axiomatic theories are, in effect, vast, complex deductive arguments. And the point has been emphasized that in considering these arguments or theories all that has been said is: *if* the premises are true, *then* the theorems are, in fact, true.

This points out the crucial thing which has been missing from all of the above discussion, namely, any reference to fact or data or the empirical world or reality. Even in the example of geometry, it is still merely an axiomatic theory, a body of interrelated propositions stating only that if the premises are true then the conclusions are true. Indeed, the point was made above that axiomatic theories, by their nature, deal *only* with "if . . . then . . ." statements, and that the actual truth or falsity of the propositions is definitely excluded from this area. Yet, of course, it is precisely this—the truth or falsity of propositions—with which the scientist is concerned.

It is folly to assume that all this is merely a frivolous mental exercise, engaged in simply for its own sake or for some inherent satisfaction it provides. Yet we cannot but recognize that it is insufficient—that axiomatic theories or deductive arguments alone are not enough. Therefore it becomes clear that before any deductive argument or axiomatic theory can be meaningful, or useful, or have any practical value, one vital thing must be done. In some way, the axiomatic theory must be brought up against the real world—its axioms and theorems must be compared with empirical data—its propositions must be "bounced against" reality. Until this is done it *is* little more than a mental exercise, and it *is* worthless from a practical point of view.

An axiomatic theory can be constructed in the silence and seclusion of a monastic cell, without ever going out into the real world to see what is actually happening. But its real test is whether it is in tune with reality. Geometry, again, has withstood the test of time not only because it is a beautiful example of an axiomatic theory, but also because it *has* been found to be in tune with the real world. It is useful, it has practical value, we navigate a ship or an aircraft or a space craft by geometric principles, we build buildings and bridges using geometric theorems, we utilize it in walking across campus or weaving a rug or doing a painting. As beautiful an example of a deductive system as geometry is, it long ago would have been abandoned or relegated to its proper place as a museum piece if it had been found to be inconsistent with empirical data. And this is precisely what must be done with any axiomatic system—we have to take it outside and bounce it against reality and see if it works. If it does, then we're in business, we have something valuable, we have a powerful contribution to knowledge with which we can not only explain actual phenomena but also predict the course of future events. This is what the scientist strives for. However, if the axiomatic theory does not jibe with reality, then there must be something wrong with either the theory or the information about reality, or both. When this situation arises, as it does very frequently in scientific activity, then one must go back and reexamine the theory and also reexamine the information about the empirical world. It may be that the argument was, in fact, invalid, or some of the propositions were faulty, or the instruments for observing reality were inadequate, or there was an error in the data-collection process, or many other possibilities. But in some way the theory and reality must be made consistent with one another. If the information about reality is found to be accurate, then the theory will have to be modified or abandoned. Obviously one can never modify or abandon reality, once it has been ascertained that the information about reality is correct. And so it is at this point that we must switch to the other side of the coin and examine *inductive* reasoning, which is of utmost importance to the whole process of comparing a theory with reality.

Chapter 3

Inductive reasoning and retroduction

INDUCTIVE REASONING

Reality-testing

The scientist, striving for explanations of natural phenomena, attempts to construct axiomatic theories as the ultimate form of explanation. But, as we saw, axiomatic theories are worthless until they have been "bounced against" reality, regardless of how beautiful, rigorous, and perfect they may seem to be. (The process of reality-testing is also known as "verification" of a theory. However, some prefer the term "corroboration" instead.)[1] Just what is done when an axiomatic theory is tested against reality? Specifically, all that *can* be done is to determine whether the various propositions in the theory are, in fact, true or false. One has a theory composed of propositions; it is assumed that the construction of the theory has been carried out in a careful and rigorous manner, and that therefore the axiomatic theory is valid; consequently the only remaining variable is the truth or falsity of the axioms and theorems contained in the theory.

Now, just what information is provided about an axiomatic theory, when we determine the truth or falsity of the axioms and theorems? We have noted that there are only three statements which can be made with complete certainty about various combinations of truth and falsity, and validity and invalidity, in deductive arguments. If these are reworded we have the following three possible kinds of information which may be obtained:

1. We may find that the axioms are true. Then, we know that

[1] Popper, 1961, pp. 32–33, 251.

the theorem is true. Thus we have a useful, productive, and fertile theory. (Of course, the theorems must then be tested against reality to further verify the theory.)

2. We may find that the axioms are true *and* that the theorem is false. Then we know that the theory is, in fact, invalid, and must be revised.

3. We may find that the theorem is false. Then we know that at least one axiom is false, *or* the theory is actually invalid, *or* both. Thus we must reexamine the axioms and the validity of the theory.

There are two other possible outcomes of examining the truth or falsity of the propositions in a theory:

4. We may find that one or more axioms is false. Then we gain no information about the theorems. The theory may be valid but it is of no practical use and must be revised.

5. We may find that the theorem is true. This is a special case and will be considered below. For the moment we merely state that this lends *credibility* to the truth of the axioms and to the utility of the theory.

Thus, depending upon the results obtained, reality-testing *may* tell something about the truth or falsity of other propositions in the theory, *may* tell that the theory is invalid, or *may* tell that the theory (whether valid or invalid) is useless for practical purposes and should be revised. But reality-testing can *never* tell that the theory is valid. It will be noted that, with the exception of outcome 5 above, this is all a restatement of what has already been examined in the section on deductive arguments.

When reality-testing shows that the theorem is true. There is a temptation, when reality-testing shows that the theorem is true, to conclude that therefore the axioms are true. However, this would be an example of the logical fallacy known as *affirming the consequent*. This fallacy can be illustrated by the following simple example:

If he jumped in the pool then he would be wet.
He is wet.
Therefore, he jumped in the pool.

Clearly, the fact that he is wet does not mean that he jumped in the pool. There are countless other possible events which could result in his being wet. In this example, the first statement, "If he jumped in the pool then he would be wet" corresponds to an axiomatic theory, with "he jumped in the pool" being the axiom, and "he would be wet" being the theorem. Then the second statement, "He is wet" is the reality-testing—the observation has been made of this particular part of reality, and the theorem has been found to be true. This observation of reality clearly does not imply that this particular axiom is true.

There is a valid form of argument, known as *modus tollens,* which is very similar to the above fallacy but should not be confused with it. Note the slight difference between the following example and the previous one:

If he jumped in the pool then he would be wet.
He is *not* wet.
Therefore, he did *not* jump in the pool.

Here the reality-testing has shown the theorem, "he would be wet," to be false. And thus the conclusion is reached that the axiom, "He jumped in the pool," is false. This is an illustration of outcome 3 above.

The difference between these two arguments may be clearer if we formalize them:

affirming the consequent:
If p then q.
q (exists, is the case).
Therefore p (exists, is the case).

modus tollens:
If p then q.
Not-q (q does not exist, is not the case).
Therefore not-p.

Returning now to the case when reality-testing shows the theorem to be true, we have seen that this does not *imply* that the axiom is true. However, we reason as follows. Let us say that there is a theory *A* (axioms, etc.) which leads to theorem *T*. It is also known that there are other theories *B, C, D,* etc., which could also lead to *T*. It is further known that there are still other theories *P, Q, R,* etc., which would lead to not-*T*, i.e., the contradiction of *T*. Now, when the theorem *T* is tested against reality and found to be true, this immediately eliminates theories *P, Q, R,* etc., by *modus tollens.* This gives us increased confidence that theory *A or B, C, D,* etc., is the correct one. It is important to note that this does not prove that A is correct, but since it eliminates some alternative theories it increases the credibility of theory A. The more alternatives we can eliminate or disprove, the greater will be our confidence in the remaining ones. If we find that a theory leads to many correct predictions, this lends credibility to the theory, but a single (verified) incorrect prediction will necessitate modification of the theory. In ordinary problem-solving situations, when we increase the credibility of a given answer by eliminating alternative answers we refer to this as the process of elimination. For example, let us say that I, as an absent-minded professor, have forgotten which of my students I have an appointment with. I believe it to be a certain young man. If, by some means, I acquire the information that the student I am to see is not a woman, this increases the credibility of my "theory" that I am to see the young man in question.

Frequently, in actual practice, we are dealing with *several* theories, all of which lead to the same theorem. Indeed, some would say that it is essential to deal with many alternative theories. In such cases, when the theorem is found to be (probably) true, we must, in some way, rank the alternative theories, or choose among them. In other words, we must assign relative *credibilities* to the various theories. For example, we might have several theories all leading to the same theorem: "Many people report having observed UFOs (unidentified flying objects)." These theories might attempt to explain this phenomenon in terms of, for example, mass deception, or in terms of mass hallucinations, or natural events such as meteors or the emission of "swamp gas," or secret military aircraft, or beings from other planets. The person with a practical interest in these theories, for purposes of reality-testing or policy-making or whatever, must in some way rank their credibilities—if only to determine in which theory to invest his research resources. But just how to assign relative credibilities is not an easy task. One view is that one should select the safest, strongest, and simplest theory, with the last-named being the most important.[2] However, the very concept of simplicity may be so complex in its meaning as to render it useless as a means of deciding among theories, at least in some circumstances.[3] Perhaps a more promising approach is to use "utility indices" and the general concepts of decision

[2] Goodman, 1968.

[3] Ackerman, 1968.

theory.[4] For example, in betting situations one is able actually to assign numerical values to the credibility of the various alternative "theories." If one is willing to bet twice as much that one horse will win a race than that a second horse will win (assuming the odds to be the same), one is saying that the "theory" that the first horse will win is twice as credible as the "theory" that the second one will win. In similar but more complicated ways, decision theory enables one to determine the relative credibility of theories which are less obviously quantifiable.

We see, therefore, that the real advances in knowledge come when we discover, through reality-testing (observing some aspect of nature), that either the axioms or the theorems of a given theory are, in fact, true. For example, it has been suggested that theories "like that of Malthus (who postulated a simple mechanism of birth frequency, which general experience told him was largely justified, and, on the basis of this, predicted population growth curves)" exemplify the situation when the axioms are found to be true, while such "theories as the atomic theory of matter, with atoms and electrons acting only as hypothesized constructs, having consequences consistent with the observable physical world" exemplify those in which the theorems are found to be true.[5]

Thus, what we strive to do in science is to *eliminate alternative* theories. This is all we can do—constantly increase the credibility of a given theory—but we must always be aware that we can never *prove* the theory to be valid, and also we must always be aware that tomorrow the given theory *may* be proved to be invalid, by some further reality-testing. Some would go so far as to *define* science in terms of the capability of the system to be *falsified* by empirical testing.[6]

One counterargument to the above line of reasoning should be noted. Some philosophers of science point out that the above view, based as it is upon the idea of eliminating alternative theories, assumes that there is a finite number of possible theories which might lead to theorem *T*, and they further point out that this is not a reasonable assumption. They say that there is, in fact, an infinite number of possible theories which could result in a given theorem *T*. We do not deny this but we note that

[4] Kemeny, 1959, pp. 109–12; also, Chernoff and Moses, 1959.

[5] Coleman, 1960, pp. 141–42.

[6] Popper, 1961, pp. 40–41.

in any actual situation, involving a practical research activity, we do not for a moment suppose that there is an infinite number of *relevant* theories. Practically speaking there is only a limited number of reasonable theories, and the more of these we can eliminate, the greater our certainty that one of those remaining is the correct one.[7]

We now must turn to the question of how we go about determining the truth or falsity of axioms and theorems, how we go about the process of reality-testing. In order to do this, we will examine inductive arguments.

Inductive arguments

We have already defined inductive arguments (the terms "inductive inference" and "inductive logic" are also used) as those in which the premises supply only *some* evidence for the truth of the conclusion. There are at least two different kinds of inductive arguments.[8] The most familiar one, and the one which we will consider first, is known as induction by enumeration, or inverse inference. This is the whole process of coming to a *probable* conclusion, on the basis of many individual observations.[9] We make a series of observations of similar events or phenomena, and, finding certain things to be true of each of these observation, we conclude that the same things are true of *all* such phenomena. To illustrate, we make the following observations:

Bat 1 has lungs.
Bat 2 has lungs.
Bat 3 has lungs.
Bat 4 has lungs.
.
.
.
Bat *n* has lungs.

On the basis of these observations we reach a conclusion:

Therefore, all bats have lungs.

---

[7] For some differing views on this see Carney and Scheer, 1964, p. 369, and Pap, 1953, p. 27.

[8] The experts are not in agreement with one another. See Carnap, 1962, pp. 207–8; Kaplan, 1964, p. 233; Carney and Scheer, 1964, p. 351.

[9] Induction should not be confused with *mathematical induction* which is a method of proof that is actually deductive in nature. See Richardson, 1941, p. 400.

We do not, in induction, observe *all* possible cases, i.e., *all* bats in the above example. We either cannot, because of practical considerations, or it is not worthwhile. (If we *did* observe all bats, or all the possible instances of a phenomenon, this would be an example of what is known as perfect, or complete, induction. Such exhaustive enumeration of all cases is really an example of deduction. This would be nice, but it is rarely possible.) In induction we merely enumerate a portion of the total possible number of cases. This is the essence of induction—the conclusion of an inductive argument refers to a *whole class* of objects, on the basis of observation of only *some* of the objects. Thus since the conclusion is based only upon the ones which are actually observed, no matter how many we may observe (enumerate) we can never be *certain* that the next one will be the same, and thus the conclusion can never be more than *probable*. That is, the evidence offered by the observations is regarded as making the conclusion more probably true than its negation.

The conclusion of this kind of inductive argument is usually a universal proposition (i.e., one which applies to all members of a given class), which is established by examining specific instances falling under it. It may be, as in the example above, that the conclusion applies to all members of the class, or it may be that it only applies to a certain proportion of the members of the class, as in the following example. Again, using bats as an example, it might be found that of all the many bats observed, two thirds were brown in color. Then the conclusion would be that two thirds of *all* bats are brown.

Now let us reexamine the above inductive argument which used bats and lungs as an example. This can be expressed as follows, letting B stand for "bat" and L for "lungs":

$B_1, B_2, B_3, B_4, \ldots B_n$ have Ls.
Therefore, all Bs have Ls.

If we substitute the words "Brooklynite" for B and "low IQ" for L, then the argument says that because we have observed a certain number of people from Brooklyn with low IQs, therefore all Brooklynites have low IQs. Clearly, we are much less willing to accept this conclusion as true than we are to accept the one stating that all bats have lungs. How do we explain this difference in our willingness to accept the conclusions of the two arguments? The answer is that we are willing to accept the conclusion in the "bat" case because, on the basis of our experience and knowledge, we believe that the bats which have been observed are, in fact, typical of all bats. In other words, we are saying that the proposition, "Whatever is true of B_1, B_2, B_3, B_4, . . . B_n, is true of all Bs" is really part of the argument. In fact, in *any* induction by enumeration argument, this proposition is implicitly part of the argument. But this proposition has even more significance because it is actually a statement of one of the fundamental assumptions of science, namely, the uniformity of nature. Our earlier discussion of the phrase "recurring relationships among phenomena" in the definition of science touched upon this. Thus when this proposition is included, the complete inductive argument is as follows:

> Whatever is true of B_1, B_2, B_3, . . . B_n is true of all Bs.
> B_1, B_2, B_3, . . . B_n have Ls.
> Therefore, all Bs have Ls.

But this is, of course, a valid *deductive* argument! Thus we see that the only difference between a deductive argument and this kind of inductive argument is that in a deductive argument we *assume* the truth of the first proposition in the above argument, while in an inductive argument we *assert* the truth of the first proposition on the basis of our knowledge or beliefs about the homogeneity of the class of all Bs. That is, we say *that* it is true.

Thus we see that the real issue here is the homogeneity of the class of all Bs. An inductive argument amounts to a deductive argument stating that "If the class of all Bs is homogeneous . . . then the conclusion is true." Thus in no way is deduction opposed to induction; they are essentially the same form of inference. But the distinguishing characteristic between the two is that in induction it becomes crucial to determine just to what extent the class of all Bs is, in fact, homogeneous. Not only does the inductive argument depend upon homogeneity of the class of all Bs, but also it depends upon how representative the observed Bs are of the class of all Bs. This introduces, of course, the question of *sampling*, which will be discussed in a later chapter. Returning now to the original question of why we accept the conclusion about "bats," but do not accept it about "Brooklynites," we see that in the latter case we are unwilling to assume the same degree of homogeneity about Brooklynite IQs that we are about bats' anatomy, and further, that we are less willing to accept the observed Brooklynites as an adequate sample than we are to accept the observed bats as an adequate sample. In practical situations it is very common among persons who engage in sloppy thinking to assert the truth of the first proposition in the example, when they have no basis for doing so. This is especially obvious in what is known as the particularistic fallacy (i.e., generalizing from one particular instance) and is the basis of many erroneous beliefs in the area of ethnic discrimination, among others.[10]

In the second kind of inductive argument which we will consider, namely, predictive inference, the evidence for the truth of the conclusion comes not from a series of *similar* observations, but from *other* kinds of observations or statements.[11] This kind of inductive argument is best illustrated by the example given in Chapter 1 of the explanation of why Cassius plotted the death of Caesar. This type fits the definition of inductive arguments in that the premises supply only some evidence for the truth of the conclusion. Furthermore, all of the essential characteristics of induction by enumeration are also true of this type of argument: we do not observe all cases, the conclusion is only probable, the conclusion is usually a universal proposition, and in some way the assertion of the proposition concerning the uniformity of nature is present in the argument, although perhaps only implicitly. Although it is actually a fairly common form of argument, this type of inductive argument is not so clearly understood by the philosophers of science.

In conclusion, then, we see that the process of induction provides us with the means of evaluating a proposition which has already been suggested—evaluating in the sense of determining the truth or falsity of the proposition. Whereas deduction is not concerned with the material truth of propositions, that is precisely what *is* the main concern of induction. While the proposition "All bats have lungs" may be premise or conclusion of a deductive argument, it is in the inductive process that we are able to determine whether or not that is a *true* proposition.

The process of induction is in common use in our everyday lives. As a compulsive record-keeper and cat lover, I note that of approximately 80 kittens of which I have information, 70 percent were born in April. I conclude that 70 percent of all kittens

[10] Cohen and Nagel, 1934, pp. 276–78.

[11] Carney and Scheer, 1964, p. 351.

(all Arizona kittens?) are born in April. As a newcomer to India, I notice a woman wearing toe rings. In response to my inquiry I am told that this means she is a married woman. I see another, and another, and another, and in each case I am told the same thing. I conclude that all Indian women who wear toe rings are married. During my first few months in a new community I notice that on Mondays I receive a disproportionately large amount of "junk" mail. I conclude that on all Mondays I am likely to receive a lot of junk mail. I am deceived by a used-car salesman. This happens again, and again, and again. I conclude that all used-car salesmen are liars. And so on and so on. (In these particular practical illustrations we recognize, of course, that all the conclusions may not actually be true—it depends upon how correct we are in asserting the truth of the "uniformity of nature" proposition.)

Hypotheses and laws

To further understand the use of inductive arguments, it is necessary to examine two additional concepts: "hypotheses" and "laws." A hypothesis is a proposition stating an assumed relationship among two or more things. Thus it expresses a tentative or conjectural or supposed or possible relationship. It may or may not be *believed* to be true, but that is extraneous to the definition. Also, it is not necessary that any evidence exist for the support of the hypothesis. It is merely assumed, for the sake of further investigation. This further investigation is undertaken through the use of inductive reasoning. In other words, the starting point of an inductive argument is a hypothesis.[12] (Note the similarity between hypotheses and axioms. Whereas a hypothesis is the starting point of an inductive argument, an axiom is the starting point of an axiomatic theory. Furthermore, both are assumed to be true for the sake of the argument, regardless of whether or not there is any empirical evidence to support this.)

In order to serve as a useful starting point for a line of inductive reasoning, there are certain characteristics which a hypothesis should have. First, it should be worded as simply and clearly as possible. Second, the terms in the hypothesis should be such that either their referents are easily recognizable or

[12] A "null hypothesis" is a hypothesis which usually states that there is *no* relationship between two things. It has a specific statistical use which will be described later.

indicators are readily provided.[13] Next, a hypothesis should be specific and precise, and not so grandiose, general, or elaborate that it would be impossible to test. Fourth, it must be capable of verification by means of available techniques. Finally, the hypothesis should provide the answer to the problem or question which initiated the inquiry.[14]

Having introduced this concept of hypothesis, we can now see how the process of reality-testing of theories or explanations takes place. We select the axiom, theorem, or other proposition which is to be tested, reword it if necessary to conform to the above criteria, and then refer to it as a hypothesis. To continue with the same example as before, let us say that the proposition, "All bats have lungs," is the axiom or theorem which we have selected to reality-test. This proposition becomes our hypothesis (no change in wording is needed in this illustration), and it serves as the start of our induction. In induction by enumeration, we then proceed to observe Bat_1, Bat_2, Bat_3, . . . Bat_n, and these observations enable us to make the statement that our hypothesis is or is not (probably) true. We say that the hypothesis is affirmed or supported or rejected, etc. There are various statistical tests which are utilized at this point which enable us to state rather precisely just how sure or confident we are that the hypothesis is true. The use of these statistical tests of significance will be considered in a later chapter. (If, on the other hand, the proposition to be tested is a singular proposition, such as "*This* bat has lungs," induction is not necessary—providing there are no observational errors—since only a single observation is necessary to determine the truth or falsity of the proposition.)

The conclusion of an inductive argument (i.e., a hypothesis which has been affirmed) is known as a *law*. Thus a law is an empirical generalization; it is a proposition concerning which sufficient empirical evidence has been collected so that we believe it to be probably true, and it is a universal proposition.[15] As was pointed out above, when defining inductive arguments, we can never be absolutely certain that the conclusion is true; we can only continue to add evidence to support it. Therefore, sci-

---

[13] See section below on Definitions and Indicators in Chapter 6.

[14] Cohen and Nagel, 1934, pp. 207–15; Goode and Hatt, 1952, pp. 67–73, Ayer, [illegible], pp. 87–88.

[15] Hempel and Oppenheim, 1953, p. 338.

entific laws must always be regarded as only probably true, or tentative. We can continue to use them until the time when a greater amount of evidence is amassed, supporting an *alternative* hypothesis. At such time the first law will be abandoned in favor of the alternative.[16]

It is this tentative character of a law (i.e., the conclusion of an inductive argument) which has led some writers to refer to such a conclusion as a hypothesis. However, there is an important distinction between a hypothesis and a law. In the case of a hypothesis we need have no reason whatsoever to actually believe it to be true. We may even believe it to be false. It is nothing more than an assumption we choose to investigate. However, when such a proposition has survived an inductive investigation there *is* considerable evidence to support our belief that it is true. It has withstood an empirical test, and thus we *assert* that it is true to the extent indicated by the probabilities involved, and so we refer to it as a law.

Methods of induction

For years, literally centuries, philosophers have struggled with what is referred to as the problem of induction. This problem has centered around two major issues, first, the attempt to devise a rigorous system of rules of procedures which would govern inductive reasoning in the same manner as traditional logic does for deductive reasoning, and second, the question of the justification of induction.

The historical name most commonly associated with the attempt to formulate a system of rules of inductive reasoning is that of John Stuart Mill (1806–1873), who drew upon some earlier efforts of Francis Bacon. Mill produced five canons, or rules, of induction which he said served as methods of discovering causal relationships, and also as methods of testing the validity of inductive arguments. The five canons are known as the method of agreement, the method of difference, the joint method of agreement and difference, the method of concomitant variation, and the method of residues. Details of these may be found in many widely-available sources.[17] However, Mill him-

[16] The term "principle" is usually used to refer to a fundamental or basic law, the truth of which is very well established.

[17] See, for example, Goode and Hatt, 1952, chap. 7; Carney and Scheer, 1964, pp. 376 ff; and Lastrucci, 1963, pp. 196–203.

self believed that although these five canons were pertinent to the physical sciences, they were not applicable to the social sciences.[18] In fact, in a detailed analysis, it has been shown that these canons are neither capable of discovering causal relationships, nor of serving as means of testing validity of inductive arguments.[19] However, they are of definite value in eliminating false hypotheses. Since, as we have seen, this is the way in which science proceeds, those who would ignore Mill's work altogether are overlooking much of considerable value in scientific research.

Currently, the question of rules of inductive logic remains unresolved. Some philosophers argue cogently against the possibility of ever establishing such rules.[20] On the other hand, the preface to one prominent volume states that the book's aim "is the actual construction of a system of inductive logic . . . that can take its rightful place beside the modern, exact systems of deductive logic."[21] Clearly, this part of the problem of induction remains as much a problem as ever.

The question of the justification of induction is equally as knotty. An eminent philosopher has pointed out that philosophers of science have long been concerned with the question of how we can know from the past what the future will be like.[22] Our strong belief that the patterns of the past will persist in the future is not based upon experience, nor is it any kind of logical necessity. Simply *because* every bat we have observed is brown does not ensure that the next one observed will also be brown. Simply *because* every group we have observed has a leader does not ensure that all groups have leaders. Simply *because* the sun has risen every day in the past does not ensure that it will rise tomorrow. Yet we have varying degrees of confidence that these events will take place. Certainly, there is little doubt in our minds that the sun will rise tomorrow, and we plan our activities on that assumption even though we are aware that some astronomical cataclysm could conceivably occur. Upon what basis do we justify our belief in the future course of

---

[18] Ryan, 1970, pp. 138–40.

[19] Cohen and Nagel, 1934, pp. 251–67.

[20] Perhaps the extreme position is that of Popper who flatly denies the existence of induction (1961, p. 40).

[21] Carnap, 1962, p. v.

[22] Kaplan, 1964, p. 20.

events? One answer to this question is the assumption, mentioned previously, of the uniformity of nature. Clearly, this is not an adequate answer. In the first place, of course, it is merely an assumption. Furthermore, in trying to specify exactly what is meant by "uniformity" it is found to be a far more complex problem than is apparent. Philosophers of science are agreed that this does not provide a satisfactory answer. Other attempts to justify, or validate, induction have proved to be equally unsatisfactory, and today there is considerable interest in trying to *vindicate*, rather than validate, induction by showing that *if* "any method of predicting the future works then induction works."[23] Thus, the most generally accepted justification of the use of inductive reasoning is not really a rigorous justification at all, but merely lies in the undeniable fact that the propositions which result from such reasoning are found, in practice, to have predictive value. Predictions derived from good inductive reasoning are found to be true. People do make predictions based upon experience, and they have always done so, and these predictions have, with varying degrees of accuracy, enabled life to progress. As Braithwaite puts it:

> The case for employing the recognized inductive policies is thus not the negative fact that there is no other systematic way of *trying*, but the negative fact that there is no other way of *succeeding* in making true predictions, combined with the positive fact that pursuing inductive policies frequently does succeed.[24]

One thing about which there is considerable agreement concerning induction, regardless of the viewpoint taken as to the nature of induction, is that it is based upon some theory of probability. However there is, alas, no agreement as to the nature of probability itself. Despite the fact that probability has come to occupy an important place in the field of mathematics, and especially the fact that it serves as the foundation for all statistical procedures, the experts in the field adhere to several different theories of probability. In a very helpful passage, Kaplan describes the three predominant approaches to probability.[25] The first is known as mathematical probability, in which probability is interpreted to mean the ratio of the number of favorable cases

[23] Smart, 1968, p. 183.

[24] Braithwaite, 1953, pp. 272–73.

[25] Kaplan, 1964, pp. 225–32.

(i.e., the cases in which we are interested) to the total possible number of cases. We associate this kind of probability, particularly, with card games, dice, roulette, and other gambling games. For example, let us say that from an ordinary deck of 52 playing cards I select one card at random. What is the probability it will be a king? There are four possible favorable cases, that is, there are four kings in the deck. And the total possible number of cases is, of course, 52. So the ratio of these is 4/52 or 1/13, which is the numerical value of the probability of selecting a king. Similarly, let us say that I am to select one student at random from a class containing 18 men and 23 women. What is the probability that I will select a man? There are 18 men, and a total of 41 students, so the probability is 18/41. In the same class, if I want to know the probability that I will select a person less than 8 feet tall, the answer—unless the class contains some unusual students!—will be 41/41 or 1. And similarly, the probability of selecting a student more than 8 feet tall is 0/41 or 0. It is easily seen that numerical values of probability will always be between 0 and 1, inclusive, with 0 representing impossibility and 1 representing certainty.

The second form of probability, recently come into prominence, is known as personal or psychological probability. This is a subjective view and is exemplified by one's willingness to place a bet on a given event at certain odds. The odds are determinants of the numerical values of the probabilities involved. An illustration of this—hypothetical, to be sure—might be a popular, utterly unsentimental, and mathematically-trained young woman who faces the task of choosing among several offers of marriage. For each of the young men in turn she considers the likelihood, for example, of his becoming financially successful, of his being a "good" father, of his continued good health, of his continuing to be a stimulating and exciting partner, of his compatibility with her family, and of whatever other criteria she personally deems important. In making her decision she must consider not only the relative importance to her of these various criteria, but also her belief in the likelihood or the odds (i.e., the probability) that they will occur. Central to this psychological approach is the so-called *Bayes' theorem* of conditional probability, which takes into account the probability of some prior or antecedent event, and its effect upon the probabilities of the various alternatives under consideration. This approach to probability has come to occupy an important place in decision theory, and other situations dealing with problems of human behavior involving choice.

Frequency or statistical theories are the third type. In these the concept of probability is applied to the relative frequencies of a sequence of events. Illustrative of this is the Weather Service's reporting that "There is a 30 percent probability of rain today." In order to make such a statement, the meteorologists collect data on the amount of moisture in the atmosphere, the stability of the air mass, the amount and frequency of recent precipitation, wind direction and velocity, and other pertinent information. From their historical records they find that on 30 percent of the days on which this particular combination of factors occurred, rain actually did fall. Kaplan points out that no one of these theories of probability is clearly preferable to the others:

> The behavioral scientist may find it useful to apply mathematical probability to the treatment of certain questions of heredity, for example; statistical probability for questions of growth and development; and psychological probability in connection with questions of choice and decision by the mature adult.[26]

Thus it is seen that some concept of probability is fundamental to the inductive process.

Despite the above serious philosophical problems concerning induction, and despite the ambiguity of the probabilistic foundation of the inductive process, induction is nevertheless an essential part of the scientific method. These areas of philosophical inconclusiveness should not lead the student to underestimate the importance of induction.

In this section we have examined reality-testing, and have shown that it is through reality-testing of some part of an axiomatic theory that advances in knowledge are achieved. Inductive arguments are used as a means of reality-testing. The various kinds of inductive inference, especially induction by enumeration, were then discussed, the intimate relationship between inductive and deductive reasoning was pointed out, and the importance of the always-present assumption of the uniformity of nature was noted. Then the characteristics of hypotheses and laws, and the relationships between them, were pointed

[26] Ibid., p. 231.

out. Finally, the problems of the quest for a systematic set of rules for induction, and of the justification of induction, were considered, along with a brief note on the probabilistic foundation of the inductive process.

Thus far we have considered axiomatic theories and inductive reasoning—two essential parts of the scientific effort. However, there is one more part to the picture, to which we now turn.

RETRODUCTION

In the preceding sections on axiomatic systems and inductive reasoning we have seen how an axiomatic theory or a tentative explanation is tested against the real world through an inductive process. The confirmed hypothesis, or law, is the final outcome of this process, and these various laws, linked with other propositions, form explanations. But little has been said about where the theory comes from, or how we devise it. To consider this, we now turn to an examination of the process of *retroduction*, which will constitute the final link in this chain of scientific procedure.[27]

It was mentioned above[28] that in devising a deductive explanation one starts with the explicandum and then works back toward the explicans. Or to phrase it differently, one starts with the theorem and then devises a theory, consisting of axioms, primitive terms, etc., which will result in that theorem. Or to put it in still different terms, one starts with an observed phenomenon and then devises tentative explanations, or theories, for the observation. This process of reasoning from consequent to antecedent is known as *retroduction*.[29]

Historically, and until recently, induction and deduction were regarded as the total extent of the processes of inference and reasoning, at least as pertains to scientific activity. Philosophers of science have devoted much time and effort to attempting adequately to describe the relationships between induction and deduction, and more importantly, to show just how these constitute the scientific method. Although many ingenious attempts have been made in this direction, none of these efforts have produced a completely satisfactory picture.

[27] It should be noted that the various writers on this subject, taking their cue from Peirce himself (see below), use the terms retroduction and abduction interchangeably. Here, the preferred term "retroduction" will be used.

[28] Page 37.

[29] Peirce, 1958, pp. 367–68.

A solution to these difficulties began to take form as a result of the writings of the philosopher Charles Sanders Peirce. Among other things, Peirce directed his efforts to the question of where theories, or tentative explanations, or hypotheses, come from. What is the source of these? A close examination of induction and deduction shows that neither one of these processes can *originate* ideas. Theories (through the process of deduction) tell us the various logical and necessary implications of the axioms, and point to new knowledge. Induction takes a hypothesis and tells us whether the theory is in agreement with reality, and to what extent. But neither of them tells us where the theory comes from in the first place. In the actual "doing" of science, the scientist does not start with a theory and then make deductions from it. The theory simply does not magically appear, full-grown, to the scientist. Similarly, the scientific research process does not *start* with a hypothesis. The scientific endeavor invariably starts with *observations of phenomena.* The scientist observes some event, perhaps (but not necessarily) an unexpected or surprising event, and *wonders* about it.

This act of wondering is of utmost importance. In the complicated world of today, characterized as it is by technological and scientific achievements which were unthinkable a few decades ago, it is easy for the scientist, and perhaps easier for the college student, to become so sophisticated and blase that he ceases to be surprised at anything. After having seen men walking on the moon, how can we bother to wonder about such prosaic things as the social structure of an anthill, or how the seating arrangement in a small group is related to the relative rates of interaction? Yet without this act of wondering, the scientist would never get beyond the simple stage of observation. The scientist must ever be alive and alert to the bewildering variety of events constantly taking place around him, and to the extent that he *wonders* about them—asks what the facts are, and seeks an explanation for them—to this extent he is taking the first crucial step in the scientific method.

The scientist first observes some phenomenon and wonders about it. *Then* he tries to devise a *tentative* explanation or theory for it. The phenomenon which he observes is a specific instance of the theorem of the tentative explanation. This reasoning from the phenomenon "backwards" to a tentative explanation, is, as mentioned above, the process of retroduction. Retroduction involves bringing together many kinds and sources of information. All the scientist's previous experience and knowledge are brought to bear upon the problem. It is here that is found the most creative part of the scientific activity. The words genius, insight, imagination, and ingenuity, as well as guess, have been used by various writers in attempting to describe the retroductive process. For example, one authority says:

> The abductive suggestion comes to us like a flash. It is an act of *insight,* although of extremely fallible insight. It is true that the different elements of the hypothesis were in our minds before; but it is the idea of putting together what we had never before dreamed of putting together which flashes the new suggestion before our contemplation.[30]

Currently there is considerable interest on the part of psychologists in the phenomenon of creativity, although at present it is not fully understood. It seems quite likely that as more is learned about the way in which creativity operates, this will also provide further information about retroduction. At present, however, there are no rules for retroduction, no handy guidelines or set of steps one can follow in order to achieve the desired results. "The critical moment," as Hanson puts it in his definitive work on retroduction, comes when the scientist "perceives that one might reason about the data in such and such a way."[31] Yet although the exact nature of retroduction is unknown, there is little question that something is operating. There is general agreement that it is more than pure guesswork or intuition, and despite a superficial similarity it is certainly not the traditional "*Verstehen*" (that special kind of insight or understanding which comes from internalization of the stimulus). There is a more complicated process operating.

Hanson describes the retroductive inference process as follows:

1. Some surprising phenomenon *P* is observed.
2. *P* would be explicable as a matter of course if *H* were true.
3. Hence there is reason to think that *H* is true.[32]

---

[30] Buchler, 1940, p. 304.

[31] Hanson, 1965, p. 88. Chapter IV of this work is particularly pertinent to the present discussion. For additional material on Peirce, and especially retroduction, see also Boler, 1963, and, Peirce, 1957, as well as the works cited in other footnotes herein. See also, H. Simon, 1968.

[32] Hanson, 1965, p. 86.

More simply this can be symbolized as:

P
if H then P
therefore, maybe H

In this description, H stands for "hypothesis" or, in our terminology, tentative explanation. It is in the third step that the existence of this tentative explanation is inferred, but as Hanson points out, this inference cannot be made unless its content is present in Step 2, which is the critical and creative step. On the other hand, those who would attempt to provide an inductive account of the source of H say that repetitions of P somehow cause H to emerge. And similarly, the deductive account of the source of H regards it as some kind of "higher-level hypothesis" which is simply taken as "given" and from which P emerges deductively. As was stated before, neither of these is an acceptable account of the origination of new ideas.

Taking an everyday illustration, let us suppose that at noontime I observe an attractive coed, very stylishly and formally attired in a white dress, walking across the campus. Being male, I need no further justification for my having taken note of her. But a few minutes later I notice another girl, similarly attired, and then another and another, and I begin to wonder, "Why are all these girls, all dressed alike and in such unusual dress for this campus, all going in the same direction at the same time of day?" My wonder increases as I see several more of them. My wondering then motivates me to construct a tentative explanation. Reflecting upon the various elements of my observation, along with my previous knowledge and experience, it occurs to me that *if* there were an important ceremonial sorority luncheon taking place, the unusual situation would be explained. So my tentative explanation is that such a luncheon is taking place. To use the above symbolic form we have:

P (many coeds, stylishly attired, walking in the same direction at the same time, etc.).

If H (an important sorority luncheon is about to take place) then P (many coeds, stylishly attired, etc.).

Therefore, maybe H (an important sorority luncheon is about to take place).

Thus we see that retroduction does not lead to anything more definite than the possibility that a given tentative explanation may be the correct one. It suggests a possibility, which then must be more formally and rigorously examined by the processes of axiomatization and reality-testing. The conclusion of retroductive inference is, thus, not asserted to be true; it is merely stated as being possibly true. Furthermore,

> the conclusion has a certain "likelihood" in relation to the premisses [*sic*], but this likelihood is not capable of numerical evaluation; it is logico-psychological plausibility rather than mathematical probability that makes the theory expressed in the conclusion an acceptable one.[33]

We note again the relationship among the three forms of inference, as Peirce describes them: "Deduction proves that something *must* be; Induction shows that something *actually is* operative; Abduction merely suggests that something *may be*."[34]

In actual practice, when the scientist engages in retroduction he may, and indeed he probably will, produce more than one tentative explanation for the phenomenon which has been observed. In this case, the process of retroduction also includes the selection of one of these in preference to the various others which might also explain the event. Here the concept of credibility enters again. In selecting one from among several tentative explanations, the scientist chooses the simplest, highly credible one, or in other words the most economical one.

The picture now is complete. Starting with observations of phenomena, the scientist, by the process of retroduction, constructs a tentative explanation, reasoning in reverse so to speak. He may actually construct several such tentative explanations. He selects one which is the most economical and axiomatizes it, deducing various implications from it. Next, he selects one or more of the propositions in the theory as a hypothesis and tests this against reality through the use of some form of inductive inference. And finally, as a result of this reality-testing, he determines that his tentative explanation is or is not useful, and that he therefore has or has not made a contribution to knowledge.

---

[33] Nidditch, 1960, p. 315.

[34] Quoted in Hanson, 1965, p. 85.

Chapter 4

The scientific method: A summary

The concept of the scientific method has become reified. Commonly, the layman thinks of it as The Scientific Method, and as consisting of a set of specific procedures or steps—usually four or five in number—which the scientist must follow, and which, when he does so, ensure that his work is truly scientific. Not so! Preferably it should be regarded instead as simply the methods of science—a bringing to bear, upon a specific problem, *any* method whatsoever so long as it is characterized by objectivity, accuracy, systematization, and so on, according to the definition of science. One philosopher puts it very neatly when he says that the "scientific method, as far as it is a method, is nothing more than doing one's damnedest with one's mind, no holds barred."[1] It is an attitude, a way of thinking about and approaching a problem, characterized by persistent criticism and skepticism regarding arguments, in the light of accepted rules for assessing evidence.[2] Thus in reality all of our previous discussion about science has described the scientific method, from its beginning with the observation of phenomena, the wondering about them, the process of retroducing a tentative explanation, to the axiomatizing of this, then the reality-testing of the theory, and finally the revision of the theory or prediction, its further confirmation, and further hypotheses.

Much of the previous discussion of science, as well as some new and important statements about relationships among the various parts, are summarized in the Flowchart of the Scientific

[1] P. W. Bridgman, as quoted in Nidditch, 1968, p. 8.

[2] Nagel, 1961, p. 13.

Method (Figure 1). (The numbers down the left-hand side of the chart appear merely for easy reference to various parts of the chart, and should not be thought of as formal steps in the scientific method.) The process starts with the more or less casual observation of some phenomenon or event, and it may end there unless there is some wondering or curiosity about the phenomenon. This wondering may lead to the formation of a question or perhaps a hypothesis concerning the observed phenomenon, which, in turn, leads to the formulation and design of a research project for the purpose of *describing*, more carefully, this aspect of nature. The actual research process, consisting of data collection, processing, analysis, and interpretation, follows this, utilizing only a single observation if the hypothesis is a singular statement, or induction if the hypothesis is other than a singular statement. The outcome of this is a finding that the hypothesis is (probably) true, or is false, but in either case the result is a *description* of some aspect of nature. Note that in some cases it is possible to go directly from the "wonder" of Step 2 to the "description" of Step 9, as indicated by the long arrow connecting these two steps. From this description it is possible to make *predictions*, using an inductive process based on the assumption of the uniformity of nature, as in the case of the IUDs or aspirin, and these predictions lead to further hypotheses or questions. Thus we see here the first illustration of the never-ending aspect of science, with the process constantly being repeated with increasing refinement. Also, of course, it is from the "prediction" step that practical applications are derived. Thus far, we see how the methods of science contribute to the first aim of science, description, and how it is possible to go directly from description to prediction. And we see also that descriptive research involves the use of induction, but not of deduction or retroduction. By far the greatest amount of sociological research to date consists of this descriptive research—a necessary first step, as we have seen, but not as exciting or productive as explanatory research, which is described in the second part of the chart.

Having a reasonably accurate description of some aspect of nature, the scientist then brings to bear his knowledge, skills, experience, and creative abilities, and, through the process of retroduction, devises a tentative explanation. This tentative explanation may take the form of either a deductive explanation, that is, one that has been cast in the form of an axiomatic theory, or a probabilistic explanation. In either case, one (or more) of the propositions in the explanation (axioms or theorems, in the case of deductive explanations; premises or conclusions, in the case of probabilistic explanations) is selected for reality-testing. This involves *prediction* in the sense that there is an implied prediction that the proposition is true. The proposition selected for reality-testing is worded as a hypothesis, and this leads to the formulation and design of a research project which will yield an *explanation* of this aspect of nature. The next few steps (23–26), representing the actual research process, are exactly the same here as they are for descriptive research (Steps 5–8). The outcomes are different, however, as seen in Step 27. If the proposition being reality-tested is an axiom, and is found to be (probably) true, then we know that the theorems are true, and we have a law. The theory or *explanation* is useful and we have an addition to knowledge. If the proposition being reality-tested is a theorem, or is a proposition from a probabilistic explanation, and this is found to be (probably) true, then this lends credibility to the truth of the axioms (or premises or conclusions of a probabilistic explanation), and lends credibility to the usefulness of the theory or explanation, and to the dependability of this addition to knowledge and scientific laws. In either of these cases—i.e., the hypothesis being found to be (probably) true—this leads then to further *prediction,* the seeking of further confirmation, and again we see that the process recycles back to further predictions, hypotheses, and research. Again, as with descriptive research, it is the prediction at this stage which leads to practical applications of this new knowledge. On the other hand, if the outcome of the research process is that the hypothesis is false, then we know that the tentative explanation must be revised, and the process returns to the "tentative explanation" of Step 16.

Several general observations about this process are important. First, it is seen clearly that science is a never-ending process, with each research effort leading to further hypotheses and research. There is a constant refinement of existing knowledge and chipping away at the frontiers of new knowledge. Secondly, there is no implication in anything which has been said that all of these activities are necessarily carried out by any one individual. Indeed, this would probably be impossible from a practical point of view, even if there were some reason to

Figure 1. Flowchart of the scientific method

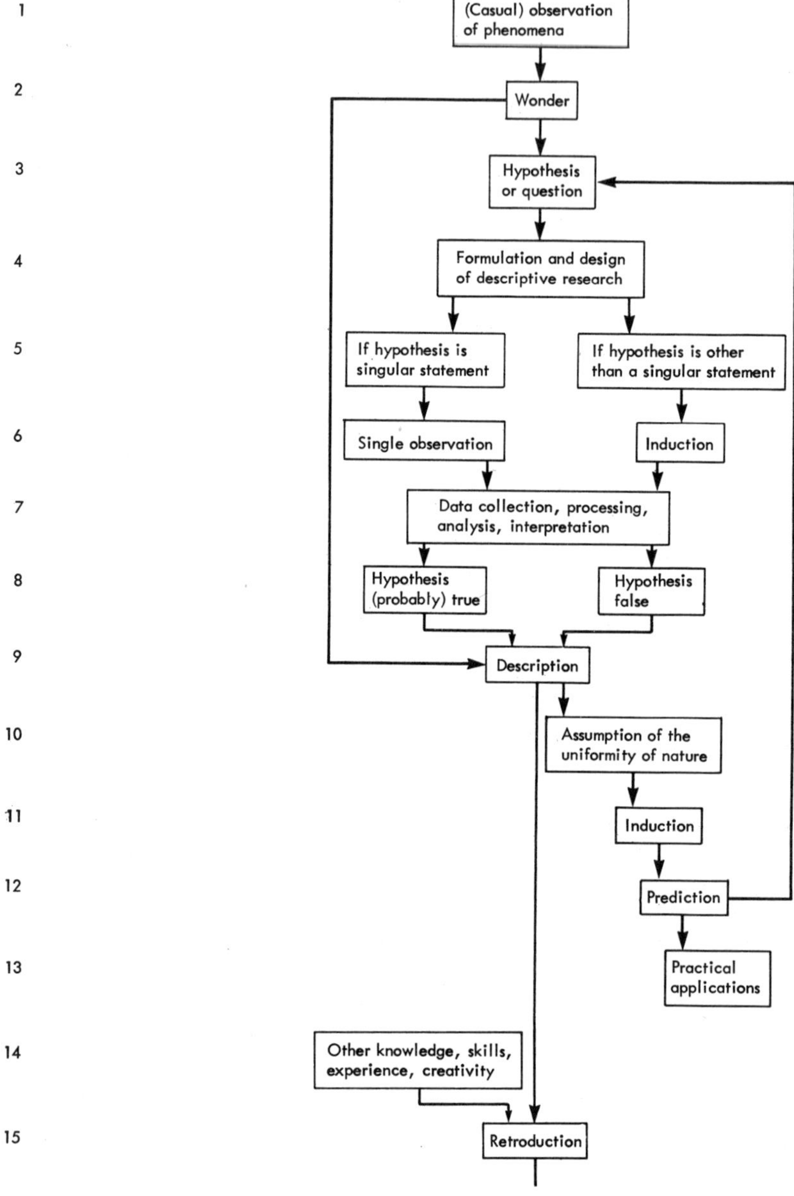

Figure 1 (continued).

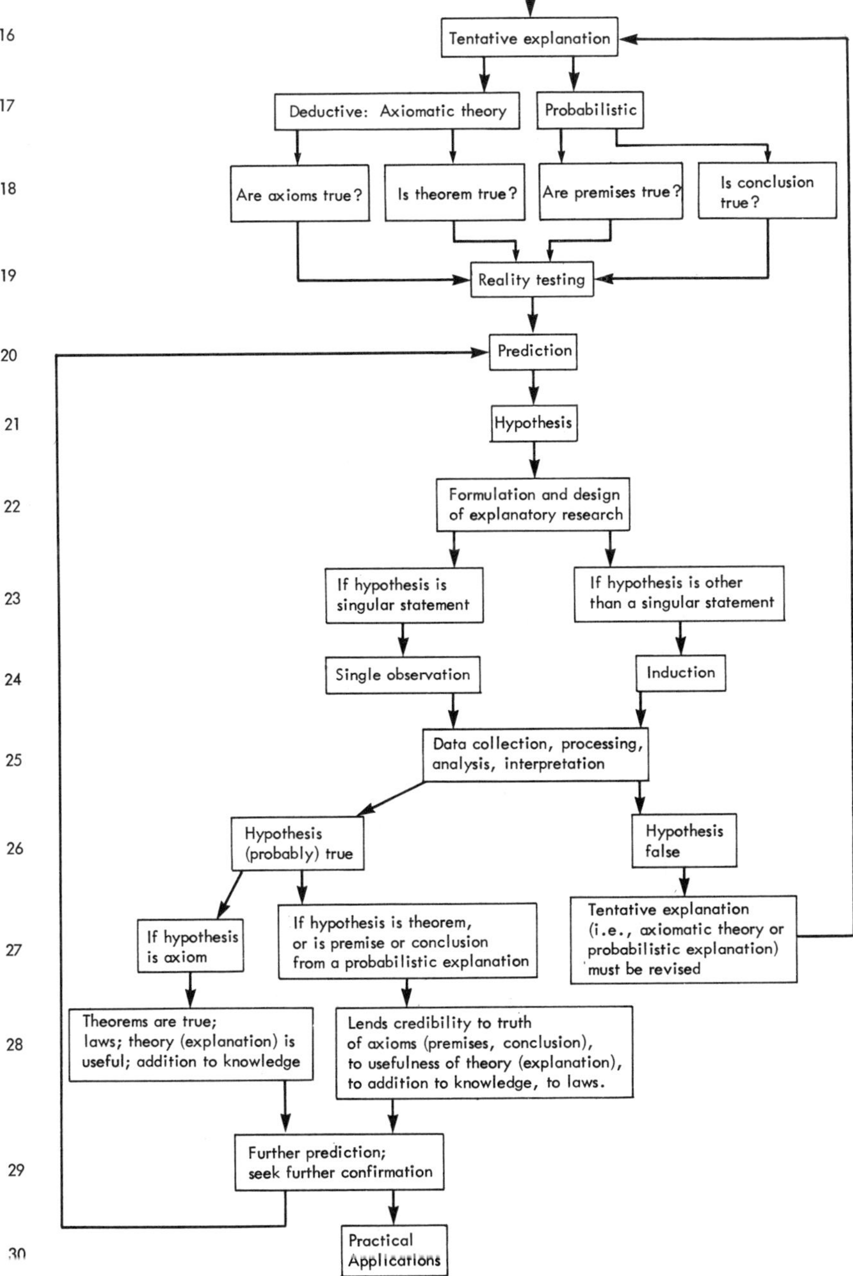

consider it to be desirable. As it is, each scientist may specialize in some aspect of this process by reason of training, skills, preferences, idiosyncratic characteristics, or fortuity, and thus we see further indication of the cumulative and cooperative nature of science.

Third, the view that theory and research are somehow opposed to each other is clearly seen as a false dichotomy. In actuality, as the Flowchart shows, descriptive research leads to theory which, in turn, leads to explanatory research which, finally, leads to either further research or revision of theory. Both theory and research are essential parts of the scientific process. Either one without the other is incomplete. This is hardly a new view, although the theory versus research debates still do continue in some quarters.[3] Finally, and of considerable importance for research design, the Flowchart shows that there are two, and only two, distinct forms of research, descriptive and explanatory. Other types which are sometimes identified in the literature (e.g., exploratory) will reduce to one or the other of these two types. The actual practical procedures of these two forms of research are the same (except as to the appropriate research designs, which will be discussed in the later section on "Basic Designs" in Chapter 8) and the only difference lies in the *origin* or *source* of the research hypothesis. For descriptive research the hypothesis originates with some wondering or curiosity about some observed phenomenon. For explanatory research, on the other hand, the hypothesis arises out of a tentative explanation (axiomatic theory or probabilistic) of some *previously described* phenomenon, event, or other aspect of nature.

The discovery of the planet Neptune is one of the most beautiful and exciting chapters in the entire history of science. A brief examination of the major events leading up to this provides an excellent illustration of the methods and aims of science, and the scientist's endeavor at its finest.[4] The Greek astronomer Hipparchus (125 B.C.) provides us with the earliest description of the solar system. It was the so-called geocentric view, with the earth at the center, and the sun and other planets revolving around the earth. Ptolemy was an Egyptian mathematician, astronomer, and geographer, who lived about 140 A.D. He fol-

[3] For one view of the relationship between theory and research, see Glaser and Strauss, 1967.

[4] *Encyclopaedia Britannica*, 12th ed., 1922.

lowed the lead of Hipparchus, and conducted extensive and important mathematical studies, especially in trigonometry. Building upon these studies he provided a more detailed geocentric description of the solar system. This description was based upon his rigorous application of geometrical and trigonometrical methods to his observations of the six planets then known (Mercury, Venus, Earth, Mars, Jupiter, Saturn). Ptolemy said that he was explaining the solar system, and it is reasonable to infer that he did use retroduction in order to devise a tentative explanation. Whether we would call this a description or an explanation today illustrates the previously-mentioned difficulty of distinguishing between the two, which arises occasionally. (Ptolemy is also noted for having originally voiced the law of parsimony.) The next significant contribution was made by Nikolaus Copernicus, the Polish student of mathematics, law, and medicine (1473–1543). He was dissatisfied with the geocentric view, and published, in the year of his death, a treatise setting forth the heliocentric view (the sun at the center, and the Earth and other planets revolving around the sun). Here again we see the retroducing of a tentative explanation based upon the available description of the solar system.

Shortly thereafter Tycho Brahe, the Danish astronomer (1546–1601), brought vast improvement to the art of pretelescopic astronomical observations, and collected a wealth of observational data which provided a much more accurate description of the solar system. He collected these data in an attempt to bridge the gap between the Ptolemaic and Copernican views, but this never materialized because of his death. In the last year of his life, fortunately, he was working with Johannes Kepler, and the latter inherited all of Brahe's materials. (Brahe also attrated some attention because of having lost his nose in a duel at the age of 20, which resulted in his having to wear an artificial one made of a copper alloy.) Kepler, the German astronomer (1571–1630), edited Brahe's principal work and published it shortly after the latter's death. This was an extremely fortunate association since Kepler, who had great speculative abilities but little in the way of mechanical skills, was able to utilize Brahe's great practical skills which had never been brought to fruition. Kepler, also influenced by the Copernican view, sought to find the reason, the explanation, for the actual disposition of the solar system. He wanted to substitute physical cause for arbitrary hypothesis. In "the greatest piece of Retroductive reasoning ever performed" Kepler did, indeed, succeed in devising three statements which accurately explain the geometrical plan of the solar system.[5] They were published in 1609. Perhaps most remarkable of all was that in the course of this retroduction he was led to abandon the view that the planets' orbits were circular—a view which had been accepted as unchallengeable for 2,000 years.

Contemporaneously with Kepler, Galileo Galilei, the Italian astronomer and physicist (1564–1642), was making careful observations of the solar system with his newly invented telescope. Although the two were in communication with each other, Galilei largely ignored Kepler's work. He, too, had adopted the Copernican view, and his observations, published around 1613, lent confirmation to this view. This is one of the most noteworthy examples of utilization of systematic observations for the purpose of reality-testing a theory. It will be remembered, too, that because Galilei's published work conflicted with Church doctrine, he was forced by the Pope to retract his views. A further—and ultimately more important—tentative explanation was retroduced by Isaac Newton, the English mathematician and philosopher (1642–1727). His formulation of what are now known as the laws of motion, and especially the law of gravitation, which were published in 1687, provided not only explanations of the whole solar system, but also accounted for various other phenomena such as the rotation of the earth and the functioning of the tides. The accuracy of the Newtonian theory was established beyond any reasonable doubt in the early 19th century, especially by the work of Pierre Simon Laplace. Laplace was a French mathematician and astronomer (1749–1827) who did important analytic work on celestial mechanics and the solar system, explaining various problems in the planets' motions. In this explanatory research he drew heavily upon the work of his contemporary and compatriot Joseph Louis Lagrange (1736–1813), the brilliant mathematician.

In 1820 Alexis Bouvard, the French astronomer (1767–1843), constructed tables of motion of Jupiter, Saturn, and Uranus

[5] Hanson, 1965 (quoting Peirce), p. 85. Chapter 4 contains a fascinating picture of Kepler's work.

(which had been discovered in 1781 by Sir William Herschel), based upon calculations made by Laplace. These predictions did in fact represent the actual observed positions of Jupiter and Saturn, but not of Uranus. The observations indicated that Uranus deviated from the predicted position to an extent beyond the likelihood of any errors in observational techniques. Here we have an axiomatic theory where reality-testing showed some of the predictions to be true and others false. This puzzle attracted growing interest and ultimately led Bouvard and others to suggest the possibility of the existence of a new planet. In our terminology, through the process of retroduction the axiom that Uranus was the outermost planet was modified, thus pointing toward a revised theory. In 1843, because of the ever-increasing attention which this problem attracted, the Royal Society of Sciences, of Gottingen, Germany, offered a prize for the full explanation. In that same year John Couch Adams, the English astronomer (1819–92), started working on the problem, having just completed his bachelor's degree at Cambridge. In late October of 1845 he presented his results to the Astronomer-Royal at the Greenwich Observatory, predicting the location, dimensions, and orbital characteristics of the new planet, but the observatory did not then undertake a telescopic search to verify his work. In another of those remarkable coincidences of history, a French astronomer, Urbain Jean Joseph Leverrier (1811–77), completely unaware of Adams' work, undertook the same problem and, less than three weeks after Adams' communication to the Astronomer-Royal, presented to the French Academy the first of three papers in which his predictions were almost identical to those made by Adams. A telescopic search was made in the summer of 1846, and in late September the Berlin Observatory discovered the new planet, later named Neptune, in almost the exact position predicted by Adams and Leverrier. In this case it was the axiom of the revised theory (namely, that Uranus was not the outermost planet) which was reality-tested and found to be true, thus lending further support to the entire theory. As would be expected, there was considerable discussion as to which of the two astronomers should receive credit for this discovery, but today they are recognized as having made it independently. It is interesting to note that the outermost planet, Pluto, was discovered under similar circumstances in 1930.

The discovery of Neptune also provides an additional illustration of the importance of perseverance, care, and accuracy in scientific work. An examination of earlier astronomical observations revealed that in May of 1795 another French astronomer, Joseph J. L. Lalande (1732–1807), had observed an unidentified star (Neptune) on two separate evenings, and, finding the two observations to be different, had concluded that one must have been in error. Had he merely made a third observation, the additional motion revealed would have led him to recognize this as a new planet rather than a star.

So we return again to the question put in the early pages of this book. Why is our interest only in *scientific* research? This entire discussion provides the answer and tells why science has acquired its honorific status. Simply because the methods of science provide a more dependable way of acquiring knowledge than do any nonscientific methods now known. Next we must look at the relationship between science on the one hand and values, applications of science, and policy making on the other.

Chapter 5

Values, science, and sociology

In our entire discussion so far we have attempted carefully to avoid the subjects of values, applications of science, and of policymaking, because they are not directly pertinent to the basic subject of science itself. However, in the business of science and in the doing of research they are of the utmost practical importance. Furthermore, there are certain pronounced implications contained in our lengthy description of science which lead us to some almost unavoidable positions on these controversial subjects. And they are, indeed, controversial: probably no other matters have provoked as much discussion, debate, and emotional reactions on the part of professional sociologists in recent years. This is not to say that these topics are of concern only to social scientists. Quite to the contrary, all sciences face these debates and individual scientists in all fields must make personal decisions as to how they will cope with these matters. However, in the social sciences the issues seem more acute—perhaps because there is great public concern for the amelioration of social problems, and this is commonly regarded as the special area of interest of the social sciences. Society has long looked to the physical scientist and the biological scientist for aid in solving many problems—problems of health and transportation and communication, for example—but it is a relatively new experience for social scientists to be asked, urged, or required to aid in solving practical problems.

Also, many sociologists and students of sociology have chosen this field largely because they were interested in bringing about social reforms and welfare. Indeed, simply because society expects the social scientists to solve many of its problems, and because an ever-increasing number of social scientists expect this of themselves, it would seem that the social sciences should move full speed ahead in attempts to do this. However, a cautionary note must be sounded because of some of the implications and significance of such a course of action. Therefore, in this chapter we will consider first, the place of values in scientific activity, then the question of the scientist's concern with applications of science, and third, the closely related question of the extent to which policymaking decisions are included in the role of the scientist. Finally, we will discuss some special characteristics of sociology as a science.

VALUES

When we talk about "values" we are not, of course, using that term in the strict economic sense, as when I say that "the value of this chair is 30 dollars." Again we encounter the familiar situation of having a plethora of definitions, but fortunately agreement on the precise definition is not crucial here. For purposes of our discussion, a value is any "thing" (objective phenomenon or subjective) which is believed, by an individual or society, to be important, to have meaning, to be desirable, and to be worthy of serving as a guide for people's thoughts, aims, and behavior. According to two authorities, examples of values which characterize the mainstream of American society include: a world at peace, family security, freedom, honesty, ambition, responsibility, achievement and success, activity and work, efficiency and practicality, progress, material comfort, and equality.[1] Of course there are many others which could be added, and of course not everyone would agree with this—or any other—list.

It is clear that, regardless of the specific values on a list, values are statements of what is regarded as right or wrong, as good or bad, of what kind of behavior one should or should not engage in. If, for example, honesty is a value, that means that honesty is believed to be important, to have meaning, to be disirable, and to be worthy of serving as a guide for one's thoughts, aims, and behavior. In other words, the statement is that honesty is right and good, and one *should* be honest.

---

[1] Rokeach, 1973; Williams, 1970.

One area of disagreement about the general nature of values is whether there are any universal values or whether they are culturally related. Most social scientists today would agree that they are culturally related. Since values are statements of what is right or wrong, and since the concept of cultural relativism is so well established, there can be little doubt that values do vary from society to society. Not only that, but they vary among groups within a given society, and from individual to individual within a group as well. In a sense, then, an individual's personal value system may be viewed as a statement of his predilections or biases. While we usually think of each individual as having *a* value system, it has been suggested that perhaps he actually has plural value systems. It may be that there is a separate value system associated with each role the individual plays. While we would expect considerable similarity between the value systems of two individuals within a given group, we would expect more and more diversity as the groups or societies become larger and larger.

Finally, most value systems are probably hierarchical in nature—most of us, as individuals, can certainly *rank* many or all of our values in terms of their importance to us and their influence upon our lives at any given time. That is to say that we can make statements such as, "It is more important to me to be honest than to be competitive," or, "For me, love is a higher value than power," or, "For this group (society) the value of material possessions takes priority over the value of integrity," and so on.

With this very brief and oversimplified description of values as background, let us now look at the place of values in scientific activity. There are three aspects to this. In the first place, not only knowledge, but also science itself, are values. In the opening pages of this book it was pointed out that the very idea of research is based upon the assumption that knowledge is desirable. This is a value statement. And science, too, as evidenced by its great importance in the popular folklore of today, conforms to the above definition of value. Both knowledge and science, and their practical consequences and fruits—wonder drugs, television, computers, space travel, sophisticated weapons systems, and so on—are regarded as important, and perhaps even essential to modern life. Yet we should not lose sight of the fact that, since values are not universal, not everyone may share our belief in the significance of the values of knowledge and science—a disquieting thought at best.

The second way in which values are related to scientific activity pertains especially to the social scientist, since values may serve as the *subject matter* of social scientific investigation. We may be interested in discovering the values of the American people, or perhaps we are concerned with how the value system of the upper class in Australia compares with the value system of the lower class Australian. Or perhaps with the way in which the value system of the Japanese influences (or is influenced by) their economy. Or with how the values of the young people of the United States are changing, or how they compare with the value systems of young people three decades ago.

Values are a legitimate subject for investigation, but according to at least one significant point of view values are not, and cannot be, empirical data. This is to say that values (as well as attitudes and motives) are intervening variables—hypothetical constructs whose existence is assumed in order to attempt to explain human behavior. It is neither necessary nor important for us to go into the details of this view, other than to say that the central thesis is that it is only through observations of overt behavior that we are led to make statements about values. The only way we have of knowing what people's values are is to observe their behavior. For example, I observe many of my students making great sacrifices to attend the university. Perhaps they are holding down full-time jobs and supporting a spouse and children, taking a full load of classes, living on the other side of town and riding a bicycle many miles a day in order to come to school—doing all this despite obstacles such as bad weather and illness, but never missing a class, always completing the assignments, and so on. I observe this behavior and on the basis of it I conclude that for such a student education is a very important value. But I cannot observe the value itself. This is not meant to imply that research on values is suspect—far from it. But it is meant to serve as a caution to the researcher that he may be making a mistake if he treats values as empirical data.

The third, and most important, way in which values are related to scientific activity has to do with the scientist's own personal value system. The importance of objectivity to the scientific endeavor has been stressed repeatedly in these pages—the scientist must be unbiased, unprejudiced, detached, impersonal, and his conclusions must not be influenced by individual characteristics which are not shared by all investigators. Yet the scientist, as any other human, has his own individual value system, his own views as to what things are worthy of serving as a guide for his aims and behavior. As pointed out above, these values are statements of right and wrong, of good and bad, of shoulds and should nots; furthermore, value systems and hierarchies vary from individual to individual. Thus it becomes immediately apparent that the concept of objectivity and the concept of values are in direct conflict with each other. Science, because of its foundation of objectivity, must deal only with what *is*, or with what *can be*. When statements are made as to what *should be* or what *ought to be*, these are, by definition, value statements (or value judgments, as they are usually called). That is, a statement that something is good or bad (right or wrong, etc.) can be traced back to a value to which it is believed to be related.

For example, when we state that "crime is bad" we are making a value judgment and not an objective statement. Also it is an incomplete statement. When we make it into a complete statement it indicates the values involved. In order to complete the statement we must show that it is bad *for* something—for the attainment of certain values, such as honesty or fair play or friendliness, for example. We can just as readily justify the statement that "crime is good" if we point out that it provides employment for policemen, parole officers, social workers, criminologists, prison guards, manufacturers of crime detection equipment, builders of prisons, and so on—all of which can be traced to values such as material possessions, working hard, efficiency, and so on. Similarly, any such statement of good or bad is a value judgment, and is arguable, depending upon one's values. Thus we see that a value statement, as differentiated from an objective statement, is a statement made within the frame of reference of a particular value system. And we would expect that scientists (or any others) would disagree on value statements but would agree as to objective statements. The objective, scientific, statements about, for example, crime, would include descriptive and explanatory statements, but would not include value statements as to whether crime is good or bad. Science must follow the truth, regardless of where it goes—whether it leads to results which the individual scientist regards as good or as bad, whether the results are consistent or inconsistent with the scientist's hopes, beliefs, and wishes. Obviously this creates problems, because it is difficult to maintain one's objectivity if one has a strong value interest in the outcome of the research.

Yet, in a fundamental way, values enter *all* research, if not in all kinds of behavior. Whenever judgments or decisions must be made there exists the possibility that they will be influenced by values. Even in something as seemingly objective as reading a meter on a piece of scientific equipment, there is always the ambiguous region where the pointer indicates a result halfway between two numbers. Is it 16.8 or 16.9 amperes? Certainly values (hopes that the research findings will be thus-and-so, or beliefs that certain findings will have desirable—or undesirable—consequences, for instance) may be one of several factors leading to a final decision or perception of the meter reading as either 16.8 or 16.9.

Aside from this kind of impact that values may have upon research, there is the larger question of whether a scientist *should* engage in research which may have consequences (or practical applications) contrary to his values. One of the most noted examples of this is the still continuing debate as to whether it was right for physicists and other scientists to participate in research leading to the development of the atom bomb, given that they knew that the bomb might be used for mass destruction of humanity. For those, if any, who supported the idea of war as a means of decision making or of settling issues, or who were not opposed to killing under those kinds of circumstances, presumably there was no conflict between their work and their values. But those whose values were opposed to such mass slaughter found themselves in a very sharp dilemma, neither "horn" of which was very tolerable. The value positions on this might range from, at one extreme, "It's OK to kill 90,000 people (the number killed and missing at Hiroshima) with one bomb" to "It's OK to kill 90,000 people with one bomb if it will end the war sooner and thus prevent further killing" to "It's not OK to kill 90,000 people with one bomb; 9,000 a day with several bombs on each of ten days is OK, but not 90,000 all at once" to "It's not OK to kill. Period." Similarly, we would probably find that the strength of the values of knowledge and science for the individual scientist would also lie along a continuum.

Despite this last illustration, the fact remains that the conflict between objectivity and values is more acute for the social scientist than for the physical or biological scientist. This is because the connection between the scientist's values and the subject of his research is usually much more tenuous for the physical scientist than for the social scientist. The way in which values are related to the strength and characteristics of a laser beam, or the crystallographic structure of minerals, or the process of photosynthesis, is not clear, but when the subject matter is crime or mental health or political systems there is an obvious connection. Furthermore, as mentioned above, many sociologists initially choose the field of sociology specifically because they have strong values related to social reform and welfare.

How is this conflict between values and objectivity to be solved? Among sociologists, two polar positions can be distinguished. There are those who urge—or insist—that sociology be value-free (and some have added that therefore sociologists must be value-free). The goal of a value-free sociology has been the dominant view of contemporary sociologists as well as of some of the most important figures of the past.[2] At the other extreme are those who say that sociologists should be guided by their values in their professional work; by virtue of their training they are in a better position to specify desirable goals than are less trained people. Recently the "activist" movement in sociology has led to an increasing concern with attempting to achieve value-oriented goals.[3] The most tenable position lies between these extreme polar views. We agree, certainly, that a value-free sociology is desirable and further believe that it can be attained (even if individual sociologists may be value-saturated) as long as there is full and free critical discourse on public results. This is the familiar "self-correcting mechanism of the community of science," and it indicates that the objectivity of science depends upon social processes rather than on the individual scientist's objectivity. Not only is a value-free sociology desirable, but despite the difficulties involved, freedom from values is a reasonable and desirable goal toward which the sociologist can strive, without any necessary expectation of actually attaining it. It can serve as a guide—a beacon, if you will—for scientific endeavors.

[2] For example, Durkheim, Pareto, Weber. For a discussion of various views on this issue, see Inkeles, 1964, pp. 101–5.

[3] For example: Hoult, 1968.

There are two things the sociologist can do which will bring him closer to this goal of objectivity. In the first place it is important that he identify his values. Many people attain maturity in their personal and professional lives without ever having undertaken sufficient self-analysis to know what their basic values are. To do this requires considerable introspection. Once the values are identified, the researcher must take whatever steps he can in order to ensure that they will not mar the objectivity of his work. In some way he must compensate for any values which might affect his research. Perhaps the mere identification of them will serve to provide this compensation. Or perhaps it may be important to work with a colleague who does not share these same values. In extreme cases, when the values are so strong that the researcher may be emotionally involved with his subject matter, perhaps he should consider abandoning that particular research topic. As an illustration let us suppose that I am undertaking some research having to do with Jews and/or the state of Israel. Furthermore, let us assume that I have identified in myself some values which have resulted in my having a strong anti-Semitic bias. Under these circumstances it might be well for me to have a Jew as a colleague, or perhaps, if I felt I could not be sufficiently objective, it might be well for me to avoid conducting any research related to Jews.

Now obviously the very choice of a research topic involves, among other things, at least an expression of interest in the subject matter on the part of the researcher. And interest is, of course, closely related to values. Therefore it is important not to misinterpret the above comments on avoiding certain research subjects. By no means do those comments imply that the researcher should not do research on a subject in which he is interested. The point is simply that if his interest is based upon strong value commitments and/or emotional involvements, he should take some precautions to avoid impairing the objectivity of his work.

The second thing is to recognize that the role of scientist is only one of many roles which affect the individual's behavior. Among the many others which affect his behavior in the daily course of his life is the role of citizen. Science makes rigorous demands, as we have seen, and so the role of scientist requires strict adherence to behaviors such as objectivity, caution, impersonality, lack of bias, and the elusive freedom from values. But the role of citizen makes no such demands; indeed, it is quite the opposite. The citizen is *expected* to take an active part in civic affairs, he is *expected* to propound his own particular views with all the legitimate force at his command, he is *expected* to be guided by his subjective views of what is right and wrong, desirable and undesirable. Adherence to objectivity is appropriate behavior for the role of the scientist. Adherence to subjectivity is appropriate behavior for the role of the citizen. And just as most of us have little difficulty in knowing which role is operating in a given situation (we behave like students and teachers in the classroom; we behave like mothers, fathers, sons, or daughters when we are at home with our families) we should expect little difficulty in keeping separate our behaviors as scientist and as citizen. As a scientist I am concerned with the fact that this particular drug will kill this person or will cure that disease, but I am not at all concerned with the value judgment that it is better to be cured than killed. As a citizen I *am* deeply concerned and strongly believe that curing is better than killing. And so I support governmental efforts to require stricter regulation of the sale of drugs, and so on. As a scientist I am concerned with the fact that a certain combination of circumstances may result in ethnic discrimination, or in a race riot, and I am concerned with the fact that another set of circumstances may lessen the probability of discrimination or of riots, but my concern is not that discrimination may lead to unhappiness, or that it is commonly regarded as being bad. However, as a citizen these things concern me deeply, and I use whatever power and persuasive abilities I have to bring about an end to discrimination and race riots. As a scientist I am concerned with the relative characteristics of various forms of government such as democratic or socialistic or fascistic, but it is only in my capacity as a citizen that I allow myself to become embroiled in debates as to which form of government is "better" or "best." In other words, it is imperative that we not confuse the world as it is with the world as we wish it were.

It is beyond dispute that the scientist *qua* scientist must follow his data wherever they lead, regardless of how much the conclusions may please or displease him. If science did not strive to be as value-free and objective as possible, the results of scientific activity would not be characterized by truth, proof, and certitude. If science did not strive for objectivity and freedom from values, the resulting knowledge, if such it could be called, would be far less dependable and accurate. There is simply no other way than the constant quest for maximum objectivity. The approach of the activists, while having highly commendable goals, would sacrifice long-range additions to mankind's store of knowledge in favor of attempts to bring about short-range amelioration of social problems. Both of these are needed, but both are not the province of the scientist.

APPLICATIONS OF SCIENCE

The above argument favoring the separation of the scientist and the citizen roles can be expanded and further supported by recognizing the distinction between science and applications of science. We have defended the view that science (all science, not merely sociology) is concerned with the pursuit of truth and knowledge, specifically as regards descriptions, explanations, and predictions of nature, and that it is not concerned with value judgments stating what should be true of nature. This gives rise to legitimate questions as to what good any science is if its resulting knowledge is not used for practical purposes, questions as to how scientific knowledge is to be used and by whom, and questions as to how social change is to be brought about, and by whom. Of course it is hoped that all scientific knowledge will be used in some way—hopefully for the betterment of mankind, however that may be defined. But if the task of science is only to supply knowledge, then it follows that if this knowledge is to be used it must be used by someone other than the scientist. This "someone" is the one who makes practical applications of scientific knowledge.

Chemistry and physics, for example, are sciences; chemical engineering and mechanical or electrical engineering are the fields which take the scientific knowledge contributed by the chemist or physicist and make practical applications of that knowledge. A test-tube reaction, or an equation or a formula, or a laboratory process, are taken as basic information, out of which a plastics plant, or a bridge, or a television system, or a military weapon, may be built. Similarly, the physician and the nurse apply knowledge from biology, physiology, anatomy, and the like, to the task of healing the sick and injured. And in the same way the field of social work applies knowledge derived from sociology, psychology, and other sciences. The task of those engaged in the applied fields—the engineers, the physicians and nurses, the social workers, for example—are not to *produce* knowledge, but rather to *use* knowledge. In general, the social worker is not concerned with adding to knowledge nearly as much as he is concerned with applying knowledge in order to add to the welfare of society. And it is here, obviously, that values come back into the picture.

Values are central to even a superficial discussion of things like the betterment of mankind, or the welfare of society, or healing the sick, or constructing a weapon. In the applications of science, value considerations are as appropriate as they are inappropriate in science, in part because the concept of objectivity is not nearly so important here. Not only are value considerations appropriate but they are necessary, since the scientific knowledge is being used *for* some goal which is deemed desirable. This distinction between the functions of science and the functions of the application of science, in society, is essentially the same distinction as was made above, between the role of scientist and the role of citizen, in the individual member of society. Needless to say, there is no implication that any of these activities is "better than," or preferable to, any other—merely that they are different.

The distinction made above between scientific research and the applications or uses of the results of that research should not be confused with the different distinction which is sometimes made between doing research on "pure" topics (i.e., topics with no obvious practical use) and doing research on "applied" or practical problems. Any topic is legitimate as a subject for a research effort; our concern here has been with the manner in which the results of the research will be used.[4]

POLICYMAKING

It follows from the above discussion that, in the practical world, many decisions must be made concerning the relationships between science and applications of science. More specifically, for our purposes, policymaking refers to the decision processes regarding which scientific knowledge will be

[4]A brief but fascinating look at some results of social science research on practical matters is to be found in Social Science Research Council, 1969.

used, how it will be used, for what purposes, and how financial and other resources will be allocated among competing goals. Such policy decisions are undertaken by administrators of governmental, institutional, corporate, and other similar bodies. Thus they involve not only the values of knowledge and science, but also values related to such things as human welfare, health, human life itself, financial solvency, political considerations, international relations, and so forth. The aims, goals, and objectives of policymaking are quite distinct from the aims of science, and are indicated by the various values just mentioned, and also by the objectives of the particular institutional (or other) body. A governmental unit may have the goal, among others, of providing services and welfare for the population; a corporation may have the goal of making profits; while a university may have the goals of providing education for the public as well as contributing to knowledge. Therefore, the task of the policymaker is more complex than that of the scientist in many ways, since the scientist is guided by the primary value of knowledge while the policymaker must follow many values, some of which are frequently inconsistent with one another.

The task of the policymaker, in other words, necessitates establishing a hierarchy of values and adhering to that hierarchy. The policy decision to go ahead with the development of the atomic bomb, for example, involved decisions as to whether the objective (developing a weapon for mass destruction) was justified in terms of the progress of the war and in terms of commonly held values about human life and killing, decisions as to whether the results to be obtained were worth the expenditure of money, time, and effort, decisions as to whether the possible peaceful uses of atomic energy were important enough to consider, and if so to what extent, and so on. Similarly, when the sociologists are able to say that "If actions A, B, and C are taken we predict that the crime rate in this city will be reduced," it becomes the responsibility of the policymaker to decide whether funds, personnel, and other resources will be allocated for this effort at reducing the crime rate, or whether they will be expended, instead, upon efforts to reduce air pollution or improve public transportation or build new schools or build flood-control projects or perhaps to try to take first steps towards all of these worthy goals. Clearly, the activity of policymaking is quite distinct from the activity of science, although it utilizes the products of science. Thus it follows, as above, that to the extent that the scientist participates in policymaking activities he does so not in his role of scientist but in the role of citizen and/or policymaker. There is no reason to believe that the scientist in his role of scientist is any more qualified than anyone else to give advice on political or policy matters as one authority points out.[5]

Despite this, there is continuing discussion within the field of sociology as to the relationship between sociological research and policymaking. The pages of *The American Sociologist* and of *Footnotes* (both published by the American Sociological Association and devoted to matters of professional concern) have contained many articles, letters, official policy statements, and the like representing all viewpoints on this issue. As one example, in 1967–68, 51 percent of the voting members of the American Sociological Association favored a resolution urging the immediate withdrawal of American troops from South Vietnam, but 65 percent voted that the Association should not take an official position on this issue. In 1969 the American Sociological Association established a Standing Committee on Public Policy, and in 1971 an entire special issue of *The American Sociologist* was devoted to the topic "Sociological Research and Public Policy."[6] Furthermore, some prominent sociologists have publicly supported each of the following diverse views, in recent years:

Sociological research should attempt to solve social problems.[7]

The American Sociological Association should not be involved in matters of public policy, and it is important that we learn "to distinguish between a social problem and a sociological problem."[8]

It is important for policymakers to consult social scientists and utilize their findings in order to make better policy decisions.[9]

---

[5] Chain, 1970.

[6] See especially, the following issues of *The American Sociologist:* vol. 2 (November 1967), pp. 213–23; vol. 3 (May 1968), p. 164; vol. 4 (August 1969), pp. 261–62; vol. 5 (November 1970), pp. 339–44, 387–91, 414–16; vol. 6 (May 1971), p. 180; vol. 6 (June 1971), entire Supplementary Issue. Also, see *Footnotes,* February 1973 and March 1973.

[7] Rose, 1954, chap. 8.

[8] Bierstedt, 1965, p. 128.

[9] Greer, 1969, pp. 189–95; Blalock, 1970, pp. 3–5.

There should be more active participation on the part of universities in attempts to solve social problems.[10]

The more extreme view, namely, that social scientists should be involved in policymaking, is also strongly defended by some.[11]

Doubtless this debate will continue for some time to come among social scientists with honest differences of viewpoint. However, within the view of science presented in this book, and the logical implications of that view, we believe that there can be even less doubt that scientific activities and policymaking activities must be separated.

SOCIOLOGY AS A SCIENCE

We return now to some of the issues raised in Chapter 1 when sociology was defined as a science. In effect, what we have done thus far is to develop a syllogism:

Sociology is a science.

All sciences have a certain set of characteristics.

Therefore, sociology has the same set of characteristics.

In other words, all that is being said, and all that follows in this book, is an elaboration of—a consequence of—the conclusion to the above syllogism. To put it another way, all that follows is based upon a definition of sociology as a science, and also on a definition of science, and these definitions are the two premises of the above syllogism. As with any syllogism, if one does *not* grant the premises then the conclusion does not necessarily follow, which is to say that the whole body of scientific procedures which characterize sociological research does not follow.

In the earlier discussion of this topic it was pointed out that some people raise the questions of whether sociology *is* a science, whether it *can* be a science, and whether it *should* be one. Now we are in a better position to respond to these issues. Is sociology a science? We here have defined it as such and from our point of view there is no doubt about it being a science. Hopefully the argument has been persuasive enough to convince others as well. All that has been said in our lengthy

[10] Backman, 1970, p. 208.

[11] Freeman and Sherwood, 1970; Parker, 1967.

examination of science contributes to that argument, and what is more it certainly demonstrates that sociology can be a science. Nothing that has been said in the whole description of science and its methods is in any way in conflict with sociology and the professional activities in which sociologists customarily are engaged. A careful analysis of the assumptions about science which are used to advance the "anti-science" viewpoint, discussed in the earlier section, reveals that none of these assumptions is compatible with the true meaning of science. The other assumptions, about human behavior, society, and social events, which are also used by the proponents of the anti-science view are also difficult or impossible to substantiate, and the student will find it an interesting exercise to critically analyze them. The question of whether or not sociology should be a science is, of course, a value judgment. Since we have seen that science is the best available method of gaining knowledge, there seems little reason to question the view that sociology should be a science, and this is obviously the reason for the "limitation" of our interest to scientific research.

While none of the above anti-science arguments is sufficiently strong to negate the view that sociology is a science, some of them do point to characteristics which complicate the task of the social scientist, as compared to the physical scientist. In addition, there are also other characteristics which differentiate sociology from other sciences. Because of the complexities and bewildering variety of human behavior, for example, it is difficult (but by no means impossible) to design research which adequately takes into account the large number of variables operating. Similarly, research must be designed so as to eliminate—or at least take into account—the possibility that the people who are the subjects of the research will consciously affect the outcomes. Another difficulty lies in the impact which the passage of time has upon human behavior. To paraphrase the ancient saying, one can't cross the same river twice, and similarly one can't interview or observe the same person twice. Still another problem results from the ethical complications involved in attempting to do any controlled experimentation on humans. And, of course, the questions of values and objectivity, discussed in the previous section, introduce further difficulties.

Another interesting point is made by the philosopher-mathematician John G. Kemeny. He notes that the process of deduction involves what is essentially the solution of mathematical problems. If the number of cases or objects is small enough, we can solve the problems by working through all the possibilities, one at a time, by the use of ordinary arithmetical procedures. If the number of cases is very large, on the other hand, say of the order of billions, or billions of billions, we can safely and reasonably assume that there is an infinite number of cases, and so make use of calculus—one of the most powerful mathematical tools. However, if we are dealing with numbers of the order of thousands, or tens or hundreds of thousands, which is exactly the range of interest for much sociological investigation, neither of the above methods is appropriate. And unfortunately, as Kemeny points out, this is an area of mathematics which has not yet adequately been developed, and so there is at least the possibility that progress in social science will be slowed until there is further progress in mathematics.[12]

Finally, social science is not yet able to achieve the high degree of accuracy which is commonplace in the physical sciences. While the latter can, and do, make predictions with such low likelihood of error that they are accepted as being completely accurate, we in social science must be satisfied with predictions having possible errors of 5 or 10 percent. Undoubtedly this has to do with the complexities of the subject matter with which we deal, and with the elementary stage of development of our measuring and observation instruments. It is reasonable to assume that as time passes we will develop more accurate instruments and more adequate methods of handling the complexities of the subject matter. In the meantime it is well to remember that our field is a very young one as compared to the physical sciences. This is vividly illustrated by noting that the entire history of sociology as a separate discipline is spanned by the lifetimes of just three men, as shown in Figure 2.[13] Auguste Comte was born in 1798, invented the term "sociology" about 1838, and died in 1857. William Graham Sumner was born in 1840, about the time that "sociology" was born, and died in 1910; his important work *Folkways* was published in 1907. Shortly before that, 1902 marked the birth of Talcott Parsons, who only recently retired from his post at Harvard University.

[12] Kemeny, 1959, pp. 249–50.

[13] I would like to acknowledge the source of this illustration but, alas, I cannot recall where I first encountered it.

Figure 2. Span of history of sociology

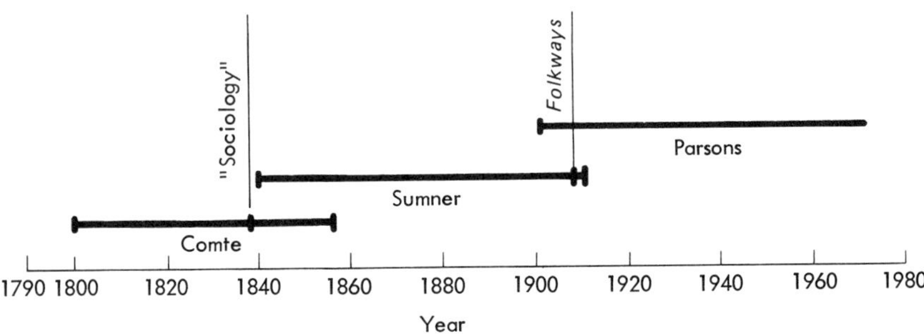

When this time span is contrasted with the history of the physical sciences (for example, the discovery of Neptune in 1846), it becomes obvious that it is unreasonable to make comparisons between the achievements of sociology and those of physical science. To expect that sociology of today should be able to explain all forms of human interaction and to solve the many problems confronting society is like expecting Kepler and his contemporaries, or Newton and his, to master the intricacies of jet propulsion or atomic fission or electronic circuits or solar energy. But it is only the faint-hearted who will be discouraged from trying. There is no reason to doubt that sociology can and will make tremendous strides in the future.

PART II

METHODS OF RESEARCH

Objectives. Part II, the final section of the book, is a general examination of the methods of doing sociological research. It offers an opportunity for the student to acquire a comprehensive overview of the techniques, procedures, and methods currently used to formulate, design, and execute research activities; to become more familiar with the use of a scientific approach to solving practical problems; and to develop enough skill in these methods so that he or she can successfully undertake a limited research project. At this point in an academic career, the student will gain greatly by undertaking such a project. This combined study-and-practice of the methods of research will contribute to the overall objectives set out early in this book, since the student may gain experience in conducting research on human interaction, will certainly be faced with the many practical decision-points of research, and will thus be in a better position to evaluate research done by others. Completion of the exercises appearing at the end of each chapter should also provide stimulating and valuable training in achieving these objectives. Remember again that this book is not intended to make the student into a thoroughly trained, competent, independent researcher. Those who will be doing independent research will almost certainly take more advanced courses in methodology during their graduate training. Thus this section definitely does not attempt to provide complete training in all available techniques. However, extensive references are included so that the student can, on his own, further investigate any subject. *The footnotes should be consulted carefully* for guides to more detailed discussions of the various topics presented.

Chapter 6

Formulation of a research problem

We have seen how the scientific process, following the casual observation of some phenomenon, really begins with a wondering about the phenomenon, or a hypothesis or question about it which in turn eventually leads to a tentative explanation and a further hypothesis. In order to proceed with research, we must transform this hypothesis (or question or vague wonderment) into a systematized statement which is sufficiently precise so that we can realistically attempt to determine the truth about it. Even if it already is a relatively precise hypothesis, this is only the first step. Much more information about the question (hypothesis, wonderment) is necessary in order that we can research it. The process of formulation consists in making explicit all available information about the question, as well as the circumstances surrounding its choice. And in the formulation process we encounter the first of the many practical decisions which must be made in conducting research.

Prior to the actual formulation itself, it is necessary to examine the considerations involved in the selection of a research topic.

DECIDING UPON A RESEARCH TOPIC

Starting point of research

The reader is reminded of what research is, namely, the careful, diligent, and exhaustive investigation of a specific subject matter, having as its aim the advancement of knowledge. Furthermore, because our interest here is in scientific research all that has been said thus far must be kept in mind. What we have discussed already are the guidelines which determine how one goes about formulating and solving a research problem.

The aim of research is to advance knowledge. It follows that the starting point of a research activity must be a gap in our knowledge of some aspect of nature. This lacuna is almost invariably expressed as a question to be answered, a hypothesis to be tested, or sometimes a problem to be solved. It was pointed out before that there are two kinds of research, descriptive and explanatory. Therefore, the research starting point may consist of a description of some aspect of nature which is desired (the "What?" question) or a tentative explanation, the accuracy and usefulness of which we want to determine by testing its predictions against reality (the "Why?").

When a description is sought, the "What?" may be expressed in any of the three forms mentioned above. For example, it might be the question, "How has the rate of murder in Calcutta changed since India attained independence?" or the hypothesis, "Ex-airline stewardesses have a lower divorce rate than the average for all women's occupational categories," or the problem, "Determine the socioeconomic background factor which is most highly correlated with success in graduate school." The source of these, as seen in the Flowchart in Chapter 4, is some "wonderment" or curiosity expressed about some observed phenomenon, or a previously-obtained description of some kind.

When we seek to test a tentative explanation, the knowledge gap is expressed as a hypothesis, e.g., "Ex-airline stewardesses have a lower than average divorce rate because of the emphasis in their training on solicitude toward people and calmness in all situations." Such hypotheses are propositions derived from a tentative explanation which we desire to reality-test.

Our definition of research clearly implies that such questions, hypotheses, or problems are the only appropriate starting points for research. However, there exist other possible starting points for sociological research which are at best questionable, even though they may sometimes have useful, beneficial, and productive outcomes. Two such *opportunistic* starting points are: a group which happens to be available, and a technique which happens to be intriguing. For example, the researcher may be leader of a Boy Scout troop, or member of a particularly interesting work group. Or new computer equipment may become available or a new familiarity with a technique such as Bales' Interaction Process Analysis may be acquired. To be sure, these groups or techniques may lead to productive, legitimate research, but the starting point of such research should still be some descriptive or explanatory question *about* the group, or one which can be answered *by* the technique. Another inappropriate starting point, in view of the earlier discussion of scientific objectivity and values, is an attempt to prove a point. Because of the likelihood of subtle or gross bias one should not engage in research to prove a hypothesis one strongly likes (or to disprove a proposition one dislikes). Rather, it is far preferable to *test* the point, without regard for the outcome.

Another starting point for research—by no means "inappropriate," but a special case—is a replication of some previous research. "Replication" refers to the repetition of a study with all circumstances and variables as nearly identical to the original as possible. Such studies are potentially of great importance, since they serve as a means of verifying research results. There is always the possibility that any research results may be due to some undetected flaw in the research design, or to some unknown peculiarity of the situation being studied, or some other unrecognized confounding factor. Replications can be of great help in eliminating such possibilities. Unfortunately, however, replications are much rarer in sociology than in, for example, the physical sciences.

Sources of ideas and topics

How do we go about deciding upon a specific research topic? Or, as students sometimes say when faced with an assignment of doing some original research, how do we know what things to wonder about? How can we decide which hypothesis to test? Clearly, one's interest is the most important single factor. The question might be phrased, What theory am I interested in? since practical research ideas may stem directly from theory, as indicated in the Flowchart (above). Given the enormous number of lacunae in our knowledge, and the premise that all knowledge is desirable, it follows that research on any such lacuna is worthwhile. There are no right or wrong topics to study, and, other considerations aside, whatever appeals to one's interest is as good a starting point as any other. There is no implication here that the question (or hypothesis or wonderment) must necessarily be original. It is quite legitimate to undertake research on hypotheses, questions, or theories which others have devised, or on questions which arise in the course of one's reading. (Needless to say, credit for such sources must be acknowledged, in the reporting of the research). Many interesting and useful observations pertaining to the source and development of research ideas are presented by Mills, although we would not agree with all his views.[1] In his essay, "On Intellectual Craftsmanship," he discusses, among other things, the use of one's life experiences in professional work, taking notes and keeping files, the imagination as the source of ideas, and the proper use of language for communicating with one's audience.

Aside from general interest, there are various other factors which may play a part in deciding upon a topic. One's experience frequently yields valuable suggestions—other courses one has studied, other subject fields one may have been exposed to, job experiences, or travel, or general life experiences. Various articles and books may present suggestions for needed research in certain areas. From time to time some professional journals devote whole issues to such accounting, and professional meetings and associations may publicize lists of desired research.[2] Various government agencies and fund-granting organizations may publicize research which they believe to be necessary—for example, the Center for Population Research of the National Institutes of Health. (Appendix A is a list of possible research topics from the author's files.)

A useful way of narrowing one's research interests is to identify two interesting variables and to select the area where they intersect each other as a research topic. For example, one might be interested in the characteristics of stratification within rural communities, and also in the relative popularity of various mass communication media. So research could be conducted on some

---

[1] Mills, 1959, pp. 215–48.

[2] The following references contain suggestions for needed research (Although some of them are old, the research is still needed): Williams, 1947; Rose, 1954, pp. 128–49; Borgatta and Cottrell, 1957; *Sociology and Social Research*, vol. 42 (July 1958) (the entire issue is devoted to articles on needed research); L. Miller, 1965; Popovich, 1966; Beshers, 1967, pp. 161–62; Brown and Gilmartin, 1969; Coleman, 1970-a; Rhoades, 1975; Dorwin Cartwright, 1965.

aspect of the relationship between—the intersection of—these two variables, such as the relative effectiveness of newspapers and television among upper-, middle-, and lower-class rural adults. Finally, ideas for research topics may be supplied by some external source. The student, for example, may be assigned a topic or given a list of potential topics. The advanced researcher may be approached by an agency or foundation requesting research on a specific subject. One particular example of this, evaluation research, will be discussed in the next section.

From one or more of the above sources—and perhaps others—the researcher now has a fairly specific topic in mind. Let us say that, in the course of his reading, the researcher has been intrigued by the following passage:

> the surgeon may "skilfully perform" the operation and yet the patient may die, a victim of forces over which the surgeon has no control. . . . In such cases the professional naturally balks at being evaluated on results, and the only basis for evaluating performance is to ask whether or not he employed appropriate methods in carrying out his work.[3]

He ponders this, wonders about it, and is interested in the research possibilities which seem to lie in it.[4] The broad idea, "evaluation of surgeons' performance" (or some similar idea) is not specific enough for the purpose of research; some particular aspect of it must be selected. For example, one might state the problem as, "Is medicine the only profession which is evaluated on criteria other than results?" or, "Is teaching similar to medicine in that performance is evaluated on the criterion of methods used rather than results?" Many other specific research problems could be derived from this same general idea, of course.

Evaluation research

In recent years a new trend has occurred in many parts of the world which increasingly serves as an important source of ideas and topics for sociological research. An enormous number of social action programs have been undertaken by public,

---

[3] W. R. Scott, 1966, p. 270.

[4] Thanks are due to the author's former student, Gregg Peterson, for suggesting this interesting research question.

semipublic, and private agencies. The focus of these varies bewilderingly—education, housing, poverty, health, family planning, agricultural productivity, delinquency and crime, nutrition, community planning, political change, and more—but they share the twin goals of planned social change and amelioration of social problems. Unfortunately, despite the best of intentions and assiduous efforts to apply the most dependable sociological knowledge to these practical issues, it cannot be assumed that the programs are therefore successful, nor even that they share the same degree of relative success. In actual fact, relatively little is known regarding the effectiveness of such programs. In view of their social importance, the large costs, the frequently controversial issues involved, and the great number of people participating and served by them, it is not surprising that there is an increasing demand for accurate assessment of the effectiveness of these action programs.

This demand provides a fertile source for research topics, and indeed, evaluation research has achieved enough prominence during the past decade and a half so that we consider it separately here. "Evaluation research" is a general term referring to research designed to evaluate the effect of social action programs, in terms of the objectives of the individual programs. One approach to evaluation research has concentrated on inputs to the program, such as numbers and qualifications of workers, proportionate amounts of equipment and facilities, recordkeeping, or dollars of budget per unit of target population.[5] An alternative—and probably preferred—approach emphasizes output or effect of the program. The rationale for this is, of course, to determine whether the program is in fact achieving its goals, and, to the extent that it is not, to enable corrective action to be taken. Clearly then, evaluation research may be either descriptive or explanatory. Given the importance and magnitude of the programs, evaluation research can not only have important practical consequences, but can contribute to the development of the whole field of sociology as well.

In doing evaluation research one utilizes essentially the same techniques and procedures as in any other kind of sociological research. However, since the research usually takes place within the framework of an ongoing program in a social action agency, there are certain methodological problems and issues

[5] Caro, 1971, pp. 2–3.

which may be peculiar to this kind of research. Among these are:

> (1) the tendency of the program to change while it is being evaluated, (2) the relationships between evaluators and program personnel, and (3) the fact that the program is embedded in an organizational system and that the nature of the system will have consequences for outcomes."[6]

Other difficulties may be encountered in identifying and measuring the goals of the program and in the relationships between the researcher and the target population of the program.

Most evaluation research has been done in the years since about 1960, and to a disturbingly large extent the results have been disappointing. In part this is because too much of the research has been subjective and impressionistic rather than rigorously scientific. Another reason lies in the very frequently encountered "dismaying tendency to show that the program has had little effect."[7] It seems clear that evaluation research offers many opportunities for further work. As an illustrative example of evaluation research, Appendix B provides a description of a project directed by this author in 1962–64.

Evaluation of a research topic

At this point, specifically, one faces what is probably the first of the practical decision-points involved in doing research. A statement of a problem—an idea for a research topic—has been obtained, or, more realistically, several such ideas have been obtained although some may be more crystallized than others. The decision must be made, therefore, as to which (if any) of the ideas should be pursued. This evaluation can usefully be divided into three questions.

Is the topic worthwhile? Since the researcher's time and energy and skills are valuable, he must expend these assets wisely. Is it worth his while to spend so much of his time and energy and other resources on a given piece of research as com-

---

[6] Weiss, 1972, p. 93. This book provides basic information for doing evaluation research. For a somewhat more advanced presentation see Suchman, 1967. See also Bernstein, 1975, and the comprehensive works: Guttentag and Struening, 1975, and Struening and Guttentag, 1975.

[7] Weiss, 1972, p. 126. For further discussion of this aspect of evaluation research see Rossi and Williams, 1972.

pared to some alternative? He will want to consider both the sociological and the practical worth of the investigation, although practical worth is by no means an essential ingredient of scientific research. (In fact, practical worth may be a detrimental factor, and may even inhibit scientific development.)[8] Will this investigation make enough of a contribution to be significant? Obviously, a definitive answer to such questions cannot be given in advance, but the researcher's general experience should enable him to decide whether or not the topic is worthwhile.

To continue with the same example, is it worthwhile to undertake research to find out whether medicine is the only profession which is evaluated on criteria other than results? Unless the researcher answers this affirmatively, he will probably not want to proceed with the research. It is not necessary that he completely identify the contributions which the research will make at this point, but his general background and experience must convince him that this will make sufficient contribution so as to merit his expenditure of time, energy, and money. In this illustration he can recognize that, in general, the topic is of potential importance to the sociology of occupations, and perhaps to the medical profession itself, so as to justify this undertaking.

Is it feasible? Several practical considerations may affect the decision as to whether or not to proceed with the project, or what form the project will take. Research involves a series of compromises between the "ideal" procedures and those which are feasible. Is sufficient time available to bring the project to a successful conclusion? Not only must any deadline for completion of the project be considered, but also the proportion of the researcher's time that he can devote to the research. In studying evaluation procedures of surgery, for example, it might be necessary to observe patients' recovery rates, which could involve relatively long periods of time. Are the necessary tools and techniques available for the research? One's familiarity with research technology which may be acquired over time helps to assess this aspect of feasibility. To continue the surgery illustration, the study might not be feasible if the research question necessitated accurate measurement of personality changes, since techniques for accomplishing this are not well developed. Are sufficient resources available? Resources may include physical space

[8] Kuhn, 1962, p. 95.

(such as office, laboratory, and data-processing space), equipment (such as computers, data-processing machines, and tape recorders), supplies, transportation facilities, and, of course, money. Any research costs money, if only in that the researcher's time has some monetary value. Time expended on research is time which therefore cannot be expended on other, perhaps more remunerative, activities. And even the simplest research will usually require at least a small amount of office supplies, postage, carfare, and the like. At the other extreme, large sums may be needed for salaries, office and other space, equipment, travel and so on. Many practical decisions are made, in the course of any research activity, on the basis of the availability or lack of availability of funds. In assessing the feasibility of a project, one must have at least a rough idea of the costs involved.[9] Finally, are the size and scope of the project feasible (aside from the limitations imposed by time and resources)? A common mistake, especially for beginners, is to attempt to research a project which is too vague, indefinite, general, or sweeping.

A different aspect of feasibility, which may be extremely hard to assess in advance, is the question of whether the study is likely to encounter opposition from certain individuals or groups. Some cases are obvious. It would be difficult, for example, to study the rituals of a fraternity, or the internal workings of a police department or a criminal organization, or the decision-making processes at the highest level of a large corporation, or the use of wiretaps or bugging by a governmental agency. For whatever reasons, many groups and organizations observe strict secrecy with regard to some of their activities. Less obvious are the cases where a study may encounter opposition by a portion of the public who view the study as dubious, undesirable, or worse. It may happen that this cannot be determined in advance, and a study which appeared to be feasible when it was formulated may have to be abandoned or severely modified. One such study of school dropouts in a Southern California community had to be sharply changed as a result of political pressure on the school administrators. Right-wing political groups objected to the so-called invasion of privacy, in part because they feared that the researchers were going to "assess the

[9] See below for a discussion of the sources of financing.

personality of students so that those with right-wing tendencies could be committed to institutions as psychotic when they reached their majority."[10] It is hard to know whether to laugh or cry in such situations! Still another form in which opposition may occur is at the individual level. Sometimes it is necessary to receive the approval or cooperation of a certain key individual in an organization—a school superintendent or a personnel manager, for example—and for personal reasons this individual may perceive the study as threatening and may not grant the necessary approval. To the extent that these aspects of feasibility can be identified in advance, they must be taken into account at this stage of the formulation procedures. It may also be necessary to take these considerations into account later when decisions about the general design of the research are being made.

Will any personal factors affect the research? It may be that there are certain personal factors of the researcher which will, in one way or another, affect the conduct of research. It is important to consider these since their effect may be very subtle and bias may be introduced into the research without the investigator being aware of its source. These factors may be of two different kinds. It is well known that superficial characteristics of the researcher, such as age, sex, race, and physical appearance, may be related to rapport and success in interviewing (as will be discussed later), but these may also affect his own frame of reference and thus his ability fully to grasp the subtleties of a situation. A foreigner, for example, may well overlook many implications of the data which a native would easily recognize, or may see more. There is always at least the possibility that a male and a female researcher would handle the study of, say, pregnant women, or childbirth, in significantly different ways. The second, and more subtle, group of personal factors consists of values and personality traits. An anxious individual, for example, may tend to be much more conservative in planning the research than will a more self-confident researcher. A researcher of a fundamentalist religious persuasion may study divorce in a different frame of reference than an agnostic would. Values may be particularly troublesome in undertaking research in a different society from one's own, but must always be considered, as noted in our earlier discussion of values and policy. Recall that the researcher's values are premises, and thus fundamental to the whole logical development of the research ar-

[10] Voss, 1966, p. 139.

gument or plan. As Werkmeister points out, the full statement of the problem must

> include the delimitation of its scope, the guiding hypothesis, the principles for the selection of data, the definitions of all terms, and a clear and concise formulation of the value premises. These premises must themselves be submitted as hypotheses, subject to future revision, and not as self-evident truths which are absolute and final.[11]

At this point in the evaluation of a research topic, the researcher should identify any such personal factors which may interfere with or help (it may work either way) the proposed research, and further, he should question whether such interference or help are of sufficient magnitude that he should consider changing or abandoning the project, or whether they will require special efforts at maintaining an objective approach.

With increasing experience some of these evaluative steps may become routine or "second nature" for the researcher: he may be able immediately to recognize whether or not the proposed research is worthwhile and feasible. However, it is important *always* to carefully inquire into the presence of any personal factors which might affect the research. If the results of this whole evaluation process are negative, then of course the researcher either abandons the proposal or modifies it. If the evaluation results in a decision to proceed with the research, he takes the statement of the problem and begins the formulation process.[12]

FINANCING

Although financing of research is not strictly related to the formulation process, it is very definitely related to feasibility. As mentioned above, many practical research decisions are made on the basis of the amount of money available. Thus the availability of funds has a definite bearing upon at least the manner in which the research is conducted, if not on the outcome.

The most obvious—if least satisfactory!—source of funds is the researcher himself. The beginning research student, or even the student working on a master's thesis or doctoral dissertation,

---

[11] Werkmeister, 1959, p. 503.

[12] A list of eight criteria of significance for sociological research is given in D. Miller, 1970, pp. 6–7.

may find that the demands of the project are sufficently small so that the financing can be managed from personal or family funds. Surely this is as much an integral part of one's education as the costs of tuition and books. In the long run it *may* even prove to be a wise course for the student to borrow money in order to finance his research, if the research is a sufficiently important part of his training, such as a thesis or dissertation.

Most American universities offer scholarships, fellowships, and assistantships for some of their graduate students, and some have additional funds to support research by graduate students. While these are usually not sufficient to completely finance a student's project, they may provide at least partial aid. Also, of course, in many academic departments there are ongoing research activities. These may be under the direction of an individual faculty member, or a bureau or organization within the department, or they may be departmentwide undertakings. Often such activities provide opportunities to employ some students. These research jobs vary considerably in the amount of autonomy the student has in pursuing his own research goal.

The researcher who is employed or otherwise affiliated with a nonacademic organization or agency may find that the organization has some provision for, and interest in, supporting research undertaken by its personnel. This is especially true in the case of organizations whose goals are served by social science research, and also by those organizations which recognize the wisdom in contributing to the further education of their employees.

For the more experienced researcher, even more sources of funds become available. Not only are there his own university or employer, but also many philanthropic organizations, foundations, semipublic agencies, government agencies, and private agencies and corporations. Some of these have funds available for any worthy project, while others may have a limited and specific list of topics in which they have a vested interest (evaluation research, for example). Some also have funds available for students. It is impossible to list here all such agencies, but most libraries maintain directories of foundations and philanthropic agencies.[13] Aside from all the above, the ingenious researcher will discover additional sources of financing.

[13] Miller, 1970, gives a very useful and comprehensive directory of agencies which support social science research, pp. 393–408.

FORMULATION

The formulation of a research problem, as mentioned above, consists of a systematized statement which serves as a prospectus, or guide, and as a basis for all the other practical decisions which must be made during the course of a research undertaking. This statement should be very carefully thought out and precisely worded. Since it is to serve as a guide for designing and conducting the research, it should be put in writing before proceeding to the following stages of research design. The formulation statement is most usefully divided into five parts, which will be considered individually.

Statement of general topic

The first part of this formulation is simply a statement of the general topic which has previously been evaluated favorably, as described above. For example, it might be, "An investigation of the criteria for evaluating performance in the medical and teaching professions." This statement should not be confused with the *title* of the research project or of the final report, although in the long run they may be worded similarly or even identically.

Goals

Here the researcher specifies his reasons for doing the study, that is, the ends being sought. All the many steps which are being taken, and which will be taken in doing research, must lead toward some particular goal. And of course, as with any other endeavor, the detailed steps taken are determined by the goal one is attempting to attain. It is entirely possible that a given specific research topic could be undertaken in an effort to achieve two—or more—goals, which might be vastly different or even contradictory. And these different goals might well impose different restrictions or considerations upon the research activities. For example, one might be interested in studying the criteria for evaluation in the medical and teaching professions because of a goal of improving the public image of the teaching profession, or because of an interest in "socialized" medicine, or to test some theory about occupational status differentiations, or simply to describe a hitherto vague aspect of society. Which goals are chosen will, of course, influence the manner in which the study is undertaken. (Among other goals which may motivate sociological research are: the development or improvement of some research technique or instrument, the generation of new ideas for further inquiry, or an exploration to find out "what would happen if . . . . .")[14] The decision as to which goals are guiding a particular study is a personal, subjective thing. There are no right or wrong goals as long as they are scientific goals, nor are there any right or wrong—or scientific or nonscientific—methods for identifying and specifying one's goals. Rather, this is a process of making a personal decision regarding research goals—the decision is made to study some particular aspect of a general topic—and this decision is guided largely by one's interests. The goals of a typical research study are divided into three types.

First, there are one's personal goals. This is a personal statement of the researcher's *reasons* for doing the study. For example, he may ask himself the following questions. Why are you interested in this topic? What is your personal rationale or justification for doing it? Why do you *care about* this topic? What personal benefits or satisfactions do you hope to derive from *doing* the study? (Note, the question is *not:* What benefits do you hope will be derived from the *results* of the study?)

Next, the researcher will identify the sociological goals, or importance, of the study. For example, of what professional use or value will it be? What will it contribute to sociological knowledge? What can or will be done with the results? How is it related to the whole field of sociology in general, and sociological theory in particular? What kind of generalizations does the researcher hope to make from his study? As with the other parts of this formulation process, these sociological goals should be spelled out quite clearly and precisely, and in detail.

Finally, some studies may have some practical goals, although this is not essential as has been seen above. Frequently these practical goals are specified by some outside agency or fund-granting source as in the case of evaluation research. It will be of value to the researcher to identify the practical uses or importance of his study, whether derived from an outside source or otherwise.

---

[14] Kaplan, 1964, pp. 148–49.

This statement of the goals of a research activity can prove to be extraordinarily helpful if it is frequently referred to during the course of designing and executing the research. Many specific and detailed decisions can be made much more easily, if the researcher constantly keeps before him his overall goals in doing the research.

Specific objectives

The specific objectives of a study consist of a precise, formal statement of the hypothesis(es) to be tested, the questions to be answered, or the problems to be solved. It may be that this statement of the specific objectives will be the same as the Statement of the General Topic previously made, although ordinarily the latter is not sufficiently precisely worded. The wording of this is of considerable importance, in order to ensure that the researcher is accurately communicating with others just exactly what his research is all about. *The same considerations apply here as were presented earlier in the discussion of the place of hypotheses in inductive reasoning.*

The statement of the specific objectives of a study should indicate whether the study is descriptive, explanatory, or both. This is because certain of the basic research designs (to be discussed below) are unsuitable for explanatory studies. (In other respects the research procedures are the same.) Sometimes it is hard to distinguish between a descriptive and explanatory study on the basis of the wording of the hypothesis or other specific characteristics of the research. However, as can be seen from the Flowchart of the Scientific method, the crucial distinguishing factor is the *source* of the research hypothesis. Returning to the illustrative example, the specific objective might be: "What are the criteria customarily used by the public in evaluating performance in the medical and teaching professions?" This clearly indicates that the study is descriptive in nature.

Usually as part of the process of stating the specific objectives, the researcher will necessarily identify and specify what the several variables are which are to be dealt with in the study. Sometimes this is more important—or more obscure—than others. In the above example, it is readily seen that there are two main variables: performance in the medical and teaching professions, and the public's criteria for evaluating this performance.

Definitions and indicators

In order to make for the utmost clarity and precision, and to improve communication, it is important at this stage of the formulation process that any ambiguity in the meanings of any of the key words used in the statements of the problems and objectives be eliminated. In sociology there is a lack of agreement within the field as to the exact meanings of many important words. Also, many of these words have quite different meanings in popular usage (e.g., society, culture, personality, group, attitude, status). Furthermore, many words used in sociology have several meanings (e.g., function) while in many cases several different words refer to the same thing (e.g., according to Goode and Hatt, structure-function, ideal-real, formal-informal, and primary-secondary all refer to essentially the same thing).[15] Obviously, if the precise meaning the researcher has in mind is not made clear, both to himself and to his ultimate audience, confusion will result. Even careful use of a dictionary may not be sufficient, as Kershner and Wilcox point out in their classic illustration:

> Consider the statement, "She was fair." Suppose there is some doubt in your mind as to what the term *fair* means. You look in the dictionary and find something like this:
>
> > fair (adj.) [AS. *faeger*, beautiful] 1, pleasing to the sight; handsome; beautiful; 2, not dark in color or complexion; blond; 3, without blemish; spotless; clean; 4, favorable; giving promise; 5, moderately satisfactory; pretty good; 6, impartial; just; 7, according to regulations; 8, allowing lawful pursuit; 9, distinct; unobstructed.
>
> This leaves you in considerable doubt as to whether she was beautiful, clean, impartial and otherwise wholly admirable; just moderately satisfactory; or simply an unobstructed blonde not above allowing pursuit, provided it is according to regulations.[16]

To avoid ambiguity and lack of clarity the researcher should select or construct definitions which are compatible with the research objectives. In doing this the differences among three

[15] Goode and Hatt, 1952, p. 46.

[16] Kershner and Wilcox, 1974, p. 9.

related things must be taken into account. First there is the *referent*. This is the actual "thing" being considered or defined. It may be some objective phenomenon, such as an object, action, or event which can be directly observed; it may be only indirectly observable and involve some inference (e.g., anger, a dream); or it may be subjective (i.e., not observable), such as an idea (democracy, government, Protestant ethic) or a quality (honesty, progress).

Second, there is the *term* (i.e., the symbol, or word) used to designate the referent. Finally, there is the *concept*, which is the whole family, or cluster, of meanings associated with a term.[17] Concepts are, therefore, abstractions carrying with them all the implications and associations customarily made with the particular term, and thus are essential for human communication, and even for thinking. To illustrate, the referent might be a man, woman and child. The term used to designate this is "family." The concept would include (in American society) such things as: it is a monogamous relationship; the parents are responsible for the physical survival and well-being of the child, as well as its socialization; the husband is expected to provide financial support; the husband is typically older than the wife but they are from similar educational and class backgrounds; sexual fidelity is expected of the husband and wife; there is legal sanction of the relationship, etc. From the illustration it may clearly be seen that concepts derive from the experiences of the individuals, and thus are culturally related. The "typical" American concept of "family" will be at some variance from the "typical" Hindu concept. Similarly, of course, concepts will vary within a society, and even, to some extent, within a profession.

If one overlooks the distinctions among "referent," "term," and "concept," various problems may result. Most serious, perhaps, is the fallacy of *reification* in which a concept is confused with a referent and treated as though it actually is an observable phenomenon. Very similar is the situation in which a referent is treated as though it actually possesses all the characteristics which are part of the concept, when in reality these particular characteristics are simply abstractions which have come to be associated with the referent.

Definitions exist for the purpose of specifying meaning and enhancing communication, as discussed in Chapter 2. An adequate definition attempts to convey the essential part of the

[17] Kaplan, 1964, pp. 48–49.

total body of meanings and implications contained in a concept. In fact, a definition may usefully be thought of as the "formal," written expression of a concept.[18] Whether or not a given definition is adequate depends upon the purpose of the definition—what it will be used for. The research definitions should emphasize those aspects of the concepts which are most relevant to the research objectives. These are usually real or operational, but may be nominal, or perhaps other, definitions.

In constructing a definition, or judging the adequacy of a given definition, *the referent must be the starting point.* Words are symbols and have no inherent meanings other than what we impart to them, while the referent exists entirely independently of whatever verbal label may be applied to it. A vital question is: exactly what is the referent which the researcher has in mind when using a certain term? To use a common example, let us say that the research involves some interviewing of "college students." It is easy to overlook the ambiguity of this familiar term. Does the researcher have in mind some distinction between college and university? Is he thinking only of full-time (whatever that may mean) students or also part-time? What about a person enrolled in only one course—is he included in the researcher's conception of the term? Is there some age limit involved—would he include middle-aged or elderly people, or only those of "college age"? Are graduate students included, or only undergrads? What about individuals who are employed full-time, and also attending college classes? The answers to these kinds of questions are determined by reference to the goals and specific objectives of the study. Clearly it is necessary, if it has not been done previously, to identify exactly what the referent is. One way of doing this is by specifying some set of operations or other objective, observable criteria which can be used in the data-collection procedures. This may be done through either an operational definition or what is called a "working definition."[19] Regardless of what it is called, the detailed criteria must be stated clearly here and now, if possible. For example, "For this research a college student is defined as any person under age 30, enrolled full-time in an undergraduate program in the Liberal Arts or Education Colleges of this university."

---

[18] In one sense, "definition" and "concept" may be synonymous. See DiRenzo, 1966, p. 9.

[19] Selltiz et al., 1959, p. 42.

After deciding upon the definitions, the researcher faces another crucial question: How will he *recognize* the referents he is studying when he encounteres them? What kinds of information will he accept as evidence of their presence? Such questions *may* have been answered if the above are operational or working definitions, but frequently they are not. In the example given of "college student," there is no problem, since this is a directly observable referent. If, however, the referent is only indirectly observable, or not observable, some *indicators* must be specified which the researcher can accept as providing evidence for the presence of the referent. He must devise some physical or symbolic operations, or identify some observable events or phenomena, which indicate that the thing being studied exists at a given place and time. The researcher's ingenuity is important here. How will one recognize "anger," for example? Indicators which might be selected include redness of the face, muscular tension, loud and abusive language, hitting, and other physical violence. If a study were being done of sailing as a hobby, indicators which could be used to recognize "sailing enthusiasts" might include subscribing to yachting magazines, visiting a boat show, membership in a sailing club, registration as a sailboat owner, and response to an advertisement offering free sailing information. Webb et al. report on a study which utilized the rate of erosion of floor tiles in a museum as an indicator of the relative popularity of the various exhibits.[20] Similarly, a value or a quality such as honesty might be recognized by the use of various specific behavioral indicators, and a specific attitude could be recognized by verbal responses to questions. Whatever the referent under consideration, unless it is a directly observable phenomenon, indicators must be selected either through operational or working definitions, or by separately devising a set of indicators. It should be noted that indicators are not the same as definitions, although a definition may provide the indicators. We would not, for example, want to *define* the popularity of a museum exhibit in terms of floor tile erosion. Ultimately it is only the indicators and the objective, observable referents which constitute the raw data of research.[21] We can never directly observe concepts.

[20] Webb, et al. UNOBTRUSIVE MEASURES: NONREACTIVE RESEARCH IN THE SOCIAL SCIENCES, © 1966 by Rand McNally College Publishing Company, Chicago. Their book contains an enormous number of other examples of ingenious indicators. This one is, perhaps, the best known.

[21] See Chapter 10.

Further, we see that the selection of the indicators which will be utilized in a study is intimately related to the data-collection methods which will be used. The decisions made in designing a study do not always occur in a simple sequential pattern; instead, there is an interlocking relationship between decisions made at various points.

To summarize, after stating the specific objectives, the key terms must be defined and indicators for the referents identified. An operational definition may fulfill both functions, or it may be that separate definitions and lists of indicators will be used.

Relationship to existing knowledge

The final step in the formulation process is to determine in what way the present study is related to the existing body of scientific knowledge. There are two functions which are served by this step. In the first place, existing knowledge must be brought to bear upon the design of any study. One thing which must be determined is whether a similar study has already been done. There is no sense in seeking the answer to a question which already has been definitively answered, or in testing a hypothesis which already has been tested sufficiently. If the study already has been done by someone else, another decision-point arises. Either the present study must be recognized as a replication study, or it must be modified in some way so as to make a contribution to knowledge, or it must be abandoned. Rather than finding that the study has already been done, a much more likely outcome is that related materials will be found. Perhaps it will be other attempts to test the same or similar hypotheses or questions, or other tests of the same or similar theories, or someone else's techniques and procedures which can be adapted to the present study. The researcher can—and should—profit from the work of his predecessors and colleagues. There is a vast body of methodological literature, and it would be an unusual study indeed which could not benefit from previously completed research.

The second function of this step is to tie the study in with existing knowledge. Since the basic idea underlying any scientific activity is to establish relationships, it is the researcher's responsibility to show just what place his study occupies in the larger scheme of things. It becomes the researcher's task to attempt to explain why his results are different from other results, or to what extent the similarity to other results is meaningful, or what the implications are for his study upon others (and vice versa), and he must elucidate the significance of his work for sociology in general.

In order to accomplish the above, it is obvious that he must have knowledge of any related material, and this can only be achieved by an exhaustive examination of library materials. By no means is this a perfunctory step, nor should it be postponed until "later when it's more convenient." In searching through the literature, the researcher must utilize his experience and knowledge in order to decide what subject headings to examine in indexes and catalogs, what sources are likely to prove fruitful, and which other authors have worked on related matters. It is never possible, of course, to make a complete search of all existing literature, because of the sheer volume of it. Thus two decisions must be made: how extensive a search to make (that is, how many different sources or different libraries), and how intensive the search will be (that is, what the time limits are). These decisions are based upon one's judgment and knowledge of the field. No library is complete—is it worth the time and money to journey to another library? Similarly, is it worthwhile to purchase or seek out one missing book or journal? One's experience and familiarity with such materials will enable one to decide. How far back in time should one search? This depends partly upon the subject matter. In the 1930s and 1940s, for instance, much was done on race relations, but little on the sociology of space travel. Also, a cut-off date must be established. New literature is being published faster than anyone can read it, and so it is not always feasible to examine the very latest materials. If the researcher waits till all the information is in, he will wait forever. An arbitrary decision must be made as to the date to stop searching.[22]

Summary

The formulation of a research problem attempts to identify the decisions which must be made to get the problem into such a form that the researcher can bring to bear upon it his repertoire

[22] See the next chapter, "The Library as a Research Tool," for suggestions on maximum utilization of library resources.

of research techniques. It should consist of a relatively precisely worded, carefully thought out, written statement, and should include: (1) the general topic to be studied, (2) the goals (personal, sociological, and practical) of the study, (3) the specific objectives or hypotheses, (4) the definitions and indicators of the key terms, and (5) a summary of existing knowledge which is related to the study. Usually this formulation statement will appear as the initial portion of the formal, final written report of the research project.

In addition, the researcher must make a statement of personal values and any other personal characteristics which might be related to the study. These should be identified by the researcher, and their possible biasing effect recognized, and dealt with in some way. This statement need not be a part of the above formal, written, formulation of the problem, but may be made as a personal statement by the researcher to himself. However, especially for those in the early stages of their research careers, it is wise actually to commit this to writing, since this helps to crystallize these often-vague ideas.

EXERCISES

1. In this chapter it was said that the aim of research is to advance knowledge and that research begins with wondering about something. Give an example of something that you have wondered about and discuss some ways that this wonderment of yours actually might lead to the advancement of knowledge.

2. Below are a number of potential research projects which a student researcher might choose to carry out. Briefly discuss the feasibility of researching each one, assuming that you would be the researcher:
   a. What is the relationship between the availability of drugs and alcohol, and the rate of addiction and alcoholism?
   b. A study of female leadership in small groups.
   c. A study of illegal-alien hiring practices.
   d. A study of the effects of energy shortages on attitudes toward politics.
   e. What makes a good parent?

3. Below are listed several projects' specific objectives. Decide whether each is more likely to be an explanatory or a descriptive research project, and briefly discuss the reasons for your decision:

a. To test the hypothesis that social isolates suffer more from anxiety than do those who are not social isolates.

b. To determine if popular magazines generally present persons of ethnic "minority" backgrounds unfavorably.

c. To determine fathers' and sons' views on politics.

d. To explore the truth of the saying: "Familiarity breeds contempt."

e. A comparative study of romanticism in Americans and foreigners.

f. To test whether or not in a hierarchy every employee tends to rise to his level of incompetence.

4. Define an abstract term such as "happiness" and then list several indicators corresponding to your definition. What were the reasons for your choosing those particular indicators?

5. An adequate definition attempts to convey the essential part of the total body of meanings and implications contained in the concept of the definition. Briefly discuss the adequacy of the following definitions in meeting these criteria:

a. "The cow is a bovine ilk, one end is moo and the other is milk." (Ogden Nash)

b. "The act is behavior of an organism stemming from an impulse requiring some adjustment to appropriate objects in the external world. The social act is that act where the appropriate object is another person." (Herbert Blumer)

c. "Hierarchiology is a social science, the study of hierarchies, their nature and functioning, the foundation for all social science." (Lawrence Peter)

d. "A society is a type of social system, in any universe of social systems, which attains the highest level of self-sufficiency as a system in relation to its environments." (Talcott Parsons)

e. Time is money.

Chapter 7

The library as a research tool

by BRADLEY A. SIMON*

"Organize, organize, organize."
Charles Stewart Parnell

Nineteenth-century Irish political leader Parnell was not speaking of libraries, but he might have been. For, just as organization was basic to the success of his political activity, so a library's organization is basic to its success in supporting research. And it follows that success for the student or researcher means understanding the library's organization, particularly that of its collections of book and nonbook materials. While this organization may vary somewhat from library to library, the basic means is the same: the use of a classification system. Such a system is designed to bring together in one place in the library all materials on a subject and—what is more—to physically locate them near materials on related subjects.

In the United States, the two most commonly used such systems are the Dewey Decimal and the Library of Congress Classification Systems.

These two systems have in common the division of all knowledge into classes or groups. Melville Dewey, himself a librarian, divided knowledge into ten different classes, which he numbered 000 to 900. The Library of Congress System, specifically developed to organize the vast holdings of the U.S. national library, is much broader; since it employs letters as class indicators, this system has the potential of using 26 divisions of knowledge. For this reason, LC is particularly suitable for larger collections and is widely used in college and research libraries.

Although LC is a broader system, it proceeds like Dewey

* City Librarian, Pomona Public Library, California

from the general to the specific. For example, at the most general level, works are classified in Dewey by three digits and in LC by a single letter. Thus in Dewey the social sciences are represented by the number 300; in LC they are represented by the letter H. The addition of numbers (in Dewey) and a combination of letters and numbers (in LC) identifies progressively more specific subjects. Thus, 301 in Dewey identifies sociology while HM does the same in LC. The longer the number in both systems, the more specific the subject it identifies. For example, a book on the aged in America bears the number 301.4350973 in the Dewey Classification and the number HQ1064.U5B87 in LC.

Quite detailed tables of these numbers have been prepared for both classification systems. For the student, however, such detail is worse than useless; it is confusing. It is enough to remember the principle that these classification numbers are synonomous with subjects and that similar subjects will bear similar classification numbers. Further, the first number or letter of the classification symbol identifies the general class to which the work in question belongs. Thus any work classified by Dewey which begins with a 3 is a work dealing with some aspect of the social sciences, just as any work classed by LC which begins with an H deals with the same subject. It may be helpful to familiarize oneself with the general classification symbols used by both systems:

Dewey		*Library of Congress*	
000	Generalities	A	General Works. Polygraphy
100	Philosophy and Related Disciplines	B	Philosophy. Psychology. Religion
		C	Auxiliary Sciences of History
200	Religion	D	History: General and Old World
300	The Social Sciences	E–F	History: America
400	Language	G	Geography. Anthropology. Recreation
500	Pure Sciences	H	Social Sciences
600	Technology (Applied Sciences)	J	Political Science
700	The Arts	K	Law
800	Literature (Belles-lettres)	L	Education
900	General Geography & History	M	Music and Books on Music
		N	Fine Arts
		P	Language and Literature
		Q	Science
		R	Medicine
		S	Agriculture
		T	Technology
		U	Military Science
		V	Naval Science
		Z	Bibliography and Library Science

At this point it may be helpful to think of the library as one large book and the classification numbers we have been discussing as page numbers in that book. To find the page we are looking for, we need an index. Such an index to a library's collections is the Card Catalog. In form this is, as its name implies, a collection of printed or typed 3×5 cards filed in trays.

Each book in the collection is represented by one or more of these cards in the catalog. Each card contains a variety of information: the author's name (last name first); the title; the imprint (place of publication, publisher and date of publication); the collation (the number of volumes or pages, the number and kind of illustrations, and the size of the book); and descriptive notes. At the bottom of the card are also the subject headings and other entries under which cards for the work may be filed. For most books in the collection, this will mean author, title, and one or more subject headings. It may also include joint authors and illustrators. Because these cards are filed alphabetically, this means that all books by one author will be filed under his name and, similarly, that cards for all books on the same subject will be filed together under that subject. When more than one card is filed under an author's name or under a subject heading, the cards are subfiled by the first word of the title.

Aside from the front door, the card catalog is the main entrance to a library's collections. It tells the library user not only what materials are in the collection but where they are located as well. For each card contains not only the information listed above but the call number for each book as well. This "call number" is a two-line entry usually located in the upper left-hand corner of the card. The first line is the classification number; the second line is the author symbol. The precise form this author symbol takes will vary from library to library. Some will use a Cutter number (taken from a table devised by C. A. Cutter about the time Dewey was devising his system); some, a modified or abbreviated Cutter number (as is used with LC); and still others, a symbol developed by the individual library. Whatever form this symbol takes, it is used for the purpose of arranging volumes within a classification alphabetically by author. This call number is of primary importance in locating a specific volume on the shelf since no two volumes will have identical call numbers. Occasionally a call number will be prefaced by a symbol indicating that the book is located in a special area. Such symbols will vary from library to library, but perhaps the most commonly used one is "R" which indicates the book is a reference book, housed in the Reference Department, and to be used (usually) only in the library.

Despite a wide variety of local variations, the card catalog remains the single most valuable guide to the library's resources, and it is the place where the library user will almost always want to begin research.

One should be aware, however, that some materials may not be listed in the card catalog. Magazines, for example, are sometimes not listed in the catalog but in separate serials lists. Audiovisual materials such as phonograph records and films may be cataloged separately as well. Magazine and newspaper articles are almost never listed in the card catalog. For these and other materials, such as many government documents, the student will want to consult a variety of other indexes.

Perhaps the most common are the various periodical guides which index popular and special interest periodicals. Among these, the most generally important are:

1. The *Readers' Guide to Periodical Literature*, published by the H. W. Wilson Company. This indexes most major, popular U.S. periodicals by author, subject, and title.

2. Prior to the inception of the *Readers' Guide* in 1901, *Poole's Index to Periodical Literature* was the principal index of this sort. It indexed both American and English periodicals from 1802 to 1908, by subject only.

3. For the student of sociology, another major periodical index is the *Social Sciences and Humanities Index* (from 1916 to 1965 called the *International Index*) which, in 1974, split into two indexes: the *Humanities Index* and the *Social Sciences Index*. In fact, this might be *the* most important index since its coverage is not limited to the popular, general interest magazines indexed by the *Readers' Guide* but includes scholarly journals as well. In addition to the overall indexing provided by the *Social Sciences Index*, most journals publish their own indexes annually or even semiannually.

4. The *Social Sciences Citation Index*, a comparatively new publication, is especially useful for researchers because it is indexed both by authors and by combinations of key words in titles of social science articles and books, and it also lists other articles which have cited a particular publication.

The importance of journals to the researcher cannot be overestimated, particularly because of the currency of the information contained in these periodical publications. In addition to the above four, there are many indexes of narrower scope, some of which, of course, index not only periodicals but books and documents of various sorts as well. Examples of these are the *Agriculture Index* (which became the *Biological and Agricultural Index* in 1964); the *Public Affairs Information Service*, which is a subject index to more than 1,000 periodicals published in English throughout the world; and the *Education Index*. Also, many of the country's major newspapers publish their own indexes which are available in many libraries. Perhaps the most important of these, because of the scope of the newspaper itself, is the *New York Times Index*.

Of major importance to researchers in the social sciences are government documents. Published by all levels of government from the federal to the municipal, these may or may not be indexed in the card catalog. Government documents can be fiendishly difficult to work with. Happily, they are often housed in a separate department where librarians who specialize in this type of material will help with their use. Failing this, a wide variety of indexes are available. Perhaps the most important is the *Monthly Catalog of U.S. Government Publications* issued by the U.S. Government Printing Office.

Using these indexes in tandem with the card catalog will give one a fairly comprehensive guide to what is available in the local library.

Not uncommonly, however, the researcher may require the resources of more than one library or may need to survey the entire literature available in a subject area. The use of indexes as described above will give a start in this direction. Also helpful will be the use of various bibliographies.

Simply stated, a bibliography is a list of books. Just as there are many different kinds of books, so there are many different kinds of bibliographies. Winchell's authoritative *Guide to Reference Books*[1] lists five basic kinds: (1) bibliographies of bibliographies, such as the *Bibliographic Index;* (2) library catalogs, particularly those of national libraries such as the Library of Congress; (3) specialized bibliographies in the manuscript and rare book field; (4) selective bibliographies used by librarians and others as tools for selection of materials; and (5)

[1] Winchell, 1967.

national bibliographies such as *Books in Print* and the *Cumulative Book Index.*

The two most useful of these are probably the catalogs of the national libraries and the national bibliographies. The former are valuable because copyright laws require that such libraries as the Library of Congress, the British Museum, and the Bibliothèque Nationale receive copies of all books copyrighted in their respective countries. Thus the catalogs of such libraries' holdings become the single most comprehensive record of publications in their respective countries. Even more useful for the average student are the national bibliographies because they offer not only author and title but usually subject listings as well of all books currently available in the country of publication.

A sixth type of bibliography is the subject bibliography. An important example of this would be the *London Bibliography of the Social Sciences,* the most extensive subject bibliography in its field. International in scope, it lists books, pamphlets, and documents in many languages. Another example, narrower in scope, would be *Current Sociological Research,* a listing of research in progress as reported by members of the American Sociological Association. And, of course, many of the books found through use of the bibliographies will themselves contain bibliographies, leading one to still other sources of information.

In fact, all three of the library tools we have discussed—the card catalog, indexes, and bibliographies—are directional in nature; that is, they direct the researcher to material and information. The card catalog directs him to materials located in a specific library. Indexes and bibliographies direct him to materials which may or may not be available in a particular library. For those materials which are not, a fourth directional tool is important—the union list, which is a "complete record of the holdings for a given group of libraries of material of a given type, in a certain field, or on a particular subject."[2] In other words, this research tool not only lists books or magazines or documents, but gives the names of libraries which have these materials in their collections. An example is the *Union List of Serials,* which lists thousands of periodicals and, for each, the names of libraries throughout the United States having back files of each periodical. It is national in scope. Other union lists may be regional or statewide, or may represent holdings of libraries in even smaller geographic areas.

[2] American Library Association, 1943.

When, through union lists or other sources, one is able to locate a specific library holding materials one requires which are not available locally, the librarian can try to borrow them from other libraries. This is called an interlibrary loan. Regulations governing interlibrary loans and the scope and efficiency of the service vary, but nearly every library offers some form of this important service. And while some libraries will not loan all materials, most will, at least, make photocopies at nominal charges. Incidentally, the researcher may find available a surprisingly large number of libraries in a community besides the familiar school, university, and public libraries. A little exploration may reveal small and/or specialized libraries maintained by businesses, governmental agencies, clubs, professional associations, museums, private individuals, and many others.

One sort of material often unavailable for interlibrary loan constitutes a major type or class of research material and includes abstracts, encyclopedias, dictionaries, biographical dictionaries, and directories. Together, these are called reference books. These are defined as books "designed by (their) arrangement and treatment to be consulted for definite items of information rather than to be read consecutively."[3]

Because of their value as sources of ready information, these books are usually housed in a separate department within the library and, as stated above, ordinarily do not circulate outside of the library.

Among the major types of reference books with which the library user should be familiar are the following:

Abstracts: This type of reference work is extremely important for researches since the abstract summarizes books, periodical articles, pamphlets, dissertations, and other works. For the researcher, works such as *Sociological Abstracts* and the now-defunct *Social Science Abstracts* might be termed scholarly *Readers' Digests* of current work in the social sciences. Using an abstract will not only give a quick overview of a subject but will enable the researcher to determine whether reference to the lengthier original is necessary.

Encyclopedias: Usually arranged in alphabetical order, these are collections of informational articles either on subjects in every field of knowledge—like the *Encyclopaedia Britannica*

---

[3]Ibid.

and the *Encyclopedia Americana*—or limited to special fields like the *Encyclopedia of the Social Sciences*, the *International Encyclopedia of the Social Sciences*, and the *Encyclopedia of Social Work*.

Dictionaries: These, also, may be general in nature like language dictionaries or topical like the *Dictionary of Social Science* and the *Dictionary of Modern Sociology*.

Biographical dictionaries: These bring together, usually in alphabetical order by surname, sketches of individuals' lives. Examples would be the various *Who's Who* volumes, the *Dictionary of American Biography*, *Webster's Biographical Dictionary*, and *American Men of Science*.

Annuals/yearbooks/almanacs: While having different names, these offer essentially the same type of information: brief reviews of the year's events or developments, statistics, summaries of information often in tabular form, and the like. These again can be general as with the *World Almanac* and the *Information Please Almanac*, or specialized like *The Statesman's Yearbook*, the United Nations *Demographic Yearbook*, the United Nations *Statistical Yearbook*, and the *Statistical Abstract of the United States*.

Directories: These are lists of persons or organizations usually arranged alphabetically or geographically. Examples would include the *Foundation Directory* and the *Public Welfare Directory*. And don't forget telephone and city directories as important sources of demographic information.

Atlases: These are collections of maps, plates, engravings, and/or charts with or without accompanying text. And gazeteers provide geographic data and information, usually arranged in dictionary form.

Of course, there are many other kinds of reference books. For an idea of the scope of the reference book field and the resources available there, the student should examine a copy of Winchell's *Guide to Reference Books*, mentioned above.

Even more important, the student should take the time to familiarize himself with the library in which he will be doing his research. Each library has its idiosyncracies, its unique collections, and its own organization. Most large libraries, for example, are departmentalized either by the type of service offered—reference, circulation, interlibrary loan, et al.—or by the type of material housed—art, architecture, law, social sciences, etc. Some of these departments are, in fact, so large as to be libraries in themselves.

With the proliferation of knowledge, the wealth of material available to the researcher may sometimes seem overwhelming. For the libraries, too, this has proved a problem. As the growth of their collections has threatened to exceed the capacity of structures to house them, many libraries have begun acquiring materials, particularly back files of newspapers and magazines, on either microfilm or microfiche. Both of these microforms greatly reduce original materials photographically. For example, it is possible to reproduce a week's run of the *New York Times* on a single roll of microfilm. Microfiche, which reproduces printed matter on sheets instead of rolls of film, permits even greater savings of storage space. While microforms are not as convenient to use as the original, hard copies (machines are needed to read them), the spectacular savings they offer in terms of space more than make up for this disadvantage.

With microforms as with all of the resources of a library, the library staff remains the single most valuable guide to their location and use. These knowledgeable professionals are not magicians, but they are dedicated to guiding library users to the information and materials needed. The more clearly the researcher has defined his needs, the more quickly the librarian can help him.

For both the novice library user and the experienced researcher, the library will continue to offer stimulating challenges. To be prepared to meet them requires a thorough familiarity with libraries in general and one's own library in particular, familiarity which must be bought with an expenditure of time and effort.

It must be remembered that the material and information one finds in the library should not be accepted as totally unbiased and reliable. Libraries cannot pretend to offer perfection in the materials they house. Also, with the current proliferation of publications, much material becomes dated very rapidly. The validity of the material is for the researcher to determine. The library can only provide the raw data.

Furthermore, it is up to the library user to have a clearcut and concise idea of what information is being sought. How this is presented to the librarian can be the key to one's success or failure in finding the material housed in that library. And from a realistic point of view, a librarian who recognizes a user's familiarity with libraries is more apt to be cooperative and generous in dealing with that person. This does not mean one should flaunt one's knowledge, but the way a question is addressed to librarians can impress them with the researcher's seriousness and motivation.

Don't ever underestimate what can be found in the library. Over the years, any library will reflect the interest and needs of its patrons as well as those of the library administration. No matter how small the library, diligent searching may well yield a storehouse of valuable and appropriate material for a research project.

This can be true of the largest university library as well as the smallest public library, but as staffs change, materials in certain areas become neglected and forgotten, and it is up to the individual to use the best investigative efforts to ferret out what is wanted, with the assistance of the librarian whenever necessary. One should be prepared to dig, search, and research for oneself. The time and effort are well worth it, for finding that hidden source of material may well provide the major impetus to the successful completion of a research project.

Successful research in any given library depends greatly upon attitude and motivation. It is unwise to feel that one can simply walk into a library and be rewarded by having the material laid in one's hands. Research requires motivation and perseverance, and a reluctance to accept "no" for an answer.

EXERCISES

1. In using the library to find published information on a research topic, the search frequently proceeds first to locating the title and author of the research and second to locating more complete information such as a summary of findings and perhaps more detailed information. Using the following topics as examples, list the reference works one would use to select about 10 to 20 sources by title and author. Next, list the references one would use to find out more specific information on the sources selected.
   a. The discussion of issues by presidential hopefuls during a given presidential campaign.
   b. The study of the relationship between social class and membership in voluntary organizations.

c. The study of campaign law violations since the law's passage.

d. The study of community expenditures for police protection for all communities in a particular state.

e. The study of alienation in modern life.

f. The study of marriage rate trends for 20-year-olds since 1950.

g. The study of educational attainment of religious leaders during the 20th century.

h. The study of growth of ethnic population in communities as that growth relates to the location of developing ethnic business enterprise.

2. In what library indexes or abstracts would one have the best chance of locating the most complete list of sources on the following topics?

    a. Opinions of college students on world affairs.

    b. The effects of mothering behavior on manifest anxiety.

    c. Electrical union strikes during the last decade.

    d. Social class and the incidence of mental illness.

    e. Teaching technique and achievement in elementary school children.

3. In what local organization specialized libraries might information be found on the following topics?

    a. Alcoholism

    b. Suicide.

    c. Drug abuse.

    d. Government expenditure on the arts.

    e. Traffic injuries and fatalities.

    f. The number of people voting for the incumbent during the last city election.

4. Below is a list of some commonly used, but important, U.S. government documents published by the Department of Commerce. What kinds of data are found in each which students might use for a research project?

    a. *Census of Population, General Social and Economic Characteristics.*

    b. *Census of Housing, General Characteristics.*

    c. *Census of Housing, Detailed Characteristics.*

    d. *Metropolitan Area Block Statistics.*

    e. *1972 City and County Databook.*

    f. *Statistical Abstract of the United States.*

Chapter 8

Design of research: Part I

INTRODUCTION

Now, if all has gone well, the researcher has a clear, specific statement which covers: the topic to be studied, the goals, the specific objectives (hypotheses, questions or problems), the definitions and indicators of the key terms, and a summary of existing knowledge related to the study. (He also has identified some personal characteristics and values which may affect his research.) In other words, he has a research problem and now faces the question of how to solve it. The answer to this question, i.e., the detailed plan of how the research will be conducted, is known as the *research design.* A good research design not only will anticipate—and specify—the seemingly countless decisions connected with planning and carrying out data collection, processing, and analysis, but also will present a logical basis for these decisions. These decisions must be made within the framework of sometimes conflicting demands of scientific objectivity and integrity, efficiency and effectiveness of the research, administrative restrictions, and ethical considerations.

It is important to try to plan every step of the project in advance—before any step is actually carried out. Doing so will help to avoid such disheartening experiences as finding that there are no simple or appropriate analytic tools available for the data which have been collected, or, even worse, that the correct data have not been collected. Thus the more familiar the researcher is with all the alternatives available to him in data collection, processing, and analysis, the better his research design is likely to be.

Some goals of research design

In designing the research some general goals should be kept in mind. First, it will be remembered from the earlier discussions of induction and of reality-testing that hypotheses can never be proved to be true. Instead, all that can be done is to amass more and more evidence in support of a given hypothesis, much of which evidence consists of eliminating alternative credible hypotheses. Planning the research so as to yield results which will eliminate these alternative hypotheses is thus a most important consideration in research design. Another consideration is that, insofar as possible, the study should be replicable. While this can never be achieved absolutely in social science research, if only because of the effects of the passage of time, the researcher should strive for this goal, and avoid situations and procedures which are clearly unique. A third consideration to be kept in mind during the design process is the nature of the desired results. That is, if the researcher continually asks himself "What kinds of statements will shed light upon the research problem?" this will aid in designing the research. For example, it might be desired to make statements such as "Surgeons' financial success is related (unrelated, related in a certain way) to the number of successful operations they perform," or, "There is a high correlation between the number of articles a professor has published and the number of his former students who have won PhD's," or, "Surgeons who perform experimental procedures are more highly regarded by their colleagues than those performing traditional procedures, regardless of the rate of cures." These or any other kinds of desired results will, obviously, be important guides in designing the whole project. Fourth, the nature of the problem may dictate that a pilot study be undertaken. A pilot study is a "small-scale study designed to provide information intended to improve a planned large-scale study, particularly in cases where the existing literature is inadequate.[1] A pilot study may be indicated not only by the nature of the problem, but also by limitations in the time or money available, as well as by the future plans of the researcher. Finally, any method of data collection will yield some useless and irrelevant data. In selecting a method, this *dross rate* should be kept to a minimum, in the interests of economy of time and money.[2]

---

[1] Hoult, 1969, p. 238.

[2] Webb et al., 1966, pp. 32–33.

Multiple methods and variables

While the traditional approach to sociological research has consisted of a single method of data collection, there are persuasive arguments in favor of the use of multiple methods. One of the most cogent views deplores social scientists' frequent dependence upon just the interview or questionnaire, and states:

> Once a proposition has been confirmed by two or more independent measurement processes, the uncertainty of its interpretation is greatly reduced. The most persuasive evidence comes through a triangulation of measurement processes. If a proposition can survive the onslaught of a series of imperfect measures, with all their irrelevant error, confidence should be placed in it.[3]

Use is made of the analogy of geologic outcroppings, that is, the familiar fact that a large underground—and thus unobservable—deposit may appear at the surface in a number of different, small, scattered forms. Similarly,

> a theory predicting a change in civic opinion . . . might be such that this opinion shift could be predicted for many partially overlapping populations. One might predict changes on public opinion polls within that universe, changes in sampled conversation on commuter trains for a much smaller segment, changes in letters mailed to editors and the still more limited letters published by editors, changes in purchase rates of books on relevant subjects by that minute universe, and so on. . . . Any given theory has innumerable implications and makes innumerable predictions which are unaccessible to available measures at any given time. The testing of the theory can only be done at the available outcroppings, those points where theoretical predictions and available instrumentation meet. Any one such outcropping is equivocal, and all types available should be checked. The more remote or independent such checks, the more confirmatory their agreement.[4]

The specifics of data collection will be discussed in later chapters. However, while designing research the advantages of using more than one method should always be kept in mind. Of course, this may well increase the costs, time, and complexity of

---

[3] Ibid., p. 3. For a beautiful example of this "triangulation" strategy, see Sales, 1973.

[4] Ibid., pp. 27–28.

the research. But these costs must be balanced against the added confidence one can have in the results. There is no one perfect method of data collection—each has its weaknesses and sources of error, as well as its advantages. When the errors inherent in a given method are compensated for by the use of other methods, the additional costs and time may be a small price, indeed, to pay.

Another characteristic of conventional sociological research is its practice of dealing with only two variables in a given research. This is largely because of the fact that, until recently, mathematics and statistics could only cope with two variables, and also the fact that it is more costly and complicated to try to deal with more than two.[5] Usually we distinguish between independent and dependent variables. Generally speaking, in explanatory research the independent variable is the antecedent, while the dependent variable is the consequent. Or, in the terminology of Chapter 1, the independent variables are the explicans and the dependent variable is the explicandum. The independent variables *explain* the dependent variables; the dependent variables comprise the *description.* That is, if we are trying to measure the *effect* of surgical success rate *on* surgeons' income, the former is the independent variable and the latter is the dependent. In other words, we hypothesize that surgical success rate (partially) *explains* surgeons' income. On the other hand, we might have a research interest in just the reverse of the above: the effect of income on surgical success rate (higher income resulting in greater psychological security which results in increased skill, for example) and here income would be the independent variable and success rate the dependent. While many times the researcher has this option of deciding which will be his independent and his dependent variables according to the research objectives, it is also just as common for there to be no reasonable choice. For example, if we are studying the relationship between age and surgeons' income, it would be unreasonable to hypothesize that income has an effect on age; clearly, in this case, age must be the independent variable. In the case of descriptive research, on the other hand, sometimes there will be only one variable, or a series of single, unrelated variables, and so none would be referred to as dependent or

---

[5] Kaplan, 1964, pp. 159, 162.

independent. Even when descriptive research deals with the *relationship* between two variables, these usually would not be identified as dependent and independent as long as the research is not attempting to study the *effect* of one variable on the other.

Increasingly, however, the importance of dealing simultaneously with multiple variables, in explanatory research, has been recognized. When studying virtually any sociological phenomenon other than the simplest, we know that it cannot be explained by examination of a single variable. Surgeons' income might be explained by surgical success rate, age, characteristics of training, personality variables, ethnic category, geographical location, parents' income, type of hospital affiliation, and patients' characteristics, to name a few. Studying the effect of any one independent variable upon a dependent variable may, of course, lead to useful and valuable information, but it may also lead to inaccurate, or even incorrect, conclusions. This is because in actual practice the independent variables may interact with one another in such a way as to produce quite different results from the "pure" situation in which only one independent variable is operating.

Let us suppose that we are concerned with the dependent variable, surgeons' success rate, and the independent variables, surgeons' personal characteristics, age of patients (let us say old or young), and type of surgical equipment (e.g., Types A, B, or C). If we conduct three separate studies linking each independent variable with the dependent variable, the resulting data may show various kinds of close relationships. However, such data would not show the effects of any interaction which might exist among the three independent variables, as in the following examples. Some surgeons might work better with old patients, regardless of the type of equipment. Or some surgeons might work better with certain equipment, regardless of patients' age. Or certain equipment might be so unsuitable for elderly patients that success rate would be small regardless of the surgeon's characteristics. And so on. In order to obtain more illuminating data, the research could be so planned as to deal with all the independent variables simultaneously. Assuming that the practical problems could be dealt with, we might want each surgeon to work under each of the possible combinations of patient's age and type of equipment, as shown below.

Surgeon	*Equipment type*		
	A	*B*	*C*
1	young old	young old	young old
2	young old	young old	young old
3	young old	young old	young old
4	young old	young old	young old
5	young old	young old	young old

Appropriate statistical analysis of the results will show how the various combinations of independent variables are related to the dependent variable.

If all of the independent variables are subdivided into an equal number of categories, another plan called a Latin Square may be used. Using the above example, with three types of equipment there would also have to be three categories of patients' age and three surgeons (or three different sets of personal characteristics). The research plan would ensure that each type of equipment was used with each different age category and with each different surgeon, as follows:

Surgeon	*Equipment type*		
	A	*B*	*C*
1	young	middle-aged	old
2	middle-aged	old	young
3	old	young	middle-aged

Here again, appropriate analysis identifies the relationships among various combinations of these three variables and the dependent variable. Latin Squares may be of any size.[6]

"Multivariate analysis" is the general term referring to the various techniques and approaches of analyzing the effects of multiple variables which have been developed in recent years. Prominent among these are multiple regression analysis, analysis of variance and covariance, multiple factor analysis, and path analysis.[7] While more will be said about the use of these in Chapter 16, the possibility of their use should be kept in mind at this stage of research design. Not only must the subsequent use of these analytic approaches be taken into account while designing the research, but of course the data collection procedures must be so planned as to yield the necessary multivariate data.[8]

A note on replication studies

In replication studies, as we have seen, the goal is to repeat the original research with as few variations as possible, in order to decrease the likelihood that the original results are due to some error or unknown confounding factor. Complete replication is not possible, of course, since even if the same individuals are studied and under the same circumstances, the passage of time itself will have introduced some change. Furthermore, the mere use of a new researcher will introduce variation to the design. Nevertheless, when a replication does duplicate the original results, we have increased confidence in the accuracy of the original. A failure to replicate the results, however, is not so easily interpreted.[9] It may mean that the findings in the original research were spurious, or it may be that the replication was not, in fact, accurate, and some other variable such as change in researcher affected the results, or it may be that the replication simply was not done competently. Some years ago Rose studied all the replicated studies he could find in the published sociological and social psychological literature, and found very

---

[6] For a full discussion of Latin Squares, see Edwards, 1968, chap. 10. See also Ross and Smith, 1968, pp. 382–85.

[7] Recent discussions of causal inference and causal analysis are frequently couched in terms of these, especially path analysis.

[8] See, for example, Dodd and Christopher, 1965.

[9] Aronson and Carlsmith, 1968, pp. 20–22.

little consistency between the replications and the original studies. In order to achieve more consistency he suggests four things should be taken into account in designing replication studies: (1) the proposition for which verification is sought should be part of a larger general theory; (2) propositions should be stated in terms which can be generalized; (3) the need for sampling should be eliminated if possible, since samples representative of whole societies are so hard to obtain; and (4) a framework of standardized definitions and assumptions should be developed.[10]

Dimensions of research

One useful means of coming to grips with the problem of how to design a study, is to consider some of the main questions or decisions the researcher faces. Ultimately, what would be most useful is to be able to specify what might be called the *dimensions of research,* that is, a minimum number of questions which must be answered in order adequately and completely to design a research project. Just as it is not only possible, but is perhaps essential for meaningful discourse, to be able to identify the complete set of variables for describing a chemical compound or for constructing a boat or for playing a clarinet, so it is reasonable to think that a complete set of dimensions for design of research would be immensely beneficial. Although the following pages do not present such a set, they do consider the most important research design decisions, and so may constitute a step in that direction.

SOME SOURCES OF ERROR

While it is not possible to anticipate and identify all the possible sources of error in doing research, the researcher should certainly ask himself what are the most likely sources. What kinds of mistakes or errors are likely to occur? What confounding factors can be identified which seem likely to affect the results? What can be done to avoid them or counteract their effect?

---

[10] Rose, 1954, pp. 262–66.

Assumptions

One potential source of error which has already been mentioned is the various assumptions which the researcher has made. Many times these are fundamental viewpoints or values of the researcher. However, assumptions are by no means always of such a deep and all-pervading nature; they are just as likely to be more limited and specific and less abstract, yet just as much a potential source of error in research. For example we might make assumptions about the importance of financial gain as a motivating factor, or about the significance of certain behavior. (Does church attendance really indicate a commitment to religion?) Or about the veracity of interviewees, or about the accuracy of crime statistics, or about the cooperation we will receive from informants, administrators, and those who control needed sources of data, and so on. If any of our assumptions prove to be false, the consequence may be additional costs (time and energy, as well as money) and confusion at best, and at worst errors in data and conclusions. The important thing at the design stage is not so much the accuracy of these assumptions but rather that the researcher *recognize* the assumptions he is making. If he does this then he can at least be prepared for possible error which may be introduced at various stages of the project. If he does not, errors may creep in in the most subtle and surprising fashion.

Reliability

It is obvious that any tool, instrument, or procedure which is used for making measurements or observations must yield the same results consistently, if it is to have any value. This capacity for consistency of results is called *reliability*. There are two different aspects to reliability: consistency of observations for a single observer, and consistency of observations among several observers using the same instrument. If a laboratory balance gave the results 15 kilograms, 20 kilograms, and 25 kilograms on three successive weighings of the same object, we would have little faith in the value of the balance. It would be said to be unreliable. On the other hand, if the successive weights were 15.9, 16.0, and 16.1, we might be quite satisfied with the reliability. It depends on the precision of results needed for the measurement at hand, and also on the degree of technological achievement in constructing instruments. Similarly, if three different observers, using the same procedures and equipment, obtained three different results, we would be dissatisfied with the reliability of the instrument. An unreliable instrument is of no value in conducting research, since one can never be certain whether the results obtained represent variations in the thing being measured, or spurious variations caused by the unreliability of the instrument.

There are three methods which can be used to measure the reliability of many sociological instruments, especially verbal and written scales. The *multiple form* method consists of using more than one form of the same instrument in succession to measure the same group, and comparing the results. If a satisfactory level of agreement is obtained, the scale will be considered reliable. The *split-half* method consists of dividing the scale items into two halves by some random procedure, and comparing the results obtained from these two halves after having administered it to a group. This is essentially a modification of the multiple form method. In the *test-retest* method, the same instrument is used to measure a group at two successive times, close enough together so that it may be presumed that the group has not changed in the interim. Here again, if sufficient agreement is obtained between the two measures the scale will be regarded as reliable.[11] If none of these three methods is appropriate, it may be that a logical analysis of the situation will shed some light as to the extent of reliability of the instrument being used. But in some way the researcher must satisfy himself as to the reliability of the instruments he is using. Adequate reliability is an essential prerequisite for validity, which we will now discuss.

Validity

In any set of measurements or observations, the question always arises as to how accurate or correct the measurements or observations are. (If they are not reliable, then of course, considerations of accuracy are meaningless.) We know that error may

[11] See Selltiz et al., 1959, pp. 166–86, for a more extended discussion of reliability.

be introduced by changes in the thing being measured, by inadequacies or inaccuracies in the measurement device, by certain characteristics or behaviors of the researcher, or by various other factors. For example, the complexity of a seemingly simple measurement in the physical sciences is indicated in the following passage:

> A measurement is a number that arises from the interaction of an observer and his instruments with the object observed. The number so obtained will depend on (1) the brain structure of the observer, (2) the state of relative motion of the observer and the object observed, (3) the physical and physiological receptors of the observer, (4) the interaction between the observer and the object observed, (5) the properties of the object observed, (6) the effect of the remainder of the universe.[12]

With the exception of (2), these observations apply equally to measurements in the social sciences.

It has been the custom to regard validity as the degree to which a measuring device measures what it purports to measure. However, today a broader view is observed, and validity is taken to mean the degree to which the recorded description of a set of data conforms to its referent. The present emphasis is thus on the *results* of the measuring or observing, rather than the measuring or observational device itself. Clearly, if a voltmeter is inaccurate it will yield invalid measurements. In the same way, if an attitude-measurement scale is poorly constructed the resulting data will not give an accurate portrayal of the respondents' attitudes. And if an observer is inconsistent or careless in his observations, his results, too, will be invalid. The problem, of course, is how to assess the validity of a set of data. There are three approaches to this which are commonly used, plus a fourth which has much to recommend it. (Validity, as discussed here, should not be confused with validity of deductive arguments, as treated in Chapter 2.)

Perhaps the simplest method is that of *face* validity, more formally known as the method of *logical analysis*. This refers to the situation in which a "commonsense" approach to the validity of the data is used—the accuracy of the data are believed to be apparent "on the face of it." This approach is useful when the data are based on direct observation of the referent, and no in-

[12] Walker, 1963, p. 51.

ferences are required. For example, if we are attempting to measure the relative swimming abilities of a group of boys, we only need stage a series of appropriate races. The results would have face validity. Similarly, if we are interested in comparing the sex ratios of a group of public schools, a simple counting operation is all that is needed to yield a valid measure. However, even in these simple illustrations error may creep in. In timing a race, we must depend upon not only scorers' integrity, accurate eyesight, and watches, but also be alert to various other factors which may influence the outcome. Illness or indisposition may affect a boy's performance on a given day. Also, his nonswimming relationships with the other boys in the race may affect his will to win, as Whyte points out in discussing bowling and baseball performance.[13] Sometimes a jury, or panel of judges, is used to assess face validity, as when we use several judges to measure boys' diving abilities. This modification of the face validity method is known as the method of *jury opinion*. In situations when the data are either not based upon direct observation or measurement of the referent, or when inference is required, such as attitude measurement or public opinion surveys predicting voting behavior, obviously this method cannot be used.

We may also determine the validity of a set of data by comparing them to some *independent criterion*. This method is also referred to as the *pragmatic*, and as the *known groups* method. The criterion may take various forms. We may compare our data with data obtained by another measure which is known to be valid. For example, we may validate interview responses to the question "Did you vote in the last election?" by comparison to known voting records of the community. With this method of independent criterion the question arises as to why we don't use the other measure, and, indeed, unless the newer measure is less costly or time-consuming or complicated, or has other advantages, the older one may be preferable. Alternatively, the criterion may consist of groups which are known to occupy opposite positions on the variable being measured. For instance, let us say we are attempting to validate a scale for measuring attitudes toward legalized abortion. If the scale adequately discriminates between a group of conservative Catholics and a group of militant advocates of women's liberation we can have

[13] Whyte, 1955, pp. 17 ff.

confidence that the scale has validity. However, this confidence is based on the assumption that the groups are similar except for their attitudes toward abortion, and that there are not other differences which would result in the disparity between the scores. If there are other significant differences between the groups, such as age or social class or marital and parenthood status, the scale may actually be measuring these things instead of (or in addition to) the attitude toward abortion. Thus this form of validation must be used with extreme caution. Finally, the criterion could be the accuracy of some prediction based upon the data being validated. For example, a medical test might be validated by its accuracy in predicting the onset of a certain disease, or a measure for predicting success in an academic program could be validated by the subsequent actual success rate in the program. This pragmatic approach to validity may be very useful.

The third means of assessing the validity of a set of data is the *construct* validation method.[14] This is particularly appropriate when the data purport to measure some personality characteristic or hypothetical trait, such as intelligence or honesty, which is not directly related to any specific behavior. "Construct validity involves relating one's measuring instrument to the overall theoretical structure in order to determine whether the instrument is logically tied to the concepts and theoretical assumptions that are employed."[15] With honesty, for example, the whole theoretical structure which defines and describes it, and which presumably the research is examining, would lead to a set of logically derived propositions. That is, one would predict that individuals who are high on the honesty scale would exhibit certain characteristics A, B, and C, and that individuals who were low on the scale would not exhibit these characteristics, or would exhibit them in a significantly lesser degree. Thus to validate the honesty scale the researcher would predict that the individuals ranked high and low by the honesty scale would exhibit these other characteristics in varying degrees. These predictions are of a different sort than those used in validation by an independent criterion, since with an independent criterion it is the accuracy of the specific prediction which is of concern.[16] Construct validity is at best a somewhat hazy concept,

[14] The term "construct" is used here as essentially synonymous with the term "concept" as defined previously.

[15] Sjoberg and Nett, 1968, p. 303.

[16] See Selltiz et al., 1959, pp. 158–63.

and is the subject of a fair amount of disagreement among sociologists.[17]

Close examination of the above three approaches to assessing validity reveals that none of them is really completely satisfactory, and this is undoubtedly the reason why considerable attention is now being given to a different approach. Essentially this consists of designing the research in such a way as to *maximize* the validity, rather than being concerned with *assessing* the validity. In this connection it is useful to distinguish between internal and external validity. In analyzing almost any set of data, comparisons are made. They may be simply a matter of distinguishing between, say, males, and females, or making statements that certain groups have more or less of a given attribute; or they may be more complex comparisons. If these comparisons are accurate—that is, if the differences among the categories of *data* being compared are accurate reflections of differences among the *referent groups* themselves—then the data are said to have *internal* validity. (This is really a restatement of our definition of validity.) Beyond this, however, the researcher is concerned with the extent to which he can generalize from his results to other populations, situations, or variables. If he can make such generalizations with confidence, the data are said to have *external* validity. The difference between internal and external validity is illustrated by the following two uses of randomization (which we will discuss in more detail later):

> When the experimentalist in psychology randomly assigns a sample of persons into two or more experimental groups, he is concerned entirely with internal validity—with making it implausible that the luck of the draw produced the resulting differences. When a sociologist carefully randomizes the selection of respondents so that his sample represents a larger population, representativeness or external validity is involved.[18]

It is clear that internal validity is the more important of the two, since without it even the highest level of confidence in generalizations would be worthless. Yet without generalization the significance of the research is sharply limited. Thus the researcher strives for a design which maximizes both types of

---

[17] Sjoberg and Nett, p. 303.

[18] Webb et al., 1966, p. 11.

validity. Since factors contributing to these two kinds of validity frequently work at cross-purposes, this is not always an easy task.

In order to maximize the validity of a research design, it is important to know the various sources of invalidity. Again we turn to Webb et al., who describe 12 such sources of error.[19]

Errors from those being studied

1. The guinea pig effect—awareness of being tested: A person's very knowledge that he is the object of scientific research may, consciously or subconsciously, affect his behavior. He may deliberately cooperate with or contravene the researcher's objectives, he may feel threatened, etc.
2. Role selection: The person's awareness of the research process may lead him to select a certain role (e.g., "student participant in an experiment") which he considers appropriate to the situation, and which may not coincide with the role the researcher expects him to select.
3. Measurement as change agent: When the person is to be measured or observed at more than one point in time, the very process of the initial measurement or observation may affect his subsequent behavior.
4. Response sets: Especially in questionnaires—but in other forms of data collection as well—certain response sets may influence the results. For example, respondents will more frequently endorse a statement than disagree with its opposite, strong statements are endorsed more than moderate or indecisive ones, the format of the questionnaire may lead to stereotyped responses, such as alternating between lefthand and righthand responses, etc.

Errors from the investigator

5. Interviewer effects: The characteristics and behavior of the interviewer may substantially affect the findings.
6. Change in the research instrument: If the research instrument changes during the course of data collection, the various data may not be strictly comparable. For example, the

---

[19] Webb, et al. UNOBTRUSIVE MEASURES: NONREACTIVE RESEARCH IN THE SOCIAL SCIENCES, © 1966 by Rand McNally College Publishing Company, Chicago. Paraphrased from pages 12–32 by special permission from the author and publisher. See also Campbell and Stanley, 1963, for an extended discussion of this.

questionnaire may be revised, the interviewer may become more skilled—or bored, methods of record keeping may change, etc.

Sampling errors

7. Population restrictions: Any given method of data collection has associated with it only certain populations to which generalizations can be made. These populations may not, in fact, be the ones the researcher desires to generalize to.
8. Population stability over time: If the characteristics of the population change over time, then data collected at more than one time will not be comparable.
9. Population stability over areas: Interregional differences of populations may result in a given method being of more use, or more effective, in one location than another.
10. Restrictions on content: As with population restrictions, any method of measurement, or data collection, has limitations as to the content areas for which it is appropriate.
11. Stability of content over time: If the characteristics of the content area under investigation change over time, data collected at more than one time will not be comparable.
12. Stability of content over area: Interregional differences in the content area being studied may result in a given method being more effective in one location than another.

An additional source of error arises from statistical regression, which may operate in the case where research is undertaken on individuals or groups which have been selected on the basis of having extreme scores on some measurement (e.g., studying school children with very low and very high IQs).

Of course, no list of sources of error can be complete. However, the items in this list are among the most common and widespread ones the researcher in sociology will encounter. In the next section, on basic designs, some specific procedures will be presented for minimizing these errors, and in the later chapters on data collection several of these sources of error will be discussed in greater detail. When planning research, one must bear in mind not only these sources of invalidity but also the errors which may result from unreliability and from unrecognized assumptions.

BASIC DESIGNS

Some fundamental questions on design

We continue our approach of considering the questions and decisions which the researcher must face. We can identify two fundamental questions, and then three other questions the answers to which will assist us in dealing with the first two. These questions are crucial to the task of designing a study that will permit sound logical analysis.

First we must know for how many different points in time data are to be collected. Will all data be collected at essentially the same time, or must some time elapse between various stages of data collection? And if some time must elapse, does it matter how much time? Furthermore, are the times of data collection related to the occurrence of any external events in which the researcher may be interested? As one obvious example, a poll predicting the outcome of an election must be conducted prior to the election itself. Perhaps the research questions will necessitate collecting data two months before the election, and again one week before.

Second, we must know how many different comparable research situations must be utilized. By research situations we refer to the individuals, groups, organizations, communities, ethnic or other categories, aggregates, societies or culture groups, institutions, etc., which are the focus of the researcher's interest. If the research calls for more than one such situation, how are these to be related to one another? Are they to be alike, similar, or different, and in what ways? For instance if the research involves a study of a whole community, will it be confined to one community or will there be two or more? Will the attempt be made to select two communities which are as nearly alike as possible, and if so what criteria will be considered most important for the likeness—size, ethnic composition, social class distribution, income, etc.? If the two (or more) communities are to differ, are there some particular criteria to be used in selecting them? Will a suburban community be compared with a rural community, or are we interested in communities from two different regions, etc.? Or perhaps the two communities may be selected by some kind of chance or random process.

The answers to these questions are dictated by the nature of the research problem, of course, as well as by certain logical considerations. One aspect of the research problem which will help to determine the number of different points in time at which data must be collected is the question of whether the study involves *change*. Change necessarily involves the passage of time, so if we are to study the change in some phenomenon, this logically implies a comparison of the phenomenon at a minimum of two different points in time. It may be possible to study change by actually collecting data at only one time, if some earlier body of data already is available. However, logically this is the same as collecting data at two times.

Another question we ask about the research problem is whether it will involve some kinds of comparisons. If so, then it is quite likely that data must be collected from more than one research situation. For instance, if the study is an evaluation of performance of surgeons and teachers, clearly a comparison is involved, and we know that data must be collected from (or about) these two occupational categories. As pointed out above, most studies involve comparisons of some kind. However, this will not inevitably require data collection in more than one situation. For example, if we are interested in comparing boys and girls in their rate of response to a new teaching technique, this could be done by collecting date in a single situation—a single coeducational classroom.

Probably the most important and useful question we can ask of the research problem is whether it is a descriptive or an explanatory study. We now turn to an examination of basic designs which are appropriate to these two different classes of studies. These designs vary chiefly in the number of times at which data are collected, and the number of situations utilized.

Designs for descriptive studies

The simplest design—and probably the most widely used in sociological research—is one in which data are collected in a single situation at a single time. This is sometimes called a *cross sectional* design, because its results may be likened to an instantaneous cross sectional view of an ongoing process. However, it is more commonly called a *one-cell* design, since it can conveniently be diagrammed as follows:

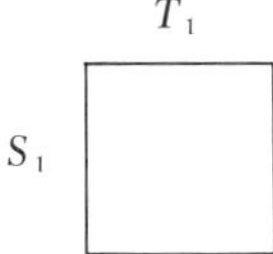

where T_1 represents a given time and S_1 represents a given research situation.[20]

The research literature abounds with examples of the one-cell design. An ordinary public opinion poll to measure the degree of approval of the government's economic policies is one example—or a study of the decision-making procedures of a small group. So is a study of students in an introductory sociology course in order to determine attitudes toward drugs, and so is a study of the distribution of new cars in a given neighborhood. The so-called "experience survey" also would typically be such a one-cell design. (An experience survey is one designed to collect and synthesize the unpublished experience of specialists such as group workers, social workers, and other practitioners, for the purpose of obtaining general background information and formulating new research activities.)[21]

All of these studies *describe* some aspect of society or nature A one-cell design may be likened to a photograph which provides a useful and accurate description of some subject at a particular time. However, the photograph portrays only a small portion of the total possible fund of information about the subject, and it is accurate at only the one single point in the total life history of the subject. The same holds for a one-cell study, and he who would generalize or draw logical implications from such a study does so with considerable risk.

There are several different two-cell designs, using either two situations or two different times or some combination of these. If we collect data from a given research situation at some particular time, and then return at a later time and again collect data from the same situation, we can diagram this design as follows:

	T_1	T_2
S_1		

[20] This form of describing these various designs originally appeared in Stouffer, 1950.

[21] Selltiz et al., 1959, pp. 55–59.

where T_2 represents a later time than T_1. This is commonly known as a *longitudinal* design. Any study of change occuring in a given situation would be of this type. For example, a study of the crime rate of a given city in two successive years; or a study of lower-class values as revealed through magazine short stories, comparing the 1930s with the present decade; or a study of the political opinions of a group of college students at the beginning of their freshman year and again at the beginning of their sophomore year. Sometimes the two data collection times are selected so as to occur before and after some particular event or occurrence. For instance, we might want to measure the crime rate of a city before the appointment of a new police chief, and then again after his first year or two in office. Or we might be interested in the rate of cigarette-smoking in a particular group, before and after exposure to an antismoking film. This particular kind of longitudinal study is known, for obvious reasons, as a *before-and-after* study.

It may be that the research interest is to make some comparisons between data collected in the present and data from some time in the past. If historical records or archives contain information which is comparable to that collected in the present, this is a feasible study design. It would be diagrammed as:

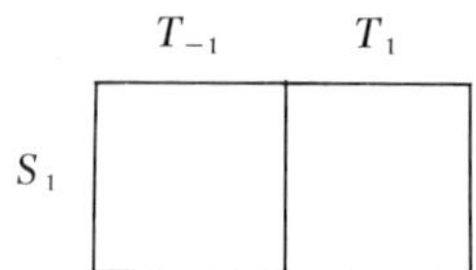

where the negative subscript is used to indicate the time in the past when the data were collected. This kind of design is known as the *ex post facto* design. Studies utilizing census data, comparing the current figures with those of a previous time, are obvious illustrations of this design. A study relating university students' current academic achievement to their earlier high-school or elementary-school grades, or other childhood experiences, would be another illustration. The ex post facto design carries an ever-present disadvantage in that the earlier data may not be readily available, or may not be complete, or may not be strictly comparable; and frequently so much time has elapsed that it becomes impossible to verify accuracy, data collection methods, and so on. However, under the proper circumstances this can be a very useful design.

Both the ex post facto and the longitudinal types can be extended, with data being collected at three or more times. These are known as three- or four- cell designs, etc., and would be diagrammed accordingly:

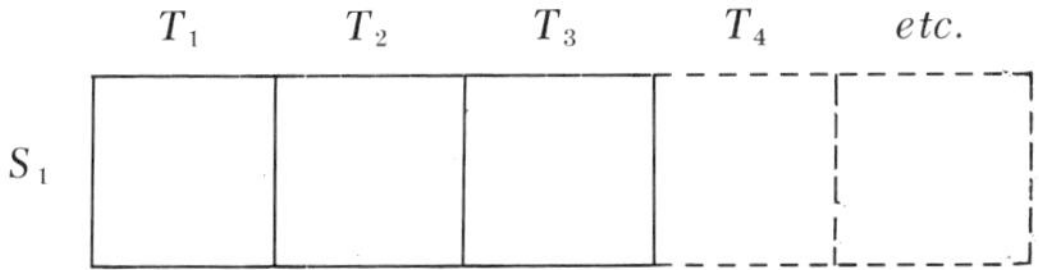

This design is known as a *panel* design, since it involves following a "panel" of individuals over a period of time. It has the advantage of facilitating relatively accurate studies of change over long periods of time, since the same individuals are being studied. However, the aforementioned class of errors originating from those being studied may be particularly troublesome here.[22] Panels have been widely used for consumer market research.

Rather than collecting data on a single situation at two times, it may be that data are collected at a single time from two situations. We diagram this design as follows:

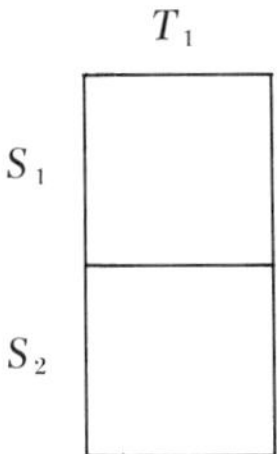

where S_1 and S_2 represent two different situations (groups, communities, etc.). The interest here is usually in comparing the data for the two situations, hence this is known as a *comparison* design. Illustrations of this design would be a comparison of the criteria for evaluating performance of surgeons and teachers, or of the relative rates of conformity of urban and rural people, or of the rates of cigarette smoking of a group of healthy people and a group of lung cancer victims, or of the personality charac-

[22] See: Lazarsfeld, Pasanella, and Rosenberg, 1972, section IV; Zeisel, 1970; Glock, 1955; and Crider, Willits, and Bealer, 1973, for discussions of the problems and techniques peculiar to this design.

teristics of Republicans and Democrats.[23] In the last-named, for example, an actual study attempted to answer the question: Are there any personality differences between typical active Republicans and typical active Democrats? Politically active people were selected on the basis of their participation in organized political activities for one party during an election campaign, combined with consistency of their prior voting records for the same party. The Guilford-Zimmerman Temperament Survey, (a widely used, standardized questionnaire which gives scores for ten personality and temperament factors) was administered to these active Republicans and Democrats at meetings of various political clubs. Thus it was possible to compare the scores for the Republicans and the Democrats. The comparison design can, of course, be expanded so as to compare three or more situations simultaneously. We will have more to say about this design later, when we discuss designs for explanatory studies.

Another two-cell design consists of collecting data from one situation at one time and from another situation at another time:

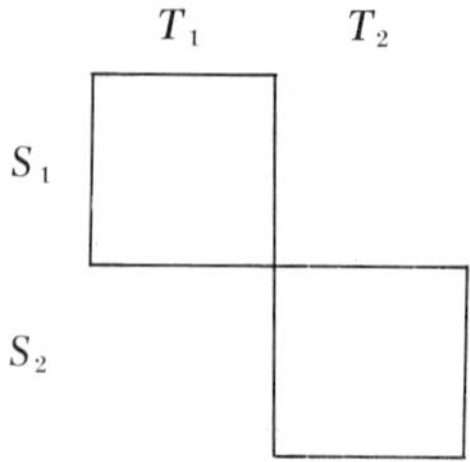

We call this a *matched-stage* study, referring to the fact that it is most appropriately used for studying two different situations that are in the same stage of their development or history. One of the most familiar examples of this is Bogardus's studies of social distance, in which he compared the level of prejudice (as measured by his Social Distance scale) of a group of college students in 1926 with a group of college students in 1946.[24] Each of these groups was at the same "stage" of its history (i.e., they were currently undergoing college training) when the data were collected. Thus it is possible to use these data as the basis for statements such as "College students in 1946 were more (or less) prejudiced than college students in 1926," and so on. Sometimes a modification of this design is used when it is de-

[23] Manheim, 1959.

[24] He also repeated the study in 1956 and 1966. Bogardus, 1967.

sired to study the more ordinary cases of change or comparison, and for some reason it is not possible to use one of the previously discussed designs so that this design becomes the best available. If we are interested in comparing two situations, for example, we see that our two sets of data are not strictly comparable since they are collected at different times, which may introduce all kinds of confounding factors. Similarly, assessment of change is not legitimate since the two situations are not the same. In order to deal with these difficulties, we modify the design as follows:

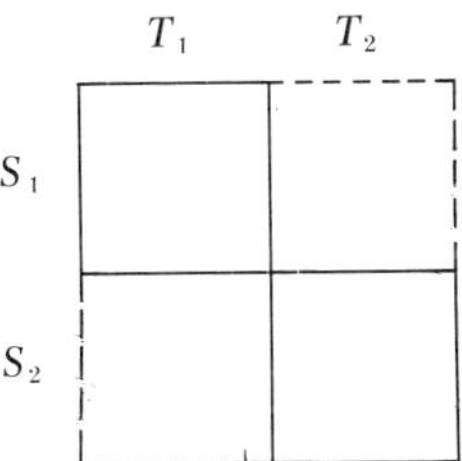

The dashed cells indicate that it is necessary to *assume* that the data from one of the dashed cells (which are not available) are equal to one of the sets of data which is available. For example, this was used, by Stouffer, in attempting to measure certain changes occurring in American soldiers as a result of being sent overseas in World War II.[25] Since he was unable to study the same soldiers at two times, he studied one group in the United States and a second group, similar to the first, at a later time overseas, *assuming* that the two groups were initially the same. As he points out, the accuracy of the results hinges upon the extent to which the two groups were in fact initially similar.

All these designs which have been discussed in this section are suitable for descriptive studies. To summarize, if the study involves both change and comparison, the most appropriate design is the matched-stage. If it involves change but not comparison, the longitudinal, ex post facto, panel, or perhaps the matched-stage design should be used. For a comparison study which does not involve change, the comparison or matched-stage design would be used. Finally, a simple descriptive study, involving neither change or comparison, uses the one-cell design. The explanatory designs to be discussed below may also be used for descriptive studies. As has been stated before, the

[25] Stouffer, 1950.

greatest proportion of existing sociological research is descriptive, and so utilizes one of these designs. This is as it should be, since it is necessary to answer the descriptive question, "What?" before we can go on to answering the explanatory "Why?"

Designs for explanatory studies

In designing explanatory research one is not so concerned with the factors of change and comparison. It will be recalled that the process of explanatory research consists of first asking the question "Why?" about some phenomenon, then retroducting a tentative answer or explanation, and then phrasing this as a hypothesis. The hypothesis, of course, expresses a relationship between two or more variables, but in the case of an explanatory research hypothesis it is an *assymmetrical* relationship. That is, we do not merely hypothesize that X is related to Y, but rather that X (and not some alternative) has some particular *effect* on Y. In other words, we specify that X is the antecedent and Y is the consequent, or that X precedes Y in time. Thus a research design suitable for an explanatory study must make it possible to collect data pertaining to these qualifications. These requirements impose some severe restrictions upon the research design, which will now be examined.

In the first place, none of the above descriptive designs is adequate for an explanatory study—with the single exception of the comparison design, and that only *under certain circumstances*. To explain why this is so we will examine each of the above designs, using the following example. Let us say that the Heart Association plans to establish a Heart Council (a group of volunteers whose purpose is to educate the public about heart disease) in a local community, and wishes to know what effect the activities of this Council (the independent variable) have upon the public's knowledge about, and attitudes toward, heart disease (the dependent variables).[26] This leads to a hypothesis such as, "The establishment of a local Heart Council will result in improved knowledge and attitudes toward heart disease on the part of the public." It has been decided that the data collection is to consist of a public opinion poll of the adults in the community.

---

[26] Manheim and Howlett, 1964. See Appendix B for a fuller description of this project.

Consider the one-cell design. We might conduct our poll at some time after the Council has been functioning, say, for a year. But what would the results tell us? Merely that the knowledge and attitudes of the public were of such-and-such a magnitude. We have no way of knowing what the magnitude was before the Council started functioning and therefore have absolutely no basis for reaching any conclusions as to what effect, if any, the Council had. Furthermore, without some other figures to compare the results to, there is no way of knowing whether the magnitude of the obtained results is "high" or "average" or "low."

If we elect to use the longitudinal design, we conduct a poll prior to the establishment of the Council and a second poll at a later time after the Council has had an opportunity to function. Or we may be able to use the ex post facto design, collecting data in the present after the Council has been functioning for some time and using some comparable data for a time before the Council was established. Both of these can be discussed together. It might seem that this design would give useful information, since it would be possible to observe the change in the dependent variable (public knowledge) over the period of time between the two data collections. However, this completely overlooks the important fact that any of the sources of invalidity which we have discussed earlier might lead to a change in the dependent variable, and there is no way of telling with this design. The cumulative effect of these might be far greater than the effect of the Council itself, and it is even logically possible that the effect of the Council operating alone might be a *decrease* in public knowledge.

The two-cell comparative design comes closer to our requirements. We might collect the data from the community under study after the Council has been functioning for an appropriate length of time, and also at the same time conduct a similar poll in another community like the first one but in which no Council is operating. We might expect that any difference in results for the two communities would be clearly due to the functioning of the Council. However, this reasoning is based upon one fundamental assumption, namely, that the magnitude of knowledge in the two communities was the same before the Council started functioning, and also that the changes in the two communities were the same subsequent to the time of the start of the Council's functioning. Again, there is no basis for making this assumption *unless* the two situations have been equated through a process of randomization (to be discussed below)—generally a completely impractical procedure when dealing with whole communities.

Finally we consider the matched stage design. We have already seen that this design cannot be used for making comparisons or studying change without making certain important assumptions, and so this design is undesirable for an explanatory study.

What kind of designs, then, *are* appropriate for explanatory studies?[27] A great many different designs exist, each having advantages and disadvantages depending upon the details of the particular research project. These designs are based on the fact that any of the sources of invalidity may be responsible for a change observed in the dependent variable. The problem is how to differentiate between a change caused by these extraneous factors and one caused by the independent variable, which is what we are trying to measure. This is complicated by the fact that sometimes it is desirable to be able to measure both the change in the dependent variable which is due to the independent variable, and also the change that is due to the action of the extraneous factors. Some designs make this more feasible than others. We will examine here only four of these many designs: two which are preferred when only the effect of the independent variable is to be determined, one which supplies additional information, and one which is very widely used when preferable ones are not feasible.

First we look at the so-called *classical four-cell design*, diagrammed as

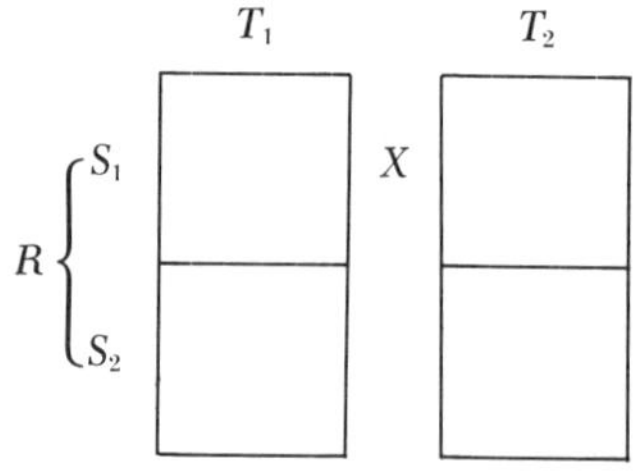

[27] There are at least two very comprehensive and excellent treatments of this subject, and the student should consult both of them for a more advanced discussion than is necessary or possible here: Ross and Smith, 1968, and Campbell and Stanley, 1963.

The X indicates that the independent variable operates on one of the two situations between T_1 and T_2. This is usually known as the *experimental group* while the other situation, on which X does not operate, is known as the *control group*. In the following discussions it is assumed for the sake of simplicity that the independent variable is either present or absent. It must be understood, however, that in actual practice the independent variable may be present in varying magnitudes. So the comparisons made may be, for example, among "much" of variable X, "a moderate amount" of variable X, "a little" of X, and no X. Furthermore, the R indicates that the members of S_1 and S_2 are assigned by *randomization*. Randomization means that the individuals are selected from a common pool and assigned in such a way that for each individual the probabilities of his being assigned to either group are equal. Flipping a coin serves admirably for this purpose. In order fully to understand the importance of randomization, we digress here to consider the subject of matching.

Matching. Any process whereby two or more research situations are made equal, in order that the effects of an independent variable can be accurately measured, is called *matching*. Usually the researcher is desirous of equating the situations only (or especially) on those certain variables which he considers to be most likely to have an effect upon the dependent variable. For instance, if we were comparing the effects of two different teaching methods upon children's learning, we would want the two groups to be matched on, let us say, age and IQ, among others, since our knowledge and experience tell us that these variables are likely to affect learning. If they were *not* matched on these, we could not be sure whether any differences in learning were due to the teaching method or to age or to IQ or to some combination of these.

We would be much less concerned to have the groups matched on religion or height or favorite sport since we do not ordinarily associate these variables with learning rate. Matching by a process of randomization, as described above, is by far the most preferable method of achieving equality. An interesting and important consideration is that randomization will result in matching not only on the desired variables (such as age and IQ) but on any variable whatsoever—religion or number of siblings or color of shirt worn, or whether or not the individual ate breakfast that day. The process of randomization does not guarantee that the two groups will be equal—there is always the possibility that inequalities will exist and will affect the research results. However, the probability of these inequalities being present can be determined by using appropriate statistical tests of significance, and thus the researcher can know how much confidence to place in his results. The larger the number of individuals in each group, the smaller will be the probability that the randomization has been unsuccessful in eliminating inequalities.

If for some reason randomization is not feasible, there are two other possible approaches to matching. *Precision matching* consists of dividing the pool of available individuals into pairs, with the two members of each pair having identical combinations of the relevant variables. Then one member of each pair is placed in each of the two groups by a random process. Thus if in the experimental group there was a highly prejudiced, middle-class, 24-year-old married male (assuming these to be the relevant variables), there would be a person in the control group with these same characteristics. And similarly, if one member of the experimental group was a nonprejudiced, upper-class, 37-year-old married female, there would again be a matching person in the control group. And so on, through all the individual members of the two groups. It should be apparent that precision matching is extremely difficult to achieve, since with more than a very few variables to match the rate of attrition is so high as to rapidly deplete the pool of available individuals. For example, if we use a two-category division of prejudiced and nonprejudiced, and a three-category division of social class (upper, middle, and lower,) a five-category division of age (20–29, 30–39, 40–49, 50–59, 60 and above) and the usual two-category divisions of marital status and sex, we see that there are 120 possible combinations ($2 \times 3 \times 5 \times 2 \times 2$) of just these five characteristics. Thus it would require an enormous pool of subjects in order to have reasonable expectations of finding a sufficient number of matched pairs.

In order to overcome this problem, *matching by frequency distribution* can be used. Here, instead of matching individual by individual, we merely ensure that the frequency distribution of the relevant variables is essentially the same for the two groups. Using the same illustrative variables as above, we would ensure that the proportions or percentages of prejudiced and nonprejudiced persons are the same for each group, and likewise the percentages of upper, middle, and lower class persons, the percentages in each of the five age categories, and the percentages of married and single, and of male and female. The matching in this method is not as close as with precision matching, because this ignores the effects of interaction among the relevant variables, but it is not nearly so costly since the attrition rate is much lower. The term "blocking" is frequently used to refer to this procedure of dividing the subjects into groups, or blocks, of homogeneous characteristics.

It is important to recognize that precision and frequency distribution matching are never to be thought of as substitutes for randomization. The reason for this is that no matter how carefully precision or frequency distribution matching is done, one can never be certain that *all* the relevant variables have been even identified, much less matched. And there is always the possibility that any differences which are found between the experimental and control groups are due to some unknown and unmatched variables. Randomization, as pointed about above, can ensure, within the statistical limits of the design, that *all* variables are matched, and therefore this randomization mainly contributes to the *internal* validity of the research.

We return now to our discussion of the classical four-cell design. The two groups, S_1 and S_2, are equated through randomization, and data are collected from each at T_1. One group is exposed to the independent variable X, whose effect is to be measured, and then at T_2 data are again collected from both groups. Thus by comparing the change from T_1 to T_2 for both groups, the effect of X can be ascertained. The understanding in this design is that all other variables, with the sole exception of X, operate equally on both groups, and the details of the design must be planned so as to make this possible. This design has long been considered the optimum for measuring the effect of an independent variable upon a dependent variable, and indeed, it has much to recommend it. It also provides information about the initial position of each individual on the dependent variable, which may be useful or necessary to the research objectives, as in the case of wanting to measure individual change as well as group change. There is, however, one disadvantage and that is the possible error introduced by the very process of measurement or observation. For example, the mere process of administering an attitude scale may result in changes of attitude in an individual, regardless of whatever research variable he may subsequently be exposed to. Thus in this design there is no way of separating out the effect of the initial data collection from the effect of the independent variable.

In order to overcome this problem, another design is increasingly recognized as being preferable. It is known as the *after-only* design,[28] and is diagrammed as follows:

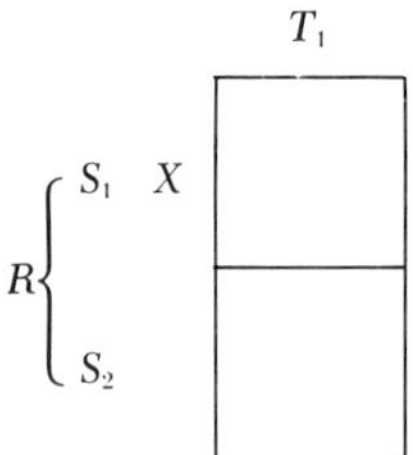

This is the same as the classical four-cell design except that here the initial data-collection is omitted. It will also be noticed that this is quite similar to the *comparison* design discussed above, but here we make the crucial specification that the two groups be equated by randomization. This similarity, and the frequent failure to recognize the important difference between the after-only and the comparison design, have led to neglect of the after-only design in the past. However, as long as there is no reason to question the accuracy and effectiveness of the randomization, this design has the advantage of eliminating the need for the initial data collection and the possible contaminating effects which can result. This is because if we can assume that initially the two groups were equated, then we can also assume that their "scores" on the initial data collection would have been equal. Thus any difference occurring between the two groups when the data are collected can be presumed to result from the effect of the independent variable. Additional advantages of this design are the saving in time and money by eliminating the first data collection step. The major disadvantage of this design is that since initial measurements

[28] Selltiz et al., 1959, p. 108. Campbell and Stanley (1963, p. 25) use the more unwieldy term, "Posttest-only control group design."

are not available, it is not possible to measure individual change, or any other such factors.

When it is desirable to *measure* the effects of the initial data-collection, and of the uncontrolled variables (such as maturation processes and contemporary events), as well as of the independent variable, and also the effect of the *interaction* between the independent variable and the initial data-collection, *Solomon's four-group* design is used.[29] It is diagrammed as follows:

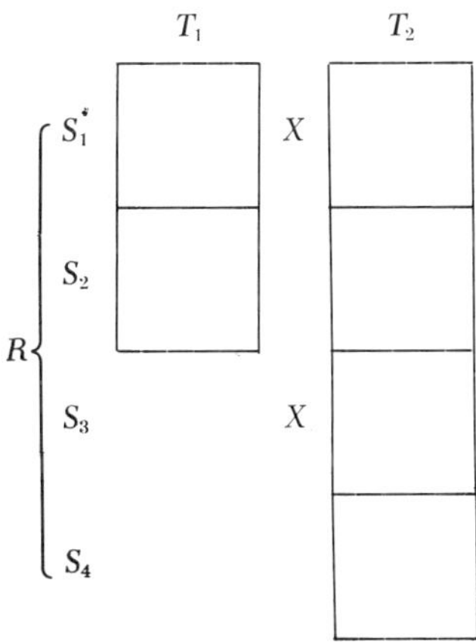

This is clearly a combination of the classical four-cell design and the after-only design. By appropriate arithmetic manipulation of the results obtained with this design, all of the above effects may be measured. This design is obviously much more costly, in terms of money, time, and other resources, than the two-group designs.[30]

Great emphasis has been placed on the importance of a random assignment of the individuals to the two (or more) groups used in the various designs discussed above, in order to increase internal validity. But a little reflection will show that this is possible only for some kinds of research situations, and not for others. If the researcher is creating the groups he usually can accomplish randomization, or if it is a matter of, for example, assigning students to one of two treatment programs, he may

[29] See: Campbell and Stanley, 1963, p. 24; Selltiz et al., 1959, p. 121. A three-group design for measuring all the above except the interaction effects is described by Ross and Smith, 1968, p. 360.

[30] Campbell and Stanley, 1963, pp. 55–56, describe one design utilizing 12 groups, which, it is claimed, effectively deals with all sources of error.

have the authority to do so. But if we are using two communities, as in the above illustration of the study of Heart Councils, it is clearly impossible to accomplish a random assignment of individuals to the two communities. This situation arises with great frequency in sociological research, since we so commonly study naturally-occurring groups or situations over which we have very limited control. The most commonly used design for these circumstances when randomization is not possible is referred to as the *nonequivalent control group* design.[31] Its diagram is as follows:

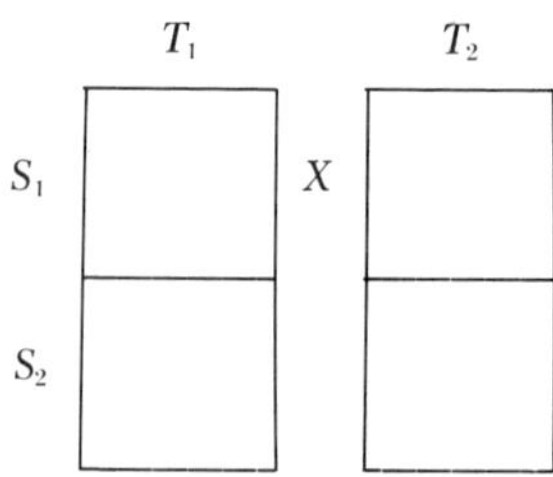

Obviously, this is the same as the classical four-cell design except that the randomization is omitted. (See Appendix B for a description of the use of this design in the Heart Councils research.) In this design the two situations are made as similar as possible, perhaps through frequency distribution or precision matching, or perhaps through careful selection of the two situations on the basis of the researcher's knowledge and judgment. (A method has been suggested for assessing how effective matching is under such circumstances, and whether it has been sufficiently effective so as to permit measurement of the effect of the independent variable.[32]) After equating the two situations insofar as possible, a random procedure is used to determine which will be the control group and which the experimental, but it is clearly recognized that these procedures will not equate the situations as accurately as randomization would. The results of the initial data collection will provide valuable information as to how similar the two groups actually are. The more similar the initial measurements the greater will be the researcher's confidence that the two groups actually are similar. On the other hand, if the initial measurements are widely divergent, regres-

[31] Ibid., p. 47.

[32] Yinger, Ikeda, and Laycock, 1967.

sion effects will almost certainly operate to confound the results of the final data collection. As stated above, the nonequivalent control group design is widely used, and it is a very valuable part of the sociologist's research repertoire, but it must not be confused with the classical four-cell design.

One particular form of this design is considerably weaker than the above. That is the situation in which *self-selection* is the basis for the formation of one or both groups. If, for example, we were attempting to determine what effect seeing an antiprejudice film would have upon ethnic attitudes, it would not do to compare a group of people who had volunteered to see the film with a group who had not. The mere act of volunteering to see an antiprejudice film would lead us to expect that such people would be more interested in the subject of prejudice than nonvolunteers, and so it would be expected that they might be more receptive (or perhaps more antagonistic) to the film's message than the average person. Despite this weakness, it may be a useful design when no stronger design is possible.

Thus we see that there are many possible answers to the questions of how many different times and situations are to be utilized in the data collection procedures. The reader is reminded again that any of these basic designs which have been discussed can be used in combination with the suggestions for dealing with multiple variables which were presented earlier.

EXERCISES

1. Discuss some of the problems that a researcher might incur in trying to replicate the following studies:
   a. A study of kinship structure and retail buying patterns in "Plainville."
   b. Birth order and sociometric status in a college fraternity.
   c. In medium-sized retail establishments, the relation between success in business and the use of modern personnel management techniques.
   d. Social class and life chances in wartime.
   e. The relation between reported crime rates and the level of education obtained by the arresting officer.
2. In the following specific research objectives, which are the independent and which are the dependent variables?

a. Student attitudes toward political leadership vary directly according to the political philosophy and activity of their parents.

b. Younger women suffer less job and salary discrimination than older women.

c. States with open shop union laws have fewer strikes and less lost work time than states with closed shop laws.

d. The amount of liquor consumed in a locality varies directly with the number of full-time employed ordained church ministers.

e. The longer a volunteer member of the military is in the service the more authoritarian that person becomes.

f. The difference between a good baseball team and a great one is the amount of support it receives from its fans.

3. Suppose you are studying the effects of sex on occupational and monetary success. This means that your three primary variables are sex (male and female), occupational type, and income. Discuss some possible interaction effects among these variables and then design a Latin Square which you might use to determine the influence of these effects on your findings.

4. Suppose you are carrying out a study of attitudes toward a current social movement or social problem and you have available as respondents the subjects listed below. Discuss the merits of using each of them in terms of maximizing *both* internal and external validity.

   a. Your immediate family and friends.

   b. The business people and shopkeepers on Main Street in your home town.

   c. A random selection of names from the telephone book in your home town.

   d. The people whom you can get to respond to you at a table that you have set up in a public place such as a shopping center or at a public concert.

   e. A 1 percent sample of homes in 10 small towns across your state (no town larger than 10,000 persons).

   f. A 10 percent random sample of all district level organization leaders of a national organization using a mail survey (sample size about 800).

5. Listed below are several descriptive studies. For each, select one of the research designs discussed in this chapter which would be

the most suitable for the research. Discuss the reasons for your selection.

a. A study to determine whether occupational mobility is the same for males as for females.

b. A study to determine what significant changes have occurred between 1940 and 1960 in the determinants of labor force participation rates of women.

c. A study to determine the morale problems of combat soldiers on duty at Da Nang, Vietnam, in 1970.

d. A study of women's fashions during economic depression and expansion using subjects who recall their youth and experiences of the period 1930–39.

e. College humor in 1930 and 1970: An investigation using a campus newspaper published by students.

f. A study of socioeconomic status and sociometric status in high school based upon a sample of 1,500 high school students.

6. Suppose you are trying to replicate a study to demonstrate that *as a group* males with muscular legs are more intelligent than males with underdeveloped legs. What variables might you select to match the groups in order to equate them and to rule out the operation of extraneous variables' effects on your findings? Discuss the reasons for your selections.

7. Suppose that the researchers of the following studies are using the classical four-cell design and are using randomization to control for operation of extraneous variables. Decide upon a randomization method for each study and explain how it is to be done.

a. The more sustained and intense the violation of the social reciprocity norm in informal groups, the greater the turnover in membership.

b. The more anxiety-provoking the social interaction situation, the greater the behavioral response of affiliation in females.

c. The "open classroom" approach to elementary education results in improved attitudes in elementary school children toward school attendance.

d. The laboratory method of teaching social research is more effective than the lecture method in transmitting research skills to beginning sociology students.

e. The higher the perceived social status of a partner, the greater the percentage of wins by a partnership in a contract bridge tournament (all hands predealt and identical for all partnerships).

8. Select one of the research designs discussed in this chapter for each of the following explanatory studies and explain the reasons for your selections.
   a. A study of the effects of sex education upon attitudes toward written pornographic materials.
   b. A study of the effects of practice with nonverbal puzzles and mathematical games upon performance in an introductory course in algebra.
   c. Highly structured task oriented groups: A study of their effects upon interpersonal intimacy of married couples.
   d. A study of the effect of a campaign speech about the issues of the environment on college students' awareness of problems with the environment.

   For which of the above studies would it be most preferable to use the after-only research design? Discuss the reasons for your selections.

Chapter 9

Design of research: Part II

Having considered the basic designs of research, we now turn to several other research design decisions.

EXPERIMENTS

The next question is one which has been implied in some of the previous discussions, namely, will it be desirable or necessary for the researcher to manipulate some of the variables which he is studying? Will he have some control over the variables or will he simply observe them as they occur naturally? A research situation in which some (or all) of the variables under observation are manipulated by the researcher is known as an *experiment*. (Some writers use the term "experiment" to refer to virtually any scientific investigation, and use terms such as "manipulative experiment" or "controlled experiment" to refer to what we here label simply "experiment.")[1] The purpose of this manipulation is to aid in determining or measuring the relationship between two or more variables. Frequently one encounters the view that scientific—or more particularly, explanatory—research *necessitates* experimentation, but by no means is this true. Astronomy, geology, and meteorology serve as excellent examples of sciences which have achieved high degrees of explanatory sophistication without engaging in experimentation—although in recent years we do see experimentation being introduced to these fields. Furthermore, experimental research is not necessarily explanatory but may be descriptive.

[1] For example, see Kaplan, 1964, pp. 161 ff; Nagel, 1961, pp. 450–53.

The decision as to whether or not experimentation will be utilized, as with many of the other decisions we have considered, depends upon the specific characteristics of the research problem. In some cases experimentation is clearly impossible for practical, moral, economic, or other reasons. In other cases it may be the only way of obtaining the necessary data.

This writer conducted an experimental investigation of the hypothesis: the greater the differentiation between groups, the greater the likelihood of intergroup conflict.[2] This was a descriptive study, utilizing the comparison design, and it will be described here as an illustration of experimentation. Sixteen matched triads were formed of hired college students, in a laboratory. Each triad had imparted to it by the researcher either a high or a low status relative to the other triads, and each either had an appointed leader or was leaderless. These two variables, relative status and leadership, were the independent variables.

Each triad was then placed in a series of situations each of which required that it interact with one of the other triads. These situations called for discussion and solution of a human relations problem. The similarities and differences of the two triads in each situation—on the status and leadership variables—served as indicators of the amount of differentiation between the groups. (That is, the two triads in each interaction situation were either: alike on both status and leadership, alike on status but different on leadership, alike on leadership and different on status, or different on both status and leadership.) The intergroup interaction between each pair of triads was recorded and analyzed by Bales' Interaction Process Analysis (see section on nonparticipant observation in Chapter 12), which provided a measure of intergroup conflict, the dependent variable. Thus it was possible to determine the relationship between the dependent and independent variables.

Since an experiment involves manipulation of variables, the distinction between an experiment and a nonexperiment is cloudy, inasmuch as *some* manipulation is almost always present. Even the act of interviewing a person is, to some degree, manipulating his environment. Therefore we can usefully identify a continuum according to the relative amount of control that the researcher has. At one extreme is the laboratory experiment in which the researcher has the maximum amount of control

[2] Manheim, 1960.

over the variables acting upon his subjects. At the other extreme are naturally occurring situations which are mostly or completely beyond the control of the researcher, but which nevertheless present him with the opportunity of designing research which approaches experimentation. These are known as *quasi-experimental* designs (or sometimes as "natural experiments").[3] Examples of such situations might include such major events as the relocation of Japanese from the west coast of the United States to concentration camps, in the early years of World War II, or local events like the establishment of a Heart Council in a local community. The experienced researcher will always be alert to the occurrence of events which may be related to his research activity. As far as the logic is concerned it is immaterial whether the scientist himself, or some external agency or force, brings about the changes in some phenomena which are observed, as long as the other requirements of the research situation are met.[4] The social scientist, much more than the physical scientist, will have to make use of quasi-experiments. Rigorous experimentation is relatively easily accomplished in the physics or chemistry laboratory. However, in the social sciences we cannot so easily—even if we would—manipulate the environments and characteristics of human beings. The social scientist does not have the same kind of power or authority over his research subject matter (people) as the chemist has over his (chemicals and laboratory equipment). More importantly, the ethical and moral obstacles may be insuperable. This is not in the slightest to imply that experimentation is inappropriate to social science or that it is a rarity—we merely say that it is more difficult than for the physical scientist.

When a true experiment can be designed, it has many advantages for the researcher. Being in a position to manipulate the variables means for the researcher that he has some—or perhaps complete—control over the independent variables as well as the other extraneous variables. He can so control the extraneous variables, such as physical surroundings, time of day or day of the week when the research subjects (individuals, groups, etc.) are exposed to the independent variables, and so on, that their likely effect is minimized, or, alternatively, so that their effect is the same upon all the subjects. This control of environmental

[3] Campbell and Stanley, 1963.

[4] Nagel, 1961, p. 453.

circumstances can have the greatest importance in experimental design. There is a myriad of these extraneous variables in any situation, any one of which may have an unanticipated and irregular effect upon the dependent variable. The presence of a pretty female research assistant or of a member of an ethnic minority, a smile or a frown on the researcher's face, a meeting just before or just after lunch, all may have differential effects upon the variables being observed. The researcher can also control the independent variables so as to vary the "treatment" in any way that he sees as desirable for the purposes of the research. This control over the variables also facilitates the later replication of the research. Probably the most important advantage of experiments, however, is that it permits the researcher to achieve the randomization which, we have seen, is so extremely important for explanatory research design.[5]

There is one particular kind of experiment which may have considerable significance, on the relatively rare occasions when it is possible to design one. This is the so-called *crucial experiment* —one which is designed to provide conclusive evidence in support of one of two competing and contradictory theories. The reason why these are so rare is that it is not only the specific propositions of the two theories which are being tested but also the whole body of premises which have gone into the construction of the two theories, and the logic of the situation requires that all these assumptions be called into question too.[6] The current development of social science probably does not include any such crucial experiments.

SAMPLE SURVEYS

We now turn to the question of whether the research will require collecting information from, or about, such a large number of people or a number that is so widely scattered geographically, that it is not practicable or not necessary to observe them all. For instance, we might desire a measure of "public opinion" of a whole community regarding some issue, or perhaps we desire to predict the outcome of a civic election, or perhaps the research involves the attitudes of students of X university toward the use of drugs, or an attitude study of the

[5] Aronson and Carlsmith, 1968, p. 7.

[6] Cohen and Nagel, 1934, pp. 219–20. See also Kaplan, 1964, pp. 151–52.

members of the American Sociological Association. If the population of the community, or the number of eligible voters, or the size of the student body, is sufficiently small, it is possible that the researcher could observe (interview, measure, etc.) each individual. However, as the population increases in size or dispersion, the practical considerations of research time and costs rapidly assume decisive importance. Under these circumstances, the researcher will use a *sample survey,* which is a systematic collection of data from or about a large number of people through the use of a sample. In turn, a *sample* is defined as a part of the population which is observed in order to make inferences about the whole population.

Sample surveys have become such an ubiquitous part of the contemporary scene that we scarcely need illustrate them. Introductory sociology students conduct sample surveys of their fellow students, as learning exercises. Professional sociologists make wide use of sample surveys in their research.[7] The National Opinion Research Center, at the University of Chicago, conducts sample surveys, for a fee, for professional social scientists who do not have the time or facilities to conduct their own. The U.S. Bureau of the Census regularly conducts sample surveys as part of its data collection procedures. Sample surveys of television viewers determine which programs will survive and which will be eliminated. Manufacturers of consumer goods, and their advertising and market research agencies, make crucial decisions as a result of sample surveys of the public. The "Gallup poll" of various public opinion issues has become virtually a household phrase around the world. And polling has become such an integral part of public elections that a former head of the U.S. Census Bureau has stated, "It would be foolhardy for any candidate for a major office in a contested situation not to have a poll."[8]

The specific procedures for selecting a sample will be discussed later, in Chapter 14. For the present it will suffice to point out that these procedures are quite exacting and complex, and that if inferences to the whole population are to be made with any degree of confidence and accuracy, the sample must be drawn with great care. By no means is it adequate for the re-

---

[7] As just one well-known example, see Lipset, Trow, and Coleman, 1956. See also Appendix B for another example.

[8] Richard Scammon, quoted in *Newsweek,* July 8, 1968.

searcher to simply interview or observe whatever individuals happen to be readily accessible.

In a sample survey the data which the researcher is seeking are seen as being located in individual people, or perhaps small collections of individuals such as engaged couples or families. This implies that the researcher will generally be utilizing such techniques as interviews, questionnaires, and the like. (The details of these, also, will be considered in the section on data collection, since their use is not confined to sample surveys.)[9] After the selection of the persons to be included in the sample, the information is collected from these persons by trained interviewers in a face-to-face situation, or perhaps by telephone or mail. Following the processing and analysis of these data, inferences can be made to the total population from which the sample was drawn, by means of the appropriate sampling statistics.

Sample surveys may be used for a great variety of research questions, and indeed they have been so widely used by social scientists that many people (including some social scientists!) mistakenly believe that this is their only, or their major, approach to research. Nevertheless, sample surveys are of great importance in those research situations as indicated above, when the number of people from whom we desire information is very large. Sample surveys can be used within the framework of any of the basic descriptive and explanatory research designs which have been discussed. For the most part, sample surveys have commonly been confined to questions about the individual respondent—census-type questions or attitudinal questions, for example. In the analysis of such data, results are totalled for various subcategories of the sample, and various statistical techniques used in order to make comparisons, test significance, and so on. Despite the great value of such studies, one problem has been that the individual respondent is always the basic unit of analysis and so the research problems which can be dealt with by this method typically are problems of what has been called "'aggregate psychology,' that is, *within*-individual problems, and never problems concerned with relations between people."[10] Yet sample surveys can be used for studying such relationships, and this is increasingly being done. Among the

[9] For a thorough coverage of the details of sample surveys, see Babble, 1973. See also: Hyman, 1955; Campbell and Katona, 1953; Backstrom and Hursh, 1963; and Moser, 1958. Regarding costs, see Sudman, 1967.

[10] Coleman, 1970-b, p. 116. See also Coleman, 1962, pp. 61–62.

techniques this involves are the inclusion of sociometric-type questions in the interview, and also of questions designed to determine the individual's relationship with some larger social unit of which he is a part, such as a school or factory; the use of certain types of sampling procedures, especially "snowball" sampling; and finally, the design of research so as to provide information about the homogeneity of belief or attitude of a group, and the various pair and clique relationships within a group.[11]

Those who are unfamiliar with the nature of sampling are frequently surprised at the idea of being able to obtain accurate information about a large population from only a very small sample. Pollsters such as Gallup regularly use a sample of less than 2,000 in order to predict the outcome of national elections in which over 70 million votes are cast, and they do this consistently, with errors of less than about 2 percent. The two notorious exceptions to this level of accuracy are now clearly understood, and subsequent survey techniques have been modified. The *Literary Digest* magazine poll in 1936, and all the major polls in 1948, made incorrect predictions on the outcome of the U.S. national elections because of errors in drawing the sample. In addition, the 1948 polls ceased their data collection too soon, and thus neglected to allow for last-minute changes in voter preference. When sample surveys are used for research purposes, the researcher does not, of course, have the same opportunity of measuring his accuracy as in the election poll. Yet there are statistical procedures whereby accuracy can be determined, and error levels of 5 percent and less are common.

Here, for the first time in this book, we must take note of intercultural differences. While everything which has been said thus far—and indeed throughout most of the remainder of the book—about the philosophy and methods of research applies to sociology wherever it may exist, there are some specific problems which may occur in conducting sample surveys in particular areas of the world. Stycos has detailed some of the problems occurring in developing areas, and says that on the basis of his experience he believes that sample surveys are feasible in such areas, as long as the researcher guards against certain problems.[12] We can generalize from his comments about developing

[11] For a more detailed description of these, see Coleman, 1970-b, pp. 115–26.

[12] Stycos, 1960.

areas to the case where the researcher is conducting a survey in any culture or subculture which is *different* from his own. (Since Stycos's views are based upon specific evidence, it is perhaps "dangerous" to make such generalizations. However, the following suggestions seem to have wider applicability.)

One of the most important steps is to overcome any initial fear and mistrust on the part of individuals by obtaining the cooperation of the community leaders. Stycos refers especially to semiliterate and lower-class communities, and says that he found the resistance to the survey was usually communal rather than individual. There are reliability and validity problems related to both the interviewers and the respondents. Some of the interviewer-related problems are as follows. Since literacy is a prerequisite for interviewing, there may be a considerable status-difference between the interviewer and the respondent. In cultures with rigid systems of social stratification, other characteristics such as sex, age, caste, marital status, religion, ethnic category, and language may also contribute to status differentials. Personality characteristics which are found to be related to success in interviewing in one culture may not be at all useful in another culture. If hired interviewers are of a different culture from the researcher, their motivations may be quite different from the researcher's expectations. Similarly, the interviewers' appreciation of the importance of objectivity in interviewing may not be the same as the researcher's. Reliability and validity problems associated with the respondent include intentional errors, such as deliberate avoidance or falsification of answers because the question violates some norms of propriety, etc., and unintentional errors due to semantic problems related to the cultural differences.

The many advantages of sample surveys have been indicated in the previous paragraphs. In research situations where it is not feasible to observe the entire population, these may be the only satisfactory research method. Furthermore, when the 100 percent accuracy provided by a complete census is not necessary, a sample survey may prove to be a far more economical way of doing research. There is another side to the coin, however. Some communities (college towns?) and segments of the population have been exposed to so many sample surveys on so many different topics that they have acquired a resistance to any new one, regardless of its importance or sponsorship. Resistance may also occur because of suspicions as to the ultimate use to which the data will be put, as has happened occasionally in some ghetto areas of the United States in recent years. A more important methodological limitation is that sample surveys are only suitable for certain kinds of research, and to obtain certain kinds of information. This is because sample surveys almost always use interviews and questionnaires, and therefore the important limitations inherent in these devices will affect the usefulness of a sample survey. These will be considered in detail later, but for the moment we merely point out that the data collected in an interview consist only of verbal behavior, and sociology is interested in far more than this. Despite the importance and very widespread use of sample surveys, we caution the student against assuming that these are *the* research method of sociology. They are but *one* of several methods available to the researcher, and some of the others may be far more productive and valid than a sample survey for a given research problem.

SITE OF RESEARCH

The final research design question we will discuss is, Where will the research be done? What type of location, place, or setting will be used for collecting the data? There are no necessary limitations—sociological research can successfully be conducted anywhere, limited only by the researcher's ingenuity. These sites can be examined under three general headings.

Field research

Field research refers to any research which takes place in a natural setting. That is, the data being collected or the behavior or activities being studied are perfectly normal or routine (or if not routine, this is their "natural habitat") for that kind of location—with the possible exception of the activities of the researcher himself. Studies of riots, for example, or of workers in a factory, or of an isolated tribe, or of the learning processes in a classroom, or of everyday interaction, or of marital success and failure, or of ethnic attitudes of college students—all of these fall under the general heading of field research.[13] So do sample

[13] See, for example, the Bank Wiring Room studies in Roethlisberger and Dickson, 1939; Mead, 1963; Locke, 1951; Bogardus, 1967.

surveys, of course, and also some experiments. Quasi-experiments are, by definition, subsumed under field research, and other experiments in which the researcher has greater amounts of control may also be done "in the field".[14] (We avoid use of the common term "field experiment," because it has two slightly different, and therefore confusing, meanings. On the one hand it is used to refer only to quasi-experiments, and on the other, to any experiment conducted in natural surroundings.)

Field research has the obvious advantage of always being relevant and immediate. It carries the aura of really coming to grips with practical matters and the "real world." However, the practical difficulties involved in studying social behavior in a natural setting, without contaminating it by the influences of the research process itself, are very great. Similarly, costs may be very high.

Field research also includes the *case study* (sometimes the rather vague word *fieldwork* is used) which is a study of some total, separately identifiable, social unit, usually over a period of time.[15] The research objective of the case study is usually an analytic description of a complex social organization. This is not simply a journalistic description, but "is primarily an empirical application and modification of scientific theory rather than an efficient and powerful test of such a theory, since only one case—however complex—is involved in the study."[16]

The research problem in a case study may call for a study of a whole community, such as the Lynds' well-known study of Middletown, or of a portion of a community, such as Whyte's study of Cornerville.[17] (When the part of the community which is studied is relatively homogeneous in its culture, and also more or less sharply differentiated from the larger part of the community, this is sometimes known as a "culture group," and special research techniques may be useful.)[18] Occasionally, in fact, the residents of a community will undertake to study their own community, in order to bring about some practical results,[19]

---

[14] For example, see the illumination studies in Roethlisberger and Dickson, 1939; and Coch and French, 1968.

[15] *Case studies* should not be confused with *case histories*, which will be discussed later.

[16] McCall and Simmons, 1969, p. 3.

[17] Lynd and Lynd, 1956; Whyte, 1955.

[18] See Young, 1966, chap. 16.

[19] For example, Wormser and Selltiz, 1951.

or an outside agency will undertake the study for similar reasons. These are all case studies, as are studies of an institution, such as the church in a given society, or studies of an organization, such as a university.[20]

Cross-cultural studies. Cross-cultural studies, as the name indicates, are studies conducted across cultural boundaries, in order to make comparisons between two or more cultures. Will independent variable *X* have the same effect upon dependent variable *Y* in two (or more) different cultures? Is our knowledge of, say, leadership in complex organizations true of all such organizations, or only of those in America and other "Western" societies? These kinds of questions have all too frequently been overlooked by sociologists, and their importance unrecognized. To a considerable extent our current fund of sociological knowledge is based upon studies conducted in North America and western Europe—a very small fraction, indeed, of the world's population or of separately identifiable societies. Thus our "knowledge" may be extremely limited in its scope. Berelson and Steiner, in their impressive inventory of such knowledge, state that "except for anthropological materials a large proportion of these findings are based upon data collected in the United States."[21] To the extent that sociology aims to make general statements about human interaction wherever it may exist, the possibility of generalizing from a fortuitous sample of less than 10 percent of the world's population is certainly questionable. Cross-cultural studies are clearly needed in order to check the validity of research findings, and yet only a relatively small number of such studies have been undertaken.

In one interesting and well-known study, a modification of the Thematic Apperception Test was used in an effort to make cross-cultural comparisons of personality on relatively large numbers of persons. The test was administered to approximately 300 college students in Hong Kong, Taiwan, India, and the United States. In addition to testing a technique, the results pointed to some personality differences among the Chinese, Indian, and American cultures.[22] Another example of a cross-

[20] For a very useful collection of articles on all aspects of field research, see Adams and Preiss, 1960. See also Zelditch, 1962; Junker, 1960; H. Becker, 1970-b, Part I; and Young, 1966, chaps. 17, 18, 19. For studies of organizations in field, laboratory, and simulated sites, see Vroom, 1967.

[21] Berelson and Steiner, 1964, p. 8.

[22] Watrous and Hsu, 1972.

cultural study will be found in the section on content analysis in Chapter 13.

While the development of such data sources as the Yale University Human Relations Area Files makes great contributions to cross-cultural research possibilities (see section on "Libraries and Archives," below) much field research remains to be done. We have already discussed the use of sample surveys in such research. There are several other problems of particular importance to this kind of study. These include the difficulty in defining the fundamental data unit (tribe, society, dialect group, culture, etc), sampling problems, the problem of defining variables so that they are applicable across cultural lines, sociolinguistic problems, and certain problems of coding and data analysis.[23]

Laboratory

In most of the social science literature we find close association between the concept of "experiment" and that of "laboratory " and frequently the two terms are even treated as inseparable. However, for clarity of thinking it is useful to make the distinction between experiment as a form of research design, and laboratory as a site of research. We have already seen that not all experimentation takes place in a laboratory, although indeed the maximum of control of variables is attained in a laboratory. It has now become commonplace for sociological research to be conducted in laboratories. Since any location which is specifically designed and used for data collection may be called a laboratory,[24] it is not possible to give any precise description of a sociological laboratory. What is essential is that the maximum number of variables with which the researcher is concerned can be controlled. At the very least, a laboratory will be isolated from the influences of unwanted interruptions from outsiders, to avoid "contamination" of the interaction or behavior under observation. At the other extreme are elaborate facilities with provisions for one-way observation, visual and sound recording, and complicated (and expensive) equipment of various kinds. (Some of this equipment will be described in

[23] For details of these, see Whiting, 1968. See also Naroll, 1968; Anderson, 1967; Rokkan, 1968; Grimshaw, 1969; Holt and Turner, 1970, and Manaster and Havighurst, 1972.

[24] In common practice, however, spaces used for data *processing* are frequently referred to as laboratories.

the later discussion of tools of research.) Probably the ingenuity of the researcher is more important than the amount of equipment available. Among the more ingenious pieces of laboratory research are the well-known study of communication patterns in small groups by Bavelas and Leavitt, and Sherif's autokinetic effect studies.[25] Sherif's widely recognized summer camp studies, although literally performed in the field, might also be taken as examples of laboratory research, since the camp situations were established for the purpose of research.[26]

In laboratory research, the attempt usually is made to utilize variables which are as "pure" and widely applicable as possible. In the study of intergroup interaction cited above, for example (and also the communication patterns study), interaction was limited to written notes. This served the purpose of providing a definite record of all the interaction taking place, and also of screening out any *intragroup* interaction which would have contaminated that particular research design. Similarly, other characteristics of the laboratory situation are usually designed to set aside many of the extraneous factors with which so much interaction is ordinarily surrounded, and allow the essential "skeleton" of the interaction to be observed. For these reasons laboratory research has frequently been criticized as being artificial and not related to real life.[27] Festinger's comments on this, some years ago, are still just as valid today. He says that such criticisms are due to a lack of understanding as to the purpose of a laboratory experiment. Laboratory experiments are not intended to be duplicates of "real-life" situations; and in fact most of them are certainly very much *unlike* everyday situations. Instead, they are designed to facilitate the study of variables "under special identified and defined conditions."[28] We would add the comment that laboratory situations are very definitely real-life situations—the individuals who are interacting in the laboratory, their interaction itself, and the physical surroundings are, of course, real. They may be more or less un-

---

[25] Bavelas, 1968; Sherif, 1958. For other examples see Asch, 1958, and Leik, 1965. Also see the experiment on intergroup interaction (Manheim, 1960) described at the beginning of this chapter.

[26] Sherif and Sherif, 1956.

[27] For an especially caustic, outspoken, and entertaining criticism of experimental and laboratory research, as well as of the uses of math in research, see Sorokin, 1956, chaps. 7–10.

[28] Festinger, 1953, p. 139.

usual, but they are nonetheless real. The fundamental elements of interaction—whatever they may be—can be studied wherever they occur. However, there is another respect in which such criticisms of laboratory research are invalid. To the extent that laboratory research is explanatory research—and much of it is—it follows that what the researcher is doing is attempting to reality-test one or more of the propositions from some theory or explanation. The purpose of the research is to supply additional evidence as to the validity of the theory, and not merely to provide some isolated bit of knowledge which may or may not have some practical application.[29]

There is an additional potential benefit to be derived from laboratory research. To some extent a case can be made for the view that a considerable amount of sociological research studies the "wrong" things. By "wrong" we merely mean secondary or derived concepts rather than fundamental concepts with universal applicability. To the extent that sociology investigates concepts which serve as original or generating sources—that is, concepts which have wide applicability and implications, concepts which deal with the essence of sociological phenomena, concepts which are general rather than specific—the more rapidly will sociological knowledge accumulate. For example, "norm deviation" is a more fertile concept to investigate than is "juvenile delinquency" which is, after all, but one instance of norm violation. Similarly, study of "social organization" or "ecology" is likely to be more fertile than study of "rural sociology," and "interaction" more so than "small group interaction." The main reason that so much research has concentrated on the "wrong" things is that sociology has yet to achieve wide agreement as to what the fundamental concepts are. When more agreement is reached about these fundamental concepts it should be possible to study these under laboratory circumstances, and so this site of research will assume even more importance.

In addition to the above, laboratory research presents various other advantages to the researcher. It makes possible the study of variables which might not feasibly be undertaken in field research. The summer camp studies, for instance, dealt with the creation and then the reduction of intergroup hostility, both of which would be extremely difficult to study under natural cir-

[29] Zelditch, 1969, makes a similar point in his intriguingly titled article.

cumstances.[30] The intergroup interaction study (described above) originated out of an interest in studying the patterns of interaction between gangs of hostile juvenile delinquents. In this case the laboratory research had the additional advantage of being physically safer for the researcher. Finally, laboratory research is frequently cheaper than comparable field research, although the actual costs, of course, depend upon many other factors. Typically, a given expenditure of funds will yield more data in a laboratory situation than in field research.

There are, of course, certain problems inherent in laboratory research. Probably the main one is that mentioned above—namely, generalizing from laboratory results to the larger social order. We have pointed out that this is not always a desired part of the research, nor is it always appropriate. However, sometimes it may be legitimate to attempt such generalizations. Since laboratory studies, as we have seen, deal with "pure" variables, usually accompanied by holding constant all other variables, these circumstances are very unlikely to occur outside the lab, and therefore the findings cannot be directly generalized to completely uncontrolled situations. Such findings must ultimately be tested in some kind of field research before they can be regarded as having any practical utility. Another problem lies in the technical difficulties of devising ways of manipulating the desired variables and of creating situations which will engender the desired responses on the part of the subjects.

There is one additional, and special, form of laboratory research, namely, simulation, about which a word should be said now, although it will be discussed in more detail in Chapter 13. Simulation refers to the use of models for research purposes, although in current usage it is usually confined to mathematical models which are studied by means of computers. With the rapdily increasing availability of computers for teaching and research purposes, and the increase (although regrettably less rapid) in mathematical training for social scientists, the use of simulation for research holds great promise.

Libraries and archives

The third general site of sociological research includes libraries and archives, and similar places where data may already be

[30] Sherif and Sherif, 1956.

collected, such as museums, hospitals, corporations, schools, government units, and private collections. Commonly, the terms "existing data" or "available data" are used to refer to data found in such sites; details of these data will be discussed in Chapter 13. There are rich sources of research material to be found in these places—census publications are only one example. Not only is the variety overwhelming, but data which otherwise might be completely unattainable—historical documents, for example—may be found in such archives. To be sure, the accuracy of archival data is not under the control of the researcher; instead he must rely upon the abilities, skills, motivation, and techniques of the original data collectors.

In addition to such primary materials, previously unused for research, archives also contain an ever-increasing body of secondary material. The latter is data originally collected (to a large extent by sample surveys) and used for some specific research purpose but still containing an abundance of information suitable for further research. Increasingly, data banks and archives are being established in order to make these materials available to researchers everywhere. This means that a vast assortment of data is accessible for research purposes at greatly reduced cost, since the researcher does not have to bear the expense of the basic data collection. Among the more well-known data archives in the United States are the following: Human Relations Area Files, at Yale University; Inter-University Consortium for Political Research, at the University of Michigan; Institute for Research in Social Science, at the University of North Carolina; and Roper Public Opinion Research Center, at Williams College. A very useful listing of important documentary resources available in libraries, and also a directory of social science data libraries in the United States, are available.[31] Information of a more technical nature on the establishment and organization of international data banks and data archives, and the problems and technology of data archiving and retrieval, is also available.[32]

ETHICS OF RESEARCH

We now turn to a matter of a different nature—one which is of concern throughout an entire research project, not just during

[31] D. Miller, 1970, pp. 68–76, 100–102. This book also contains a wealth of useful information on all aspects of research design.

[32] See Rokkan, 1966.

the design stages. Ethical considerations must always be kept in mind, but for the sake of convenience we can discuss them here in three separate contexts: in relation to research subjects, to the scientific community, and to the larger society.

Most sociological research, whether it be a sample survey or an experiment, whether it be field research or laboratory research—in fact all except library or archive research—necessarily involves the study or observation of people. And the researcher must never forget that these subjects of his research *are* people—individual humans with their own dreams, wishes, desires, personal lives. They have their own rights—rights to privacy, to freedom from interference in their personal activities, and to be treated with a full measure of human dignity. This applies, of course, regardless of who the subjects are—regardless of their social status or ethnic background, or whether they are from the researcher's own culture or a bewilderingly different one, regardless of the extent of their deviance from the norms, regardless of how much their values and beliefs and philosophy differ from the researcher's. Needless to say, the previous sentences are value statements, based upon a value of individual human worth and /or dignity. For the researcher, ethical problems arise in that often there is a conflict between the aforementioned value and the values of knowledge and honesty and perhaps others. Scientific research is devoted to attaining knowledge, and for the social scientist this implies knowledge about human beings and their interaction and behavior. For example, when the researcher is seeking knowledge about a certain form of interaction or behavior, and in order to attain that knowledge his research methods must interfere with his subjects' lives or involve deception, the resulting dilemma is a value conflict. As with any other instance of value conflict, or disagreement about values, there can be no simple answer. People of goodwill always have, and always will, disagree as to a hierarchy of values.

Let us first see how these ethical problems arise in connection with research subjects, and then we will look at the ways in which social scientists deal with these problems. The most common instance is that of deception of subjects. It is frequently considered to be necessary to disguise the exact nature of the research—either its purposes or its sponsorship or the specific things in which the researcher is interested. For example, in Sherif's famous studies utilizing the autokinetic effect, if the subjects had been told that in reality the light did not move, this knowledge probably would have had a greatly confounding effect upon the research results.[33] In a study of public knowledge about heart disease, the interviewees were told that it was a study of health sponsored by a university, rather than being given the full information—that it was sponsored in part by the American Heart Association.[34] It was believed that if the interviewees were aware of the sponsor and the specific nature of the research, it might bias their responses to some questions in which they were asked to rate the severity, extent, and importance of certain diseases. Other forms of limited information or deception might involve giving the subjects false information about, for example, the source of a quotation, or the details of some public event of current interest. In a somewhat more pronounced form of deception which has sometimes been used, the subject is given false information about himself, such as his IQ, emotional stability, personality characteristics, and the like. Here again, this is done for what are regarded as sound research design reasons. In the study of intergroup interaction, for example, the subjects were led to believe that their IQs were either lower or higher than was actually the case. The purpose of this was to aid in imparting a relatively low or high status to the group, since the research interest was in differential status as an independent variable.[35] In more extreme forms of deception, subjects have been placed in situations in which they were made to believe that some event was taking place which resulted—or might have resulted—in extreme upset or psychological trauma on the part of the subject. In one well-known experiment, subjects found themselves locked in a windowless attic room of an old building, and by the use of smoke pots were deceived into thinking that the building was on fire—so that the researcher could study behavior under conditions of fear.[36] More recently, in a study of obedience to authority, subjects were led to believe that they were administering large, and even lethal, electric shocks to another person as punishment for failure to learn rapidly.[37] In all of these illustrations the value of honesty,

---

[33] Sherif, 1958.

[34] Manheim and Howlett, 1964.

[35] Manheim, 1960, p. 418.

[36] French, 1944.

[37] Milgram, 1974. See also A. Miller, 1972, Part 2.

at least, was being set aside temporarily in order to obtain scientific knowledge. We will say more about this shortly.

Another way in which ethical problems may arise is in research situations where the subjects are completely unaware that any research is being conducted. This has usually been done in order to obtain information about behavior or interaction which, presumably, would be modified if the subject knew that he was being observed. For example, reactions to invasions of "personal space" were studied by having the researcher sit in a chair immediately next to a student in a library, when there were many other vacant seats available.[38] Concealed research which stirred up considerable controversy was a law-school-sponsored study of the judicial process, which included an attempt to record jury deliberations without the knowledge of the jury but with the knowledge and consent of the judge and all attorneys involved.[39]

Deception and concealment are not the only ways in which ethical matters enter into research design. There is also the question of eavesdropping in general, and particularly the use of various kinds of electronic and recording devices without the knowledge of the subjects. A hidden microphone or TV camera may enable the researcher to study certain variables in a more "natural" or uninhibited situation, but ethical questions of the propriety of so invading the privacy of the subjects cannot be ignored. The anonymity of subjects is another area involving ethical decisions and actions. To make public any information which might be harmful or embarrassing to research subjects, is contrary to the "human worth and dignity" value mentioned above. Yet complete and honest publication of research results sometimes may seem to necessitate identification of at least some of the individuals. This would be especially true of anthropological investigations, studies of small communities or organizations, and the like. Related to this is the question of what use the research results will be put to. Even though individuals may not be identified or directly harmed, the publication of some kinds of research data pertaining to a given group of individuals may enable other individuals or groups to wield undue power over the research subjects. The researcher cer-

[38] Felipe and Sommer, 1966.

[39] Vaughan, 1967.

tainly desires to avoid this kind of intrusion into his subjects' lives, and yet, again, the norm of full and accurate reporting of research is also operating.

Most social scientists are acutely aware of the many ethical problems inherent in social science research, and consequently make great efforts to respect the rights and sensitivities of the people they study. The vast majority of such research is accomplished without harmful intrusion into the lives of the subjects, infringement of their rights, or ethical problems of any other kind. It will be valuable to the student to consider how social scientists handle ethical dilemmas—some of which have been described in the preceding paragraphs—in their research. A partial answer is to take great pains in designing the research so as to minimize the likelihood of such problems arising. But this is not always as easy as it sounds. The researcher can never be sure that some minor, mild research variable will not have great impact upon one—or more—of his subjects. He must constantly be alert to such possibilities. As we have said, research involves a constant series of decisions among alternatives. Not only do the alternatives vary as to efficiency, ease, cost, and practicability, but they also may vary according to the ethical problems which result. Some decisions will be reached on the basis of trading off ethical problems for some other kind of problems. Another attempt at coping with these ethical problems is the suggestion that the privileged relationship between the physician and patient be extended to the social science researcher and his subjects, in order to protect the confidential nature of this interaction.[40]

A step which is almost always taken when any deception has been employed is to debrief the subjects at the close of their participation in the research. This can be more complicated and difficult to achieve than at first it appears.[41] At the absolute minimum, debriefing consists of apprising the subjects of the true facts of the situation, explaining the reasons for the deception and the purposes of the research, answering their questions, and dealing with any untoward reactions which may have been caused. Milgram, for example, in his electric shock experiments

[40] Gross, 1956.

[41] For a good discussion of ethical problems in laboratory research and the problems of debriefing, see Aronson and Carlsmith, 1968, pp. 29–36. See also A. Miller, 1972, part 3.

mentioned above, went to extraordinary lengths to debrief his subjects and to ensure that no harm befell them.[42]

In the last analysis, however, solving these ethical dilemmas becomes a matter of value hierarchies, as indicated above. At one extreme, there are those who take the view that under no circumstances should the slightest deception, dishonesty, or withholding of information be practiced. One authority, for example, would not allow any "observations of private behavior . . . without the explicit and fully informed permission of the person to be approved," nor even the simulation of warmth by the interviewer in order to establish rapport.[43] This viewpoint regards the value of human worth and dignity as clearly superior to the value of scientific knowledge. The opposite extreme, of holding the attainment of scientific knowledge as being of such importance that individual human welfare should be sacrificed to it, probably exists only in unusual situations such as totalitarian societies. Most social scientists hold views between these two polar ones. The former view is generally regarded as imposing such severe restrictions upon social science research as to render such research almost useless.

We take a more moderate position here. All of these ethical decisions must be made on the basis of the particulars involved. Any intrusion upon the individual's rights must be justified as being an acceptable "cost" in view of the scientific benefits obtained thereby. If there is an alternative design available which would involve less intrusion, this should be selected. Never, of course, should the researcher engage in any manipulation of his subjects for the ego-gratifications which may accompany such demonstration of "power" over others—an occasional temptation for beginning research students. He must ask himself whether the nature and extent of the possible harm to the subjects is sufficiently mild so that it is overbalanced by the importance of the research results. And he should be well prepared to defend his decision to impartial outsiders. As for the problem of deception in particular, we do not believe that deception, per se, causes any harm to research subjects. Indeed, anyone living in a society characterized by advertising and salesmen may well *expect* deception, at least in certain circum-

[42] Riecken, 1974; Milgram, 1972.

[43] Edward A. Shils, as quoted in Webb et al., 1966, p. vi.

stances. However, the researcher must constantly be aware of these kinds of problems, and seek alternative techniques which will minimize and/or eliminate deception.[44]

It is not the extreme cases which are difficult to handle. Most people—social scientists as well as laymen—would agree that no significant harm is likely to result from sitting "too close" in the library, or from not telling interviewees that the main focus of the interview is heart disease. And similarly, there would be virtually universal agreement that locking people in an apparently burning building, or revealing damaging information to one's employers, are completely unethical for the researcher. But when the nature of the research design is such as to cause the subject *some* embarrassment or anxiety or similar discomforts, who can say what is the dividing line between ethical and unethical conduct? It seems likely that this will remain a question that the individual researcher must decide for himself. Certainly as he gains in research experience the probability of his violating any ethical norms will decrease.

The ethics of the relationship between the researcher and the scientific community, and between the researcher and the larger society, involve somewhat different problems. By scientific community we mean the researcher's collaborators, students, assistants, his university or employer, the sponsoring agency, and his professional colleagues and associations. The larger society includes not only the local community but may also, depending upon the research, include the national or even international level. One question which arises is with regard to the possible impact that the research will have upon the larger society, and to a lesser extent upon the scientific community. The search for knowledge may have many and varied practical consequences for society, including some which may be "undesirable" according to popular value systems. Sjoberg and Nett discuss this in the context of conservative and liberal approaches to social science research. They suggest that the conservative view would avoid chosing research topics which would lead to controversy within the scientific community, or to an upsetting of the moral order. The liberal view, on the other hand, which the authors support, is that, since knowledge is preferable to ignorance, the social scientist should feel free to pursue his re-

[44] Kelman, 1967.

search interests regardless of what controversy may result.[45] The well-known furore over Project Camelot illustrates this particular ethical problem as well as many others. Project Camelot was a large-scale social science research project undertaken in Chile, under the sponsorship of the U.S. Army. This erupted into an international incident which led to the project's cancellation, and to a continuing debate within the social science community over the ethics of the project.[46]

An ethical problem about which there is considerably less disagreement is that of assuring that all appropriate persons are given proper recognition for their part in conducting the research. Scientific honesty and integrity would demand that those who make significant contributions to a project should be given public recognition. However, disagreement may arise on this issue; the most likely context, but by no means the only one, is that of student participation in the conduct of research. Student assistance has occasionally not been given proper recognition, either deliberately or because of a genuine disagreement as to the extent of the student's contribution or because of the view that to the extent that the student has received financial support for his participation further recognition is unnecessary. A useful criterion is whether the student (or other assistant) has contributed innovative ideas to the design of the project. If, for example, routine clerical or interviewing assistance (whether paid or unpaid) is not acknowledged, there is no violation of ethical principles, although common courtesy might call for some recognition. But one whose contributions altered or otherwise affected the course of the research procedure should clearly receive proper recognition.[47]

In these and the countless other research situations where questions of ethics may arise, the competent researcher will always rely on the two basic ideas woven through the above discussion. The first is a diligent and careful attention to the details of research design. The second is a penetrating examination of the hierarchy of values involved in his research. And he will constantly strive, by every means available to him, to maintain the highest ethical standards in his work. Just as these mat-

[45] Sjoberg and Nett, 1968, pp. 120–28. These authors also discuss many other aspects of the ethics of sociological research throughout their book.

[46] See Horowitz, 1967, and Sjoberg, 1967-b.

[47] See Sjoberg and Nett, 1968, for further discussion of this.

ters are of great concern to the individual sociologist, so are they to the profession as a whole. After considerable deliberation, effort, and time, the American Sociological Association recently adopted a Code of Ethics to serve as a guide in sociological inquiry. This is reprinted in its entirety in Appendix C. The American Psychological Association has also published a set of ethical principles.[48]

ADMINISTRATION

The problems involved in administration of a research project are usually not of major concern to the beginning researcher, so they will only briefly be touched upon here. In addition to all the formulation and design procedures which have already been discussed, the administrator of a large-scale project will have various additional responsibilities related to the size and complexity of the project. Initially a time budget will have to be prepared, specifying when the various steps of the research process will occur. In very complex projects a flow chart and the techniques of critical path analysis may prove beneficial.[49] A cost budget will have to be prepared, and once the project is underway various accounting and disbursement procedures will have to be maintained.[50] An area of concern with which most projects must deal is that of personnel. Decisions must be made as to how many persons are to be hired and what skills are needed. The recruitment and hiring of competent personnel must be accomplished, and training programs devised and carried through. The employees must be supervised in general, and particularly with regard to honesty and accuracy.[51] The logistics of the project must be managed. Supplies, equipment, and office space must be obtained. Transportation needs, and perhaps even housing of personnel, must be provided for. Office procedures must be established and maintained. And finally,

---

[48] American Psychological Association, 1973 (and related articles in later issues). For general treatments of the subject of ethics, see: Kelman, 1968; Shils, 1959; and Reissman and Silvert, 1967. For details of some of the important recent ethical controversies in social science research, see Sjoberg, 1967-a. See also Denzin, 1970-b, pp. 447–48, 527–30.

[49] For example, see Lockyer, 1969.

[50] See D. Miller, 1970, p. 409.

[51] See Roth, 1966.

attention will have to be given to public relations with the community.[52]

CONCLUSION

We have considered at some length the *general* aspects of the design of sociological research. But the planning of high-quality research also includes the specifics of how the data will be collected, processed, and analyzed, and these topics will be discussed in the following chapters. The reader is reminded again of the desirability of accomplishing all these steps, insofar as possible, before any data are actually collected.

In conclusion, it is important to recognize that research design is not a static, unchanging thing, any more than sociology itself is. As new techniques of data collection, processing, and analysis are developed, they will undoubtedly have an impact upon the basic design of research. Furthermore, the whole direction of social science research may change—some would even say that this is necessary for the survival of the discipline. The kinds of things being studied, the scope or scale of the investigations, the relative emphases upon "pure" and "applied" research, intensive versus extensive research, and the methods and control of the financial sponsorship of research—all of these are important current issues in the planning of social science research.[53]

EXERCISES

1. Below are several sets of variables which could readily be studied using the experimental research design. For each set, make up a research hypothesis relating the variables and outline an experimental procedure one could use to test it.
   a. Work productivity and strictness of supervision.
   b. Intensity of anxiety and participation in religious activities.
   c. Positive verbal reinforcement and team performance.

[52] For some detailed suggestions on dealing with various administrative problems, see: LeClair, 1960; Selltiz et al., 1959, Appendix A; and Parten, 1950, chap. 5.

[53] For a discussion of these issues, see Blalock, 1970, chap. 6. For a review of recent developments, and needed developments, in sociological research, see Coleman, 1970-a.

d. Sociometric status of a team member and his success in sports activities.

e. Self image and the number of current intimate role relationships.

2. Listed below are several populations' samples and the research topic about which the respondents in the samples are being surveyed. Suppose the researcher obtains accurate, reliable, and valid results. To what general population may the researcher legitimately make inferences about the results of each study?

   a. A 10 percent random sample of students at the college you presently attend—students were interviewed on their attitudes toward marijuana.

   b. A 10 percent random sample of the residents in your home town—residents were telephoned and asked to recall childhood experiences of parental discipline.

   c. A 30 percent return of mailed questionnaires to all chairpersons of sociology departments in U.S. universities—respondents were asked to relate major academic influences on their careers.

   d. A 100 percent sample of teachers at your home town high school—teachers were interviewed on their reasons for originally choosing teaching as a career.

   e. A sample of 1,500 ghetto residents—500 in Detroit and 1,000 in Los Angeles. Respondents were interviewed on the adequacy of health care in their neighborhoods.

3. Discuss some of the major difficulties a researcher might incur in trying to obtain information from subjects in the following studies:

   a. A study of the use of modern management techniques by chief administrators, and resultant organizational efficiency.

   b. Religious piety and authoritarian personality traits.

   c. The happiness of suburbanites and their use of tranquilizers.

   d. A study of the incidence of drug abuse by Mexican-Americans.

   e. A comparison of attitudes of librarians and janitors toward pornographic writing.

4. Suppose a researcher wants to test the hypothesis that the mode of production used by factory workers is related to their feelings of alienation toward themselves, their jobs, and their futures. For one part of the study the researcher travels to Sweden where auto production is done in a very unspecialized way and where each worker participates in all phases of the production of the finished automobile. Next the researcher uses an instrument to measure

"alienation." For the second part of the study the researcher goes to the United States to an automobile factory where production is carried out by workers who are responsible for only a small portion of the finished product and who must repeat the same task day after day and week after week. Again the researcher uses the same instrument to measure alienation of the workers.

The researcher finds that there are significant differences between alienation levels in workers in the two countries. Based on the discussion in this chapter of cross-cultural studies, what may be concluded about the results of this study?

5. The following are some possible research projects. In each the researcher must be aware of his own value priorities and then make decisions as to whether he will carry out the given piece of research. Assume that you are the researcher, and the state several values you hold which are of a high priority. Using these values as a guide, discuss whether or not you would carry out the study.
   a. A study using confederates to give the perception to a subject that he has a certain status level in a group.
   b. A study to determine the kinds of sexual conflicts subjects have in their marriages.
   c. A study to determine general attitudes toward stealing by providing the subject the opportunity to steal something.
   d. A study of the characteristics of female Aid for Dependent Children welfare cheaters.
   e. A study of group interaction characteristics using one-way mirrors and hidden microphones.

Chapter 10

Introduction to data collection

Having made the various decisions discussed in the previous chapters, the researcher now must decide precisely how he will go about collecting the necessary data. What method or methods of data collection will be utilized? Some of these methods have been mentioned already, and undoubtedly others are also familiar to the student through his previous training. We will attempt here to present some general guidelines which are useful in deciding among the available alternatives.

TYPES OF SOCIOLOGICAL DATA

The data which the sociologist uses can be classified into three main *types*, with some subclassifications.[1] The first type is *human behavior and characteristics*. This is subdivided into two categories, the first of which is one particular form of verbal behavior, namely, any *oral or written response to questions* given by the researcher. This includes the familiar interview or questionnaire situation.

The second category is *all other overt behavior and observable characteristics*. Thus this second subtype includes individual behavior, interaction among two or more individuals or groups, and observable characteristics such as number or sex of individuals, physical location, skin color, type of clothing worn, stature, gestures, and so on. Common examples of such data in sociological research include: discussions within a group of subjects, behavior and scores in a bowling match or other game or contest (as indicators of status), patterns of interaction in

[1] These should not be confused with the three *levels* of data which were discussed with the definition of science in Chapter 1.

families and other groups, individual responses to receiving contradictory information from two respected sources, and the number, sex, race, social class (as estimated by clothing), etc. of people in a given location or situation. Webb et al. give many more unusual illustrations of human behavior and characteristics as data, such as tattoos, hair length, clothing, seating arrangements, changing physical proximity in a group (as indicator of fear), unobtrusive sampling of casual conversations, and eye movement when looking at certain objects.[2] These, of course, give only a small sample of the various kinds of data which can be used. The author is not aware of any sociological research using tastes as data, and there is only limited reference to the use of odors.[3] However, interesting possibilities come to mind, such as cultural, age, or sex differences in preferences for perfumes and foods.

The second type of sociological data is *the products of human behavior and characteristics*, and this, also, can be subdivided into two categories, *physical traces* and *archives*.[4] *Physical traces* include any kind of physical evidence (other than archives) surviving from past behavior. Webb et al. distinguish two kinds of physical traces, *erosion* and *accretion* measures. The former are illustrated by the earlier example of the rate of wear on floor tiles, and also by the wear on library books (as an indicator of their popularity). Examples of accretion measures are the counting of empty liquor bottles in trash cans (as an indicator of liquor consumption in a "dry" town), and the measuring of the number and height of noseprints on a glass exhibit-case (as an indicator of the number and ages of children viewing the exhibit). We use the term "accretion measures" more broadly than do Webb et al. so as to include the characteristics and location of buildings, highways, railroads, parks, hospitals, schools, farms, wells, grain storage facilities, and other ecological features. These examples are only a few of the enormous number of such kinds of data which might profitably be used by the sociologist.

Archives refers to the vast accumulations of records, documents, library collections, and mass media materials which are extant. These include familiar materials such as census data,

[2] Webb et al., 1966.

[3] See Largey and Watson, 1972; and Dawson and Gettys, 1948, pp. 361–62.

[4] Webb et al., 1966.

vital statistics, other ecological and demographic data, statistical records of all kinds, personal documents such as autobiographies, diaries, and letters, and case histories (also known as "life histories," which are records of facts—almost always subjective—about an individual or group, collected either by the subject or by an external source). It also includes the various mass media materials such as newspaper and magazine files, and the content of radio, television, and movies. Less familiar archival materials which have been used, according to Webb et al., include tombstone inscriptions, sales records, suicide notes, nurses' records of patients' conditions, legislators' voting records, variations in city water pressure, and the height of pilots involved in jet plane accidents. The distinguishing characteristic of archival data is that they were originally produced for some other purpose—the researcher has no control over them.

A special word should be said about library collections. Many of the above archival materials may be found in libraries, of course. But in addition, it should not be overlooked that libraries also may serve as a *source* of sociological data—that is, in our earlier terminology, second-level data. (For example, the number of books on a given topic as an indicator of community tastes, or a comparison of social characteristics of successful authors in two different periods of time.) With the emphasis on "empiricism" in recent years it has become almost unfashionable to undertake "library research" and consequently, this kind of data is often neglected.

A final note on the use of archival data. Since these are generally third-level data as compared to all the others we have discussed, which are second-level, there is a greater likelihood that archival data will contain "built-in" errors.

The third type is *simulated* data, meaning any kind of data which is the product of a simulation process. In the usual context of simulation today, these data will consist of computer outputs. While simulated data have considerable potential for sociological research, simulation has not yet achieved wide use. The nature of such data will be clearer after the discussion of simulation in Chapter 13.

Reflection upon these five types of sociological data (verbal behavior in response to questions, all other behavior and characteristics, physical traces, archives, and simulated) shows the not-surprising fact that, in general each type of data is associated with different methods of data collection. These will be considered in the following chapters, after a few more general comments about data.

CHARACTERISTICS AND SELECTION OF DATA

As pointed out in our earlier discussion of definitions and indicators, the raw data of research consist of objective, observable referents or of indicators. And we have also seen that the use of multiple forms of data and data collection is highly to be recommended. It may be that all the raw data of the research have already been completely identified, in the process of constructing definitions, but if not it must be done before proceeding any further. These raw data—whether observable referents or indicators—may consist of any of the previously discussed five types. Considerable ingenuity may be exercised here in identifying different forms of data which will bear upon the problem, and also in identifying the location of these data. (Are they to be found residing in individual people, in groups, in families, in archives, in interaction situations, in simulators, etc.?) It is also well to remember that there is frequently a considerable amount of emotional involvement—on the part of the researcher, his subjects, and his audience—in the raw data of sociological research. People tend to become much more emotional about things like religion, sexual behavior, political behavior, or the treatment of criminals, than they do about the currents flowing through wires, balls rolling down inclined planes, the temperature of a chemical reaction, and other data with which the physical scientist deals.

Whatever the data, it is probable that the researcher will not be able to use all that is available, but must, in some way, make a selection from it. One way of achieving this is by *sampling*, an idea which was introduced in the previous chapter and which will be more fully discussed later. Another useful means of selecting from among the available data is through the use of a *cohort*, which is "the aggregate of individuals (within some population definition) who experienced the same event within the same time interval."[5] Cohorts have mostly been used for studying people who were born, or married, within the same year, but the concept could just as well be applied to the study

[5] Ryder, 1965, p. 845.

of all those entering school, or a career, or who travelled abroad, or who experienced any other event at the same time. Whether or not a cohort will be a useful device depends, of course, upon the research objectives. The use of *"insight-stimulating"* examples is another means of selection, especially for descriptive research.[6] For example, the reactions of strangers, newcomers, or marginal individuals who are moving from one group to another may point out group characteristics which might otherwise be overlooked. Similarly, individuals or groups in transition from one developmental stage to another may provide useful insights, and so may deviants, isolates, or pathological cases. The study of "pure" cases of some phenomenon, when available, may also prove very useful. Also, individuals who fit well in a given situation, those who do not fit well, those who represent different positions in the social structure, and finally, self-study by the researcher—all of these may be constructive means of selecting from among the total body of available data. Again, the researcher's common sense and ingenuity, will suggest other means of deciding just what data will be utilized.

A special kind of selection problem frequently exists when the data are of the first type —human behavior and characteristics. Obtaining the necessary cooperation of human individuals—whether for an interview or some other kind of data collection—frequently turns out to be a very frustrating experience. The general public simply cannot be counted upon to have the same interest, desire, and motivation to contribute to scientific knowledge (or to the researcher's progress toward a Ph.D.) that the researcher has. Interviews are refused for countless reasons. It may prove not only surprising, but perhaps devastating, to find that students will not volunteer to take part in an experiment, or that even the incentive of money will be insufficient to attract enough subjects. Some years ago the author attempted to hire about two dozen students to participate in some research at a small state college where poverty was a particularly acute problem among the students as well as the surrounding community. The project was well-advertised, required only a small amount of time at the student's convenience, would not cause him discomfort or embarrassment, and the rate of pay was about 50 percent higher than the going campus rate.

[6] Selltiz et al., 1959, pp. 59–65.

Yet out of a student body of approximately 2,000, it was not possible to obtain more than about 10 volunteers! Undoubtedly many reasons exist for this kind of difficulty—fear, apathy, who knows?—but the researcher must anticipate the problem when selecting the data.

EXERCISES

1. In a study of the relationship between age of driver and attitudes toward the recently lowered speed limit on a given state turnpike, a researcher decides to collect data (using appropriate sampling) of two types: verbal behavior and archival. For each type give some specific examples of data he might collect to carry out his study.
2. In a study of family decision-making a researcher hypothesizes that in formal structured situations the father is most likely to make decisions binding upon family members and in informal unstructured situations the mother is most likely to make decisions binding upon family members. To test his hypothesis the researcher decides to collect data of three types: verbal behavior in response to questions, other overt behavior and characteristics, and simulated. For each type give some specific examples of data he might collect to carry out his study.
3. In a study of the effects of using advertising using the "celebrity identification" approach on actual contributions to a nationwide research program to eradicate a crippling disease, a researcher decides to collect data of two types: overt, non-verbal behavior and physical traces. For each type give some specific examples of data the researcher might collect to carry out his study.
4. As discussed in this chapter, obtaining volunteers for studies and securing their cooperation in providing data for a study is one of the difficult problems in the research process. Suppose you were the researcher in each of the studies outlined above. Assume that in each case you have adequately chosen a sample of potential respondents. Next, describe how you would proceed in meeting the problem of obtaining their cooperation.

Chapter 11

Data collection: Questioning

As mentioned in the previous chapter, the five different types of sociological data may be associated with five different methods of data collection. The first of these will be described in this chapter and the others in the next two chapters.

INTERVIEWS AND QUESTIONNAIRES

The most common form of data collection used by sociologists is asking questions of people, the data being, of course, the oral or written responses. If the researcher does this questioning in a situation that necessarily involves direct interaction between himself and his subject, *during* the data collection—whether in a face-to-face situation or by telephone, and whether with a single individual or a group—the situation is known as an *interview*. The research to measure the public's attitudes toward, and knowledge about heart disease—referred to previously and described in Appendix B—is an example of the use of face-to-face interviews.

Sometimes the questioning takes place *without* the necessity of any direct interaction between the researcher and the subjects during the actual data collection. Examples include questioning by mail and face-to-face situations (again, with either an individual or a group) where the subject(s) simply write(s) out the required information. Although interaction *may* take place, as in giving instructions to the subject, it is not an *essential* part of the actual data collection. This form of data collection is known as the questionnaire. (We think it is important to distinguish between the data collection method which makes use of a questionnaire, and the questionnaire itself. However, the custom in contemporary sociology is to use the one term for both referents, so we bow to this custom with the hope that the reader will heed the distinction.)

As mentioned previously, interviews or questionnaires are used for data collection in the great majority of sample surveys, and in many other designs as well. Most studies of attitudes use questioning as the primary means of data collection.[1] Questioning also may be used to collect a wide variety of other kinds of data—demographic and other factual information, beliefs, knowledge, opinions, feelings, information about present or past behavior, the reasons for present or past behavior, information about the characteristics of groups and organizations of which the individual is a member, and so on. Information about personal or private behavior such as sexual activities, religious practices, or voting patterns, and about unobservables such as feelings, beliefs, and dreams, and about events which took place in the past, and about deviant behavior, may well be obtainable *only* by means of one of these kinds of questioning.

Interviews

Interviews may vary in several ways. As indicated above, the researcher may interview one individual at a time or several people simultaneously. The latter procedure is not so commonly used, but would most likely be useful for collecting information from a whole family, etc. Interviews are also most commonly conducted in a face-to-face situation. (Some special comments will be made later about telephone interviews.) One of the most important ways that interviews may vary is on the continuum from *structured* to relatively *unstructured* in format. This refers to the degree of structure, or flexibility, or rigidity in the interview. At the one extreme, a structured interview will present exactly the same stimuli, insofar as this is possible, to every respondent (the person being questioned). This means that the precise wording and sequence of the questions will be specified in advance, with no deviation permitted. It also implies that the respondent's replies will be in terms of *fixed alternatives,* a limited number of predetermined responses of which the respondent selects one. Furthermore, in a structured interview

[1] See W. A. Scott, 1968, for a comprehensive review of attitude measurement.

the interviewer strives to avoid giving any additional information or explanations to the respondent.

In an unstructured or *depth* interview, on the other hand, the interviewer is permitted—in fact, encouraged—to vary the manner and wording of the questions in order to suit the peculiarities of the situation, and he may follow up on opportunities suggested by the respondent's replies. (The most unstructured form of interview is the psychoanalytic interview, usually characterized by free association in which the respondent is free to report anything whatsoever that comes to his mind, with no set topic or subject. These, however, are rarely used for sociological research, nor are other kinds of clinical interviews.) In an unstructured interview the interviewer will use *open-end* questions, in which the respondent is free to reply in his own words.

Fixed-alternative and open-end questions on the same topic may be illustrated by the following:

Fixed-alternative

Which one of the following do you think is the most serious health problem facing our nation today?

1. Tuberculosis.
2. Heart disease.
3. Cancer.
4. Muscular dystrophy.
5. Mental illness.
6. Arthritis and rheumatism.
7. Polio.
8. Cerebral palsy.
9. Drug addiction.
10. Alcoholism.

Open-end

What do you think is the most serious health problem facing our nation today?

Fixed-alternative questions have the obvious advantage of permitting relatively easy tabulation of the responses from many respondents. However, they do not permit the respondent to give his own replies, and there is no assurance that the predetermined responses will include the one he believes to be correct. Furthermore, the respondent is forced to select from among a limited number of possibilities and is not given the opportunity to qualify or elaborate upon his reply. The open-end question, on the other hand, enables the respondent to reply in exactly his own words. One difficulty, however, is that this puts a much greater burden upon the interviewer who must endeavor to record verbatim all that the respondent says, and with the unusually garrulous respondent this can become a real problem. The analysis and tabulation of such data are also much more difficult, since categories must be established into which the multitude of possible responses may be placed. Finally, the use of open-end questions requires a more skilled and highly trained interviewer who must ensure that he obtains the needed kinds of responses and not merely a lot of verbiage. He must be able to follow up any reply with *probe* questions, designed to elicit further and deeper information from the respondent. These comments about the differences between the use of the two kinds of questions also apply to the two kinds of interviews, structured and unstructured.

Another way in which the two types of interviews vary is in the amount of inference which the interviewer will make. The research requirements may permit a skilled interviewer in an unstructured interview to make some inferences along with his recording of the respondent's words, thus shedding some light upon the respondent's emotional state, etc.

In actual practice an interview may fall between the two polar extremes, and may utilize both kinds of questions. In fact, this is probably the typical research situation. Much will depend upon the subject matter of the interview, the more personal and psychologically deeper kinds of material being elicited more effectively in an unstructured interview.[2]

A special form of interview, developed by Merton and Kendall for studying the effects of mass communication, is the *focused* interview.[3] The "focus" of such an interview is on some particular experience which the respondent is known to have had. In their mass communication studies this consisted of a radio program the respondent had heard, a film he had seen, or some printed matter he had read. The researcher had previously analyzed the content of the experience. Thus he could study the subjective experiences of the respondent and compare these with the objective stimuli to which the respondent was exposed.

---

[2] For a further discussion of structured and unstructured interviews, see Selltiz, chap. 7.

[3] Merton and Kendall, 1955. See also Merton, Fiske, and Kendall, 1956.

Focused interviews are not, of course, limited to mass communication studies, but may be used in studying the effects and characteristics of any known previous experience.

A telephone interview differs from a face-to-face interview in some important ways. Generally it must be quite short since people may become impatient or suspicious, and/or give inaccurate responses. Therefore it is usually suitable only for relatively superficial questions, and probably the most common use has been in audience surveys for television and radio. In these the respondent is asked what program, if any, he is watching (listening to) at the time, and a few other related questions. However, there have been some studies which successfully have obtained rather personal information. One research team conducted telephone interviews with a probability sample of the adult U.S. population with regard to beliefs and practices concerning a series of health problems.[4] The interviews lasted about five minutes but included questions on toothbrushing on the previous day, recent visits to dentists and physicians, and certain medical tests. It must be noted, however, that all the respondents had previously been interviewed personally on similar topics 16 months earlier, and they all had received letters advising of the forthcoming telephone interview two weeks ahead. In this case, the researchers found very low refusal rates and the data obtained were consistent with what had previously been obtained in the face-to-face interviews.

Telephone interviews tend to be relatively structured since there is only limited opportunity for the interviewer to attempt to probe into any subconscious or personal factors, and almost no opportunity to establish rapport with the respondent. An advantage is that they are very inexpensive since no travel costs are involved, and because one interviewer can complete so many in a given length of time. Even long distance calling may be relatively inexpensive, as in the above example. Sampling problems are frequently involved, however, since not all households or businesses have telephones. In 1974, in the United States, 6 percent of households had no telephone service, and in many parts of the country, as well as in other countries, the figure may be much higher.

---

[4] Kegeles, Fink, and Kirscht, 1969. For a full, albeit dated, discussion of the techniques, advantages, and disadvantages of telephone interviewing, see Parten, 1950.

Questionnaire data collection

Data collections by questionnaire, since they do not necessarily involve interaction between the researcher and respondent, have some significant differences from interviews. As with interviews, they may be conducted with one or more than one person at a time, they may or may not be conducted in a face-to-face situation, and they may be more or less structured. However, in an unstructured questionnaire data collection there is no opportunity for the researcher to follow up on the responses he gets nor to do any probing, nor to ask any questions for purpose of clarification of misunderstandings. He must be prepared to accept whatever responses the respondent writes, and must be prepared to analyze them in some suitable manner. For these reasons, questionnaires are not so commonly used as interviews when personal, complicated, or sensitive material is desired.

A typical questionnaire situation is found in the common practice of administering a questionnaire (or other paper-and-pencil "test" or inventory) to a group of people simultaneously —in a classroom, at a meeting, or in some similar situation. The study comparing personality characteristics of Republicans and Democrats, which was described in the section on designs for descriptive studies in Chapter 8, is an example of data collection by questionnaire. There may be interaction between researcher and subjects while the procedures are explained and instructions given, but in the actual data collection the respondent responds only, or primarily, to the written stimuli of the questionnaire. Since questionnaires lend themselves so well to group situations, they represent a relatively easy and economical means of obtaining information. The skills required of the data collector are not as complex as those needed by a well-trained interviewer, and the advantage of being able to obtain information from relatively large numbers of people simultaneously is an important factor.

Questioning by mail presents some unique advantages and disadvantages. As with telephone interviews, one of the chief advantages is the relatively low cost. In a population which is geographically scattered over a very wide area this may be the only practical means of collecting data, regardless of any other advantages or disadvantages involved. If, for example, one wanted to collect data from a sample of all the members of the American Sociological Association, which has members residing in more than 70 foreign countries in addition to the United States and Canada, interviewing would be out of the question.

In contrast to an interview situation, or a face-to-face questionnaire data collection, a mail survey has only the most minimum opportunity to secure the cooperation of the respondent. A covering letter of explanation is always included (or perhaps it forms the introductory portion of the questionnaire), and the impression which the respondent gains from a (frequently) casual reading of this is what will determine whether or not he will respond or throw it in the wastebasket. Thus not only the covering letter but the appearance and, especially, the length of the questionnaire may be decisive factors. Even the most cooperative person may be deterred from replying by a lengthy or complicated questionnaire. If a glance at the questionnaire gives the impression that it can be easily or quickly completed, this may make the difference. On the other hand, if it looks as though it will require a great deal of pondering, writing, and decision making, the respondent may well be inclined to set it aside until "later when I'll have more time." Of course, "later" never arrives, especially for busy people, and so the questionnaire may be forgotten.

Related to this is the fact that responses may be biased, insofar as it is the busy people who refrain from replying, while the replies which are received may overrepresent those respondents who have "nothing better to do" than fill out questionnaires. It is also known that respondents with intense opinions are more likely to reply to a mail questionnaire, and there are other differences in response rate according to such factors as education and economic class.

Overall response rates with the general public tend to be low with mailed questionnaires, generally running below 40 percent. In 1964, *Trans-Action* magazine undertook a mail survey of all the individual subscribers to the *American Sociological Review* to study sociologists' attitudes toward their profession, and obtained approximately 51 percent replies.[5] With specialized populations (e.g., those known to be interested or involved in the specific subject matter), on the other hand, response rates may run to 90 percent or higher. There is evidence that, under

[5] J. Timothy Sprehe, personal communication, Feb. 28, 1972.

some circumstances, even with subject matter of a very general nature, response rates of about 75 percent can be achieved through careful attention to every detail of the data collection. Among other things this includes the physical appearance of the questionnaire, the wording and order of the questions, and especially an intensive followup of the first mailing with as many as three subsequent mailings, even using certified mail.[6] The low response rates and the likelihood of biased responses may prove to be almost insurmountable obstacles under some circumstances, and these disadvantages should be borne in mind whenever considering use of a mail questionnaire. On the other hand, as pointed out before, these problems may be outweighed by the advantages of the method.[7]

Limitations of questioning

Questioning as a method of data collection has probably contributed more to the advancement of sociology than other data collection methods. Yet questioning is suitable only to certain kinds of research, and for obtaining certain kinds of information. *It must never be forgotten that the data collected by questioning consist only of verbal behavior,* and furthermore, that the sociological and psychological literature provides ample evidence that the relation between verbal behavior and other forms of behavior is neither simple nor completely known. Inasmuch as sociology *is* concerned with other forms of overt behavior, and more particularly with social behavior and interaction, this limitation of the questioning method must not be overlooked. In addition,

> Interviews and questionnaires intrude as a foreign element into the social setting they would describe, they create as well as measure attitudes, they elicit atypical roles and responses, they are limited to those who are accessible and will cooperate, and the responses obtained are produced in part by dimensions of individual differences irrelevant to the topic at hand.[8]

The comment, "If I want to learn about your behavior I'd much rather observe it myself than have you describe it to me"

[6] Manheim, 1961, p. 5; Catton, 1965, p. 76; Dillman et al., 1974.

[7] For a useful discussion of the techniques of conducting a mail survey, see Babbie, 1973, chap. 8. See also Parten, 1950, chap. 11; Goode and Hatt, 1952, chap. 12; McDonagh and Rosenblum, 1965; Robin, 1965; and F. Scott, 1957.

[8] Webb et al., 1966, p. 1.

may seem cynical, but it is a view which merits consideration by the careful researcher. This is not to say that questioning should not be used—there is no substitute for face-to-face interaction—but rather that its limitations should be clearly kept in mind. More important, this means of data collection should be *combined* with other methods, if the researcher wants to get anything like a comprehensive picture.

We now turn to a consideration of some of the instruments and techniques used in this form of data collection.[9]

SCHEDULES AND QUESTIONNAIRES

The set of questions which the interviewer will ask when conducting an interview is usually printed or otherwise duplicated, and the interviewer himself records the answers to the questions directly on the form. Such a form is known as an *interview schedule*, or simply a *schedule*. This is distinguished from a *questionnaire*, which is a similar set of questions designed to be self-administered, that is, filled out by the respondent. Both are constructed so as to elicit the required information from the respondent in a cordial and efficient manner—a considerably more exacting task than may at first be apparent. In the more extremely unstructured interviews an *interview guide* may be used, which is simply a list of questions or topics which the interviewer is expected to cover, with a considerable amount of leeway permitted as to just how the topics should be handled.

The fact that a schedule is usually intended for the eyes of a trained interviewer, whereas the questionnaire is to be seen by the respondent, necessitates certain differences in their construction. Physical appearance and attractiveness are more important for the questionnaire than the schedule since this may prove a major factor in securing the respondent's cooperation; similarly with a questionnaire which appears to be short and easily completed. The wording of a questionnaire must be such

[9] For the student desirous of more detailed and exhaustive treatments of all aspects of questioning, there are four references which are especially to be recommended: (1) Babbie, 1973: a thorough coverage of all aspects of survey research; (2) Backstrom and Hursh, 1963: a brief and easily understood book with practical suggestions for survey design and data collection; (3) Cannell and Kahn, 1968: an extremely thorough and systematic compilation of extant knowledge about interviewing, with a slight emphasis on psychological viewpoints; (4) Parten, 1950: although this is somewhat dated it is still a very complete source of practical instructions on all phases of the subject.

as to be easily understood by the respondents for whom it is intended, with no opportunity for clarification or explanation. On the other hand, a schedule may contain relatively complicated instructions to the interviewer for asking certain groups of questions in the event that certain answers are received on previous questions, and so on. Aside from differences such as these, however, the construction of schedules and questionnaires involves essentially the same considerations, and the following comments apply to both.

Physical appearance and size are important insofar as these contribute to legibility, clarity, and ease of handling and filing. Three types of questions are usually included: information which identifies the particular interview and interviewer; demographic information such as age, sex, marital status, education, occupation, and income; and the substantive questions which are the focus of the questioning. The sequence of these three kinds of questions, as well as the sequence of questions within each of these three categories, is important. There should be some kind of logical pattern to the questions, personal or sensitive questions must be located so as to be least likely to provoke resentment or resistance, early questions should be so designed as to lead the respondent easily into the interview, and transition from one kind of question to another must be accomplished smoothly.

Questions should be worded simply, concisely, and unambiguously. (The classic example of ambiguity is the seemingly innocuous questionnaire instruction, "Check your sex," where "check" may be variously interpreted as meaning: restrain, verify, or indicate.) One should also usually avoid using words with emotional connotations. The content of the questions is another crucial factor. Questions must be so selected as to obtain all the needed data, but on the other hand the tendency to include extra questions just because they "sound interesting" should be avoided. Each question must justify its inclusion in the schedule by making a direct contribution to the hypothesis or research problem. Perhaps the only exception to this is for questions which are included simply as devices to change the respondent's train of thought to a new topic. The length of the schedule or questionnaire should be kept within reason, according to the subject matter and the respondents. One half hour is commonly thought of as a reasonable maximum time for an interview. The opening and closing statements (including thanks to the respondent) should be included, especially in questionnaires, and provision should be made in schedules for the interviewer to make any comments he considers to be of importance. In both types it is frequently valuable to encourage the respondent to amplify or qualify his responses, although this may not always be desirable. Finally, if the data-processing and tabulation procedures are anticipated appropriately when constructing the schedule or questionnaire, great amounts of subsequent labor may be avoided. Such *precoding* and other related procedures will be discussed later.

Regardless of the amount of care and skill which have gone into the construction of the schedule or questionnaire, there will still be some ambiguities, confusing questions, and inefficient questions. In order to identify these, the instrument must be *pretested.* This is done by administering it to a number of people who are *similar* to those who will actually be studied later, under conditions which are as near as possible to the actual interview or questionnairing situation. Never should the pretest be done on the actual research subjects or respondents, nor on people who are likely to discuss the interview with the research subjects. The pretesting will turn up ambiguous and confusing questions. Also, if everyone responds the same way to a given item it *may* mean that the question is useless or unnecessary. On the other hand if there are many "don't know" responses or refusals to answer, it may indicate a poorly worded or offensive question.

Checks for the reliability and validity of the instrument, as described in Chapter 8, should also be made. According to the subject matter of the questioning, these may vary in importance.[10]

Although *projective techniques* are more appropriate for psychological than for sociological research, we should take note of them. While these may fit the definition of interview schedules, they are sufficiently unique to be considered separately. Projective techniques are characterized by the presentation to the subject of an ambiguous stimulus, his response to this stimulus

[10] Details of most of these steps in schedule and questionnaire construction are given in Babbie, 1973, chap. 7, and Parten, 1950, chap. 6. Another very complete coverage, especially for the beginner, is Oppenheim, 1966. See also Goode and Hatt, 1952, chap. 11, and, Selltiz et al., 1959, Appendix C. An outline especially for mail questionnaires is contained in D. Miller, 1970, pp. 76–84.

being taken as data pertaining to his self-perception and other basic aspects of his personality. Projective techniques have been most widely used for clinical diagnosis, and some of them require a considerable amount of training for successful use. One of the most familiar examples is the Rorschach test, in which the subject describes what he sees in a series of ink blots. In the Thematic Apperception Test (TAT) the ambiguous stimuli consist of a series of pictures and the subject is asked to tell a story about each one. In the sentence completion test, the subject is asked to complete a sentence starting off with, for example, "I wish that . . ." or "People my age should . . .". Similarly, in the word association test, the subject is asked to respond immediately with the first word that comes to mind after he is presented with each of a series of standard stimulus words. In addition to their wide use for diagnosis, projective tests have also successfully been used in cross-cultural studies of personality (see section on cross-cultural research in Chapter 9) and in studies of social attitudes.[11]

INTERVIEWING

The interview itself may vary from a very brief, structured one requiring only a minimum of training of the interviewer, to a lengthy, relatively complicated session lasting perhaps as long as a few hours. The latter demands considerable skill and experience on the part of the interviewer. In surveys involving these more complex interviews, especially those large enough to use several interviewers, the interviewer training program may frequently be combined with the interview schedule pretesting. Following are some general procedures for the typical interview.

Whenever the interviewer will be interviewing strangers, he should be provided with a letter of introduction from the responsible person of the research project. This may be the director of the project, a classroom teacher, the university department chairman, or someone of similar position. The letter will serve to authenticate the interviewer's reasons for "intruding" into the personal life of the respondent. He should, of course, carry with him the necessary pens, clipboard, and other equipment, and should present a favorable physical appearance.

[11] See Selltiz et al., 1959, chap. 8.

The first thing the interviewer must do is to ensure that he has located the desired respondent. Sometimes his instructions will be to conduct an interview at a specific address, and perhaps with a specific individual at that address. He must determine that he has, in fact, found the correct address, and that the respondent is the correct one. This may mean asking the individual whether he is of a certain age, whether he is a resident of that address, etc., and it may mean returning at a later time to interview the desired person.

Sometimes the time and day of the interview will be specified in advance, but more often these are at the option of the interviewer. Depending upon local custom, certain times and/or days may be preferable to others. In some cultures, for example, the custom of an afternoon nap or siesta makes these hours undesirable for interviewing. Morning hours may find the housewife at home, but resistant to interruption because of her household activities. Working men may be absent from home most of the day, but again, depending upon local practices and distances, may be home at lunch time. People who work nights or other unusual hours may sleep during the day. Early evening hours may be more likely to find people at home, but effort should be made to avoid interrupting the dinner hour. Sundays and holidays are usually undesirable times for interviewing, but in some cases may prove to be desirable. Interviews conducted in work or school or other situations, instead of at home, will have their own good and bad times. Common sense and knowledge of local circumstances will be important in making these kinds of decisions. If the research design permits, making an advance appointment for an interview may be the best procedure providing that it is not important to conduct the interview without the respondent having the opportunity to think about the subject in advance.

The door-to-door salesman is so common in the United States—and generally so unwelcome—that it is important for the interviewer to avoid giving the impression that he may be a salesman. His appearance, manner, mode of dress, and the materials he is carrying, may all be taken into account in avoiding this impression. In his initial interaction with the respondent he must establish the fact that his presence is connected with some legitimate research activity, and he must attempt to establish sufficient rapport with the respondent so that the latter will agree to the interview. However, every interviewer will encounter some respondents who refuse, regardless of how convincing the interviewer may be, and he must expect this and not allow himself to feel either discouraged or angry. Sometimes it may even be that the interviewer will find himself the target of some hostility from the proposed respondent, but a skilled interviewer who manages not to let his ego become involved may be able to turn this into a successful interview.

In conducting the interview the immediate environment can be important. Some interviews can be handled successfully while just standing at the door, but for others—especially longer ones or those which require the respondent to do some writing—it is preferable to sit down. Interference from other people is frequently the most bothersome environmental factor and may require great tact on the interviewer's part. Regardless of such interference, the interviewer must follow his instructions as carefully and accurately as possible, and should make a note of any unavoidable deviations. The responses should be recorded not only accurately but legibly, and at the time of the interview, not later.

Without fail, the interviewer should thank the respondent at the close of the interview and do anything he can to ensure that the respondent is left with a favorable image of not only this particular interview but research interviews in general.

Appendix D consists of a set of interviewer instructions which were used in the heart disease study mentioned earlier. These may serve as a useful illustration of some of the details of the typical survey interview conducted in the respondent's home and lasting about a half hour.[12]

The more unstructured interviews require somewhat different techniques in the actual conduct of the interview, although the general procedures, the locating and approaching of the respondent, and the closing, may be quite similar.[13] Among the additional problems presented by the unstructured interview are: ensuring that all the necessary points are covered and questions asked, encouraging and facilitating complete and open responses on the part of the respondent, and recording the responses. Since the interview schedule may be very general in

---

[12] For a comprehensive and very useful book on interviewing, see Gordon, 1969. See also Babbie, 1973, chap. 9; Parten, 1950, chap. 10; and Goode and Hatt, 1952, chap. 13.

[13] For practical suggestions on conducting such interviews, see Whyte, 1960.

form, and the sequence of asking questions may be entirely determined by the interviewer at the time of the interview, he must have some means to be certain that he obtains all the required information. Perhaps a skilled interviewer can rely upon his memory, but more likely a checklist, at least, will be needed. Since open-end questions are used, the respondent's replies may be lengthy, devious, or completely off the subject. This will necessitate the interviewer's judiciously asking probing questions, or interrupting, or bringing the respondent back to the subject, without offending him.

The recording of the responses in an unstructured interview presents a problem since they tend to be so much lengthier than with fixed-alternative questions. The use of a tape recorder may inhibit the respondent, although there is disagreement as to just how widespread this effect is, and using a hidden recorder of course presents serious ethical problems. Accurate and complete note-taking during the course of the interview may require that the interviewer frequently has to ask the respondent to repeat his remarks, and this may slow down the interview considerably. On the other hand, trying to depend upon memory and write up the notes after the completion of the interview will probably result in the loss of much of the data.

Some kinds of interviews, because of their unusual length or format, may require different procedures and more specialized training. Nondirective interviews, in particular, were developed by Carl Rogers as part of his nondirective, or client-centered, therapy. As a technique for use in sociological research interviews, the nondirective approach has its greatest use in encouraging a free and spontaneous flow of deep-seated ideas and feelings, without any more than the minimum of stimulus (direction) from the interviewer. The essence of the technique is that the interviewer presents a neutral image to the respondent, and by the use of appropriate echoings or reflections of the respondent's ideas, or expressions of understanding and interest, or "expectant pauses," he encourages the respondent to probe deeper into his own thinking, and to amplify his responses.[14] For example, if the respondent states "I've worked here for two months now and still have to eat lunch by myself," the nondirective interviewer might respond with "You still have to eat by yourself." The expectation is that this would encourage the re-

[14] Rogers, 1942, and Rogers, 1945.

spondent to say more about his attitudes and feelings toward his work group (assuming this was one of the purposes of the interview).

Special interviewing procedures may also be called for when interviewing elite or other specialized categories of respondents such as political candidates, government officials, heads of state, justices of high courts, diplomats, lawyers, physicians, corporate heads, and the very wealthy.[15]

Regardless of the nature of the interview—whether structured, unstructured, long, short, nondirective, or whatever—it will always involve interaction between respondent and interviewer, and this very interaction may itself be a biasing factor in data collection. Remember that the purpose of the interview is to obtain certain data in the form of verbal behavior. The verbal behavior *desired* consists of responses to questions or other stimuli put by the interviewer. But since an interview is an interaction situation, the stimuli actually received by the respondent consist not only of the question itself but also the entire body of stimuli presented by the interviewer (as well as the immediate environment of the interview). Thus it includes all the physical characteristics and appearance of the interviewer (age, sex, race, stature, physiognomy, deformities and scars, height, weight, hair, attractiveness, dress, and so on), demeanor, language patterns, gestures, and all the other countless stimuli given by the interviewer, as well as the questions themselves. Not only are all these stimuli of great intrinsic importance, but even more important is the respondent's perception of them and of the entire situation, or in other words his role expectations. Especially in a society such as the United States, where interviewing has become a familiar aspect of ordinary life, there is ample reason to think that the role of interviewee or respondent carries with it a whole set of expectations, some of which may be acting at cross purposes with the research needs.

Thus it is clear that the response given by the respondent is a result not only of the question put to him, but also of his perceptions of all these other stimuli and roles. Furthermore, the interviewer's behavior, in turn, must be affected by all the similar stimuli he receives from the respondent, as well as his perceptions of them and of the appropriate roles, and these, of course, may well have an impact upon the manner in which he proceeds

[15] See Dexter, 1970.

with the interview. To be sure, the skilled interviewer, being aware of these factors, attempts to compensate for them, but there is an obvious limit to the extent to which this can be accomplished. An extreme case of such biasing factors is the situation in which the respondent deliberately falsifies his answers.[16] The biasing effects of this interviewer-respondent interaction can be so serious that we hypothesize that to the extent that interaction takes place in a data collection situation, it is a disruptive factor in objective research. Considerable attention has been devoted to such factors in recent years. It should be noted that similar comments apply to any interaction between researcher and subject—this is not limited to the interview situation.[17]

SOCIOMETRY

Although *sociometry* makes use of a questionnaire, as defined above, we treat it separately because it differs so much from other questionnaires and because sociometric and related techniques have been so very widely used since they were first developed by Moreno in the 1930s.[18] The most complete, comprehensive, and up-to-date coverage of all aspects of sociometry, including an extensive review of the literature, is contained in the article by Lindzey and Byrne, and some of the following comments draw upon this source.[19]

Basically, sociometry is a method of ascertaining the choices and/or rejections which the members of a group express toward one another. The individual members are asked, privately, to name the other group members with whom they would prefer (would prefer not) to engage in some specified activity, such as membership on a committee, sharing a social activity, having as a co-worker, or perhaps simply liking and disliking. The results of this questioning may be very illuminating with regard to group organization and structure, internal social relationships,

---

[16] See Farber, 1963, and Harper, 1973.

[17] The most comprehensive view of this is in Hyman et al., 1975. See also: Cannell and Kahn, 1968; Rosenthal, 1966; Riecken, 1962; and Cannell and Fowler, 1964.

[18] Moreno, 1953. See Moreno, 1960, for a collection of articles on sociometry. The journal *Sociometry* was founded by Moreno in 1937 and was devoted to articles pertaining to sociometry; however, since 1956 it has been published by the American Sociological Association and contains articles on all aspects of social psychological research.

[19] Lindzey and Byrne, 1968.

and other characteristics of small social systems. This is a simple, rapid, and inexpensive technique to use; it is suitable to various age levels, and presumably is not culture-bound.[20] It may be used with groups of virtually any kind and of various sizes, although most generally they are small enough to permit face-to-face interaction. The criterion for choices and rejections may be varied to suit the research purposes, and so may the number of choices and rejections which each individual is asked to make. The most important restriction upon the use of sociometric measures is that the privacy of the individuals' responses be respected, and that when, and if, the results are presented to the group it should be impossible for the members to identify specific individuals.

There are several forms in which sociometric data can be presented, the most common being the *sociogram* which is familiar to every student of introductory sociology. A sociogram is a graphical, or pictorial, presentation in which the individuals are represented by symbols, and their choices and rejections expressed by appropriate arrows or lines linking the symbols. Figure 3 is a sociogram showing first choices of a small group of college undergraduates who were asked whom they would like to work with on a group research project. Figure 4 shows both first and second choices for the same group. There are various ways in which these same sociograms could be drawn, since there is no standardization of the symbols and conventions which are in use, and in some cases this leads to considerable variation in the interpretations which can be made from the same data. This is one of the major drawbacks of sociograms, the other being that as the group and the number of choices becomes larger the increasing complexity of the diagram makes it begin to look like a plateful of spaghetti.

An alternative means of presenting the same data, which has the advantages of being both easier to construct and suitable for larger groups, is the *matrix*. In a sociometric matrix, the group members are listed down the left-hand column, and, in the same order, across the top row. Then the choices made and received by each individual are indicated in the appropriate cells, as shown in Figure 5, which presents the same information as Figure 4. Usually the group members are instructed to not choose

[20] Lindzey and Byrne's bibliography lists some half dozen reports of utilization of sociometric techniques in Latin America and Europe.

Figure 3. Sociogram showing first choices (double-headed arrows represent mutual choices)

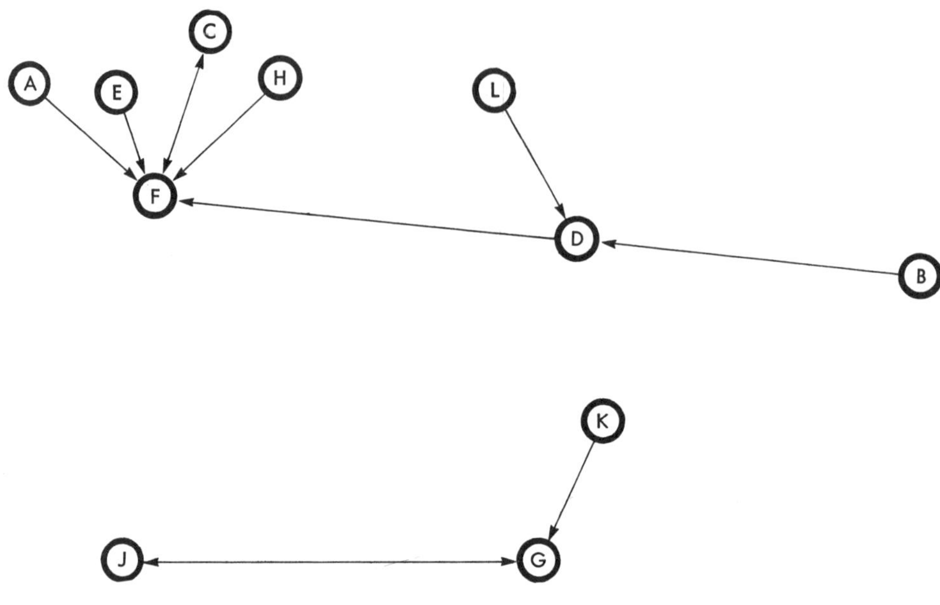

Figure 4. Sociogram showing first and second choices (double-headed arrows represent mutual choices)

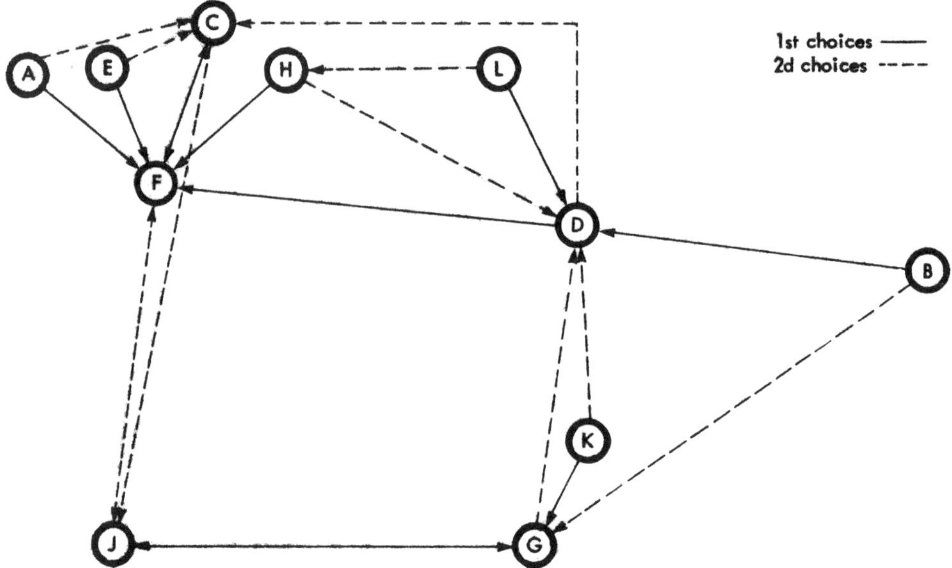

Figure 5. Matrix showing the same data as Figure 4

		Choices received											
		A	B	C	D	E	F	G	H	J	K	L	
Choosers	A			2			1						
	B				1			2					
	C						1			2			
	D			2			1						
	E			2			1						
	F			1						2			
	G				2					1			
	H				2		1						
	J						2	1					
	K				2			1					
	L				1				2				
Number of 1st choices rec'd		0	0	1	2	0	5	2	0	1	0	0	11
Number of 2d choices rec'd		0	0	3	3	0	1	1	1	2	0	0	11
Total choices rec'd		0	0	4	5	0	6	3	1	3	0	0	22

1 = 1st choice.
2 = 2d choice.

(or reject) themselves, and therefore the main diagonal will be empty. The distribution of choices received is easily obtained by adding the figures in each column. If rejections are also shown, appropriate symbols such as minus signs are used. If the number of choices made by each member is not constant, the distribution of these may be obtained by summing across rows.

In addition to these most common means of presenting sociometric data, there are various scores and indices (e.g., ratio of attractions to rejections), statistical methods (e.g., comparisons of the number of choices received by each individual to the number he could be expected to receive by chance), factor analysis, matrix multiplication, and other mathematical techniques.[21] The manipulation of the sociometric matrix by the procedures of matrix algebra indeed holds great promise in the

[21] Lindzey and Byrne, 1968, pp. 463–74; Roistacher, 1974.

analysis of group structure, as does also the use of graph theory.[22]

The research uses of sociometric measures may be divided into two categories, sociometric status and interpersonal attraction. The former consists of "the generalized tendency to evoke positive or negative interpersonal choices from one's peers. . . . [and] establishing the antecedents and correlates of individual differences in this tendency,"[23] and includes such factors as leadership and personal adjustment. The latter deals with the question: "Why is a particular individual attracted or repelled by specified other persons?"[24] and includes studies of propinquity, demographic variables, and prejudice among others. There is a wide range of possible uses for sociometric measures and also a wide variety of means of presenting and analyzing the data, ranging from the simplest to the most complicated. A glance at even such a simple sociogram as Figure 3 shows a possible leader or powerful individual (F), a clique (J, G, and K), and isolates (A, B, E, K, and L).

EXERCISES

1. Suppose you are conducting a descriptive study of students attending your university or college who are "out-of-state" residents. In order to obtain certain data you decide to use a structured interview with fixed alternatives for the following questions:
   a. What is your present classification?
   b. Why did you choose to attend this university?
   c. What are the most disagreeable aspects of attending this university?
   d. What improvements would you like to see made in this university for out-of-state residents?

   List the fixed alternatives you would use for each of the questions and discuss the reasons for your choices.

2. As discussed in this chapter, fixed alternatives facilitate ease of analysis of data once it has been collected, but limit the kind and extent of the responses that may be made. Given this consideration discuss the advantages of *not* using fixed alternatives for the questions listed above.

[22] Flament, 1963; Harary and Norman, 1953.

[23] Lindzey and Byrne, 1968, p. 483.

[24] Ibid., p. 496.

3. In light of the discussion in this chapter of the use of structured and unstructured interviews discuss the advantages and disadvantages of using an *unstructured* interview for the above study.

4. A researcher is testing the hypothesis that male youths aged from 12 to 15 years who feel loved by their mothers are less of a discipline problem in their high schools than those who feel less loved. In a pretest the researcher uses a questionnaire with open-ended responses to determine how loved each youth in his sample feels. The results of the pretest show that responses are generally "I don't know" or "Mom loves me" or the item is left blank. The researcher decides that these responses will be inadequate to test his hypothesis and begins searching for alternative data collection techniques. Suppose that you are the researcher. Decide upon an alternate data collection technique and then briefly outline how your alternative will provide improved results.

5. The following are studies proposed by beginning researchers. In each the researcher plans to use either the interview, questionnaire, or both to collect his data. Suppose you are the researcher. Decide upon the data collection technique you would use to complete each study and discuss the reasons for your decision.
   a. A study of political affiliation and attitudes toward world Communism. The sample will be businessmen who are members of the local chamber of commerce in all towns with populations of 10,000 to 25,000 in your state.
   b. A study of marital happiness and husband's job satisfaction for a 10 percent random sample of a middle class section of a community with a population of 75,000 in your state.
   c. A study of specialized vocabulary use by blue collar workers, and their job satisfaction, in manufacturing firms employing 100 to 150 workers in a nearby metropolitan area in your state.
   d. A study of scholastic success of elementary school children and parental participation in the school's Parent-Teacher Association for all elementary schools in a town of 10,000 in your state.
   e. A study of the relation between socioeconomic status level and participation in the organizational activities of united appeal charities for a 10 percent random sample of heads of households in ten representative blocks in a nearby metropolitan area in your state.

6. At the beginning of each month Congressman Smith in your legislative district sends out a blanket letter and questionnaire to all resident constituents. On last month's questionnaire he asked

whether or not Bill Number 601 on environmental control should be passed. This month Congressman Smith sends out his letter and reports that 85 percent of his district feel that Bill 601 should be passed. In view of the characteristics of mailed questionnaires as discussed in this chapter, discuss the accuracy of Congressman Smith's statement.

7. A researcher is trying to test the hypotheses that females who strongly rebel against their parents as teenagers are more likely to *(a)* marry at younger ages, *(b)* have children soon after getting married and *(c)* get divorced soon after having one or more children. The sample for this study includes about 200 female divorcees of less than 30 years of age, the names of whom are selected from a membership listing of a regional association of divorced persons. To obtain the data necessary to test the hypothesis, the researcher decides to use both the structured and unstructured interview. Suppose you are the researcher. Decide upon a minimum number of questions which could be used to test the hypothesis as stated above and outline briefly how you would proceed in conducting your interview. For the structured portion of your data collection you will need an interview schedule. For the unstructured portion you will need an interview guide.

Chapter 12

Data collection: Direct observation

INTRODUCTION

When the type of research data to be collected consists of interaction, some other overt behavior, or observable characteristics, rather than the verbal behavior discussed in the previous chapter, the data collection method will be some form of *direct observation of human behavior and characteristics.* Of course, *all* scientific data collection involves some kind of observation—whether Tycho Brahe looking at the stars without benefit of telescope, or the nuclear physicist with the most modern and sophisticated equipment; whether the marine biologist tagging fish or the archeologist collecting potsherds; whether the pollster conducting an interview or the social psychologist watching a discussion group through a one-way glass. In fact, much of our ordinary daily life activity consists of some form of observation of our surroundings. We use the term "direct observation" here to indicate our concern with behavior and characteristics which are directly observable, as distinguished from verbal reports of them. (We are *not* making a distinction, as some do, between observation and experiment as two different methods of data collection.[1] As pointed out in our earlier discussion, the distinguishing mark of an experiment is that the researcher's manipulation of some variables presumably affects the phenomena *being observed.* But as far as the *methods of observation* are concerned, it makes little difference whether the phenomena being observed are a result of the researcher's manipulation or occur "naturally.")

[1] See, for example, Weick, 1968, pp. 358–62.

To illustrate what is meant by direct observation: If we are interested in studying kindergarten children's acts of aggression toward one another we might *interview* the teacher (or possibly the children), or we might *directly observe* the children in their play area or schoolroom (with or without manipulation by the researcher), watching for such indicators as hitting, pushing, pinching, hair-pulling, ostracizing, taking playthings, verbal abuse, grimacing and other gestures, and hiding from or avoiding one another. Such observation, however, consists of much more than merely standing around and watching. "Scientific observation is deliberate search, carried out with care and forethought, as contrasted with the casual and largely passive perceptions of everyday life."[2] This implies that the systematic observation which marks the scientific endeavor must be distinguished from anecdotal observation (the casual observation of scattered episodes or phenomena which should not be assumed to be typical). Above all, scientific observation must be accurate, the observer must know what to observe, and he must do the observing objectively. Such observation does not necessarily entail the use of instruments or other aids, although these may be very beneficial when they are available. But it does entail some systematic means of selection from among the vast number of stimuli which are potentially observable. And it also implies that definite steps will be undertaken to ensure the objectivity of the observations.

Part of the problem of achieving objectivity in observation is that the perceptual processes of the observer must always be taken into account. As one writer puts it, "After the moment of the observer's birth no observation can be undertaken in all innocence."[3] The observer's entire psychological history, including his language, socialization, culture, experiences, and so on, necessarily affect his perceptual processes at any given time. More specifically, "Observation of x is shaped by prior knowledge of x," according to Hanson.[4] To use his example, one's prior experience (or lack of it) with X ray tubes will determine whether one *observes* the glass-and-metal object to be: an X ray

---

[2] Kaplan, 1964, p. 126.

[3] Ibid., pp. 132–33.

[4] Hanson, 1965, p. 19. His entire first chapter is devoted to an interesting discussion of observation. For a discussion of observation and the question of physical reality, see Nagel, 1961, pp. 145–52.

tube dangerously overheating, simply an X ray tube, or a complicated lamp bulb. This implies that different observers will not necessarily have the same perceptions of any given phenomenon. Clearly, the above considerations indicate that considerable training and experience may be required for accurate observation and to ensure observer reliability. Various procedures for accomplishing these ends will be outlined later in the chapter.

Observational methods differ from one another along several variables or dimensions, which will now be considered. First is the question of *what* is to be observed. Presumably this decision will already have been made, as discussed in the section on definitions and indicators in the chapter on formulation, and in the early pages of this chapter.

Some observational methods are more *structured* than others. As in the case of interviews, this refers to the degree of formality, rigidity, flexibility, and specificity involved. These variations may occur in the phenomena under observation, or in the selection of which data will be observed, or in the recording of these data. At one extreme, the most structured situation might permit the subjects in a laboratory experiment to engage in only certain precisely specified forms of behavior; the observer might be concerned with only certain aspects of such behavior; and these might be recorded either with some physical equipment (e.g., cameras, tape recorders, other recording devices, counters, etc.) or with some precise checklist or other similar instrument. The other end of the structured/unstructured continuum is exemplified by some forms of social anthropological investigation in which observation is made of a relatively limited group or society in an attempt to provide a complete description of its activities or daily life. The members of the group continue to behave as they ordinarily do, the observer attends to as much of the individuals' behavior as is possible, and the recording consists of a running, anecdotal account of what is observed. The only equipment likely to be used in such a situation consists of tape recorders and cameras. The nature of the data being sought and the research objectives will usually determine how structured the observation methods will be.

Related to the above is the variable of inference (in the ordinary, not the statistical, sense). To what extent will the observer engage in making inferences from the data he observes? Inferences are, of course, one step removed from the data; they are a result of the observer's perceptual processes acting upon the data. The datum, in observing children at play, might consist of "Gerry hit Harold on the arm." A statement making an inference from this would be "Gerry is angry at Harold." An even greater inference would be "Gerry dislikes Harold." These simple examples illustrate the importance of the question of inference. As more inferences are made, the information becomes richer and richer—but also is subject to more and more error. There is not much likelihood of error in recording the basic statement "Gerry hit Harold on the arm," given that the observer is not mentally ill and has adequate vision. But the statement "Gerry is angry at Harold" may or may not be accurate. Certainly the act of hitting may be a friendly gesture, as well as a hostile one, or it may consist of a socially-acceptable and routine sanction against some deviant behavior. To state that "Gerry dislikes Harold" implies that Gerry has an ongoing, temporally stable, attitude toward Harold, which conclusion is not justified on the basis of a single expression of anger. As in so many other cases, we must pay a price for increased benefits. Whether the benefit of the richer data is worth the price of a greater likelihood of error will depend, again, not only on the research objectives but also on the researcher's views on risk-taking.

Another variable on which observation methods differ is whether or not the subjects are aware that they are being observed. If they are aware of it, there is always the possibility that this awareness may have an effect upon the very behavior the observer is interested in. The subjects may get "stage fright," or the simple fact of drawing attention to routine behavior may alter or disrupt the behavior, like the familiar story of the centipede who, when asked about the sequence in which he moved his legs while walking, became so confused trying to figure out the answer that he was rendered completely incapable of walking at all. Furthermore, awareness of being observed may result in the subjects deliberately altering their behavior in order to "cooperate with," or confuse, the researcher. A multitude of means have been used to conceal from the subjects the fact that they are being observed. For example, the researcher might actually join the group (see the following discussion of participant observation). Thus one researcher got a job at a post office in order to study various aspects of interaction among postal employees. Or the researcher may observe interaction from behind a one-way glass or through the use of concealed microphones; or he may observe people's reactions when he invades their "personal space" by sitting or standing "too close" to them.

While concealed research may solve the problems mentioned above, it of course presents ethical questions, most of which were discussed in Chapter 9. Two additional ethical points are particularly pertinent to concealed research.[5] In the first place, the use of concealment would be ethical in cases where the behavior being observed is public behavior anyway, such as in the reactions to invasions of personal space—but could be questioned if the behavior is *not* public, such as in the studies of jury deliberations. Second, in the case of a researcher joining a group for the purpose of studying it without informing the other group members, the ethical question might hinge upon *all* his motives for joining the group. Thus the ethics of a researcher who obtained a post office job because he needed a job, and then decided to study the work group, would not be questioned. But the ethics of a researcher who "joined" a small, informal, friendship group for the sole purpose of doing research upon it, could be questioned. As stated earlier, there is no simple rule—in each case the "profit" from a research method must be weighed against the "cost" of any ethical intrusions.

Very closely related to the question of whether or not there is concealment in the research is the variable of whether the things being observed are taking place in their "natural" setting or in a laboratory or other "artificial" setting. This is the familiar distinction between field research and laboratory research, already discussed.

Two general variables among observational methods remain to be discussed. These are: the extent to which the researcher participates in the situation he is observing, and the specific means whereby the researcher records the data which he observes. Since these two are closely linked to each other they will be discussed together in the next two sections.

PARTICIPANT OBSERVATION

The term *participant observation* has at least three separate meanings in current sociological literature. In one it refers to

[5] Weick, 1968, p. 374.

exploratory research in which either the sociologist has no advance information about the situation, or there are many misconceptions about it, or the situation is so familiar that there are aspects of it which are likely to be overlooked.[6] In the second, "participant observation is most sensibly regarded, operationally, as the blend of methods and techniques that is characteristically employed in studies of social situations or complex social organizations of all sorts."[7] As such it typically involves at least five specific techniques:direct observation, interviewing of informants, interviewing of respondents, analysis of documents, and direct participation. The third—and most widely accepted—view of participant observation is that it is that method in which "the investigator is or becomes a part of the situation he is studying,"[8] over a period of time, either with or without revealing to the members that he is engaged in research. This is the same as the "direct participation" in the second definition, and it is the sense in which the term is used in this book.[9] We do *not* include as participant observation those situations in which the researcher briefly interacts with the subject under some ruse, such as the above-mentioned studies of invasion of personal space.

The method of participant observation has been extensively used in case studies and anthropological research, and indeed, some of the most widely known sociological research falls into this category. One of the best known is Whyte's study of "Cornerville," an Italian slum in the Boston area.[10] Whyte lived in Cornerville for three and a half years, and participated in most of the activities of the groups of young men he was studying. They knew that he was engaged in research, although some had more detailed knowledge of his objectives than did others, and this knowledge seemed not to hamper his research activities in any way. Perhaps it even facilitated them.

---

[6] Blalock, 1970, p. 41.

[7] McCall and Simmons, 1969, p. 3.

[8] Hoult, 1969, p. 233.

[9] Although the definition used here of participant observation is much narrower than that of McCall and Simmons, 1969, their book is highly recommended as the most useful compilation of information on the subject. On data analysis, see Becker and Geer, 1960. For an approach to participant observation quite different from the one presented here, see Bruyn, 1966.

[10] Whyte, 1955. This edition includes a very informative and engagingly written appendix in which Whyte gives details of the methods he used and the experiences he had. For a more recent similar study, see Liebow, 1967.

On the other hand, participant observation when the subjects are not aware that research is being conducted presents practical problems in addition to the ethical problems which have already been discussed. If persons are unaware the research is taking place, it may be very difficult for them to accept the probing and personal questions which may be asked, or the reluctance of the researcher fully to participate in all the group's activities (e.g., illegal or immoral activity), and thus the desired data may not be so readily available. Furthermore, the influence of the researcher upon the group may be extremely difficult to assess under such circumstances. An example of participant observation research in which the members were unaware that research was taking place is the study of a small group of American suburbanites who believed that they had definite information that the world was going to be destroyed by a flood on a certain date.[11] In both of these illustrations the researcher directly participated in the ongoing activities of the groups being studied, which, as we have seen, is the defining criterion of this form of observation. There is no theoretical or general limit to what kinds of groups can be studied by this means, although there are obviously practical limits to gaining entry to some groups (intimate groups such as engaged couples or families, deviant groups such as criminal or "immoral" groups, secret groups such as military or industrial boards of directors, etc.).

The techniques used to record data obtained through participant observation will depend upon whether or not the subjects are aware of the research. If they are, it may be that the maximum use will be made of mechanical aids such as cameras, tape recorders, and video recorders, in addition to note-taking. However, these mechanical aids have certain disadvantages along with their obvious assets. They may be sharply inhibiting to the people under observation. They are expensive, and the transcription of taped material is time-consuming even for the most skilled typist. And any kind of cinema or video process is so dependent upon lighting conditions as to render it unsatisfactory in many circumstances. Concealed participant observation obviously restricts the use of these mechanical aids. It may be that they can be used openly under some pretext or other, and

[11] For a brief account of some of the difficulties of concealed observation, see Riecken, 1956. For a full account of the whole study: Festinger, Riecken, and Schachter, 1956.

there is always the possibility of using hidden cameras and microphones. In the latter case the ethical problems are so extreme as to usually override the advantages of their use.

Thus in most situations ordinary note-taking remains the paramount means of recording data—possibly aided by use of a dictating machine or tape recorder. Also, checklists, coding systems, rating scales, mapping, and the like may be used. Whether notes should be taken during the observation, or only afterward, is a debatable point, and also depends upon the specific research situation. If the notes are not taken during the observation they should be written up as soon as possible afterward—the greater the time lag, the greater the probability of errors or omissions. Regardless of when the notes are taken, the observer must be alert to the question of inference, discussed above.

Participant observation provides the researcher with the opportunity actually to take part in the ordinary activities of the group. He

> receives the same socialization as ordinary members, acquires similar perspectives, and encounters similar experiences. In this way the scientist acquires some sense of the subjective side of events which he could less readily infer if he observed *without* taking part.[12]

This first-hand experience is one of the chief advantages of this method. The researcher obtains data which he could not get otherwise. Probably no amount of interviewing or the use of any other technique of data collection would have provided Whyte with the same insights as he obtained from having joined the other Corner Boys in illegal voting. And the researcher's introspection upon his experiences may also be a valuable source of ideas and hypotheses. Such advantages make this extremely useful for some kinds of research. Indeed, it is hard to imagine an anthropologist studying an isolated tribe or society *without* engaging in participant observation.

The above quotation points to some of the additional problems of this kind of observation. In order to gain knowledge about the subjective side of events by means of participant observation, one must assume a common frame of reference between the observer and the observed—or at least a certain similarity between their frames of reference. These frames of ref-

[12] McCall and Simmons, 1969, pp. 4–5.

erence are, of course, a function of the entire psychological histories of the individuals, and thus include the socialization and the culture which they have experienced. Even in cases where these are essentially the same, they will never be identical. Ultimately, gaining knowledge of subjective events through participant observation is based upon the assumption that *Verstehen* (see section on "retroduction" in Chapter 3) is a legitimate method of data collection—an assumption which we reject, regardless of what other merits *Verstehen* may have.

The length of time occupied by the typical participant observation study may also create problems. The affective bonds which may arise between the observer and the observed are one example, to the extent that they interfere with the observer's role as researcher. This problem is certainly not limited to participant observation, but given the longer period of time that the participant observer interacts with the members of the group, it is reasonable to assume that the effect of affective relationships would be a more acute problem than with the pollster or the laboratory experimenter. Along with these effects of prolonged interaction, the researcher may also find that as he becomes more and more assimilated into the culture he is studying, he increasingly loses his sense of wonder and thus misses many important phenomena. Finally, the mere length of time involved greatly increases the costs of the research.

The most serious problem related to participant observation is occasioned by the participation itself. By definition, the observer interacts with the members of the group being studied and thus he necessarily influences the behavior of the group members (this is what is meant by "interaction") and they influence him. Thus the participant observer is observing a total situation *which includes himself.* To be sure, this is true of any data collection method in which interaction takes place, but the problem is more extreme in participant observation since the observer is acting not only in the role of researcher but also in the role of group member. This presents a two-fold problem. In the first place, the observer cannot help but have some impact upon the situation he observes, no matter how hard he tries not to. To the extent that there is interaction, this influence must exist.[13] Thus the data obtained are not as "pure" as would be

[13] Whyte, 1955, comments upon such difficulties in the appendix of his volume, pp. 335–36.

desired. The other part of the problem is the difficulty—if not impossibility—of the observer maintaining an objective approach to studying a situation which *includes himself*. We hold this to be such a serious obstacle to obtaining accurate and valid data that the researcher should carefully consider alternative means of data collection in designing a project. At least the attempt should be made to supplement the participant observation by some other means of data collection. Again, the objectives of the study will be the deciding factors. We are by no means saying that participant observation should not be used. We are saying only that, as with any other procedure, it is an advantage to the researcher to be clearly aware of the pitfalls he may encounter.

NONPARTICIPANT OBSERVATION

Nonparticipant observation (often referred to simply as "observation") refers to any observation situation in which the researcher does not act as part of the situation which he is observing. He functions only in the role of researcher, although on occasion this role may be disguised. The variety of forms which such observation can take is enormous and limited only by the researcher's inventiveness. Webb et al. describe countless examples of ingenious uses of observation.[14] Nonparticipant observation may be used in such diverse situations as a laboratory experiment, or recording the number of biracial couples on a college campus in a given time period, or recording the content of overheard conversations, or studying the interaction patterns of workers in a factory unit or of boys in a summer camp, or measuring the weight and height of traffic offenders or the seating patterns in a classroom.[15] Much of the recent research subsumed under the labels of "personal space," (such as that described in the earlier section on research ethics), "territoriality," "everyday interaction," and "ethnomethodology" has used nonparticipant observation for data collection.[16]

---

[14] Webb et al., 1966, chaps. 5–6.

[15] In addition to those contained in Webb et al., 1966, there are many examples of nonparticipant observation studies in Hare, Borgatta, and Bales, 1965. Other widely reprinted examples include: the "Hawthorne studies" (Roethlisberger and Dickson, 1939), the "autokinetic effect" studies (Sherif, 1958), the "Asch experiments" (Asch, 1958), the "pajama factory" study (Coch and French, 1968), the "Robbers' Cave summer camp" studies (Sherif and Sherif, 1956), as well as many cultural anthropological studies.

[16] For examples see: Sudnow, 1972; Garfinkel, 1967; Hall, 1966; Sommer, 1969.

The development of some of the specific techniques of observation was given considerable impetus, some years ago, by the increasing interest on the part of sociologists in the objective study of interaction and group processes, as differentiated from individual behavior. Some of the early efforts in this direction include the development of a system for recording interaction in group therapy,[17] a system of scales for measuring the dimensions of groups,[18] a system using the Stenotype shorthand machine for recording interaction,[19] a modification of the TAT for studying group properties,[20] and a paper-and-pencil method for measuring interaction and activities in certain limited situations.[21] As can be noted, these vary in, among other things, the instruments or tools which are used, ranging from relatively simple paper-and-pencil checklists or procedures to the use of machines. More recently the technology in use has expanded considerably, and also includes rating scales ("a scale with a set of points which describe varying degrees of the dimension being observed"),[22] category systems (such as Bales' Interaction Process Analysis, described below), mapping,[23] counting and recording devices, and the more complex and sophisticated electronic equipment, video and photographic equipment, and tape recorders. The development of new instruments proliferates, and each successful one, as it is more and more widely used, *influences* the course of future research.[24] When instruments become available, many researchers turn to problems which are amenable to study by the new instruments. Following is an example of this.

Bales' Interaction Process Analysis (IPA), has had this kind of impact upon recent sociological research, and is one of the most widely used systems for observing interaction.[25] The heart of the system is a series of twelve exhaustive categories into which all interaction occurring in small groups can be placed:

1. Seems friendly.
2. Dramatizes.

---

[17] Joel and Shapiro, 1949.
[18] Hemphill and Westie, 1950.
[19] Carter et al., 1951.
[20] Horwitz and Cartwright, 1953.
[21] Atteslander, 1954.
[22] Heyns and Zander, 1953, p. 393.
[23] Melbin, 1960.
[24] Kaplan, 1964, p. 135.
[25] Bales, 1951.

3. Agrees.
4. Gives suggestion.
5. Gives opinion.
6. Gives information.
7. Asks for information.
8. Asks for opinion.
9. Asks for suggestion.
10. Disagrees.
11. Shows tension.
12. Seems unfriendly.[26]

Bales provides lengthy definitions of these categories, so the above are to be regarded only as labels. One or more trained observers observes the interaction while it is taking place, and on a specially prepared form—or a moving paper tape—records each bit of interaction as it occurs, classifying it into one of the 12 categories and noting who initiated the act and who was the target. Various forms of analyses of such data are possible. The percentage of acts occuring in each category may be graphed as a "profile" of the interaction. Breakdowns can be made for various time periods—say, the beginning of the session, the middle, and the ending. "Who-to-whom" analyses can be made to indicate the kinds and quantities of interaction initiated and received by various group members. Furthermore, the categories themselves may be subdivided as follows: Categories 1 through 3 are Positive (and Mixed) Actions, categories 4 through 6 are Attempted Answers, categories 7 through 9 are Questions, and 10 through 12 are Negative (and Mixed) Actions. Comparisons of the numbers of acts falling in each of these four areas may also yield valuable information. For example, comparing the number of Positive and Negative Actions may be thought of as giving an indication of the emotional "tone" or "friendliness" of the interaction.

This system has been widely used in the years since its inception, and consequently there is a large body of literature reporting a variety of research uses. This acceptance is in itself a considerable research advantage since it contributes to the

[26] From PERSONALITY AND INTERPERSONAL BEHAVIOR by Robert Freed Bales. Copyright © 1970 by Holt, Rinehart and Winston, Inc. Adapted by permission of Holt, Rinehart and Winston. This list reflects the revision of the names of the categories recently introduced by Bales. See Bales, 1970, especially chapter 6 and appendix 4. Except for these changes and changes in the content of the various categories, the system remains the same as the original.

comparability of any new results utilizing the technique. As differentiated from many of the earlier systems, as well as more recent ones, IPA is not limited to specific kinds of groups or topics, but can be used to study interaction of any kind or topic in any kind of small group situation. Some of the wide variety of types of groups for which it has been used include members of Alcoholics Anonymous, discussion groups, hospitalized patients, club members, college students, and military personnel. Furthermore, although the practical problems presented are considerable, there is no theoretical reason why the system cannot be used for large groups as well.

There are difficulties with the system, however, and it has been subject to significant criticism.[27] One difficulty, namely that of obtaining observer reliability, can best be overcome by means of extensive observer training. The same is true regarding the problem caused by the amount of inference which the observer must use in deciding which category to use for a given act. Another criticism of the system has been that the 12 categories themselves do not permit of fine enough distinctions, and to this end some revisions and refinements of Bales' original system have been proposed.[28]

Statistical investigation of IPA results by means of factor analyses, as reported by many investigators, have repeatedly yielded what Bales refers to as "three fundamental *dimensions of social evaluation* involved as one person views another in a group setting."[29] These three serve as the basis for Bales' recent work linking personality and the functioning of groups.[30] They may also widen the scope and utility of IPA as a research tool.

Although it is the best known single technique for nonparticipant observation, IPA is by no means the only one, nor should it be regarded as the preferred method. Nor are "category systems" in general, of which this is but one example, necessarily the most useful. As indicated above, there is no limit to the ways in which observation may be conducted. Observational methods will vary according to the nature of the phenomena being observed, the location or setting for the observation, the techniques used for recording the data, and the

[27] For a brief review of this, see Strodtbeck, 1973.

[28] Weick, pp. 398–99.

[29] Bales, 1968, p. 467.

[30] Bales, 1970.

objectives of the research. Because of the enormous variety of methods in use it is not practicable here to provide any kind of list or inventory of observational methods.[31]

PROBLEMS IN OBSERVATION

As with any other procedure, there are various problems and sources of possible error which may arise when using an observational method of data collection. The nature of these problems and the likelihood of their occurrence will vary according to whether the observation is participant or nonparticipant, structured or unstructured, whether the research is concealed or not, and the amount of inference to be used. Most of these have already been considered in our earlier discussion of sources of error, but there are some additional ones which pertain especially to observation.

One class of problems is occasioned by the interaction between researcher and subjects, and especially by the subjects' knowledge that they are under observation. To the extent that an individual sees himself as functioning in the position labelled "research subject" his perception of the *role* of research subject will necessarily affect his behavior. This may include attempts to cooperate with (or confound) the researcher's intentions, insofar as he believes he understands them, and it may lead him to engage in behavior which he "ordinarily" would refuse. These are similar to the whole class of problems already discussed in connection with interviewing.

Even more important—and disturbing—is the fact that bias may be introduced into the research situation subconsciously and unintentionally, not only by the subjects but *by the researcher* as well, as has been so forcefully demonstrated recently by Rosenthal.[32] He describes many ways in which the researcher's behavior—unintentionally—may influence the results which he obtains. Among his more dramatic findings were those connected with learning in rats, summarized as follows:

> . . . each experimenter was randomly assigned a rat after being told that the animal had been specially bred for brightness or dullness. Lo and behold, when the results were tabulated, it was

---

[31] The most comprehensive discussion of all aspects of observational methods is to be found in Weick, 1968. See also Reiss, 1971. For carrying out a laboratory experiment, a very useful article is Aronson and Carlsmith, 1968.

[32] Rosenthal, 1966.

> found that the so-called bright rats learned more quickly than the so-called dull rats.[33]

While this is an unusual example, it certainly points up the care which the researcher must exert if bias and error are to be kept to a minimum.

Other similar sources of error may lie in the subjects' suspiciousness of the researcher's intentions, in the subjects' perceptions of the characteristics of the demands made upon them by the researcher, and in the subjects' apprehensions that the researcher may, in some way, be evaluating them.[34] A related problem, about which less information is available, is the influence that the research situation, and the subjects, have *upon* the researcher and his research. Some writers have raised several questions in this connection, especially with regard to emotional involvement between researcher and subject, and the possible consequences this might have for the research.[35] Although they do not have answers to these questions, they suggest the possibility of T-group training for researchers as a means of coping with the problem.

How can these interaction problems, in general, best be dealt with? In the case of laboratory experiments, Aronson and Carlsmith make several suggestions.[36] To counteract the biases caused by the subjects' role perceptions, they suggest that the researcher take specific steps to prevent the subject from identifying the true purpose of the experiment. One way of achieving this is to devise procedures which appear the same to all the subjects involved, even though they are actually being exposed to different independent variables. Another means involves providing the subjects with a false or misleading explanation for the activities which are required of them. To handle the problem of the researcher's influence, they suggest an analogy to the medical "double-blind" model, in which the observers are research assistants who are kept at least partially ignorant of some crucial aspect of the independent variable. In direct observational research other than laboratory experiments, some of these same procedures may prove useful. In the case of concealed research, at least the subjects' role perception problems will not

---

[33] Aronson and Carlsmith, 1968, p. 67; also see pp. 61–70 for a discussion of avoidance of bias in experiments. See also Kaplan, 1964, pp. 136–44, and A. Miller, 1972.

[34] Rosenthal and Rosnow, 1969.

[35] Glass and Frankiel, 1968.

[36] Aronson and Carlsmith, 1968, pp. 61–70.

arise—although alternative problems may arise from whatever role a subject does perceive as being appropriate. The suggestion, frequently heard, of striving for complete standardization on the part of the researcher's behavior, even to the extent of using taped or other mechanical stimuli, may present its own problems inasmuch as this does not take into account the differences among subjects.[37] Ultimately, as before, we are forced to return to our earlier admonition that caution and alertness must be constant companions to the process of designing research.

A second class of problems stems from the difficulties inherent in the human qualities of the observer. He is not always operating at peak efficiency, sometimes he is tired, lazy, bored, upset, or hungry, and if he is *hired* for the observation task his commitment to the project may be minimal.[38] His values and personal history affect his perceptual processes, and in some forms of data recording his memory may play an important part. These kinds of problems may best be dealt with by appropriate modifications in the research design, and by careful training of the observers.

These problems are by no means sufficient to negate the great value of direct observation of human behavior and characteristics as a means of data collection. The importance to the sociologist of dealing with data other than simply verbal behavior cannot be ignored. We have previously discussed the inadequacies of the use of questioning as a means of data collection. Given the fact that sociology is especially concerned with human interaction, it behooves the sociologist to give special attention to direct observation as a means of data collection. Considering the amount of error which may be introduced by the subject under questioning, the sociologist may wish to depend more upon his own intellect in direct observation rather than upon the subject's intellect. To those sociologists who adopt a strong behavioristic approach, the advantages of direct observation over questioning become even more important.

EXERCISES

1. Suppose you are researching the effect of informal socialization processes at social gatherings held by two groups: one a business

[37] Ibid., p. 46.

[38] For some hair-raising examples of the latter, see Roth, 1966.

majors' fraternity at your college or university (of which you have been a member for about 2 and one half years), and the other a businessmen's association, some of whose members are fathers of the members of the fraternity. As researcher you have attended meetings of the fraternity on many occasions, but have yet to attend the meetings of the businessmen's association. To collect data for your study you decide to use unstructured participant observation. In view of some of the problems in using participant observation as discussed in this chapter:

a. Discuss the difficulties you might encounter in achieving objectivity in studying each of the groups since "observation of *x* is shaped by prior knowledge of *x*."

b. Discuss in the case of each group whether or not you should conceal the fact that you will be attending meetings as a participant observer for a research project.

c. Describe and discuss the way in which you would record the data obtained from your observations (once you have taken the necessary steps to assure objectivity and have decided whether or not you will reveal your reasons for attending the meetings of the two groups).

2. Suppose that the hypothesis being tested in the study above on socialization processes is that socialization is more intense and strict in the college business fraternity because of the high degree of role ambiguity of members and because social roles in the businessmen's association are highly defined. Decide upon the level of inference needed to adequately test this hypothesis in view of the data collection technique being used (i.e., participant observation); next discuss the reasons for your decision.

3. Several or all of the following studies could be researched using Bales' Interaction Process Analysis for data collection. Select those which you think could be best studied using the technique and discuss the reasons for your selections. Next discuss how the data collected using Bales' IPA might be used to help understand the relationships between the variables being studied.

   a. Amount of group consensus and level of work efficiency.

   b. Type of task performed and degree of group cohesion.

   c. Male versus female leadership in informal groups.

   d. Sex differences in response to invasion of social space.

   e. Achievement of elementary school pupils and affective versus instrumental presentation of learning materials by teachers.

   f. Satisfaction with group membership and level of outgroup hostility.

g. Degree of deviant behavior by members of informal groups and level of acceptance and rejection of deviant member.

h. Degree of deviance of discussion group members and the amount of communication received by the deviant members.

4. Describe some of the potential "researcher effects" in the following studies which could affect the overall outcome of the data collected:

   a. In a study of student attitudes toward "big business," the interviewers talking to student activists are dressed in suits and ties, and use a highly visible clip board in recording results.

   b. In a study of the effects of changing the lighting intensity level on the output of workers in a factory workroom, the researcher observes worker behavior while seated near the workers.

   c. In a study of attitudes toward parents, researchers use video tape to record interview sessions where the high school counselor interviews high school students aged 14 and 15 years about their home life.

   d. In a study of attitudes toward gun control laws, a researcher uses concealed unstructured interviews to obtain data. The actual interviews are conducted by persons who hold very strong views in regard to gun control laws.

Chapter 13

Data collection: Physical traces, archives, and simulation

OBSERVATION OF PHYSICAL TRACES

"Physical evidence is probably the social scientist's least-used source of data . . ."[1]—really a rather surprising state of affairs, when one stops to think of it, inasmuch as physical evidence is a product of human behavior and human characteristics, and these are of overwhelming interest to us. Certainly much can be learned about human behavior by studying its products. The archeologist, of course, has always done this. Ecologists, too, have concerned themselves with the size, characteristics, location, and distribution of physical evidence like buildings, roads, transportation systems, hospitals, parks, schools, churches, farms, wells, storage facilities, and so on. But aside from these two specialties, social scientists have made little use of this potentially rich source of data.

It is not possible to delineate a completely separate set of procedures for observing physical traces. In many ways this kind of observation is similar to direct observation of human behavior—the essential difference being, obviously, that here inanimate things are the target. Therefore, all the problems and complications occasioned by dealing with people are eliminated—this is the chief advantage of this method. Many of the same general comments made in the preceding section about accuracy, objectivity, system, and perception apply equally to the observation of physical evidence. Inference, too, may be involved, and the same cautions follow. The specific techniques used by the social scientist for this kind of observa-

[1] Webb et al., 1966, p. 35.

tion are almost completely determined by the nature of the data themselves, and they tend to be relatively ordinary procedures for both erosion and accretion data. The studies described in Webb et al. (virtually the sole source of information about this type of data) made use of: (1) measuring—such things as physical dimensions, amount of wear, amount of dirt, (2) counting, (3) weighing, (4) chemical analysis, (5) fingerprints, and (6) direct observation of the settings of radio dials and of graffiti. Instruments and equipment for recording may be used, as appropriate, although complex devices are probably not needed. The difficulties of this method of data collection lie in the ambiguities surrounding the reasons for the initial production of the physical trace, the possibility that some biasing factors determined which traces have survived and which have not, and the temporal and spatial variations in populations which produced the data.[2]

STUDY AND ANALYSIS OF ARCHIVAL DATA

By and large, archival data tend to occur in written form (including such "writing" as tombstone inscriptions), although they also include pictorial materials and sound recordings of various kinds. Far more than physical traces, archival data provide vast and varied information about the people who produced the data, so it is not surprising that social scientists have long made use of such data. In particular, the use of case histories and other historical documents comprises an important part of much of the early sociological research. Outstanding examples are the use of letters and other documents in Thomas and Znaniecki's monumental study of the Polish peasant[3] and the various University of Chicago studies of the 1920s and early 1930s.[4]

The term "case histories" (or "life histories") is used to refer to both the basic data—largely *historical* in nature—such as letters, diaries, autobiographies, or other collections of facts about an individual or a group, and also to the sociological analysis which the researcher makes of these data. In either usage it is

---

[2] Ibid., pp. 50–52.

[3] Thomas and Znaniecki, 1958.

[4] For example: Shaw, 1930; and Thrasher, 1927.

well to keep in mind that the data are subjective in nature. As distinguished from many other forms of data collection, here the researcher is frankly in search of subjective data to provide information about the way in which the subject perceived his world and thus to give clues for understanding and explaining his behavior. Four uses of life histories have been suggested, the first being that they provide a concrete example for reality-testing theories.[5] The second use is that they provide information about related fields of research, and the third is that they can stimulate further research. Finally, life histories can provide clues about the meaning of phenomena which otherwise are difficult to understand. Case histories have been relatively rarely used by sociologists in recent years, and probably the main reason for this is the difficulty of generalizing from information about a single case—a sample of one. This makes the method less suited for descriptive research, although it should still be possible to test theories against case histories.[6]

In addition, wide varieties of archival data have been used.[7] These studies are quite different from case histories, and make use of data which are generally much less subjective. There is no single method of data collection, and the techniques used are typically such simple ones as counting, measuring (e.g. size of tombstones), plotting (layout of graveyards), and various mathematical manipulations. Most of the comments made in the previous section on physical traces apply here also.

Whether case histories or other archival data, the evaluation of the original data is always important. Usually there is only minimum information about the purposes, motivation, and accuracy of the original producer of the data, and about the surrounding circumstances under which they were produced. Sometimes, of course, some library "detective work" can shed some light on the problem, but not always. Letters and diaries, for instance, may deviate considerably from accurate portrayals of events and feelings, depending upon whom they are addressed to and what the writer hoped to achieve. A letter to a

[5] H. Becker, 1970-a.

[6] For one of the few recent writings on this subject, see Denzin, 1970-a, chap. 10. A standard work is Gottschalk, Kluckhohn, and Angell, 1951. See also Young, 1966, chap. 10.

[7] See, for example, Manheim, 1961-b, which used responses to an advertisement in a newspaper personal column, and the many examples in Webb et al., 1966, pp. 53–111.

lover and a letter to one's parents would probably give vastly different pictures of the same events.[8] On the other hand, the use of archival data makes it possible to study phenomena occurring at remote times and places, which otherwise might not be researchable.

It was pointed out in Chapter 9 that archives contain an ever-increasing body of sample survey data, and that these in turn contain a wealth of material suitable for additional research on topics other than those for which they were originally collected. Such research is known as "secondary analysis." The advantages of secondary analysis are the obvious economies of money and time, the avoidance of possible public resistance to additional surveys, the contributions to theory through enlarging the number of cases and comparisons which can be made, and the opportunity to construct replication studies.[9] The sheer quantity of such data available, and the relative infrequency of their use, probably offer the greatest incentive, however. Secondary analysis presents some peculiar research design problems, on the other hand, since the researcher must *select* those sample surveys which are most appropriate to his needs, possibly choose portions of several such surveys, and rearrange these and eliminate extraneous segments.[10] In addition, such data suffer from the same questions of accuracy as any other archival data.

Content analysis

One particular form of archival data which has been studied extensively is the content of messages. Since communication plays such a central part in all social behavior it is not surprising that the content of communication in any form has been subject to much scrutiny, and a whole body of research techniques has resulted. *Content analysis* refers to "any technique for making inferences by objectively and systematically identifying specified characteristics of messages."[11] More simply, it is the

[8] For an interesting and useful account of means of evaluating documentary evidence, sources, and credibility, especially in the field of public affairs, see Newman and Newman, 1969.

[9] Hyman, 1972, pp. 6–24. This is probably the definitive work on secondary analysis.

[10] Ibid., p. 26.

[11] Holsti, 1969, p. 14. This book provides a recent and comprehensive discussion of all aspects of content analysis. See also: Holsti, 1968; Berelson, 1952; Pool, 1959; North et al., 1963; and Markoff, Shapiro, and Weitman, 1974.

study of "who says what, to whom, how, and with what effect . . . [and] why?"[12] It is a means of objectifying the sometimes casual and superficial judgments of communication content which we frequently make, and supplements the subjective examination (casual or detailed) of a given message.

The early uses of content analysis were in studies of the nature and effects of propaganda, and this type of analysis later spread to studies of news media, education, and then communication in general. Content analysis is usually thought of in connection with the mass communication media, but it is by no means limited to these—it may be used with virtually any kind of written material, and pictorial and sound materials as well. As the name—and definition—imply, content analysis refers to both the collection and analysis of data.

Generally there are three main emphases of content analysis. First, it may provide information about the characteristics of the originator's culture or about the originator himself—including, for example, the intriguing case of unknown or disputed authorship. Second, the interest may be in the message itself, such as the relative effectiveness of alternative messages, or a comparison of messages from a single source at different times or under different circumstances. Finally, a content analysis study may tell something about the effects of the message on the target audience. The researcher's main decisions in such a study have to do with the selection or sampling of the messages, the determination of the categories to be used in analysis (e.g., subject matter of the message, or treatment of the subject matter), the selection of units of analysis (single words, sentences, paragraphs, theme, etc.), and the units used for enumeration (such as the frequency or intensity of various kinds of units of analysis).[13]

In one interesting example the researcher analyzed the contents of German and American school song books. The authoritarian personality theory had previously been used in some studies of the German family, so the researcher was able to (1) reality-test some of the axioms of that theory, and (2) make a cross-cultural comparison of the national character of Germans and Americans. Individual songs or stanzas were used as the units of analysis, and each of these was classified

[12] Holsti, 1969, p. 24.

[13] Holsti, 1968.

according to which of 14 dimensions it pertained to. These dimensions were seen as applicable to all societies and included such things as nation/society, authority, manhood, work, family, night time, folk festivities, and so on. The units were then further classified according to the attitude or orientation toward the dimension. For example, songs concerning "night time" might express either "peacefulness" or "melancholy and nostalgia." The German and American songs were then compared as to the number of units in each of the various subcategories.[14]

Other illustrations of the kinds of research problems which have been studied through content analysis are: attempts at identifying the source of messages by analysis of sentence length and frequency of various classes of nouns; studies of the content of messages by counts of words and symbols, by amount of space devoted to various topics, by presence of different types of bias, and by comparison of the frequency of occupations portrayed on television with the frequency of those occupations existing in society; studies of the differential content of advertising messages as related to the audience toward which the magazines were aimed; and study of frequency of items in a message as an indicator of the author's personality traits.[15] Obviously, content analysis does not consist of any one particular method of data collection, but is typically a counting or measuring of certain carefully selected items.

It was pointed out above that content analysis is both a method of data collection and of data analysis. It can be seen from the above illustrations that—here, at least—the dividing line between collection and analysis is hazy indeed. However, one approach to content analysis which has attracted considerable attention is the use of computers, especially where word counts or word meanings are central to the analysis. The most widely used computer approach is the "General Inquirer" system.[16] In this system, the researcher prepares a dictionary of words which are central to the theory under investigation (e.g., "attack," "security," "nuclear," "defense," etc.), or uses one of several special-purpose dictionaries which have already been prepared. The text to be analyzed is then fed into the computer

[14] Sebald, 1962.

[15] Holsti, 1968, pp. 610–44.

[16] Stone, et al., 1966.

which is programmed to recognize these key words and any pertinent word sequences. The computer output may consist of word counts, sentences meeting certain required specifications, expressions of attitudes, and many other variables.

Demographic and ecological studies

The inclusion of a discussion of the specialized areas of demographic and ecological research under the general heading of "archival data" may offend—or even anger—some readers, and indeed there may be some justification for such feelings. Those who specialize in such research do not necessarily utilize archival data at all, but may collect their own data. Ecological research, especially, may depend heavily upon physical trace data such as location of buildings, railroads, highways, parks, schools, hospitals, and the like. However, the majority of such research does use some archival data, particularly census materials, and so we discuss it here. Due to the specialized nature of this research, to the fact that many nonsociologists make this their specialty, and to the fact that there are several excellent and widely-available texts in these areas, we will not here attempt any more than a brief overview of demographic and ecological research methods.[17]

Demographic research consists of the statistical description and analysis of human populations, and is primarily concerned with the age and sex compositions of a given area and their changes over time. Thus the basic variables with which the demography researcher deals are fertility (number of births), mortality (number of deaths), and migration. Other variables of interest are race and ethnic characteristics, educational level, marriage and divorce, and economic characteristics. These may be treated as either dependent or independent variables, depending upon the research interest, and can yield much information about, for example, the processes of social change:

[17] Probably the most complete discussion of demographic methods is Shryock and Siegel, 1971, and the one-volume condensation, 1976. Other very useful works are: Bogue, 1969; Hauser, 1965; and Spiegelman, 1968. See also Taeuber, 1964. A very good volume, of especial interest to the non-American reader, is Barclay, 1958. A brief introduction to demographic research is contained in Goode and Hatt, 1952, chap. 18. For both demographic and ecological urban research, see Gibbs, 1961. For a very good introduction to research methods in ecology, see chap. 14 by Calvin F. Schmid, in Young, 1966; for a more advanced view see Desmond Cartwright, 1969. For a comprehensive picture of ecology and ecological methods, see Duncan, 1964.

> The increase of youth in a peasant village or the increase of aged in a mature society necessarily alter the balance if not the forms of social functioning. . . . The hopes and frustrations that send peasants cityward alter the balances of births and deaths and the rural-urban distribution of the population.[18]

A glance at any census publication (the most common source of demographic data) will show the great variety of data which are available, the various ways in which they can be expressed, and the numerous cross-comparisons which can be made. These may be even further manipulated by the researcher. Common tools of analysis include population pyramids, crude and age-specific rates of mortality and fertility, and life tables.

A population pyramid (so-called because of its typical shape) is merely two bar graphs back to back, showing the distribution of a population by age and sex. The overall shape of the graph and comparisons of various parts of it can give interesting and useful information. Figure 6 shows population pyramids for two census divisions of the United States for 1950 and 1970. The two 1950 pyramids strikingly show the differences between highly urban and highly rural areas. School-aged persons (5 through 19) comprised a much higher proportion of the East South Central population than of the Middle Atlantic states. Conversely, the Middle Atlantic states had a relatively larger labor force (ages 20 through 54 comprise the bulk of the labor force). Since the labor force pays the taxes which support the schools, the Middle Atlantic states would have been expected to have more money available per child for educational costs. By 1970 the East South Central had become significantly more urban and the patterns typical of rural areas had diminished, but the ratio of labor force to school age was still larger for the Middle Atlantic. The proportion of the population over 60 (who are more likely to be dependent) also increased sharply over the 20-year period. These are only a few illustrations of the kinds of information which can be derived from population pyramids.

The crude mortality rate is usually defined as the number of deaths per thousand population in a given time period. *Specific* mortality rates may be computed for various segments of the population designated by, for example, occupation, age, sex, or marital status. For example, the following figures show age-

---

[18] Taeuber, Irene B., "Population and Society," from Faris, Robert E. L. (Ed.), HANDBOOK OF MODERN SOCIOLOGY, © 1964 by Rand McNally & Company, Chicago. Page 83.

Figure 6. Population pyramids for two U.S. Census divisions in 1950 and 1970

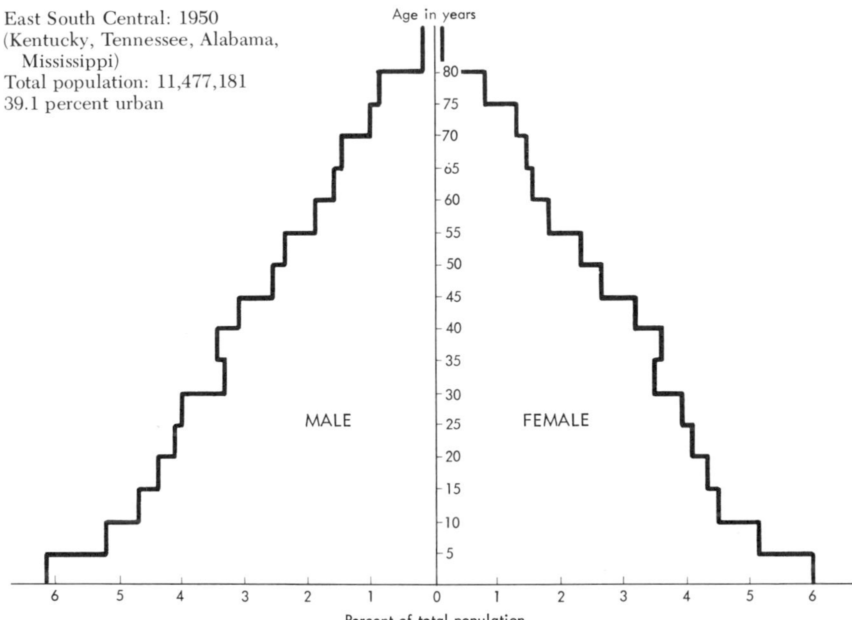

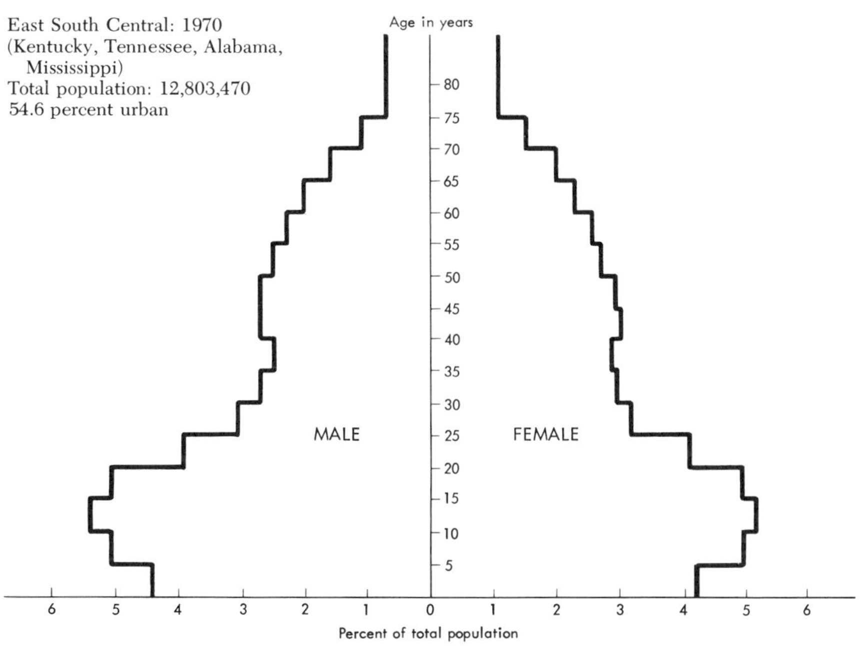

Figure 6. (continued)

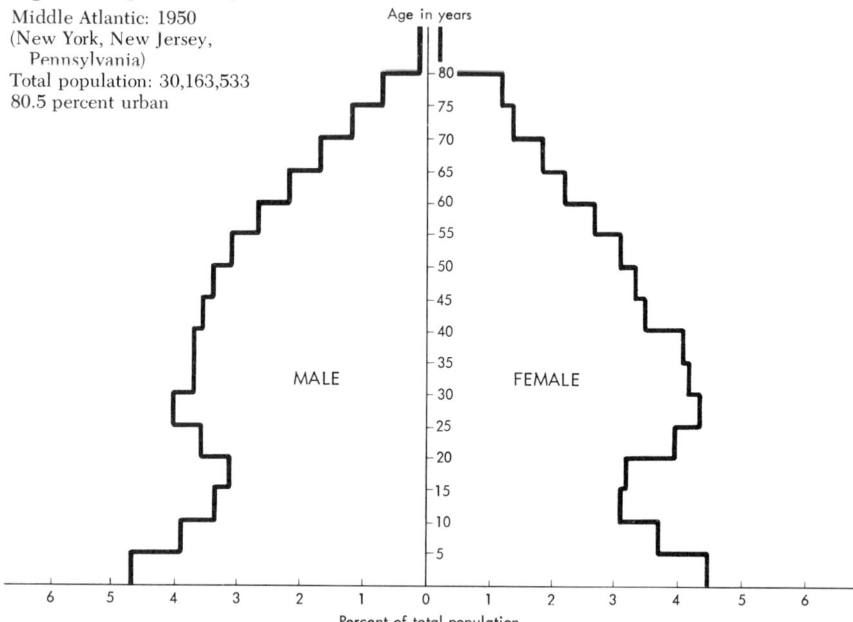

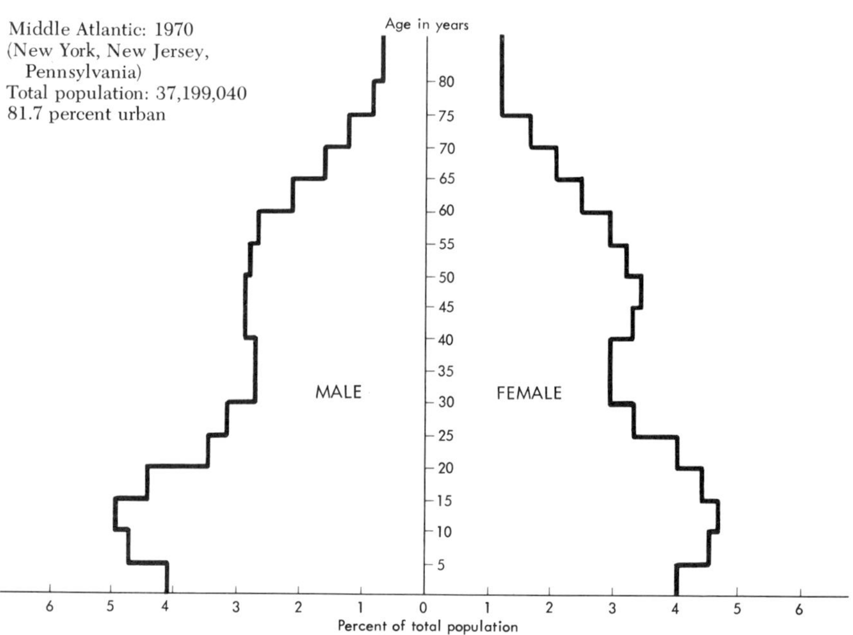

specific mortality rates (i.e., the number of deaths for every 1,000 persons) in the indicated ages and categories, for 1973, in the United States.

	White		Nonwhite		
Age	*Male*	*Female*	*Male*	*Female*	*Total*
20	1.94	0.62	3.14	1.14	1.40
21	2.01	0.62	3.58	1.26	1.46
22	2.04	0.62	3.95	1.36	1.50
23	2.01	0.63	4.20	1.41	1.50
24	1.93	0.64	4.36	1.45	1.48

Source: U.S. Bureau of the Census, *Statistical Abstract of the United States: 1975*, Table no. 84.

Crude and specific birth rates may be calculated in similar fashion. However, *fertility* rates are much more useful. These are based on either the total female population or the total female population of child-bearing ages (usually regarded as 15 through 44 in the United States). Comparison of age-specific fertility rates among various nations or religions or ethnic categories, for example, can provide much useful information about future population trends, economic characteristics, educational needs, and so on, and can also provide clues to the reasons for such differential rates. The following selected figures, for instance, illustrate some of these possibilities.

Country	*Fertility rate (births per 1,000 females, age 10–49)*	*Year*
German Democratic Republic	38.7	1973
USA	50.9	1973
USSR	55.5	1973
Japan	61.3	1973
France	61.6	1972
Chile	81.5	1970
China (Taiwan)	81.5	1972
Israel	95.1	1972
Sri Lanka	105.4	1971
Thailand	114.1	1970
Mexico	153.6	1970
Iran	160.0	1971

Source: U.S. Bureau of the Census, *Statistical Abstract of the United States: 1975*, Table no. 1392.

A life table is based upon age-specific mortality rates and yields various measures of life expectancy. For an individual of a given age it can show, among other things, the probability of surviving to some other given age or of surviving a given number of years, or the average number of years remaining until death, or it can show the average number of years a newborn infant can expect to live.[19] As one example, the following figures show the change from 1940 to 1973 of the life expectancy, in years, of newborn infants in the United States.

Year	*Total population*	*Male*	*Female*
1940	62.9	60.8	65.2
1950	68.2	65.6	71.1
1960	69.7	66.6	73.1
1970	70.9	67.1	74.8
1973	71.3	67.6	75.3

Source: U.S. Bureau of the Census, *Statistical Abstract of the United States: 1975*, Table no. 82.

These figures mean that the expected average length of life of, for example, all females born in the United States in 1950, is 71.1 years. Another way in which life expectancy can be presented shows the average number of years of life remaining for a person of a certain age, as illustrated in these figures for the United States in 1973.

Age	*Life expectancy in years*	*Age*	*Life expectancy in years*
5	67.8	50	26.3
10	63.0	55	22.3
15	58.1	60	18.6
20	53.4	65	15.3
25	48.8	70	12.2
30	44.1	75	9.5
35	39.5	80	7.3
40	34.9	85 and over	5.4
45	30.5		

Source: U.S. Bureau of the Census, *Statistical Abstract of the United States: 1975*, Table no. 84.

Ecological research—from the sociological frame of reference—consists of any research which looks at the spatial distribution of phenomena. In the broadest sense this may be

[19] Bogue, 1969, pp. 551–52.

seen as an examination of the flow of materials or energy or information in a system, which system (the "ecosystem") consists of the human plurel and its environment.[20] Spatial distribution may be described in terms of natural areas, census tracts or other census subdivisions, economic or political areas or jurisdictions, or many others. There is really no limit to the kinds of phenomena whose distribution may be studied: housing, transportation, retail sales, services, mass media coverage, ethnic category, age and sex, deviant behavior, disease, divorce, illegitimacy, land use, recreational facilities, voting behavior, child-rearing patterns, and on and on.

For instance, one study of the distribution of crimes in a city was not especially revealing until the researchers hit upon the idea of taking the physical and social characteristics of the *immediate setting* into account. The particular crime they studied was the vandalizing and/or stripping of automobiles, and in each instance of this crime the type of land use and behavior setting were noted. A set of six categories of settings emerged, each of which "reflected both the land use type of the space adjacent to the vehicle, and also the presence or absence of territorial control exerted over that space by the local control system."[21] The categories were: institutional, vacant house or store, doorless flank of a building, vacant/parking lot, occupied apartment or store, and occupied house. The findings showed that car stripping was more likely to occur adjacent to settings with little territorial control, such as factories or vacant houses, than settings with much territorial control, such as occupied houses. Another kind of ecological research, namely microecology, has attracted attention in recent years. This intriguing category uses as a variable the way in which persons are distributed around a limited physical space—seating arrangements around a conference table or in a classroom, or the work stations in a military aircraft, for example.[22] All of these may be studied over time, thus shedding light on various aspects of social change as well as population mobility. Various kinds of indexes, typologies, and techniques have been devised for manipulating and analyzing these data.

---

[20] Duncan, 1964, p. 41.

[21] Ley and Cybriwsky, 1974, p. 61.

[22] For some recent illustrations see: Batchelor and Goethals, 1972; F. Becker et al., 1973; Cook, 1970; and Sommer, 1969.

SIMULATION

Simulation "refers to the construction and manipulation of an *operating* model, that model being a physical or symbolic representation of all or some aspects of a social or psychological process."[23] The emphasis on the word "operating" implies that the model must be dynamic, rather than static; that is, that it must incorporate the changes taking place over the passage of time. In Chapter 2 we have discussed the various kinds of models, and it was indicated there that symbolic models, especially mathematical models, are the ones of greatest interest to social scientists. Simulation has probably been most widely used for training purposes, particularly in business and management situations and by the military. But whenever it is possible to express the characteristics of a social system, or some part thereof, in the language of mathematics, the resulting model becomes a powerful tool for research as well.

There are five kinds of research situations in which simulation is especially useful:[24]

1. To reproduce and study rare, costly, or destructive states, such as war.
2. To provide many, exact, replicates of a unique situation.
3. To provide contrasting situations so that confounding contaminating factors may be studied.
4. To simplify by reducing the number of variables and reducing environmental influence.
5. To provide a more readily observable situation than the real system.

In addition, simulation may be valuable whenever it is desirable to be able to expand or compress time.

In the typical use of simulation for research purposes, a math-

[23] Dawson, 1962, p. 3. This article provides a good and easily understood introduction to simulation. For a more advanced and very comprehensive view including a section on "Methodology of Computer Simulation," see Abelson, 1968. Also: Naylor et al., 1966, and Cohen and Cyert, 1965. For suggestions on the need for and use of simulation, see: Bales, 1959; Coleman, 1964-b, and Raser, 1969. For examples of the use of simulation in social science research, see: Abelson, 1965; Coleman, 1962; Drabek and Haas, 1969; Guetzkow, 1962-a; Rome and Rome, 1962; and Zelditch and Evan, 1962. See also the journal *Simulation and Gaming*. For the use of simulation in teaching, see Gamson, 1969.

[24] Zelditch and Evan, 1962, pp. 49–51.

ematical model of some social system is constructed, and then that model is manipulated by a simulator in such a way as to generate data. Usually, but not always, the simulator involves a computer. The simulation may involve only human actors, functioning as simulated decision makers (e.g., of large corporations or nations); these are known as "gaming," or "all-man" simulations. Simulations in which human actors interact with a computer are known as "man-machine" simulations, and those in which the entire simulation is carried out by a computer are known as "all-computer," or "pure-computer" simulations.

The "all-man" kind of simulation is perhaps best illustrated by the "inter-nation" simulations by Guetzkow.[25] In these, five teams of one, two, or three persons each, represented a hypothetical "nation." Each nation was allocated certain resources, had certain internal and international goals, and the leaders (i.e., team members) had the personal goals of remaining in power. The nations were provided with a flow of information and were allowed to communicate with one another in order to solve various international problems. One of the main purposes of this simulation was to study theories of international relations.

An illustration of man-machine simulation is provided by the management game developed at Carnegie Tech.[26] In this "game" each team of players represents a company engaged in manufacturing and selling detergents. Each "company" has a factory located in a specified area, warehouses for raw materials and finished products, offices, and research and development facilities. In addition it has transportation and sales facilities, a specified financial position, and so on. These companies are competing against one another, as in a real-life economic situation, and each must make decisions regarding prices, output, location of new facilities, etc. A computer is programmed to represent the (economic) environment, providing information relating to demands for products, outcomes of each company's decisions, and the like. By varying the parameters of the simulation, it is possible to do research upon many pertinent economic and business problems.

All-computer simulation is illustrated by a study designed to attack the practical problem of minimizing the lengths of pas-

[25] Guetzkow, 1962-b.

[26] K. Cohen et al., 1962.

senger waiting lines at a bus terminal.[27] Largely because of the many variables involved (scheduled bus arrival and departure times, deviations from schedule, different routes, limited loading space, limited waiting space for buses, blockage of bus movement by other buses, variations of demand from peak to off hours, number of passengers arriving per unit time, length of time to load a bus, passenger willingness to board a bus where all seats are taken, etc.), probably the only feasible way to study such a situation is by use of an all-computer simulation. To do so, in this case, required the construction of four models for passenger arrivals, bus arrivals, loading of buses, and bus dispatching. This is illustrative of many studies of queues which have attracted considerable attention in recent years.

Since the use of computer simulations requires a fairly sophisticated knowledge of mathematics and computer usage, a detailed discussion of simulation as a means of data collection is beyond the scope of this book.[28] The first and most important step in such an approach to data collection is, of course, construction of the model. This is also usually the most difficult part. Then the determination must be made as to whether simulation is the most suitable technique. It may be that a nonsimulated analysis of the model may be more productive or efficient. Once it has been decided that simulation is appropriate, the remainder of the data-collection procedure becomes the same as any other use of a computer. First a "flowchart" must be constructed, then a program is written and "debugged," and finally the model is run on the computer. It is to be hoped that those students with the requisite background will utilize this potentially very powerful kind of data collection in conducting their sociological research.

EXERCISES

1. Below are listed physical traces which could be the products of individual and group activity. Select five of them or make up several of your own and use them for variables for a study which you might carry out. For your study decide upon a specific objective or hypothesis and then briefly describe a research design in which

[27] Jennings and Dickins, 1962.

[28] See Abelson, 1968.

the indicators you have chosen could be used to test your hypothesis or demonstrate your specific objective:

a. The number of rooms in houses.

b. The number of automobiles with attached commercially printed signs ("bumper stickers").

c. The amount of graffiti on walls in public buildings and rooms.

d. The number of automobiles five years old or older in parking lots.

e. The extent and homogeneity of tans on different beaches.

f. The number of children's play articles in front and back yards.

g. The number of battered fixtures in public buildings and business establishments.

h. The percentage of total clothing articles in a closet that are "out of style."

i. The amount of broken glass in different areas of a public park.

j. The contents of pockets of boys of different ages.

k. The number of different types of recreational equipment found in garages.

l. The number of personalized coffee cups in a break area in different kinds of business establishments.

m. The number of automobiles and other motorized vehicles found in driveways and yards of homes.

n. The number of picture windows per home in differing neighborhoods.

2. Below are listed several types of archival data which could be used to conduct a research project. For each decide on some appropriate variables which could be used and the specific objective to be accomplished, and then discuss how the data obtained from the listed sources might be used to fulfill the specific objective:

   a. A diary of a Methodist minister in colonial America who systematically recorded vital statistics and important events of the members of his church over a 50-year period.

   b. A collection of letters from home obtained from a random sample of students in each class level in your college or university.

   c. Telephone log lists of subjects of calls for persons on different levels of a given organization's hierarchy.

   d. High school yearbook remarks about career aspirations for rural and urban high school students for a 20-year period.

e. City budget allocations for various functions during the last 20-year period.

f. Log books and minutes of meetings kept by social groups.

3. Below are several indicators of research variables and sources of data for group activities and individual behavior which might be researched using the technique of content analysis. For each decide upon a specific objective and other indicators as needed and then outline briefly a research design which could be used to carry out the study.

   a. Group photos of informal social functions taken at several neighborhoods representing different social classes.

   b. Types of roles played by women as seen on television shows at different times during the broadcast day.

   c. The number of hesitations and degree of nervousness evident on tape recordings of interviews of subjects on seven types of deviance.

   d. The number and kinds of retained facts about a controversial subject read to subjects from a standard text.

   e. In official memos, the numbers and kinds of orders and suggestions given and received in communications between a departmental director and the section heads who report to him in a given organization.

   f. The degree and kinds of anti-school aggressiveness of high school students as determined by graffiti.

4. Below are several indicators and sample descriptions which could be used to conduct ecological studies. For each decide upon a specific objective or hypothesis which could be tested, briefly outline a research design which you feel would be appropriate to test it, and then discuss how the data obtained might be used to support or reject the hypothesis or demonstrate the specific objective:

   a. The average value of homes at given elevations above sea level (using a 10 percent random sample of homes in a metropolitan area of about 500,000 persons).

   b. The average age of residents in homes with identical market values in neighborhoods in different parts (central, midtown, suburb, etc.) of a metropolitan area of about 500,000 persons (sample size about 3,000 households).

   c. Community retail sales per capita and proximity to metropolitan areas (using an inventory of all communities of 2,500 or more persons within a 100-mile radius of three selected metropolitan areas).

d. Out-migration of persons aged 18–30 from countries for the 1960–70 period and the percentage of persons employed in agriculture in 1960 (using a 10 percent random sample of all non-metropolitan counties in the United States).

e. The natural habitat of low-income neighborhood informal groups (using snowball sampling and participant observation).

5. As described in this chapter, simulation refers to a model of a social or psychological process. One type of simulation is gaming or "all man" simulations. They are various kinds of informal games with which one is ordinarily familiar such as parlor games, the boxed commercial games one can get in stores, sports activities, and even short stage plays one could perform. Doubtless there are others which might be used for research. Decide upon two different types of these kinds of "simulations" which you might use for conducting a research project, make up a hypothesis or specific objective for each one, and briefly outline study designs which could be accomplished using these simulations.

Chapter 14

Sampling

GENERAL COMMENTS

In the earlier section on sample surveys in Chapter 9, it was pointed out that a sample is used when the research design calls for the collection of information from or about a population which is so large or so widely scattered as to make it impractical to observe all the individuals in the population. It has been observed that in one sense *any* data collection procedure involves sampling since it is only one of all the possible observation which could conceivably be made. However, we will confine ourselves to the more limited idea above. (Other data selection procedures besides sampling were considered in the discussion of characteristics and selection of data.) There are many excellent books and articles, at various levels of difficulty, on sampling and no attempt will be made here to duplicate those. The reader who is actually going to construct a sample or who wants more information about sampling should consult a more detailed work.[1]

Since a sample, according to our earlier definition, is a part of the population which is observed in order to make inferences about the whole population, it becomes clear that in order for the researcher to decide whether or not to utilize a sample the first step must be to identify and unambiguously describe the population. "Population" is defined as the aggregate of all the elements, that is, the entire group or collectivity about which

[1] Following are some sources which are among the best and which are also widely available. They are listed roughly in order of increasing degree of required background in statistics: Chein, 1959; Parten, 1950, chaps. 4, 7, 8, 9; Raj, 1972; Stephan and McCarthy, 1958; Lazerwitz, 1968; Yates, 1960; Kish, 1965; Raj, 1968; and Hansen, Hurwitz, and Madow, 1953.

information is sought. "Elements" are those individual units about which one seeks information. Sampling is not, of course, confined to people since we may sample buildings in a community for instance, or automobiles in a parking lot.

The description of the population must include not only the elements, accurately delineated, but the time as well. For example, the population might be the entire full-time undergraduate student body at Arizona State University in October 1974, and hence the elements are the individual full-time undergraduate students at that university at that time. Or, as another example, the population might consist of farm families (however that might be defined) in the state of Kansas on a given date, and here the elements are individual families rather than persons. The importance of the time at which a sample is drawn is sometimes overlooked. If the population being studied was department store employees, for example, one would expect both a larger population and a higher proportion of inexperienced employees in the pre-Christmas weeks. Furthermore, the timing of a sample might have more impact upon certain kinds of samples than others. If a sample were being drawn from payroll records of a population of factory workers there might not be much day to day fluctuation. But a sample drawn from workers actually on the job on a given day might be sharply affected by absenteeism on, for instance, the days immediately before and after a holiday or the day of an important baseball game. Finally, as little time as possible should elapse between the drawing of the sample and the data collection, since changes might occur in the population in the interim.

Given the description of the population, one uses a sample when the population is so large or so dispersed that a complete census (i.e., a collection of information from 100 percent of the elements) is too costly in time and/or money. There may also be other reasons for using a sample, such as in industrial quality control where the process of examining the elements results in their destruction, or in situations where there is sound reason for believing that the elements are identical or similar to one another with respect to the qualities of interest, such as in the study of molecular particles, or when the loss in accuracy (which is a part of any sampling) is relatively unimportant.

Since the purpose of sampling is to make inferences, or statements, about a whole population, an adequate sample must meet two criteria. In the first place, the sample must provide an accurate portrayal of the characteristics of the population. This is commonly referred to as representativeness. And in the second place, the sample must be such that it is possible to determine the accuracy of the inferences made from it. The body of theory and procedures known as statistical inference (or sampling statistics or inductive statistics) enables us to achieve this second criterion.

To illustrate the first criterion, if I am to interview a sample of adults in a "typical" community in order to determine their attitudes toward, and knowledge about, heart disease, the sample would obviously *not* be representative if it contained only women, or if it contained no members of the lower classes of the community structure, or if it contained no elderly persons, or if it contained no individuals with more than a high school education, and so on. Similarly, to illustrate the second criterion, let us say that as a result of my survey I find that 27 percent of the sample has no accurate knowledge about heart disease, and I make the inference that 27 percent of the adult population of the community has no accurate knowledge about heart disease. It is imperative that I be able to specify the degree of accuracy of that statement (do I mean 27.0 ± 0.05, or 27 ± 1, or 27 ± 5, or less than 28, or more than 26, etc.), and also how certain I am that this is an accurate statement. In any scientific context, the importance of obtaining accurate and dependable results is so obvious that it need not be repeated. But it becomes even more important when the subject matter of the research is itself of great significance, and/or when decisions and actions based upon these results are of such a magnitude that error would be very undesirable and perhaps even catastrophic.

In order to meet these two criteria it is important to distinguish between probability and nonprobability samples. In probability samples, "every element in the population has a known nonzero probability of being selected,"[2] while in nonprobability samples there is no way of knowing the probability of an individual element being selected. Since statistical inference, as it is known today, applies only to probability samples, and since the use of statistical inference is necessary for making

[2] Kish, 1965, p. 20.

accurate inferences about the population, it follows that only probability samples meet the second criterion above.

NONPROBABILITY SAMPLES[3]

Despite this limitation, nonprobability samples can have a substantial place in research. Depending upon the specific type of sample, they may be quite representative of the population. Frequently they are cheaper, in both time and money, and almost always they are easier and more convenient to construct, use, and analyze, than probability samples. Sometimes there is no feasible probability sampling method available, such as when the entire population is unavailable and/or unknown in size. Mobile populations, of animals or fish for example, may be studied by the "capture-tag-recapture" method[4] and this method could be used for sociological research as well. Another example would be the case where one is attempting to make some generalizations about a category of deviants (e.g., transvestites) based upon observation of, or interviews with, a few cases. In such situations the researcher must make judgments as to whether such admittedly atypical information is better than no information at all. Similar to these are the situations where the use of a probability sample might necessitate compromises in some other aspect of the research. Designing of research, as we have said, involves a seemingly endless series of choices among alternatives, each of which carries with it both advantages and disadvantages. For example, the choice might be between using a probability sample with a less desirable method of data collection or a nonprobability sample with a more desirable method. Again, the researcher must bring to bear all his experience, knowledge, and judgment in order to make such decisions.

Finally, and perhaps most frequently encountered, there are situations when a probability sample is simply not needed, or would be inappropriate. In much sociological research a sample is used with no attempt to make inferences about a larger population—or only the vaguest kind of inferences are made. It

---

[3] Chein, 1959, gives a very good (and one of the few) discussions of the advantages of nonprobability sampling. This section draws upon his article.

[4] Kish, 1965, pp. 19, 387–88.

may be that a theory is being tested, or that the research is describing some characteristic of a part of society from which it is hoped that the generalization to the whole society, or "people in general," can be made, or it may be that members of a local union are interviewed, with the vague expectation that the results will be typical of all union members. Or perhaps the research attempts to answer some questions about the relationship between parents' recreational interests and children's recreational interests, and interviews are conducted with several groups of high school students, the emphasis here being on the kind of relationship rather than the representativeness of the sample. The countless number of researches being reported upon in the current journals provide ample additional examples of research in which a probability sample is neither needed nor used, and indeed in many of them the term "sample" is not even appropriate since there is no intent to make inferences to a larger population. The literature is full of references to samples where, in fact, what the researcher is really doing is a complete census of an entire population consisting of only those individuals who are actually interviewed or observed.

Three different types of nonprobability sampling can be identified. The first is known variously as *accidental*, or *convenience*, or *fortuitous*, or *haphazard* sampling. In this the individuals who are observed are selected merely on the basis of their availability. They may be the first 100 persons the researcher encounters on the street, or students in the researcher's classes, or individuals who volunteer to participate in the study for various reasons, or cab drivers, barbers, waiters, and others who the interviewer thinks represent public opinion, or business men located in a neighborhood conveniently close to the researcher's headquarters, and so on. Clearly there is no way of knowing how representative such a sample may be of a larger population—if indeed any such larger population can be identified. This, coupled with the fact that statistical inference techniques do not apply, renders such accidental samples quite unsatisfactory when the design calls for generalizing to a larger population, and it is safe to say that they should be used only as a last resort.

The second type of nonprobability sample is *quota* sampling, in which cases are selected for the sample on the basis of a quota system. Where the researcher has information about the distribution of certain characteristics which are believed to be related to the research at hand, within the population, it is possible to establish quotas for their inclusion in the sample. For example, instructions for a quota sample of a university student body might specify that one graduate student be interviewed for every four undergraduates, two females for every three males, and liberal arts, engineering, and business students in the ratio of 3 to 2 to 1, respectively. Perhaps the quotas would involve combinations of the various characteristics, such as six male graduate students for every one female graduate student, etc. Quota sampling, obviously, can increase the representativeness of the sample, and this usually would make it more desirable than accidental sampling. However, as the number of characteristics upon which the quota is based increases, the difficulty of finding the appropriate cases also increases. Furthermore, this still remains basically an accidental sample.

Purposive sampling, sometimes known an *judgment,* or as *expert choice* sampling, is the third type. Here the researcher selects the cases to be included in the sample on the basis of his familiarity with the situation combined with his presumed expert judgment. Sometimes this may be a very advantageous way to proceed, especially when the researcher is truly familiar with the situation and does in fact have expertise in the matter. For example, Kish states:

> If a research project must be confined to a single city in the United States, I would rather use my judgment to choose a "typical" city than select one at random. Even for a sample of 10 cities, I would rather trust my knowledge of U.S. cities than a random selection.[5]

Purposive sampling may, then, be quite representative of the population, but this depends upon the researcher's skill and experience, and perhaps his luck, too.

Regardless of the reasons favoring use of a nonprobability sample, and regardless of all the other considerations discussed above, the fact that inferential statistics cannot be applied to this type of sample should always be kept in mind. This may be the overriding—or even the sole—consideration in deciding upon the type of sample to be used. There is no denying the fact that probability samples, which are known to meet the two criteria of representativeness and permitting inferences to be made, are

---

[5] Kish, 1965, p. 29.

preferable to nonprobability samples for the purposes of making accurate and dependable contributions to knowledge—which is of course what research is all about. Nonprobability samples should be used only in those circumstances when their advantages as described above are sufficiently large to outweigh the basic superiority of probability samples.

PROBABILITY SAMPLES[6]

As mentioned before, only probability samples enable the user to make accurate and dependable inferences from his sample results to the population in which he is interested. Basically, the reasoning is as follows. What the researcher desires is information about the population—candidate A is favored by 52 percent of the registered voters, the mean number of years of formal education of adults in this community is 9.5, and so on. But such *population values*, or true values, are of course unknown. The only data which the researcher has upon which he can base such statements are the data obtained from his sample, known as the *sample value*. The sample value is based upon his observation of all the individual cases in his sample, and is, of course, only an *estimate* of the population value. So the big question is, how good is this estimate, or more precisely, how much does the sample value deviate from the population value?

In order to answer this, we take note of the fact that the particular sample which was actually selected is only one of many (usually a very large number) similar samples which might have been selected from the same population. Each one of these samples would yield a sample value which would also deviate from the population value by some unknown amount. The array of all the *possible* sample values is known as the *sampling distribution*, and generally speaking this sampling distribution assumes the shape of a normal curve (the familiar "bell-shaped" curve). The mean value of the sampling distribution is either equal to the population value or deviates from it by a negligible amount as long as the sample size is large enough. But of course the mean value of the sampling distribution is not known either. Fortunately, sampling statistics permit us to compute estimates of the mean of the sampling distribution when a sample value is known. This estimate of the mean of the sampling distribution

[6] This section draws heavily upon Kish, 1965.

can be considered to equal the population value, as mentioned above, and thus it provides a measure of the accuracy of the sample value. This is really the purpose of sampling statistics—to enable the researcher to make inferences to populations, based upon samples. The specific procedures and formulas for this will vary with the different types of probability samples.

Types of probability samples

The fundamental type of probability sample is the simple random sample (SRS), typified by the familiar procedure of putting each individual's name on a separate slip of paper, mixing them all in a bowl, and then selecting the desired number by blindly drawing slips from the bowl. (More rigorously, the slips must all be the same size, each individual's name must appear on one and only one slip, and the slips must be thoroughly mixed.) Clearly, the total population is represented by all the slips in the bowl, and each element is represented by a single slip. If we let N stand for the total number in the population, then on the first draw the probability of selecting any given element is $1/N$. In SRS *without replacement* (i.e., where each element selected is not replaced in the bowl before the next draw), on any given draw all the elements remaining in the bowl have an equal probability of being selected. Thus on the second draw the probability of a given element being selected is

$$\frac{1}{N-1},$$

on the third draw it is

$$\frac{1}{N-2},$$

on the fourth draw it is

$$\frac{1}{N-3}, \text{ etc.}$$

In the case of SRS *with replacement* (i.e., where after each draw the element selected is replaced in the bowl, and thus has a chance of being drawn again), the probability of selecting any given element remains $1/N$ throughout the entire selection process. Either way, since the probability of selection of each element is known it is seen that these conform to the definition of a probability sample.

In actual practice a simple random sample as described above is rarely used, and there are two reasons for this. In the first place, it is very rare that the researcher would have available a complete and accurate listing of all the elements, with each element appearing once and only once, and with no nonelements appearing on the list. In the second place, the physical labor of transcribing all the elements onto separate slips of paper, and then mixing them thoroughly enough in a large enough container, is tedious to say the least.

All the other types of probability samples are merely modifications of the SRS—modifications which are introduced in order to make the sampling more practical or less expensive or more accurate. One very simple modification of the SRS which eliminates the tedious labor mentioned above is to utilize a table of random numbers. This requires that each element in the population be assigned a unique number (and preferably, that these numbers run serially) before using the table. Then, one enters the table in some random manner (perhaps choosing the page by a roll of a die, then blindly pointing to a number on the page), and proceeds through the table from this starting point until the desired number of elements have been selected. Obviously however, even this procedure becomes more and more laborious as the sample size increases, and other modifications of the SRS which will be discussed shortly provide easier procedures.

From the above it must be clear that it is necessary to have some kind of listing or all-inclusive description of the elements in the population. This may take the form of an actual list, or it may be in the form of a deck of file cards, or a map showing all the blocks where the population elements reside, or perhaps a description of procedures to follow, etc. The term "*frame*" is generally used to denote the above. Without an adequate frame it is not possible to construct a good probability sample. Ideally, each element should appear separately in the frame, should appear once and only once, and the frame should contain nothing else other than the elements. It is rare that such a frame would be available, and the researcher must use the best that is available and determine the adequacy of his frame by local inquiries and his own investigations.

Problems which are most likely to occur in frames are that

some elements will be missing, several elements may be clustered into a single listing, some elements may appear more than once, "foreign" elements may be included, and, blanks may appear on the list. As examples of these problems, if a telephone directory were used as a frame, some individuals might have gotten telephones after the directory was printed, all the members of a family might be represented only by the father's (husband's) name, a married woman might be listed under both her maiden name and her married name, business and commercial establishments will probably be included along with private individuals, and some people will usually have unlisted telephone numbers. One obvious way of dealing with such problems is to correct the entire list or frame, but this may be an extremely costly and time-consuming process. There are various other means of dealing with these problems, but two possibilities which may be appropriate—regardless of the specific nature of the individual frame deficiency—are (1) to ignore the problem if it is known to be very small and if it would be very costly to correct, and (2) to redefine the population so as to conform to what is actually in the frame, providing the differences will not seriously affect the research outcome (e.g., "a firm's payroll list may exclude recently hired employees; but these may be few and the researcher may prefer to exclude them"[7]). A particularly interesting and unusual way of dealing with some kinds of frame problems is *snowball* sampling, which may be especially useful for studying sociometric relationships within a community.[8] In this technique, one might interview a small sample of people in a community, ask them who their friends are, interview the friends asking them who *their* friends are, and so on.

Undoubtedly the simplest, most foolproof, and most widely known modification of SRS is *systematic* sampling. In this procedure the population size, N, is divided by the sample size, n, in order to yield the sampling interval (or selection interval) k. Then, one selects a random number r, from 1 to k. The rth element on the list or frame then becomes the first element selected for the sample, and thereafter, going down the list, every kth element from r is included in the sample. To illustrate, suppose that $N = 5100$, and $n = 250$. Then $k = 20.4$, which

[7] Ibid., p. 55.

[8] Coleman, 1970-b, pp. 118–19; and Kish, 1965, p. 408.

we round to 20. We select a random number between 1 and 20, which, let us say, turns out to be 14, and so the sample includes element number 14 and every 20th element thereafter: 14, 34, 54, 74, 94, ... 5,054, 5,074, and 5,094. (In this illustration the sample size turns out to be a little larger than necessary, due to the rounding of *k*.) Once *k* and *r* have been determined it is a very simple and routine clerical procedure to determine which elements are in the sample.

There are, however, two kinds of problems which may arise in systematic sampling. The first occurs when the elements are listed in a steadily increasing (or decreasing) order with respect to some variable of interest. For example, if the elements consist of individuals, and are listed in order of increasing income, then if *r* happens to be from early in the interval *k*, the mean income of the sample will be smaller than if *r* approaches *k*. The second type of problem occurs if there are some periodic fluctuations within the list, which take place in some multiple of *k*. Suppose, for instance, that we are interested in sampling daily newspapers over a period of time, and suppose further that *k* equals 7 or some multiple of 7. Then it would turn out that the newspapers selected in the sample would all be drawn from the same day of the week. Since we know from our ordinary daily experience that the content of newspapers varies according to the day of the week (in some communities Sundays are the largest editions, Mondays are the smallest, Fridays tend to emphasize recreation and entertainment, Thursdays carry much social and homemaking news, etc.), we would expect considerable bias to be introduced.

Stratified sampling is another widely used type of sampling. To use this method, the population is first divided into separate subpopulations, or strata. After the strata have been formed, a separate sample is drawn from each stratum—SRS, systematic, cluster, or some other type—and the resulting statistics for the various strata are computed, properly weighted, and combined. Since stratification obviously results in an increased amount of work, it should not be done unless there is something to be gained by it. One reason for stratifying is to decrease the variance (a statistical measure of dispersion of data) of the sample estimates. This can be achieved by making each of the strata as homogeneous as possible with respect to one or more of the (usually demographic or independent) variables of interest to the researcher. Furthermore, the strata should be as different from one another as possible with respect to these same variables. If we were studying, for example, patterns of library use among college students, we could stratify into lower division undergraduates, upper division (advanced) undergraduates, and graduate students, since our ordinary experience tells us that sophomores and seniors, say, differ considerably in their library use patterns. On the other hand, if the research interest is in, let us say, college students' parents' family mobility patterns, we would have no reason for stratifying in this way.

Another reason for using a stratified sample is if it is found to be advantageous to use different methods and procedures within each strata. For example, separate selection procedures might be used for those residing in private dwellings and those in various institutions, or different lists or frames might be available for different segments of the populations, or if there are different kinds of elements in the population such as white-collar and blue-collar workers different procedures might be appropriate. Finally, stratification would be used if information is desired about the various subpopulations, as part of the research design.

The fourth and last of these major types of sampling is known as *cluster* sampling. In cluster sampling the population is first divided into clusters, that is, units containing several sample elements. These clusters may be geographic areas, work groups, busloads of travelers, shelves of books in a library, classrooms, army barracks, time intervals, or the like. They need not even be the same size. The only requirement is that each element in the population be included in one and only one cluster. After the clusters have been formed, a sample is drawn from among the total group of clusters. Again, this may be an SRS, a systematic, a stratified or another cluster sample. It may be that the sample will consist of all the elements contained in the selected clusters. However, a more common procedure is to draw a second sample from among the total number of elements in the selected clusters. Possibly a third, fourth, or even a fifth sample will be drawn, each time from the previously selected elements. The successive samples may be of a variety of types. For obvious reasons, these are called *multistage* samples.

When the clusters used are geographic areas, this type of sample is known as an *area* sample; these have been widely used by social scientists. Let us say, for example, that the research design calls for a sample of the adult population of a given city. An area sample could be constructed as follows. First we make the reasonable assumption that every adult can be associated with a specific place of residence or dwelling unit. (In some communities the number of hoboes, migratory workers, and other homeless people may be large enough to render this assumption unreasonable.) Then, using a map, the entire city is divided into subareas, usually blocks, and a sample of these blocks is selected. The second stage consists of selecting a sample of the dwelling units in the selected blocks (this usually involves actually visiting the blocks and compiling a list of all the dwelling units), and the third stage is a sample of the adults residing in each dwelling unit. The big advantage of area sampling is that the cost per element is greatly reduced since the nonproductive time used for travel between elements is so greatly reduced. On the other hand, the disadvantages associated with it are that there is usually a much higher variance in the obtained statistics, and also the cost and difficulty of the statistical analysis are higher than with other types of samples. (See Appendix B for an example of the use of this kind of sample.)

How does the researcher decide which type of probability sample to use? Generally speaking, the nature of the research problem will rule out—or require—certain types of samples, and practical considerations will impose additional requirements. As in so many of the other points in our whole discussion of research, this decision is usually found to be a compromise between the ideal and the feasible. Economy is an important consideration—one must pay for accuracy, and sampling plans will be found to vary in how much accuracy they provide, some plans providing too much accuracy and others too little in terms of the objectives of a specific research project. In actual practice the decision is usually made in one of two ways. Either the researcher determines the level of accuracy he must have and then selects a sample design which will minimize his costs, or an acceptable cost level is selected and then that sample design is chosen which will maximize the accuracy.

There are many variations and details of the above types of sampling which have not been discussed here, but which are covered in the sources cited earlier. In particular, special procedures are called for when the research design requires repetitive sampling (time series sampling) of the same population, as with a panel design for example.

Sample size

One decision which must be made by everyone who uses a sample is the size of sample to be selected. The procedures for making this decision may be of surprising complexity to the sampling neophyte. Intuitively we expect that sample size can be specified as a percentage of population size. However, this is not the case. A little reflection quickly illustrates why this is so. Since the sample must be representative of the population, it becomes apparent that the homogeneity/heterogeneity of the population is of crucial importance. If the population is *completely* homogeneous with respect to the research variables, then a sample of size one is all that is needed. As the population increases in heterogeneity with regard to the research variables, a larger and larger sample is needed in order to be representative.[9] Thus it can be seen that the population variance (which is a measure of its homogeneity/heterogeneity) must be a far more vital factor than population size in determining sample size.

As mentioned above, there are various formulas and equations associated with the sampling statistics procedures for the different types of probability samples, and among these are formulas for computing sample size. Generally speaking, these formulas give sample size as a function of some or all of the following variables: population variance, population size, the desired accuracy of the results, and costs. In the actual use of these formulas, however, it would be a very unusual situation indeed if the researcher knew the values for all of these variables. Population variance is, of course, an unknown—this is part of what the research is designed to determine! Yet it seems that one must know the answer in order to determine the answer. One way of coping with this contradiction is to make an estimate or a guess of the variance—perhaps based upon a pilot study or on other similar previous studies. An alternative is to make an estimate or a guess of the actual population values of the means, proportions, or whatever is to be measured. This would be a matter of the researcher's judgment, based upon whatever experience and information he has, and usually he would make the most conservative estimate possible.

[9] Lazerwitz, 1968, pp. 285–87.

The population size, it turns out, is a relatively unimportant variable in the sample size formulas. When the sample size is less than 5 or 10 percent of the population (some say 20 percent), the term containing population size (usually referred to as the *finite population correction*) drops out of the formula for all practical purposes. When the sample is a *larger* percentage of the population, omission of the finite population correction simply produces more conservative results. (These comments on population size are simply a somewhat more precise statement of the earlier remark to the effect that sample size cannot be specified simply as a percentage of population size.)

The desired level of accuracy of the results is another decision which the researcher must make. This is determined by the objectives of his research—its importance, the uses to which the results will be put, the requirements specified by the funding agency, if any, the magnitude of the harm which might be a consequence of inaccurate results, and so on. Finally, sample costs typically must be either minimized or held below a specific set figure, and these can be determined only in relation to the overall budget.

In the use of the above formulas, it is probably the determination of the variance which causes the most difficulty. As a practical matter, however, it is common to select a sample size by using conservative estimates of the population values which will yield results of at least a given, specified level of accuracy, regardless of the population size. Very useful tables have been constructed to aid the researcher in making these choices,[10] and greatly simplified formulas have been developed.[11]

Having concluded our discussion of the various aspects of data collection, in our next chapter we will briefly examine some of the tools which can be of aid to the researcher at different stages of the project.

EXERCISES

1. For each of the studies listed below, decide whether each can best be researched using a probability or nonprobability sample. Discuss the reasons for your decision. Next, select one of the sampling techniques discussed in this chapter which might be used to ob-

[10] Parten, 1950, chap. 9.

[11] Lazerwitz, 1968, pp. 285–87.

tain respondents and describe how you would go about obtaining them by using the sampling technique.

a. A study to determine if juveniles with high "pick-up" rates have a high perceived family conflict as measured by a standardized family conflict scale. (The study is being carried out in a community of 50,000 people).

b. A study to test the hypothesis that children's scholastic success varies directly with parental participation in Parent-Teacher Associations in a community of 10,000 people.

c. A study of socioeconomic and attitudinal characteristics of persons who own citizen's band mobile unit radios in a medium-sized metropolitan area.

d. A survey of congressional district residents' attitudes toward proposed environmental control laws.

e. A study to determine the general priorities of the students at your college or university regarding long-term world problems.

2. Suppose you are conducting a survey to determine dormitory residents' opinions of the quality of food served in the dormitory cafeteria. The dormitory to be surveyed is a high rise building with ten floors and has 500 residents. Construct a sampling frame and describe how you might select a sample of 100 residents for the survey using a simple random sample.

3. A researcher is conducting a descriptive study to compare political ideologies of precinct leaders in medium-sized communities to those ideologies of the constituent members of their precincts. In the first community being studied there are 50 precincts with five elected precinct leaders per precinct. Within each precinct there are from 100 to 200 party members who participate occasionally in precinct political activities. During the last two local elections voters elected city officials (council members) and passed several bond proposals by very large majorities (two of them by 20-to-1 margins.

   Suppose you are the researcher and have decided that it is only feasible to collect data on a sample totalling 300 persons for the research. In view of this, describe how you might use the stratified sampling technique described in this chapter to choose respondents.

4. A researcher has indicated on a map of the city the location of 7,500 single family residences. The residences are located on about 300 city blocks and each residence and block has been assigned a unique number. The research objective is to test the

hypothesis that household economic level is related to residence health hazards. The researcher decides that he needs a sample of 600 residences to adequately test his hypothesis and that he will use systematic sampling to choose which residences he will use for data collection. Suppose you are the researcher. Describe briefly, but in some detail, how you might carry out the sampling and then discuss some of the sampling biases you would have to be alert for when using the systematic sampling techniques in this study.

5. A researcher hypothesizes that grades on midterm exams vary according to the level of income of students' families. He sets out to test his hypothesis in a class of 250 students where 80 students come from families with very low annual incomes (under $2,500) and 60 students come from families with very high annual incomes (over $50,000). If the researcher uses a sample size of 30 students, discuss the likelihood of achieving accurate results once he collects his data. What might be the best sample size to use for this study (other than a complete or near-complete census) so that accurate results may be obtained? Discuss your answer.

Chapter 15

Tools for research

In this day of rapid technological advance, almost anything written about specific research tools may be obsolete before it appears in print—at least as far as the most affluent research undertakings are concerned. But there are many researchers in this country and throughout the world who do not have access to the newest—and most expensive!—equipment, even if such equipment were necessary for their research. It is important to remember that tools are merely *aids,* and therefore rarely "necessary." Undoubtedly research tools may facilitate research, they may make it easier or faster or more accurate, and perhaps more productive. But a lack of tools should never be used as an excuse for not doing high-quality scientific research. It may be more difficult to undertake the research without certain tools, but then the person in search of an easy task would do well to avoid sociological research.

Many of the world's great antiquities—works of art, engineering feats, handiworks—serve as excellent examples of the magnificent work which can be achieved using tools which, by today's standards, were completely primitive and undeveloped. Consider the Taj Mahal (17th century), the Great Wall of China (15th–17th centuries), the famous 57-foot-tall, monolithic statue at Sravanabelgola in India (10th century), the Parthenon (400 B.C.), the amazing drainage systems of the ancient Indus cities of Harappa and Mohenjo-daro, and their ocean-going vessels (2000 B.C.), and the Egyptian pyramids (3000 B.C.). In the contemporary world, works which are just as remarkable are accomplished by many peoples who do not have access to power tools, computers, labor-saving devices, and the technology which accompanies them, but who do have—and make use of—manpower, ingenuity, patience, intelligence, and experience. So it is with sociological research. More and more tools for data collection, processing, and analysis are being developed all the time, and undoubtedly they will become more widely available as time passes. Whether the individual researcher has access to such tools or not, it should always be kept in mind that they are merely tools.

Another qualification is that the tools which are used will affect the course of the research being done.[1] A decision to collect data by use of a questionnaire, for example, necessarily means that the people being studied must be literate. If a tool or instrument is consistently used over a long period of time, or is found to be particularly useful in researching a given type of problem, this is likely to affect subsequent decisions as to which problems to research. Consider how the development of small-group laboratories has not only made it possible to study interaction within small groups, but it has also stimulated further interest in this kind of research. The mere existence of such a lab may intrigue and encourage students and other researchers to such an extent that they devote their research energies to these kinds of studies rather than to some alternative.

Let us look at some of the tools which may be useful in sociological research.

In a great many data collection procedures, whether questioning, observation, or study of archival data, much time and energy can be saved and the chance of error reduced by using some kind of standardized form or procedure for the actual mechanical or physical aspects of recording the data. The most obvious examples are homemade forms in which a specific space is provided for recording each item of information, with no ambiguity. For example, the common question concerning marital status might be provided for as follows:

Marital status: ______ Married
______ Divorced
______ Widowed
______ Separated
______ Single, never married

When the researcher places a check mark in one of the blanks there is much less chance of confusion than if he merely records

[1] Kuhn, 1962, p. 59; and Kaplan, 1964, p. 135.

the marital status somewhere in his field notes. Special forms for keeping track of interviewer assignments, supplies and purchasing, personnel records, and the like, may also play an important part in research procedures. Homemade forms, checklists, and the like are relatively quickly, easily, and inexpensively produced using familiar office duplicating procedures such as the mimeograph (e.g., A. B. Dick or Gestetner) or spirit duplicating (e.g., Ditto).

Sociograms, as described previously, may also be considered to be data collection tools.

Maps, both published and homemade, can be very useful in recording certain kinds of data. With published maps it is important to ascertain their accuracy and recency. Homemade maps, especially of small areas showing, for example, seating patterns at a table or patterns of movement around a room, may display data in a much more productive way than mere written descriptions.[2]

A great number—literally thousands—of paper-and-pencil scales and indices designed to measure a wide variety of sociological variables are available.[3] Most common are scales for measuring attitudes—toward virtually anything one can think of: divorce, mathematics, farming, religion, menstruation, internationalism, movies, old people, vivisection, chivalry, and so on. There are also instruments for measuring social status, group structure, job satisfaction, leadership, marital adjustment, and a host of others. Many of these have been widely used and their reliability and validity assessed. Therefore a researcher making use of one of these already-existing scales is not only saved the laborious task of constructing and testing a new scale, but more important he has the opportunity of comparing his results with those obtained by previous researchers. This comparison process and the resulting identification and verification of relationships among variables is, of course, the ultimate purpose of scientific research. It is probably safe to say that a new scale should not be constructed until and unless there is believed to be some inadequacy in already existing scales.

An earlier form of the Kuder Preference Record[4] utilized an

---

[2] Melbin, 1960.

[3] For descriptions of many, see D. Miller, 1970, pp. 88–99, 161–391. For the most recent complete listing of sociological scales, see Bonjean et al., 1967.

[4] Kuder, 1946.

Figure 7. Machine-scored answer sheet

NAME ____________ LAST ____________ FIRST ____________ MIDDLE ____________ DATE ____________ AGE ________ SEX ______ M OR F DATE OF BIRTH ____________

SCHOOL ____________ CITY ____________ GRADE OR CLASS ____________ INSTRUCTOR ____________

NAME OF TEST ____________ PART ____________ 1 ____________ 2 ____________

DIRECTIONS: Read each question and its lettered answers. When you have decided which answer is correct, blacken the corresponding space on this sheet with a No. 2 pencil. Make your mark as long as the pair of lines, and completely fill the area between the pair of lines. If you change your mind, erase your first mark COMPLETELY. Make no stray marks; they may count against you.

SAMPLE

I. CHICAGO is

I - A a country	I - D a city
I - B a mountain	I - E a state
I - C an island	

I A B C D E

SCORES

1 ________	5 ________
2 ________	6 ________
3 ________	7 ________
4 ________	8 ________

IDENTIFICATION NUMBER

0	1	2	3	4	5	6	7	8	9
0	1	2	3	4	5	6	7	8	9
0	1	2	3	4	5	6	7	8	9
0	1	2	3	4	5	6	7	8	9
0	1	2	3	4	5	6	7	8	9
0	1	2	3	4	5	6	7	8	9
0	1	2	3	4	5	6	7	8	9
0	1	2	3	4	5	6	7	8	9
0	1	2	3	4	5	6	7	8	9
0	1	2	3	4	5	6	7	8	9

1	A	B	C	D	E	2	A	B	C	D	E	3	A	B	C	D	E	4	A	B	C	D	E
5	A	B	C	D	E	6	A	B	C	D	E	7	A	B	C	D	E	8	A	B	C	D	E
9	A	B	C	D	E	10	A	B	C	D	E	11	A	B	C	D	E	12	A	B	C	D	E
13	A	B	C	D	E	14	A	B	C	D	E	15	A	B	C	D	E	16	A	B	C	D	E
17	A	B	C	D	E	18	A	B	C	D	E	19	A	B	C	D	E	20	A	B	C	D	E
21	A	B	C	D	E	22	A	B	C	D	E	23	A	B	C	D	E	24	A	B	C	D	E
25	A	B	C	D	E	26	A	B	C	D	E	27	A	B	C	D	E	28	A	B	C	D	E
29	A	B	C	D	E	30	A	B	C	D	E	31	A	B	C	D	E	32	A	B	C	D	E
33	A	B	C	D	E	34	A	B	C	D	E	35	A	B	C	D	E	36	A	B	C	D	E
37	A	B	C	D	E	38	A	B	C	D	E	39	A	B	C	D	E	40	A	B	C	D	E
41	A	B	C	D	E	42	A	B	C	D	E	43	A	B	C	D	E	44	A	B	C	D	E
45	A	B	C	D	E	46	A	B	C	D	E	47	A	B	C	D	E	48	A	B	C	D	E
49	A	B	C	D	E	50	A	B	C	D	E	51	A	B	C	D	E	52	A	B	C	D	E
53	A	B	C	D	E	54	A	B	C	D	E	55	A	B	C	D	E	56	A	B	C	D	E
57	A	B	C	D	E	58	A	B	C	D	E	59	A	B	C	D	E	60	A	B	C	D	E
61	A	B	C	D	E	62	A	B	C	D	E	63	A	B	C	D	E	64	A	B	C	D	E
65	A	B	C	D	E	66	A	B	C	D	E	67	A	B	C	D	E	68	A	B	C	D	E
69	A	B	C	D	E	70	A	B	C	D	E	71	A	B	C	D	E	72	A	B	C	D	E
73	A	B	C	D	E	74	A	B	C	D	E	75	A	B	C	D	E	76	A	B	C	D	E
77	A	B	C	D	E	78	A	B	C	D	E	79	A	B	C	D	E	80	A	B	C	D	E
81	A	B	C	D	E	82	A	B	C	D	E	83	A	B	C	D	E	84	A	B	C	D	E
85	A	B	C	D	E	86	A	B	C	D	E	87	A	B	C	D	E	88	A	B	C	D	E
89	A	B	C	D	E	90	A	B	C	D	E	91	A	B	C	D	E	92	A	B	C	D	E
93	A	B	C	D	E	94	A	B	C	D	E	95	A	B	C	D	E	96	A	B	C	D	E
97	A	B	C	D	E	98	A	B	C	D	E	99	A	B	C	D	E	100	A	B	C	D	E
101	A	B	C	D	E	102	A	B	C	D	E	103	A	B	C	D	E	104	A	B	C	D	E
105	A	B	C	D	E	106	A	B	C	D	E	107	A	B	C	D	E	108	A	B	C	D	E
109	A	B	C	D	E	110	A	B	C	D	E	111	A	B	C	D	E	112	A	B	C	D	E
113	A	B	C	D	E	114	A	B	C	D	E	115	A	B	C	D	E	116	A	B	C	D	E
117	A	B	C	D	E	118	A	B	C	D	E	119	A	B	C	D	E	120	A	B	C	D	E
121	A	B	C	D	E	122	A	B	C	D	E	123	A	B	C	D	E	124	A	B	C	D	E
125	A	B	C	D	E	126	A	B	C	D	E	127	A	B	C	D	E	128	A	B	C	D	E
129	A	B	C	D	E	130	A	B	C	D	E	131	A	B	C	D	E	132	A	B	C	D	E
133	A	B	C	D	E	134	A	B	C	D	E	135	A	B	C	D	E	136	A	B	C	D	E
137	A	B	C	D	E	138	A	B	C	D	E	139	A	B	C	D	E	140	A	B	C	D	E
141	A	B	C	D	E	142	A	B	C	D	E	143	A	B	C	D	E	144	A	B	C	D	E
145	A	B	C	D	E	146	A	B	C	D	E	147	A	B	C	D	E	148	A	B	C	D	E
149	A	B	C	D	E	150	A	B	C	D	E												

IBM 1230 DOCUMENT NO 511 WHICH CAN BE USED IN LIEU OF IBM 805 FORM NO 1000 A 445

PRINTED IN U. S. A.

answer pad in which the respondent, instead of using a pencil, was instructed to record his responses by making pin pricks in appropriate spaces on the pad. *Providing it is not in violation of copyright or patent restrictions,* this is a form which might be usefully adapted for data collection purposes under some circumstances.

The widespread use of machines to score tests and examinations holds considerable potential for data collection. Special answer sheets are used, one example of which is shown in Figure 7, on which the data are recorded by blacking in the appropriate space with an ordinary pencil. The answer sheets are scored by means of an optical scanner, which can be set up to print the test score directly on the sheet and also to accomplish various other tasks such as statistical computation (giving, perhaps, the mean, standard deviation, and an item-analysis of the whole set). They may also readily be scored by hand by using a stencil overlay. These answer sheets may be easily adapted for use in recording responses to questioning or other types of research data. An enormous advantage is that it is possible automatically to transfer the data on the answer sheets directly to punched cards, which may in turn be manipulated by card handling equipment or used as inputs to a computer. If questioning is the data collection method in use, and if furthermore it involves any kind of "test" in which the purpose is to assess the respondents' knowledge about, or attitude toward, some object, it is thus possible to score the answers directly by these means.

An older variation of the above is mark-sense punched cards—cards of the same size as the ordinary punched cards, on which the data are recorded in the same way as on the machine-graded answer sheets, as in Figure 8. However, these usually require the use of a special pencil, as they are read by an electrical sensing device rather than an optical scanner. Another limitation is that because of their smaller size less raw data can be put on a single card. In the ordinary use of these cards, they are automatically punched according to the data put on them in pencil. These can then, as above, be used on card handling equipment or as computer inputs.

Machines, instruments, tools, and other devices originally made for other purposes may sometimes be adapted for data collection uses. Some years ago, for example, an office

Figure 8. Mark-sense card

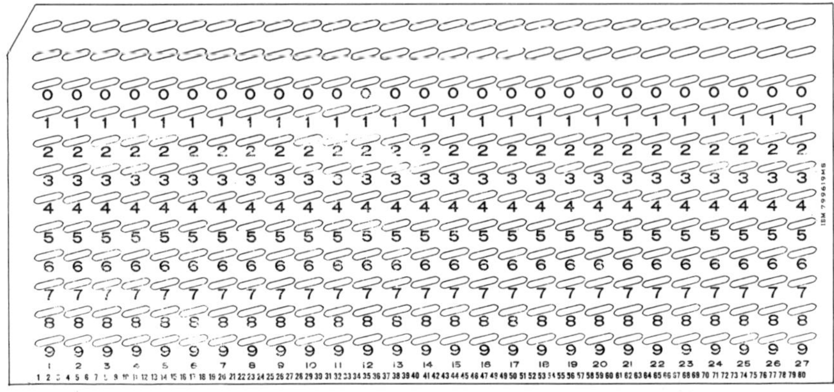

Stenotype machine was used for recording interaction in a research situation involving direct observation of behavior.[5] Undoubtedly many other machines—office and otherwise—can be adapted for data collection use, depending only on the nature of the research and the ingenuity of the researcher.

Cameras, tape recorders, video-recorders, stopwatches, timers, and the like are obvious and familiar examples of tools which may be of considerable value in data collection.

There is virtually no limit to the kinds of tools, equipment, and facilities which may be especially designed for data collection. The advent of laboratory studies of small groups in the 1950s, gave rise to much emphasis upon development of equipment. Among the first was Chapple's Interaction Chronograph, a machine for recording and evaluating personality characteristics.[6] Another early, and very important, one was Bales' Interaction Recorder, designed for use with his system of Interaction Process Analysis.[7] In the intervening years a great variety of equipment ranging from very simple to the most complex has been designed by many researchers. An example of the more sophisticated efforts is the Interaction Screen. This is described as:

> an electronic system consisting of five major components: two consoles, one for each subject, through which, by operating dials and switches, they interact with one another; an experimenter's

[5] Carter et al., 1951.

[6] Chapple, 1949.

[7] Bales, 1951, pp. 3–5.

> console for monitoring subjects' interaction; a control unit for altering the response possibilities open to the subjects; and a card punch that records all interaction by both subjects.[8]

Not only has there been much effort in developing such equipment, but entire laboratory facilities have been constructed in many locations for the purpose of conducting research, especially in the areas of small groups and industrial management.[9]

Most of the tools discussed thus far are especially suited for data collection. Others may be more useful for data processing and analysis. At the simplest and most inexpensive level are various hand-held mechanical devices. These include counters (especially useful for counting several different things simultaneously), pocket adding machines, slide rules, and abacuses. The slide rule is a particularly powerful and useful tool in the hands of a skilled user.

More expensive, but far more versatile, are electronic pocket calculators. These can provide great savings in time and labor in many of the common mathematical and statistical procedures.

Desk calculators which perform a great variety of functions are available. As would be expected, these are considerably more expensive than pocket calculators. They may be mechanical, electrical, or electronic in operation, and the output may be in either printed or visual form, or both. Some electronic calculators have memory circuits and can be programmed to perform various complex routines automatically, according to the user's needs, thus serving as miniature computers.

Punched cards and the various pieces of equipment designed to handle them have become common and useful tools for all kinds of research. The standard card has 80 columns and 12 rows of figures (see Figure 9). The user punches holes through the card at the appropriate figures, thereby permitting electrical contacts to be made through the holes when the card is passed through a machine. The holes are punched by use of a keypunch, a machine similar to a typewriter. A familiar illustration of the use of punched cards would be for questionnaire data where, for example, each respondent's marital status could

---

[8] Sawyer and Friedall, 1965, p. 447. See Hayes, 1969, for description of a similar apparatus.

[9] For example, see: Noël, 1969; Fromkin, 1969; Hoggatt et al., 1969; Rijsman, 1969; and Shure and Meeker, 1969. A useful reference for constructing psychological laboratory equipment is Sidowski, 1966.

Figure 9. Standard punched card

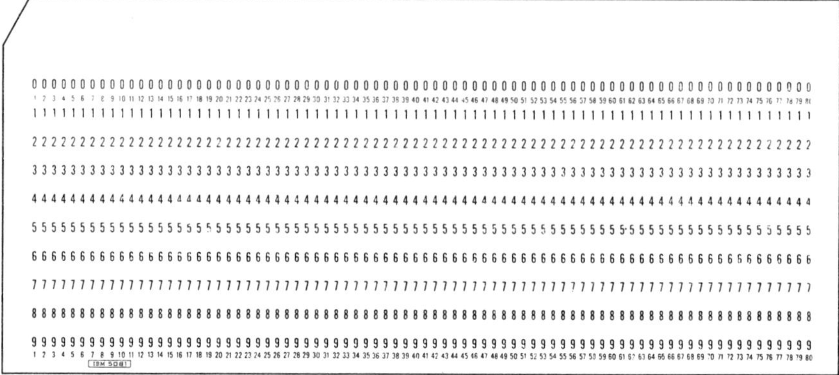

be punched in a specified column, using "1" for married, "2" for divorced, "3" for widowed, and "4" for single. After being punched, the cards may be sorted, duplicated, collated, counted, or otherwise manipulated, or the information from them may be read, tabulated, and processed, by means of various machines. Punched cards also serve as one of the most useful forms for input of information to computers. These cards have the advantage of being easily handled, economical, and able to store large amounts of information in a relatively small space. The machines which process them operate at extremely high speeds; however, the machines are quite expensive.

A simple and inexpensive system for sorting data is the patented McBee Keysort system (of Litton Industries). This system also makes use of cards, but they may be of any size and shape to suit the research. Holes are punched around the periphery, leaving the center free for entering any kind of written information. To use the system, the edges of the card are notched by either a hand punch or a machine (see Figure 10). To sort the cards, a heavy needle is inserted through the appropriate hole in a stack of cards. Whichever of the cards have been notched, as in code positions 5 and 8 in Figure 10, will fall away from the rest of the stack when they are lifted by the needle. One hundred or more cards may be sorted at a time, and therefore this system would probably best be used when there is a maximum of about a thousand cards to be sorted. It is probably also most useful for situations in which repeated use is to be made of the data cards, and/or when they must be sorted over and over again on various items, rather than when a single sorting will suffice.

Figure 10. McBee Keysort® card

Electronic computers, the most versatile and powerful of the research tools, are becoming increasingly available not only in the United States but throughout the world. The distinguishing characteristics of a computer are that it has a memory or storage unit and can automatically execute instructions contained in the memory, and that it can make logical decisions. The input to a computer consists of two kinds of information, the data and the *program* which tells the computer what operations it should perform on the data. The program is written by a skilled technician in one of several special languages, depending upon which specific computer is used and what the research problem is. The most common physical forms of inputs are punched cards, magnetic tape, paper tape, magnetic ink, optical scanners, and special typewriter keyboards. The output usually takes the form of a printout, an information sheet printed automatically by the computer.

As indicated in our earlier discussion of data collection, computers may be used for simulation of data. In some cases computers have even been used to *design, construct,* and *control* the research, as well as to analyze the data.[10]

The main advantage of the computer for data analysis is that it can perform enormous numbers of calculations with extreme rapidity, and that it can perform these on great masses of data. The considerable cost of computers and the skills necessary for their maintenance and operation may be disadvantages. Despite the speed and power of these tools, they may be inappropriate for some small-scale research. Although the computer time required is short—usually a matter of seconds—the time spent in punching cards, writing a program, and interacting with computer personnel may add up to quite a bit. Furthermore, in research of any size there may be a temptation to use a "shot-gun" approach—for example, programming the computer to produce correlation coefficients among all possible combinations of data items, in the hope that "something significant" will turn up. When wisely used, however, computers are of inestimable importance. (See discussion of SPSS in the next chapter.)

Undoubtedly the alert, experienced researcher can suggest many other possible tools for the collection, processing, and analysis of data.

EXERCISES

1. Several means of processing data were discussed in this chapter. They ranged from simple manual processing (e.g., using the McBee Keysort system) to machine processing (e.g., using mark-sensing cards and a counter-sorter) to electronic computer processing (e.g., reading data into a computer memory and analyzing it using a computer program). Below are listed several studies which researchers might carry out. Assume that you are the researcher and must decide in each case what kind of processing is appropriate for your study. Decide whether you will rely primarily upon manual, machine, or computer processing, and discuss the reasons for your decisions.
   a. A study designed to determine the difference in socioeconomic characteristics and attitudes toward current race problems of two groups of persons having different political orientations. Subjects will be chosen randomly from membership lists of persons active in the local Democratic and Republican

[10] Cooperband, 1966.

parties (in a town of about 50,000 persons in your state). Sample size will be 50 for each party. The data will be collected by questionnaire and will include 6 items on socioeconomic characteristics and 15 attitude items.

b. A study to determine the attitudes and practices of college sophomores in regard to personal use of marijuana. Subjects for the study will be those in a 10 percent random sample of all students at a college of about 15,000 students in your state. Data will be collected by interview and will include 20 items on current practices and 20 attitude items.

c. A study to determine the situational characteristics associated with college students' first acquaintance with vulgar words, i.e., "four-letter" words. Subjects will be 100 students enrolled in an introductory sociology class. Data will be collected by asking students to write one-page descriptions of their first recollection of the situations in which they heard a particular four-letter word and knew or found out that the word was "taboo." Descriptions will be analyzed to determine situational characteristics, and a coding system will be developed to categorize them.

d. A study to determine if oldest children with younger siblings are more aggressive than only children. Subjects will be chosen from a random sample of about 50 children taken from all kindergarten classes in a town of about 25,000 people in your state. Data will be obtained by direct observation and ratings by the researcher on five to ten different occasions in the kindergarten setting, and by asking teachers to rate children on a 10-point scale of aggressiveness.

2. Scales and indices which have been previously developed and published by other researchers constitute a valuable research tool. Several sources which describe these tools were discussed in this chapter. Using one or more of these sources, *(a)* select an appropriate scale or index for one of the above studies or for a study which you make up, *(b)* list the items contained in the scale or index, and *(c)* discuss how the data obtained by using it could help to fulfill the objectives of the study (include in your discussion the relevance of the individual items, measures of reliability and validity, etc.).

Chapter 16

Data processing, analysis, and interpretation

At this point in the research project, having utilized one or more of the many data collection procedures which have been discussed, the researcher has collected his data. He now faces the task of arranging these data so as to provide the answers to the questions, the solutions to the problems, or adequate tests of the hypotheses, which appeared in his statement of specific objectives, and which served as the starting point of his research. There is a temptation to think that the collection of data is the major activity of a research project, and that once it has been completed the project is almost finished and everything else will just "fall into place." To be sure, data collection is usually the most interesting and exciting phase of any project, but it is by no means the final phase. Probably almost as much work remains to be done after the data collection as was done up to that point.

Regardless of the type of data collection or the form in which the data exist, they will not automatically indicate whether the hypothesis is supported or refuted, or give the answers to the research questions or solutions to the research problems. Indeed, some systematic analysis of the data almost always is required to attain the researcher's specific objectives. This analysis must include not only the answers or solutions or tests of the hypothesis, but also some statements of just how certain the researcher is of the correctness of these results. To the extent that it is feasible, the experienced researcher will have already determined many of these analytic steps, since what is done at this stage and the way it is done will depend upon what has gone before. However, unforeseen events always occur. "Murphy's Law" (if something can go wrong, it will[1]) always seems to operate in research activities, and so the initial plans for data analysis may have to be modified.

In those relatively uncommon researches in which the amount of raw data is very small—for whatever reason—it may be that some or many of the following processing and analysis steps may be omitted. The following pages, however, apply to the great majority of sociological research undertakings.

DATA PROCESSING

In order to analyze the data, it is usually necessary to first manipulate or handle the raw data in some manner so as to render them amenable to analysis. This is what is meant by the general term "data processing."

The physical form of the raw data which have been collected may vary considerably. They may be, for example, in the form of interview schedules, questionnaires, tally sheets or other forms from some observation process, punched cards, audio tapes, video tapes, photographs, computer printouts, or many others. Most commonly the data probably appear as something *written* on pieces of paper and thus the first—obvious but necessary—part of the data processing will be to provide some means of storing, transporting, filing, and otherwise manipulating these pieces of paper. (In the event that the data are on audio tapes an important preliminary processing step will usually be to prepare a transcript of the material.) In an interview study of only moderate size this can necessitate a considerable amount of filing space. Some form of identification of the various "pieces of paper" is needed, too, in order to maintain or create any necessary chronological or other sequences or order to the data. Using different colors of paper or punched cards can be useful in such situations. Depending upon the specific nature of the material, other storage precautions may be advisable. For example, tapes should not be kept closer than about two feet from ordinary domestic electric power cords. Humidity and temperature may be important considerations, too.

Editing is customarily the next step. This is essential when the data have been collected by questioning, and probably of

---

[1] Martin, 1973, p. 4 (a book not to be ignored).

only slightly less importance when one of the other methods of data collection has been used. Editing refers to the more or less mechanical and commonsense procedures of going through the data to ensure that they are complete, that there are no inconsistencies or omissions, that all the blanks have been filled in, that everything which is supposed to be there is actually there, that any important sequences are maintained, that no glaring errors have been made, and so on. Editing also includes ensuring that the data are in the appropriate form for coding, or keypunching, or tabulating, or whatever the next step may be. In any research other than the small-scale, one-person project, it is quite possible that the data collection and the editing, as well as subsequent steps, will be accomplished by different persons. In such a case it is during the editing that any comments, elaborations, suggestions, or explanations written by the data collector will be noted and appropriate action taken.[2]

By the time the editing has been done the researcher must have a pretty accurate idea of what kinds of analytic procedures he will be using. If even the simplest of mathematical or statistical procedures will be used, such as graphs, tables, charts, frequency distributions, or even sorting (manual or mechanical) into categories, or if the data will be processed by card sorters or counters, or if a computer will be used, then coding will be the necessary next step. Coding is the process of assigning a number or other symbol to every bit of data, each of which symbols designates a specific class or category.

Let us take, for illustration, the familiar question on an interview schedule, "What was the last grade you completed in school?" The responses to this, in the United States, might range anywhere from zero to 12, for high school graduation, or more if the respondent has completed some years of college. Usually, however, it would be not only unnecessary, but confusing or worse, to report the responses to this question as they were received. Instead, the replies would be placed into classes or categories which have some meaning in terms of the research objectives, for example:

No school.

1st through 7th grade.

8th grade.

Some high school.

[2] See Parten, 1950, chap. 13, for detailed instructions on editing interview schedules.

High school graduation.
Some college.
College—bachelor's degree.
Graduate study.

The most simple and obvious way of coding here would be to assign the numerals 1 through 8 to the eight categories, (although 0 through 7 or some other sequence could be used instead), and the coding operation would consist of assigning the appropriate number to the response to that question on each of the interview schedules. In this illustration, it is obvious that life would be much simpler for the researcher if these categories are actually printed on the schedule, instead of merely the original open-ended question. An even further convenience is to have the category numbers 1 through 8 printed as well, and thus the interviewer need only encircle the appropriate number. When this is done the schedule is said to be precoded. Obviously, only fixed-alternative questions can be precoded. After all of the responses to this question have been coded to indicate the appropriate one of the eight categories, it becomes a relatively simple matter to construct a frequency distribution, or to put the data on punched cards. This illustration is quite simple and straightforward, mainly because it is possible for the researcher to determine in advance what categories he will use.

In some instances the coding operation may require greater amounts of judgment and more difficult decisions on the part of the coder, and this is especially so when, because of the nature of the question, it is not possible to anticipate the responses which will be received.

For example, in the study of knowledge about heart disease[3] one area of interest was whether the respondent had seen any educational movies dealing with heart disease, and if so, who had sponsored the movies. An open-end question was used in order not to influence the respondent's answers: "Do you recall who presented the movies?" It was not possible to anticipate the various replies which would be received to this question, but after examining the responses five categories emerged. The instructions to the coders were as follows:

Code 1 for any answer indicating that the film was presented through the efforts of the Heart Association.

[3] Manheim and Howlett, 1964.

Code 2 for any answer indicating that it was presented by health personnel and/or health associations, other than the Heart Association.

Code 3 for any answer indicating the film was presented by a school, club, fraternal or civic organization, business, etc., other than the above.

Code 4 if the film was presented at a commercial movie theater.

Code 5 if "don't know."

Clearly, in this situation the coder must have, as a minimum, a working knowledge of the various clubs, health organizations, movie theaters, and so on in the community.[4]

If machine processing of one kind or another will be used, the next step will likely be to put the data on punched cards. The keypunch operator needs only to know what numeral(s) or alphabetic letters are to be punched into each column, and so a completely precoded data form makes this quite easy. One simple way of doing this is to punch the data for a given item number into the column of the same number—the response to item number 16, for example, being put into column 16, and so on. By so doing, up to 80 responses may be put in a single card (although this would not leave any columns for identifying information). There are, of course, many other patterns for keypunching. This operation may be a source of considerable error since it is a slow and purely routine clerical step. Generally the keypunch operator has no other contact with the research operation, and is therefore not in a position to exercise any judgment or make any decisions in the event of ambiguities or omissions in the coded data. Increasingly, however, technological innovations point toward the bypassing of the keypunch operation through such means as doing the coding on mark-sense or optical scanner forms which can be automatically read and punched onto cards.

DATA ANALYSIS

There is no distinct separation between data processing and data analysis; as used here the former tends to emphasize the preliminary steps, but the specific nature of the research and the

[4] For more detailed suggestions about coding for sample surveys, see: Parten, 1950, chap. 14; and, Babbie, 1973, chap. 10.

data may blur the distinction even more. In this section we will first comment on some general characteristics of measurement, and then will discuss some of the common procedures used for the analysis of sociological data. This coverage will consist of a broad overview rather than a detailed examination, for three reasons. First, there is no precise, specific list of procedures included under the heading of data analysis. As with so many other things we have previously discussed, these will be determined by the particulars of the project and the data. While some procedures are widely used—perhaps too much so—others may have only occasional and special applications.

In the second place, the general area of data analysis is currently in a great state of flux. The past five or ten years have seen the introduction and development of a variety of new approaches—path analysis, causal inference, multivariate analysis, smallest space analysis, and a reexamination of measurement assumptions, to say nothing of the proliferation of computer use, to name a few—and the average researcher is hard put to keep abreast of all of these. The changes and new developments in data analysis overshadow by far any changes in the other aspects of research methodology. For example, in 1969 the American Sociological Association issued the first of a series of annual publications designed to enable the social scientist to keep abreast of the methodological changes in the field, and it is interesting and significant to note that, to date, these volumes have been devoted almost entirely to articles concerned with the analysis of data.[5] Finally, many of these newer analytic approaches are related to the familiar statistical procedures, and hence are things which the student is likely to have studied (or will study) in his training in statistics, and so there is no need to repeat them here.

The distinction which used to be made between qualitative and quantitative (usually termed "statistical") research or analysis is really not a particularly useful or important distinction today. And as with so many other dichotomies, it probably never was a valid distinction. Usually it was conceptualized in terms of one approach *versus* the other, and each side had its adherents and detractors. However, a little examination of these two reveals that they are not really in opposition to each other.

[5] Borgatta, 1969; Borgatta and Bohrnstedt, 1970; Costner, 1971; Costner, 1972; Costner, 1974; Heise, 1974; Heise, 1975.

Speaking generally, "qualitative" is taken to mean that the things being considered are not obviously numerical in nature, nor can they be put in numerical form, whereas "quantitative" implies that they are and can be. However, this distinction largely disappears through the use of content analysis, and the formation of categories and typologies, which will be discussed below. Furthermore, statistical procedures are tools which can, and indeed *should*, be utilized *whenever they are appropriate*, but they are not the goals or end products of research. The use of statistical procedures, or more generally of numerical data, is most definitely *not* to be taken as an indication of the quality of research.[6]

Measurement

Most, if not all, sociological research involves some kind of measurement. Measurement may be as simple an operation as determining whether two entities are the same size or are unequal, or it may be a very complex and accurate procedure. Basically, measurement consists of assigning numbers to a series of objects. This means that there must be rules which determine *what* numbers to assign to the objects. Sometimes this is more important than others. *What* my telephone number is, is of no consequence as long as the people who wish to call me know the number. But what my age, or bank balance is, is of considerable importance. In a numerical grading system utilizing the numbers 4, 3, 2, 1, and 0, it makes little difference whether 4 is the highest or lowest grade, as long as the people using the system are in agreement.

Furthermore, there must be some rules stating which mathematical operations can appropriately be performed on the numbers once they have been assigned. Obviously it is ridiculous to think of multiplying or adding telephone numbers, nor do we say that one telephone number is twice another one. A *measurement scale* is essentially a rule which specifies the kind of circumstances under which it is appropriate to perform certain mathematical operations. The practical problem in measurement becomes that of determining which measurement scale is

[6] For a general discussion of social psychological data analysis, see Mosteller and Tukey, 1968.

isomorphic to the set of rules which had been used to assign numbers to the objects.[7] (The scale which permits the use of multiplication is clearly not isomorphic to the set of rules used to assign telephone numbers.) There are four scales which are commonly used: the nominal, ordinal, interval, and ratio scales (in order of increasing "strength").

The nominal scale is merely a classificatory scale. A number is assigned to each object or class of objects purely as a means of identification. Examples are telephone numbers, automobile license plates, and the use of the symbol "1" for male and "2" for female (or vice versa) in coding questionnaires. No ordinary arithmetic procedures may be performed on such numbers; we do not, for example, say that two males equal one female, etc. The numbers may be completely reassigned without altering the meaning or usefulness of the scale.[8]

The ordinal scale consists of a *ranking* or *ordering* of the objects. Examples are the usual social class rankings, the hardness of minerals, military ranks, and the ranking of job applicants. The essential relationship here is that any object on the list is "greater than" (more than, higher than, etc.) any other object lower on the list, with respect to whatever criteria are being considered. Again, the ordinary arithmetic operations are not appropriately performed on these numbers; thus it makes no difference whether we use the numbers 6, 5, 4, 3, 2, and 1, or 25, 23, 16, 10, 5, and 0, to represent the six social classes, so long as the order is not changed.[9] As long as the order of the assigned numbers remains unchanged, the scale remains useful. *It is important to remember that the great majority of sociological data is isomorphic to nothing stronger than the ordinal scale.* (It has been suggested that ordinal data can be advantageously treated as interval data, but there is some question about this.[10])

---

[7] See the discussion of isomorphism in the section on mathematical models in Chapter 2.

[8] The basic description of these scales appears in Stevens, 1951. See Siegel, 1956, pp. 21–30, for a good discussion of the scales and the admissible operations and appropriate statistics. See also any standard statistics textbook.

[9] A variation on this is the "fixed-origin ordinal" scale which is useful when dealing with a bipolar attribute, such as favorableness of attitude, which has a meaningful zero point. See Torgerson, 1968, p. 26. He also discusses two other less common scales which are of potential importance for social science research, the "log interval" and the "difference" scales. See also Coombs, 1953.

[10] Labovitz, 1970-a.

Elaboration on these distinctions and on all the following matters can be found in any standard statistics book.[11]

An interval scale has the characteristics of an ordinal scale plus the fact that the intervals or distances between numbers on the scale are equal. Sociological examples of interval scales are rare, but the most familiar are the Fahrenheit and Celsius temperature scales. Not only is there a ranking of temperatures as indicated by the numbers assigned, but the interval between, say, 20° and 45° is equal to the interval between 60° and 85°. The operations of addition and subtraction may be performed on points on an interval scale. In the temperature scales, as in any interval scale, there is an arbitrary zero point, and of course the zero point of the Celsius scale is equal to 32° on the Fahrenheit scale.

The strongest scale is the ratio scale which has the characteristics of an interval scale plus a true zero point. There are many common examples including weight, distance, amounts of money, numbers of people, or any counting operation. Here any of the familiar mathematical operations may be performed on the numbers.[12]

How does one determine which scale is appropriate for a given research activity? A partial answer is provided by the statements of goals and specific objectives. Sometimes the kinds of statements needed to answer the research question will indicate that an interval or ratio scale is needed. In that case, special efforts will have to be made to design the data collection instruments so as to provide data which are isomorphic to the interval or ratio scale. On the other hand, the nature of the raw data themselves and of the available instruments may determine what kind of scale is appropriate—or possible. A third consideration is the degree of precision and accuracy required. If the weaker statistical tests, which are appropriate to ordinal scales, are adequate for the given research, it may be uneconomical to strive for interval or ratio data. Again, it is a matter of reconciling the ideal with the feasible. The following section

[11] For example: Mueller, Schuessler, and Costner, 1970; Blalock, 1972; also Siegel, 1956; and D. Miller, 1970, part 3.

[12] There is continuing discussion as to whether there is a meaningful distinction between interval and ratio scales. From a practical point of view it is not too important since interval scales are so rare in sociology. For discussion of this issue, see: Blalock, 1972, pp. 18–20; Siegel, 1956, pp. 26–30; and Coleman, 1964-a, pp. 57–70.

considers some more formal aspects of assigning numbers to objects under certain circumstances.

Scaling

"Scaling" refers to the various procedures which have been devised to enable the researcher to assign numbers to a series of objects. Practically all of the many techniques of scaling have been developed since the late 1920s in connection with research on attitudes, and, to a lesser extent, psychophysical and psychometric research. Research on attitudes usually takes the form of questioning, and thus the tasks involved include the precise and proper wording of the question items, decisions about the number and sequence of items, and the scoring and mathematical treatment of the results in order to yield a quantifiable measure. These, in turn, depend in part upon the particular theory of attitudes upon which the research is based—a varied and complex subject, indeed, and one about which there is considerable disagreement.

Among the most commonly used types of scales in sociological research are the following. *Judgmental* scales are typified by the so-called Thurstone scale, in which the subject is asked to indicate whether he agrees or disagrees with each of a series of statements. The statements previously have been selected from a much larger number by a panel of judges (hence "judgmental") to represent a range of different positions on the attitude under investigation. One such statement, from a scale for measuring attitudes toward the church, was "I believe in what the church teaches but with mental reservations." The most widely-known example of a *summated* scale is the Likert scale. In this, the subject responds to each item by indicating whether he strongly agrees, agrees, is undecided, disagrees, or strongly disagrees with it. The items have been chosen by the researcher to be unmistakably either favorable or unfavorable toward the object. The subject's responses are scored according to the degree of favorableness or unfavorableness, and thus this method has the advantage of measuring intensity of attitude. The earliest example of a *cumulative* scale is the familiar Bogardus Social Distance scale. More recently the Guttman Scalogram has attracted much interest. Presumably the items on such a scale measure only a single attitudinal dimension, and thus if an individual agrees with a given item he will also agree with all other items which represent a less (or more) extreme attitude.

The above three are the most widely used scales, but there are others of some interest. In Lazarsfeld's *latent structure analysis* the assumption is that an individual's place along an assumed continuum representing the attitude will determine the probability of his agreeing with the individual items. In *rating scales* the respondent places the item being judged at a point along a continuum, which point represents the degree to which he agrees with the item. Finally, in the *semantic differential* model the subject judges an object on each of a series of bipolar continua, such as "masculine-feminine," "desirable-undesirable," "friendly-unfriendly," "strong-weak," etc.

There are, of course, many variations upon these six types, and many other scales, as well, which have not been mentioned here. Details of how to construct and use these various scales are beyond the scope of this discussion. Scoring of scales may be done either manually or, in some cases, by computer.[13]

Categories and typologies

In some research it is possible, at this point, to tabulate the data, construct frequency distributions if needed, and perform various kinds of statistical procedures. But in other projects it will be necessary to classify the data in some way before going on to these other steps. This is more likely to occur in so-called qualitative studies, or in others where it is less possible to know in advance what broad patterns the data will assume. For example, in a sample survey designed to answer the question, "What is the place of astrology in the daily lives of urban people in India?" the typical Western researcher would have little to go on if he attempted to predetermine categories for analyzing his data. In such a situation—and in many, many others—it becomes necessary to create some kind of classification of the data after they have been collected. This means that in some

[13] One of the best "how-to-do-it" sources for scale construction is still Green, 1954. See also Upshaw, 1968, and Edwards, 1957. For brief but useful outlines of scale construction, see D. Miller, 1970, pp. 88–99. For a more advanced book, see Torgerson, 1958. For general discussions of attitude measurement and the theory of scaling, see: Torgerson, 1968, and W. A. Scott, 1968. For Guttman Scalograms in particular, see: Stouffer et al., 1950; Guttman, 1954; and Hagood and Price, 1952. For latent structure analysis, see: Stouffer et al., 1950, and Lazarsfeld and Henry, 1968.

way—by some criteria—the data must be arranged into a manageable number of categories. Consider the above example of astrology—it is easy to see that the answers to that question might vary over an enormous range of possibilities, and furthermore that these would not necessarily lie along a single dimension. Clearly, if the data are to be dealt with in any kind of feasible manner, some kind of system of categories must be established—a system such that each respondent can be placed in one of a relatively small number of separate categories.

Three different kinds of research situations have been identified in which categorization of data must be accomplished.[14] In the first, the data are completely unstructured or undifferentiated, as in the example of classifying newspaper editorials commenting on a major political event. Obviously, the researcher must condense or focus these materials in some way, in order to make sense out of them. The second type of research situation in which the data must be categorized is termed the "numerically supported" variety. "Here we begin with a rather arbitrary list of categories and observe the frequency with which they occur in various subgroups. Then we form a smaller number of more systematic categories, guided by our preliminary numerical findings."[15] In the third type of situation, the researcher forms categories on the basis of the theoretical considerations underlying the research, or some other information available before the data are collected. Such categories are known as *typologies*. More formally, when an object can be described along a number of (n) different dimensions, this can be thought of as an n-dimensional space. The various regions or combinations of dimensions are referred to as typologies, while the n-dimensional space itself is known as the attribute space.[16]

In constructing or using typologies, the processes of *reduction* and *substruction* are important. The former refers to the situation in which, for whatever reason, certain combinations of positions on the dimensions are combined into a single category. For example: individuals are being classified along the dimensions of education, race, and birthplace (i.e., native or foreign-born) and for some reason the data analysis calls for placing all foreign-born whites in the same category. In other words, some

[14] Lazarsfeld, Pasanella, and Rosenberg, 1972, pp. 13–15.

[15] Ibid., p. 14.

[16] Lazarsfeld, 1962, p. 759.

of the cells in the original array are collapsed. *Substruction*, on the other hand, refers to the reverse procedure of finding the original attribute space from a given system of types. This is particularly important because, according to Lazarsfeld, any system of types utilized by a researcher can be shown to be the result of a reduction of an attribute space, and it is only by knowing the original attribute space that the researcher can be aware of what is logically implied in his typologies.[17] The technique known as *smallest space analysis* is increasingly being used for the study of such multidimensional attribute spaces.[18]

Statistical analysis

It is at this point in the research process where the researcher is most likely to make use of various statistical procedures. Two crucial questions will help determine which procedures to use: What measurement scales are isomorphic to the data? How many variables are being studied? (Generally, statistical procedures are designed to be used with either one, two, or more than two variables.) The first step almost always will be to utilize some descriptive statistics to summarize and describe the data which have been obtained. As was emphasized in Chapter 1, the descriptive part of science must precede the other aims. Descriptive statistics are needed in the many cases in which there are so many individual bits of information that it is beyond the individual's capacity to assimilate them all or make sense of them. The simplest and most common first step is to arrange the data in a frequency distribution. The data may also be displayed in graphs, tables, or charts. It will almost always be important to have some measure of central tendency of a distribution, such as the mean, median, or mode, as well as a measure of the dispersion such as the variation, range, or standard deviation. If two or more variables are involved, it may be useful to know the extent to which they are related to one another, and so some measure of relationship such as the coefficient of correlation, lambda, gamma, Goodman and Kruskal's tau, or perhaps multiple regression analysis, may be selected. In attitude studies and similar research, factor analysis may be a very useful analytic technique.

[17] Lazarsfeld, 1972. See also McKinney, 1966. For construction and use of category systems when using direct observation of behavior, see Weick, 1968, pp. 421–27.

[18] Bailey, 1972; Laumann, 1969; Nutch and Bloombaum, 1968; Levine, 1972.

It is worth calling attention to a simple, but very confounding, mistake which is encountered all too often in the use of one of the simplest procedures, namely, the computing of percentages. When using, or reporting, percentages it is essential that one keep in mind the *base* of the percentage computations. For example, the statement "Sixteen percent of A's are B" is a *very different* statement from "Sixteen percent of B's are A." This is obvious when put this way, but consider the following case. A study of suicide in one community found that "Ten percent of the suicides are blacks." This finding tells us something about suicides, but not about blacks. Conversely, the statement that "Ten percent of blacks are suicides" (if such were the finding) would tell us far more about blacks than it does about suicide. Similarly, a recent newspaper article stated that "breast cancer strikes 27 percent of the women in the country," but later a corrected statement was published which was that "27 percent of all cancers occurring in women will be breast cancer." The first statement (if it were true) would convey information mainly about *women* and also about their susceptibility to breast cancer. The second statement conveys information about *cancer* (in women) and the prevalence of one specific type of cancer.

If the research deals with more than one variable (and therefore bivariate or multivariate statistical procedures are being used), and if the specific objectives of the research include a determination of whether two (or more) of these variables are related, the next step will likely be a test of the *null hypothesis.* The null hypothesis is a hypothesis of *no* relationship between the variables; hence it is the "opposite" of the substantive hypothesis (the hypothesis being researched). For example, if the substantive hypothesis were, "There is a positive correlation between surgeons' income and their surgical success rate," the null hypothesis would be, "There is no relationship between surgeons' income and their surgical success rate." The reason for using the null hypothesis is that, as the reader will recall from our earlier discussion of inductive reasoning, the credibility of theories and hypotheses is established and increased only by the elimination of alternatives. When the researcher makes the decision to accept or reject the null hypothesis—usually on the basis of some statistical test—he must give attention to the possible consequences of making an erroneous decision. In this connection, there are two kinds of errors: Type I (or alpha) is the error of rejecting a null hypothesis when, in fact, it is true, while

Type II (or beta) is the error of accepting a null hypothesis when, in fact, it is false. The practical consequences of making these two kinds of errors will depend upon the specifics of the research, and will thus play an important part in how conservative the researcher will be in making the decision whether to accept or reject the null hypothesis.

Finally, when the research design has included the use of a sample, it will be necessary to specify the probability that the obtained results are truly representative of the population. Even when a sample has not been used, the researcher is interested in knowing the probability that the results could have occurred by chance. In such cases use will be made of inductive, or inferential, statistics.[19] This may necessitate specifying what kind of distribution is isomorphic to the data, as for example the familiar normal curve, or the binomial distribution, among others. Such information may determine whether or not nonparametric statistical procedures should be used. Various tests of significance, such as the *t* test, or chi-square, or analysis of variance or covariance, are widely used, although considerable controversy surrounds the use of tests of significance in general.[20]

Currently there is a great deal of interest on the part of sociologists in some methods of analysis usually known as path analysis, causal analysis, or causal inference. While some of these techniques have been used in other fields, notably biology and economics, for some years, they have only recently attracted the attention of sociologists. Basically they consist of constructing a mathematical model of some aspect of reality, and expressing this model in the form of equations which predict causal relationships among the variables being considered. Causal paths may then be traced through the network of relationships among the variables. The specific procedures used are beyond the scope of this book.[21]

The development and publication of the *Statistical Package for the Social Sciences (SPSS)* in recent years has had an impact of much consequence and significance upon sociological research. Created in the late 1960s, it was first published in 1970 and revised in 1975.[22] SPSS is "an integrated system of com-

---

[19] For a new and promising approach to inferential statistics see Finifter, 1972.

[20] Morrison and Henkel, 1970; Labovitz, 1970-b, Labovitz, 1971.

[21] Blalock, 1964; Blalock, 1971; Blalock and Blalock, 1968; Nygreen, 1971; Borgatta, 1969; Borgatta and Bohrnstedt, 1970; Costner, 1971; Costner, 1974.

[22] Nie, Bent, and Hull, 1970; Nie et al., 1975. A short, introductory overview is also available: Klecka, Nie, and Hull, 1975.

puter programs designed for the analysis of social science data."[23] This system enables the researcher to perform numerous different kinds of data analysis much more easily, rapidly, and conveniently than was possible previously with the piecemeal programs and dissimilar computer languages then in use. With SPSS, the data need be entered into the system only once and then the computer can be instructed to perform whatever procedures are needed, in any sequence desired. The available procedures include the ordinary descriptive statistics, frequency distributions, cross-tabulations, various correlations and partial correlations, analysis of variance, multiple regressions, factor analysis, scatter diagrams, and Guttman scaling, among others. SPSS can be adapted for use on computers of several different manufacturers.

It is worth noting that there are at least two nonstandard approaches to social science statistical procedures, both of which hold considerable promise. The first is the use of "Monte Carlo" probability methods in place of many of the more ordinary procedures. These consist essentially of using random procedures (from computers, tables of random numbers, etc.) to generate a sample from which can be determined the probability of specified events. By this means it is possible to calculate, for example, the probability that two research statistics (e.g., means, ratios, etc.) are significantly different, or that a given independent variable is actually related to a given dependent variable.[24] The other approach, Bayesian statistics, emphasizes the use of conditional probabilities. This is especially useful for inductive statistics, since it is concerned with the changes in belief that a statement is true after receipt of additional information.[25] Another uncommon procedure, of somewhat more limited value, is the use of a special Binomial Probability graph paper for certain kinds of statistical problems.[26]

INTERPRETATION

The final important question the researcher must answer is "What does it all mean?" What is the real significance of the research? What has the research contributed? In what way has

[23] Nie et al., ibid., p. 1.

[24] For a brief description of Monte Carlo methods, see McCracken, 1955; for applications of these methods to sociological research, see J. Simon, 1969, chaps. 23, 24.

[25] Phillips, 1974; Mosteller and Tukey, 1968, pp. 160–83; Savage, 1968.

[26] Mosteller and Tukey, 1968, pp. 183–99.

man's knowledge been advanced? The measures of association or tests of significance or other statistical procedures used in the data analysis may indicate that the research results are extremely unlikely to have occurred by chance or that a relationship does indeed exist among the variables. That is, the results may be *statistically significant*. But statistical significance is by no means the same as *substantive* significance. A chi-square which is significant at the 99 percent level is neither the supreme accolade nor the be-all and end-all of research. The various statistical procedures are merely decision-making aids which the researcher utilizes to support the statements he is making; they are tests used to indicate the likelihood of his statements being true. But somehow the substantive significance of all the research findings must be separated out, and "data interpretation" refers to all the means of achieving this. After the fun and excitement of data collection and perhaps of using a computer and dealing with the statistical challenges, the researcher must now sit down with his data in front of him, think about his results, ponder them, scrutinize them, and grapple with the often elusive question, "What does it all mean?"

In interpreting the data one is restricted by the necessary qualifications on the one hand, and the desire to generalize on the other. It has been suggested that three qualifications apply to almost all social science research.[27] "Under certain circumstances" refers to the fact that any piece of research is performed under a specific set of circumstances which cannot be ignored. "Other things being equal" is also a frequently-made assumption, despite the fact that we know that, in fact, all the other things are neither equal nor inoperative, but that we are merely ignoring them during the research. Third, it was pointed out earlier that, except for anthropology, the great majority of social science research findings are applicable only "in our culture." On the other hand, constructing generalizations is an inherent part of any scientific activity, and these and other qualifications should not be adhered to so rigorously or blindly that one is afraid to make a generalization. This is true even if we have only a single test of a hypothesis "under certain circumstances," "in our culture," and with "other things being equal." In trying to generalize from such a case to a different population it is proba-

[27] Berelson and Steiner, 1964, pp. 7–8.

bly safe to say that the same results are more likely to be true of the new population than are opposite results.[28]

At the very least, interpretation consists of the *conclusions* the researcher has reached with reference to the specific objectives of the research. Were the objectives attained, and to what extent? Was the original research problem solved, or the question answered? Was the hypothesis affirmed? And at what levels of accuracy and confidence are these conclusions held? If it was explanatory research, these conclusions will, of course, indicate the way in which the research findings are related to the theory from which the original hypotheses were derived. Whether explanatory or descriptive research, it is the researcher's obligation to explain—or at least attempt to explain—just how his findings are related to other sociological knowledge. If his results are similar to other research results, what does this signify? To the extent that his results differ from other research findings, how can this be explained? To be sure, these explanations may be speculative at best—perhaps little more than educated guesses—but the attempt should be made, even if he feels he is "sticking his neck out." It would be relatively unusual research which yielded definitive results. What is more likely is that there will be some ambiguity, or perhaps even contradiction, in the results, and that these will lead to new research questions or hypotheses, and, in the case of explanatory research, to possible revision of the theory.

Furthermore, what are the *implications* and *inferences* resulting from these conclusions? "Given that these findings are correct, then one should expect to find thus-and-so, in such-and-such a situation." Here again, the broader the range of experience the researcher has, the easier it will be to recognize convergences between his research and other topics. Here, too, new and revised hypotheses and questions may emerge.

If the researcher fails to come to grips with this question of the broad meaning of his research then some may doubt the professional value of his work, and perhaps even his professional integrity. This may sound like too strong a statement, but consider the opposite case, where the researcher does not provide an adequate interpretation. Then, the less charitable reader of the run-of-the-mill research report may be left wondering

[28] Zetterberg, 1965, p. 128.

whether there is any real contribution to knowledge in the research, or whether it was undertaken for other reasons such as the personal advancement of the researcher.

Thus we see again the cyclical and never-ending aspect of scientific research which was shown earlier in the Flowchart. Research produces as many questions as answers. Over time, with repeated efforts by many scientists, the questions become more and more refined, precise, and detailed, but the quest for additional knowledge goes on and on.

EXERCISES

1. Below are listed a number of responses to the open-ended questionnaire item "If I could change one thing about my home life when I was a senior in high school it would be. . ." For the list (*a*) decide upon a coding system which a researcher could use to collapse the responses into from three to five categories, (*b*) make up a coding sheet which the researcher could then use to code questionnaire responses and (*c*) discuss the reasons for your constructing the coding system in the way you did.
   a. The number of rules I had to follow.
   b. The arguments I had with my father.
   c. To be more loving with my mother.
   d. To have a room of my own.
   e. Help out with the chores more.
   f. Go out with Dad more often.
   g. To ask Dad for the car more often.
   h. Tell my sister off once and for all.
   i. Be more understanding of my younger sister's problems.
   j. Ask Mom's advice on getting married.
   k. Get a job and help out with the money.
   l. Take an interest in my brother's boat.
   m. Nothing.
   n. I had an ideal home life except for religion.
   o. Learn to cook.
   p. Be more considerate with my remarks.
   q. To make Dad be more considerate with Mother.
2. For each of the following studies decide upon (*a*) the indicators you feel are best for each study variable and (*b*) the level of measurement you feel is the most appropriate for the indicators to

adequately demonstrate the specific objective; next discuss the reasons for your decisions.

a. Metropolitan newspapers' front-page headlines are more sensationalistic than corresponding lead stories in local evening television programs.

b. Younger women today are happier than older women.

c. The higher the socioeconomic level of a neighborhood, the lower the population density (number of persons per standard geographic unit).

d. The greater the number of educational years obtained, the greater the job satisfaction of employees who have been working in the same occupation for five or more years.

e. For every additional dollar spent for public welfare programs in your home state, a new welfare recipient is added to the list of those receiving public welfare payments.

3. For each of the studies listed above you have already decided upon simple indicators for each of the study variables. Next make up some appropriate categories and typologies for your indicators and construct sample data tables within which collected data might be displayed.

4. Listed below are several variables which might be measured at one of the four different levels of measurement (nominal, ordinal, interval, ratio) depending upon what indicators are used. For each decide upon indicators which you feel would be appropriate for two different levels of measurement and then briefly state a specific objective which might be demonstrated using the indicators (for each of the two measurement levels):

a. Economic well-being.

b. Comfortableness of living conditions.

c. Degree of occupational preparation.

d. Degree of urbanness of locality.

e. Happiness.

5. One of the assumptions made when researchers try to construct scales is that social variables can be represented as real or measurable attributes which reside in individuals, groups, or some other meaningful research unit. Furthermore, it is assumed that these attributes are possessed in differing degrees, much as individuals possess in differing degrees the attributes of height and weight. Below are listed several variables. Assume in each case that the variable has an attribute which is like height or weight. Next decide what this attribute might be, describe its characteristics, and discuss how a researcher might go about measuring it.

a. Bigotry.
b. Masculinity.
c. Socioeconomic level.
d. Intelligence.
e. Mechanical aptitude.

6. State the null hypothesis for each of the following and discuss why the null hypothesis may be true in each case. (Remember, the null hypothesis is *not* the opposite of the stated hypothesis.)
   a. Middle- and upper-class girls with one older sister and no older brother (that is, second-born females) are more approving of their fathers than are oldest girls.
   b. In a two-month treatment program for hospitalized patients suffering from acute arthritis using (*a*) a new drug to ease pain having moderately undesirable side effects (e.g., nausea) and (*b*) a standard drug to ease pain with a minor side effect (occasional but mild dizziness), the group using the new drug will show greater easing of pain than the group using the standard drug.

   Suppose statistically it is shown that a researcher would be correct in rejecting the null hypothesis for each of the above in 95 percent of samples (of 100 subjects each). What would this mean in terms of the stated hypothesis? Discuss. Suppose it was shown that the null hypothesis had a probability of being true in 1 in 1,000 samples; what inferences might a researcher make in the case of each study above?

7. The following is a list of numbers of suicides in two hypothetical Census tracts of differing socioeconomic levels, each with populations of about 8,000 persons, for a ten-year period. Discuss whether in each case the number of suicides is substantively and/or statistically different:

Year	*Tract A*	*Tract B*
1960	1	2
1961	2	2
1962	1	1
1963	1	1
1964	2	2
1965	2	1
1966	2	1
1967	3	2
1968	1	1
1969	2	1
Total	17	14

Chapter 17

Dissemination of results

No matter how well-executed the research has been, and no matter how important the findings, they are of little value until they have been communicated to their intended audience. Almost invariably this communication will be by means of a written report, but the content, format, and language of the report will vary with the audience. There are several possible audiences: it may be the teacher who has assigned the research project, or a faculty thesis committee, or a sponsoring agency which has requested and/or supported the research, or other sociologists attending a professional meeting, or the readers of a professional journal, or the sociological community in general.

Although the readers of this book will probably be engaged in their initial research activities as part of their learning process, students should not overlook the possibility of presenting their results at a professional meeting and/or of publishing them in a journal. Most professional journals make publication decisions on the merits of the paper alone, without regard to the prestige, age, or experience of the author. And many professional associations not only accept, but actively solicit, papers from students for presentation at the annual meetings. This is especially true of the regional associations in the United States.

CONTENT

Regardless of the audience, the report must be complete, detailed, and unbiased, and must convey to the reader an honest and accurate portrayal of what was done, why it was done, and what the results were. Needless to say, it would be unethical to conceal any mistakes or weaknesses which the researcher is aware of, or to deliberately deceive the reader.

The report usually will open with a clear statement of the topic being investigated, the importance of the investigation, and the specific questions, problems, or hypotheses being examined. This is followed by the definitions of the terms used, and a discussion of the way in which this study is related to existing sociological knowledge. Obviously, the formulation statement prepared at the start of the research may serve as this first portion of the written report. After this introductory material should appear a detailed description of the procedures which were followed in collecting and analyzing the data. Then the results are presented and the interpretation of the results. Finally, a report will usually contain a short one- or two-paragraph summary of the entire foregoing report. The bibliography and any appendix material (copies of interview schedules, tables and data of peripheral importance, etc.) will conclude the report.

The language of research reports is expected to be scholarly, objective, and dispassionate. They are usually written in the third person, and personal narratives are avoided. The articles appearing in any professional journal may be used as models for report-writing. A style manual is an invaluable aid in the mechanics of writing reports, and the use of one is strongly advised. There are many excellent manuals and most academic departments have their own preferred one. However, one of the most widely used is by Campbell and Ballou.[1] A useful checklist of specifications for research report writing is also available.[2] Usually, of course, there will be specific requirements regarding style, format, and so on, laid down by the academic department, agency, or journal for whom the report is being written. One note of caution: regardless of the audience or the ultimate disposition of the report, one copy of it should *always* remain in the researcher's possession, to guard against loss and other mishaps.

PROFESSIONAL MEETINGS AND JOURNALS

The student who is seriously committed to a career in sociology will, sooner or later, find himself joining professional associations and attending their annual meetings. And when he is still involved in training in research it is not too early to think about presenting a paper at a meeting. It is by no means unheard of for

[1] Campbell and Ballou, 1974. Also, L. Becker and C. Gustafson, 1968, will be very useful for the beginning student.

[2] D. Miller, 1970, pp. 411–13.

a high quality undergraduate research paper to be accepted for a meeting of a regional association. The excitement and thrill of presenting one's first paper at a meeting, and surviving the criticism and discussion which follows, are long remembered.

After a paper has been presented at a meeting, and perhaps revised as a result of the criticism, it may be submitted to a professional journal for possible publication. Or, of course, it may be submitted directly to a journal without prior presentation at a meeting. (However, once a paper has been accepted for publication it would be unethical to submit it for a meeting, since it may be presumed to have already reached much of the audience once it has been published.) It can be sent to any journal which the researcher deems appropriate in terms of its content, prestige, location, and so on. Since most journals have their own individual requirements for style, format, etc., it may be that if the paper is not accepted by the first journal it will have to be retyped before being sent out to a second or third. If the paper has any merit it will probably eventually be accepted for some journal, and so some initial rejections should not be too discouraging.

Once a research report has been presented at a professional meeting or published in a professional journal the researcher can take some measure of pride in the fact that he or she may have made some small contribution to mankind's knowledge.

EXERCISES

1. Using the general format discussed in the section on "Content" in this chapter, write a brief description of a study (leaving out conclusions, of course) you would like to make or one which you feel should be conducted that would add important information to sociological knowledge. Next, suppose that the study has been completed successfully and that the research findings were significant. Given the nature of the research, list some journals or other scholarly publications which accept research such as the one described for publication. In addition, list some studies you have read in these publications which are similar to the study you have described.

   If you feel that no publication for the study described is appropriate, list some other audiences and discuss why they might benefit from learning of the results of the study (e.g., members of professional associations attending meetings, members of social service associations, members of student groups, members of a class of graduate students, etc.).

SOLATIUM

While you and i have lips and voices which
are for kissing and to sing with
who cares if some oneeyed son of a bitch
invents an instrument to measure Spring with?

e e cummings
Is Five, 1926

APPENDIXES

Appendix A

Selected research topics

Presented here is a listing of possible research topics from the author's files. Probably the only thing they have in common is that at some point in time they seemed interesting. They range from the important to the trivial; some may have already been done; some may not be worth doing; certainly many of them are not original—but perhaps the reader will find some of them intriguing.

1. Is there a relationship between an individual's level of empathy and willingness to give aid to strangers?
2. If it is true that the economics of today's mass society results in a loss of individuality and uniqueness in mass-produced products, does the same thing apply in the selection of national political candidates?
3. Assume that heart disease victims are mainly middle-aged or older men. Then assume that most of them are married. Further assume that after the heart attack their activities are restricted, and that therefore the wife starts to assume some of the husband's former responsibilities. Then one might hypothesize that to the extent that the victim's self-image (of his masculinity, etc.) is related to his responsibilities and tasks, his self-image would be damaged by having to relinquish these responsibilities and tasks.

   Corollary 1: Under these circumstances he would experience an increase in psychological tension.

   Corollary 2: The more traditional husband would experience this to a greater extent than the husband who accepts the feminist viewpoint.
4. Is it true that many "classical" or "monumental" works in a given field are cited more often than they are read with care?

   Corollary: Can one devise a hierarchical scale of reading

books (e.g., mastered it, read it thoroughly, read most of it, skimmed it, read a review, etc.)?

5. What determines whether accommodation or rebellion occurs in reaction to the power structure?
6. There is a high rate of assaults against police officers responding to domestic quarrel calls. Does this imply that the partners are releasing pent-up hostilities which could just as readily be vented against *any* convenient and remotely legitimate target?
7. Are there significant similarities between crowd behavior and the Maxwell-Boltzman theory of kinetics of gas molecules?
8. What is the place of ethical considerations in decision making by business and professional men?
9. Is ethnocentrism exhibited in the placement of one's own country (region, city, etc.) on locally-produced maps?
10. Is it true that in typical (American?) families the husband's role emphasizes external relations while the wife's role emphasizes internal relations? If this is true there are similarities with large organizations where the president (commanding officer) is concerned with external relations while the second-in-command is concerned with internal relations. Is this coincidence or are these similarities significant?
11. Assume that marital interaction can be divided into "task oriented" and "social-emotional oriented," or more generally, "work" and "play." Are the proportions of time together spent in "work" and in "play," and of time apart spent in "work" and in "play" related to marital success?
12. At what age or stage of life do individuals achieve the highest standard of living?
13. What determines the allegiance and support by fans of athletic teams?
14. What are the dimensions of research referred to in the first section of Chapter 8 above?
15. An investigation of the number of friends (close personal relationships) an individual has, as related to the size of the population of eligibles. Hypothesis: there is a critical minimum population size which will enable a given individual to establish his own characteristic number of relationships.

    Corollary: A given college student will have the same number of close relationships on a campus of 40,000 students as he would on a campus of 2,000, provided the smaller figure is greater than the critical size.
16. What percent of marriages per year are first, second, third, etc., marriages for the individuals involved?

17. Are Asch's three types of independent subjects and three types of yielding subjects characteristic of all norm conformity situations?
18. Is it true that children tend to look to the opposite sex parent for affection but to the same sex parent for authority? If so, is this similar to the concepts of task leader and emotional leader of a group?
19. Is it so that high-level business executives and other similar leaders are taller and more physically impressive than average? If so, is this due to the fact that such boys (girls?) are more likely to be selected as leaders by other children, and thus they early acquire more leadership experience and training, poise, self assurance, etc.?
20. Can the concept of disaster behavior be studied by means of small groups?
21. Can the great man theory of historical leadership be studied in a laboratory situation?
22. Studies of the extent and cause of political apathy on college campuses.
23. Comparison of the success rate of mixed marriages in the United States and in other countries.
24. To what extent are stereotypes accurate descriptions? To what extent do stereotypes agree with self-appraisals?
25. Comparison of members of different political parties by IQ, education, income, general achievement, and other demographic variables.
26. Is there a relationship between social class and bodily figure and stature? (See: Susan Chitty, ed., *The Intelligent Woman's Guide to Good Taste*, 1958, chapters by Mary Tuck.)
27. Is there a relationship between intelligence and physique or figure in infertile women? (See: *Newsweek*, 9/14/64, p. 61.)
28. The more tension there is within a group, the less cohesiveness will there be, and the more people will think of themselves as individuals.
29. What percent of candidates fail the final oral doctoral examination? Assuming the figure is extremely small, can the exam be regarded as an initiation ritual rather than a serious exam?
30. Is there a functional difference between attitudes and opinions?
31. Apparently certain personality characteristics are associated with different cultures; and furthermore, it is commonly assumed that the personality differences are explained by the cultural differences. However, is there evidence to support the latter?
32. Under what circumstances do people fear, or welcome, new experiences?

33. A study of group influence upon individuals' attitudes in an educational situation (e.g., knowledge versus no knowledge of own group's attitudes).
34. Under what circumstances will economic and psychological insecurity have positive as compared with negative effects for the individual?
35. Are there cultural factors which are related to whether an individual perceives a given issue in terms of a dichotomy or trichotomy or continuum or multidimensional space or etc.? That is, do some cultures tend to think in terms of dichotomies whereas other cultures think in terms of some other scale? If so, why?
36. To what extent do the society's characteristics provide an explanation for the large number of instances in which parents inflict severe physical injury upon infants because of the latters' "incessant crying"?
37. Can odors and tastes successfully be used as data sources for sociological investigation?
38. A study of the relationship between power (financial) which parents have and the dependency of college-age children.
39. A comparison of college athletes and general student body on demographic characteristics, motivational factors, academic abilities and achievement, etc.
40. Study of reference groups of college students at different points in their academic careers.
41. A comparison of social classes with regard to amount of exposure to—or first-hand contact with—crimes of violence, different types of crime, police, etc.
42. How accurate are horoscopes and other astrological predictions?
43. Do students who have met the academic prerequisites for a course get better grades than those who have not?
44. Is there a relationship between breed and characteristics of pets and social characteristics of the owners?
45. Study of the socioeconomic characteristics of a small community which is about to be bypassed by the relocation of a major highway or freeway.
46. A study of the distribution of automobile accidents and traffic citations by religion of driver.
47. Studies of the occult, black magic, exorcism, magic, witchcraft, etc.
48. Studies of ESP, parapsychology, and psychic experiences.
49. Study of the belief in UFOs.

50. Attitudes toward acupuncture.
51. Since they are in the minority, do left-handed persons experience the same kinds of discrimination and frustration as members of ethnic minorities?
52. Attitudes toward burial, cremation, and less traditional death ceremonies.
53. How much truth is there in the old saying that education enables one to worry about things all over the world instead of just locally?
54. Hypothesis: persons who wear mirrored sunglasses are more insecure (or more hostile) than persons who do not.
55. Is there any empirical evidence to support the beliefs in a home-court or home-team advantage in sports?
56. The sociological implications of the energy shortage, with especial regard for solar energy. For example, if the efficient use of solar energy will require changes in the construction of homes and buildings in order to make better use of solar energy, will this produce changes in life styles, etc? What effects will this have upon families, neighborhoods, and communities?
57. Do middle-class women feel the feminist movement is a threat to their womanhood?
58. Are the rich getting richer and the poor getting poorer?
59. To what extent are college students (or the general public) concerned about the long-range prospects of humankind, i.e., global survival problems such as nuclear war, environmental pollution, overpopulation, energy shortages?
60. Do children from permissive families get into trouble more than children from strict families?
61. Are people who live in rural areas happier, or more satisfied with their lives, than people in urban areas?
62. Are college-educated persons happier, or more satisfied with their lives, than non-college-educated persons?
63. What is the relationship between the amount of time spent studying and the grades one receives?
64. In sports, do winning teams have loyal fans, or do loyal fans generate winning teams?

Appendix B

Example of sample survey interview research

The following is reprinted from the final report, written by the principal investigator (this author) and his assistant, of an evaluation research project.[1] It appears here to serve as an illustration of evaluation research, and of the design of a typical sample survey research using face-to-face interviews as the main method of data collection. The project was conducted in 1962–64, and was supported by the American Heart Association, the Arizona Heart Association, the National Institute of Health, and the U.S. Public Health Service, through the Arizona State Department of Health.

INTRODUCTION

The problem

During the last several decades in the United States there has been a great proliferation of nationally organized voluntary health associations. Though the organizations themselves differ in terms of methods of procedure and operation, there are some basic similarities common to most or all. For example, the goals of each are similar in that they seek to abolish or alleviate certain health problems or diseases which affect countless numbers of people. In addition, these associations are financed, at least partially, through voluntary contributions on the part of the public. Finally, in many cases a basic part of the program consists of clubs, councils, or committees at the local level composed of

[1] Manheim and Howlett, 1964, pp. 1–17.

individuals who voluntarily give of their time and effort in order to help the association in the realization of its goals.

Generally these volunteer committees conduct programs in their local communities which are designed to educate the general public (as well as certain professional categories) with regard to at least three fundamental objectives:

1. To instill in the general public an awareness that a problem exists which can be alleviated or abolished.
2. To reduce public fears and misconceptions with regard to the problem.
3. To get across to the public an understanding that something can be done, but not without their help.

In many instances a fourth objective would be to make the public aware of, and familiar with, the national association and its goals. In general, it is assumed that programs of this type are of value not only in terms of public education but also in engendering increased financial support on the part of the public. It may also be assumed that there exists a high degree of commitment to the goals of the organization on the part of the volunteer personnel. However, it cannot be assumed that commitment to these goals is synonymous with effective action at the local level. And, whether the assumptions with regard to the value of these local committee programs are valid or not, can only be ascertained through an objective, scientific evaluation of the effectiveness of their programs.

Surprisingly, there have been very few attempts to evaluate such programs, although there has been a considerable amount of research done on related matters. Most of what has been done consists of one-time public opinion surveys of specific populations. Typical of these are the 1948 survey done for the American Cancer Society and the 1961 study done for the American Heart Association.[2] This type of study can contribute much useful information to the administration of an organization. However, since there are so many extraneous variables which may affect the public's attitudes, a study of this nature generally will not

[2] "The American Public Discuss Cancer and the American Cancer Society Campaign" (Ann Arbor: University of Michigan Survey Research Center, 1948), 92 pp. (mimeographed), and "Fund Raising: A Study among the Public and Heart Volunteers for American Heart Association, Inc." (Princeton: N.J.: Opinion Research Corporation, 1961), pp. vii, 89, and Appendix (mimeographed).

provide a measure of the effectiveness of a specific program unless the study involves at least a control group and/or a follow-up public opinion survey.

Perhaps the prime example, from a methodological if not substantive viewpoint, is Dodd's study of the effects of a program of education in hygiene on the hygienic practices of rural families in Syria.[3] Two other more recent studies did attempt evaluation of parts of a program. The Office of War Information made use of control and experimental cities in an attempt to determine the general level of knowledge of the security campaign and the effectiveness of a particular pamphlet as a means of helping people to understand security problems.[4] A study by Krauss suggests a three-step approach of *(a)* identifying the goals of a public service organization, *(b)* examining the organization's day-to-day activities, and *(c)* comparing these two. The example used by Krauss emphasizes the first step.[5] No other studies, however, seem to have attempted a rigidly-controlled experimental evaluation of a public education program.

This is a final report of a two-year research project, undertaken in order to attempt to provide such evaluation of the effectiveness of local volunteer groups whose efforts were aimed at educating the public about heart disease.

In several communities in Arizona, and in many throughout the country, local Heart Councils are functioning under the aegis of the American Heart Association. With varying degrees of enthusiasm they conduct various types of programs, and meet with varying degrees of success. Much time and effort go into these activities, not only by local volunteers but by professional Heart Association personnel as well. Unfortunately, knowledge has been generally unavailable as to the effectiveness of such local programs in terms of the three stated objectives of the Heart Association: research, education, and community services. This project was designed to provide such evaluation of the program of a local Council in a city of about 10,000 people in Arizona.

---

[3] Described in F. Stuart Chapin, *Experimental Designs in Sociological Research* (New York: Harper & Brothers Publishers, 1974), pp. 55–57.

[4] "The Effectiveness of the Security Pamphlet—'A Personal Message' " (Surveys Division, Bureau of Special Services, U.S. Office of War Information, July 3, 1943), 6 pp. (mimeographed).

[5] Irving Krauss, "An Approach to Evaluating the Effectiveness of a Public Health Program," *Journal of Health and Human Behavior*, vol. 3, Summer 1962, pp. 141–46.

This information, it is expected, will be of value to local Councils and chapters, state affiliates, and the national organization. It is anticipated that the results will provide a means of determining the extent to which the Association's objectives are being realized, and of weighing alternative procedures designed to achieve these objectives. This should facilitate the more effective use of personnel and funds.

The role of the local Heart Council

There are well over 3,000 local Heart Councils and committees in the United States today. Administratively, the local Council is seen by the American Heart Association as an autonomous group assisted by a professional staff member of the Heart Association. The staff members serve only in an advisory capacity, providing guidance and information about various aspects of the Association and its program. *What* is done, and *how* it is done, are entirely up to the local Council. This relationship is described in one of the many publications of the American Heart Association:

> When the main strength of an organization rests on the good will and efforts of its entirely unpaid people, as aided and served by a small paid staff, and when its income comes through contributions freely made in each of many communities, it is of the utmost importance that local units with local leadership and much local autonomy be created and preserved.[6]

However, the American Heart Association and the state affiliate (in this case, the Arizona Heart Association) offices have certain conceptions of the most effective organizational aspects of these local Councils. These conceptions of the local Council as it should be are made clear to the members of the local Council, with the idea that this may serve as a *guide* in the effective organization and performance of the Council on the local level.

The organizational structure of the ideal local Heart Council is similar to the structure of any large-scale bureaucratic organization. There are many offices, ranging from the general chairman to other offices with more specific and limited responsibilities. Each office has certain functions which set it apart from all other offices. Specific duties, obligations, and tools

---

[6] *The Heart Future* (New York: American Heart Association, 1961), p. 50.

characterize each office. One view describes 18 offices for a local Council: Community Heart Chairman, Vice Chairman, Secretary, Treasurer, Assistant Treasurer, Medical Advisors, Publicity Chairman, Public Education Chairman, Public Education Chairman for Clubs and Organizations, Public Education Chairman for Schools, Professional Information Chairman, Chairman of Information and Referral, Memorial Gifts Chairman, Campaign Chairman, Heart Sunday Chairman, Coin Containers Chairman, Business Chairman, and Special Events Chairman.

As is indicated by the foregoing, the structural organization of the ideal local Council is carefully spelled out by the Heart Association. Whether the Council chooses to follow the above organizational suggestions or not is a decision which rests with it. In general, it may be assumed that the Heart Association feels the closer a local Council's organization resembles this ideal organization, the more effective it is likely to be.

The functions of the local Council are predominantly in the areas of education (both professional and lay), community service, and fund raising. There is no exact division between the three areas, and in many cases they overlap. Following are the functions in each area in accordance with the ideal image of the local Council:

Education. This is a year-round program of education aimed at both the professional members of the community and the general public. "The purpose is to eliminate fears and misconceptions about the heart and circulatory diseases and to encourage people to apply preventive measures; they are to be stimulated to seek early diagnosis and treatment."[7] It includes the distribution, at the local level, of selected pamphlets, booklets, and other reading materials, and the showing of motion picture films to clubs and the general public, in schools, and to any other interested organizations or audiences. With regard to this the Committee on Future Role of the American Heart Association says:

> The year-round educational program is intended . . . to maintain and improve the health of the American people so far as it can be done without invading the field of medical ethics or giving ad-

[7] Ibid., p. 18.

vice which, in certain instances, should be given by the physician.[8]

Community service. By community service is meant ". . . the provision of facilities in the local community to assist physicians in patient care and to help people help themselves."[9] This includes not only the setting up of new clinical facilities within the community, but also such aids as are seen as helpful to both physicians and the general public, such as directories of what local services are available, and "reference libraries" (a collection of pamphlets and leaflets designed to aid the patient suffering from cardiovascular disorders) which are furnished to physicians who in turn use them in counseling patients, etc. In addition,

> In its community program, the Heart Association seeks to establish policies and plan programs which will apply at the community level the knowledge obtained from basic and clinical research in prevention, diagnosis, treatment, reduction of disability, and rehabilitation.[10]

Fund raising. The local Council is an indispensable agent with regard to fund raising activities. It is their responsibility to recruit volunteers, to provide the motivation required of the volunteers in order that the fund-raising activities be successful, and to undertake the actual mechanics of collecting funds.

RESEARCH DESIGN AND DATA COLLECTION

General design

The general design took the form of a "before-and-after" study comparing two cities. In one city a local Heart Council had been established (this was the "experimental" city and has been given the code name "Exeter") while the other city did not have a local Heart Council (this city served as a "control" and has been designated "Concord"). At the beginning of the research both communities were studied in order to establish a baseline of knowledge and attitudes, for purposes of compari-

[8] Ibid., p. 38.

[9] Ibid., p. 39.

[10] Ibid., p. 18.

son. During the following year, the Heart Council was active in Exeter. At the end of that time, both communities were studied again to determine what changes had taken place during the previous year. By comparing the "before-and-after" differences in Exeter (which had an active Heart Council) to the differences in Concord (where no Council was functioning), the effect of the Council's activities for the year could be ascertained.

Data were collected regarding five areas of interest: research, education, community services, fund raising, and the Exeter local Council. The first three of these are widely stated by the American Heart Association to be their fundamental objectives, and fund raising, as mentioned above is also an important function of the local Council.

Progress toward the goal of *research* was measured by obtaining information from the local Council, health personnel, and the state affiliate office regarding efforts toward supporting heart research. It was not anticipated that this would be a major part of the study.

The measurement of the Council's effectiveness in the area of *education* was the largest part of the research. At the beginning of the project a sample survey was made of the general population of the two cities to assess knowledge about, and attitudes toward, heart disease and its treatment, and the Heart Associations. Following a season of activity by the Exeter Heart Council, a second sample survey was conducted of the two cities in order to determine the changes in attitudes and knowledge. In addition to this survey of general public educational efforts, physicians and other appropriate health personnel in both cities were also interviewed following the "after" sample survey.

Movement toward the goal of furthering *community services* was measured primarily through careful record keeping at the state affiliate office. This provided means of comparing the two communities in terms of referrals to the low-cost penicillin program, to the work-simplification for handicapped homemakers program, physicians' requests and referrals for information services, publications, and similar materials, and through observation of the extent of establishment of new services and facilities, such as clinics, information and referral services, rehabilitation services, and so on.

Statistical information about *fund raising* activities, which was available from the state affiliate office, was examined in order to evaluate the efforts of the local Council in this area and to determine the relationship between this function and the achievement of the above three formal objectives of the Association.

In order to explain the results gained from the above four parts of the study, the Exeter local Council was carefully studied. Following the "before" series of interviews, members of the research staff attended all meetings of the Council, had interviews and meetings with various Council members, and conferred regularly with the professional staff members of the Arizona Heart Association who were responsible for Heart Association activities in Exeter. The members of the local Council were unaware of the exact nature of the research, having been told only that follow-up information was needed after the sample survey interviews. Had they known that a second sample survey was to be made of their community a year later, it might have affected their activities (as in the well-known "Hawthorne effect"). The local newspapers of the two cities were carefully read and clipped in order to provide general knowledge of local events, heart cases of public interest, and similar unanticipated factors which might have affected the local Council members or the general public.

The communities

Several considerations went into the selection of the two cities to be studied. It was important that they be matched as much as possible in terms of social and economic characteristics so that the independent variable (the existence of the Heart Council in Exeter) could be regarded as the primary factor related to any changes in knowledge about and attitudes toward heart disease. That Exeter and Concord were, in fact, very similar may be seen from Table 1, adapted from 1960 U.S. Census data. The total populations are quite close, and the age and racial distributions are very similar. The percent married and the median school years completed are very closely matched. The economic characteristics (median family income, occupation distribution, unemployment rates, and median value of housing) are also substantially the same in the two cities.

It was decided to choose cities of approximately 10,000 population, for two reasons. This size made a sample survey practical,

Table 1. Summary of social and economic characteristics of Exeter and Concord

	Exeter	*Concord*
Total population	8,311	9,531
Percent nonwhite	6.7	7.2
Percent 18 to 64 years old	49.8	52.2
Male, 14 years old and over, percent married	71.8	71.8
Female, 14 years old and over, percent married	70.2	72.3
Persons 25 years old and over, median school years completed	10.8	10.8
Median family income (dollars)	5,311	4,875
Employed males, percent in various occupations:		
Professional, technical and kindred workers	10.4	9.0
Farmers and farm managers	4.9	2.0
Managers, officials, and proprietors, except farm	17.3	13.9
Clerical and kindred workers	5.3	3.8
Sales workers	8.5	7.9
Craftsmen, foremen, and kindred workers	16.8	20.5
Operatives and kindred workers	15.5	14.6
Private household workers	—	—
Service workers, except private household	5.1	6.1
Farm laborers and foremen	7.4	10.0
Laborers, except farm and mine	6.4	7.6
Occupation not reported	2.3	4.7
Civilian labor force, percent unemployed	8.0	5.9
Median value, owner occupied housing units (dollars)	10,500	10,400

Source: Based on U.S. Census, 1960.

within the limits established for the study, and furthermore, this being approximately the modal size community for the United States, it was believed that this might make the results more widely generalizable. It was also important that the two cities be separate entities, and relatively free from the influence of any other larger nearby cities. The distances of Concord and Exeter from Phoenix, the major metropolis in central Arizona, are 25 and 55 miles, respectively. Furthermore, it was required that each community have no "unique" features or characteristics which would set it off from other communities (e.g., it should not be a "one-industry" city, such as a mining town)—again in order to permit generalizations about the results.

Each city has a hospital, and approximately the same number of professional health personnel (Exeter: 12, Concord: 16). Also, each has access to the following health services:

1. A low-cost penicillin prophylaxsis program, to which any physician may refer patients whom he feels cannot or would not pay the retail price of penicillin.

2. Referral to the State Office of Vocational Rehabilitation, whereby any resident for more than one year may seek assistance in the diagnosis, treatment, and rehabilitation for any correctable condition.

3. Referral to the Department of Crippled Children's Services whereby any child under 21, who has been a resident for one year, may seek assistance for the diagnosis and treatment of any correctable heart disease.

4. The information and referral service of the Heart Association which attempts to work out a solution for each applicant's individual problem.

5. Heart Association staff assistance in developing the local Council program through films, exhibits, educational pamphlets, and special guides, such as, e.g., for surveying community resources and services for cardiac patients.

6. Homemakers Work simplification Program, for easing the burdens of homemaking for cardiac patients.

7. The Visiting Nurses Services, providing nursing care in the home for cardiac patients.

Finally, Concord had had no contact with the Heart Association, other than in the annual fund-raising drives, while the local Council had been established in Exeter some months before the start of the research. It should be noted that the Exeter Council in no way received any special or unusual treatment by the Heart Association and its staff.

The sample

In order to assess the Exeter Council's effectiveness in the area of education, sample surveys were conducted in both cities to measure the public's attitudes toward and knowledge about heart disease. The universe surveyed consisted of all persons having passed their 20th birthday. According to the 1960 U.S. Census, this numbered 4,441 persons in Exeter, and 5,203 in Concord. The sample was a multistage cluster sample, with the first stage being a systematic sample of blocks and the second stage a systematic sample of housing units. Between 2 and 3 percent of the universe were included in the sample. This description fits both the "before" and the "after" series of interviews, although the same individuals were *not* interviewed both times.

Interviewing

The interviewing for the sample surveys was conducted in person by trained interviewers, at the homes of the interviewees. The interview schedule contained questions designed to determine the interviewee's attitudes toward heart diseases, both as an illness and as a cause of death, his knowledge about heart disease, his information about the Heart Association, the sources of his information, and the usual identifying information. The content of the questions was obtained largely from publications of the Heart Associations. *It should be noted that this research in no way attempted to evaluate the publications or the programs of the American or Arizona Associations. These were taken as "given." What was evaluated was the local Council's efforts to implement these programs and to get across the messages contained in the publications.*

A preliminary version of the interview schedule was pretested in another community, and also served as part of the training program for the interviewers. Minor changes were made in the schedule after this pretesting.

In addition to the above sample survey of the general adult public of the two cities, doctors were interviewed in order to determine what impact, if any, the local Council had had on them in their professional dealings with heart disease. Questionnaires were sent by mail to all MDs, osteopaths, chiropractors, and dentists listed in the telephone directories for both cities in May 1964. A total of 12 questionnaires was sent to Exeter, and 17 to Concord.

Appendix C

American Sociological Association code of ethics

PREAMBLE

Sociological inquiry is often disturbing to many persons and groups. Its results may challenge long-established beliefs and lead to change in old taboos. In consequence such findings may create demands for the suppression or control of this inquiry or for a dilution of the findings. Similarly, the results of sociological investigation may be of significant use to individuals in power—whether in government, in the private sphere, or in the universities—because such findings, suitably manipulated, may facilitate the misuse of power. Knowledge is a form of power, and in a society increasingly dependent on knowledge, the control of information creates the potential for political manipulation.

For these reasons, we affirm the autonomy of sociological inquiry. The sociologist must be responsive, first and foremost, to the truth of his investigation. Sociology must not be an instrument of any person or group who seeks to suppress or misuse knowledge. The fate of sociology as a science is dependent upon the fate of free inquiry in an open society.

At the same time this search for social truths must itself operate within constraints. Its limits arise when inquiry infringes on the rights of individuals to be treated as persons, to be considered—in the renewable phrase of Kant—as ends and not as means. Just as sociologists must not distort or manipulate truth to serve untruthful ends, so too they must not manipulate persons to serve their quest for truth. The study of society, being the study of human beings, imposes the responsibility of respecting the integrity, promoting the dignity, and maintaining the autonomy of these persons.

To fulfill these responsibilities, we, the members of the American Sociological Association, affirm the following Code of Ethics:

CODE OF ETHICS

1. *Objectivity in Research*

In his research the sociologist must maintain scientific objectivity.

2. *Integrity in Research*

The sociologist should recognize his own limitations and, when appropriate, seek more expert assistance or decline to undertake research beyond his competence. He must not misrepresent his own abilities, or the competence of his staff to conduct a particular research project.

3. *Respect of the Research Subject's Rights to Privacy and Dignity*

Every person is entitled to the right of privacy and dignity of treatment. The sociologist must respect these rights.

4. *Protection of Subjects from Personal Harm*

All research should avoid causing personal harm to subjects used in research.

5. *Preservation of Confidentiality of Research Data*

Confidential information provided by a research subject must be treated as such by the sociologist. Even though research information is not a privileged communication under the law, the sociologist must, as far as possible, protect subjects and informants. Any promises made to such persons must be honored. However, provided that he respects the assurances he has given his subjects, the sociologist has no obligation to withhold information of misconduct of individuals or organizations.

If an informant or other subject should wish, however, he can formally release the researcher of a promise of confidentiality. The provisions of this section apply to all members of research organizations (i.e., interviewers, coders, clerical staff, etc.), and it is the responsibility of the chief investigators to see that they are instructed in the necessity and importance of maintaining the confidentiality of the data. The obligation of the sociologist includes the use and storage of original data to which a subject's name is attached. When requested, the identity of an organization or subject must be adequately disguised in publication.

6. *Presentation of Research Findings*

The sociologist must present his findings honestly and without distortion. There should be no omission of data from a research report which might significantly modify the interpretation of findings.

7. *Misuse of Research Role*

The sociologist must not use his role as a cover to obtain information for other than professional purposes.

8. *Acknowledgement of Research Collaboration and Assistance*

The sociologist must acknowledge the professional contributions or assistance of all persons who collaborated in the research.

9. *Disclosure of the Sources of Financial Support*

The sociologist must report fully all sources of financial support in his research publications and any special relations to the sponsor that might affect the interpretation of the findings.

10. *Distortion of Findings by Sponsor*

The sociologist is obliged to clarify publicly any distortion by a sponsor or client of the findings of a research project in which he has participated.

11. *Disassociation from Unethical Research Arrangements*

The sociologist must not accept such grants, contracts, or research assignments as appear likely to require violation of the principles above, and must publicly terminate the work or formally disassociate himself from the research if he discovers such a violation and is unable to achieve its correction.

12. *Interpretation of Ethical Principles*

When the meaning and application of these principles are unclear, the sociologist should seek the judgment of the relevant agency or committee designated by the American Sociological Association. Such consultation, however, does not free the sociologist from his individual responsibility for decisions or from his accountability to the profession.

13. *Applicability of Principles*

In the conduct of research the principles enunciated above should apply to research in any area either within or outside the United States of America.

14. *Interpretation and Enforcement of Ethical Principles*

The Standing Committee on Professional Ethics, appointed by the Council of the Association, shall have primary responsibility for the interpretation and enforcement of the Ethical Code. The Committee shall

(a) Advise members of the Association of its interpretation of the ethical propriety of professional conduct through formal opinions of the Committee published from time to time in *The American Sociologist*, which opinions shall omit all references to the names of individuals or institutions;
(b) Recommend amendments to or clarification of the Ethical Code when they appear to be advisable;
(c) Receive complaints of violations of the Ethical Code by members of the Association, endeavor to settle complaints privately, and, if private settlement cannot be effected, investigate such complaints as the Committee shall determine to investigate, under Rules of Procedure from time to time adopted by the Committee and approved by the Council and the membership of the Association. If on the basis of its investigation the Committee by two-thirds majority of all its members determines that an ethical violation has occurred, the Committee shall communicate to the complainant and to the member charged with the violation the finding of the Committee, and it shall impose one or more of the following sanctions:

(i) Reprimand the member;
(ii) Suspend the membership of the member for a period to be determined by the Committee;
(iii) Request the resignation of the member; or
(iv) Terminate the membership of the member;

and

(d) Receive requests that sanctions imposed herein be modified or revoked after a period of time, and take such action, including modification or revocation of the said sanctions, as the Committee in its discretion shall determine.

The Council of the Association shall:

(a) Constitute from among its members a committee which shall decide appeals from findings of ethical violations by the Standing Committee on Professional Ethics, on the record and without further hearing.

(b) Receive reports from the Committee on the disposition of complaints received by it, and approve the Committee's report to the membership of the Association of the types of complaints that have been filed with the Committee. The report to the membership shall not disclose the name of any person or persons whose past or proposed professional conduct has been called into question.

Appendix D

Health survey: Instructions for interviewers

A. GENERAL

1. You will need a clipboard and a pen (or pens). Use only blue or black ink—no other colors, and no pencils.
2. A letter of introduction has been furnished to you. Keep it with you thruout all your interviewing, and do not hesitate to show it to anyone who questions you.
3. Needless to say, interviewers should make a good impression. This means being clean and neat (including fingernails, haircuts, etc.), wearing clean, plain, conservative clothing (but don't appear too prosperous) and also presenting a confident, businesslike, and pleasant appearance.
4. Confidence is quite appropriate since people are usually flattered to be asked their opinions. Experience indicates that even inexperienced interviewers usually meet with an adequate reception, so don't be apologetic! However, keep in mind that the informant does not have the same interest in the interview that you have, and that you are taking his time.
5. Remember that both you and the informant are used to social relationships in the form of "conversations." So do nothing to give the impression that you are conducting a quiz program, or testing the informant's intelligence. There is absolutely no reason to mislead the informant or misrepresent yourself.

6. Be interested in what the informant says, but avoid time-consuming tangents leading away from the subject. Bring the informant back on the track tactfully.

7. *Be neutral in your entire manner.* Remember that you should not talk too much, no matter how tempting the opportunity. It wastes time and may bias the responses. You should always remain calm and composed, and avoid showing anger or surprise. Never indicate disbelief, disapproval, or approval. Even your voice inflection or facial expression may reveal your personal views and thus bias the informant. If you are asked your view either say frankly that you're not allowed to say, and that it's the informant's views that are important, or give a noncommital response such as, "Well, I've heard so many different answers today that I'll have to make up my mind all over again."

8. Your function as an interviewer is solely to collect information and *not* to educate the informant, influence his attitudes about the survey subject matter, sell magazines or talk him into attending the University next year. Therefore, even *after* you have completed the interview, do not give your opinions about the correct answers or related materials.

9. Under no circumstances are copies of the interview schedule to be distributed to informants or anyone else. Always keep all of them in your possession. Never leave one for the informant to fill out for you to pick up later. If for any reason one must be discarded because of an error, mark it "void" and return it to the office at the end of the day. Needless to say, you may not have anyone else do the interviewing for you. It is your sole responsibility.

10. The necessity of keeping *confidential* the information obtained in interviews cannot be stressed too strongly. The information or opinions secured should not be disclosed or discussed with anyone outside of members of the survey staff. You will have assured the informants of their anonymity. It would be immoral, as well as possibly biasing the results, to violate this.

11. Please keep accurate written daily records of your time—time of leaving the University in the morning, lunch, arrival back on campus at the end of the day, and so on. Also keep accurate mileage records from the University and return.

12. Return all completed interview schedules to the office at the end of each day, or before starting interviewing the next morning. Be prepared to spend a few minutes in checking them in.

B. LOCATING THE INFORMANT

1. You will be given Assignment Sheets showing the interview numbers and addresses where you are to conduct your interviews. *One* interview *must* be obtained at *each* address. UNDER NO CIRCUMSTANCES ARE YOU TO CONDUCT AN INTERVIEW AT ANY ADDRESS OR LOCATION WHICH IS NOT ON YOUR ASSIGNMENT SHEET. These specific addresses have been chosen as part of an overall sampling plan. Each one was chosen for a definite reason. Interviews must be conducted in person, not by telephone or mail.

2. You will receive a separate Assignment Sheet for each block. The number of interviews to be conducted per block varies from block to block. Remember that a block is an area *bounded* by streets (and canals, tracks, etc.). Therefore you should never have to cross a street while working on any given block. This may help in finding hard-to-locate addresses.

3. Each line on the Assignment Sheet is intended to be a separate housing unit. It is possible that in some rare cases this will turn out to be two (or more) housing units, when you actually get inside. If so, conduct as many interviews as there are housing units. Use the original interview number, but add the letters A, B, C, etc. to designate the separate interviews. Also *be sure* to make a note of this on the Assignment Sheet.

4. Some of the housing units on your Interview Assignment Sheet may be described as being a certain color.

It is always possible that a house has been painted since the lists were compiled, so if the color is the only thing different from the description given you, go ahead with the interview.

5. If you absolutely cannot locate a given address, make a note to that effect and report it to the survey office at the end of the day.

6. If nobody answers the door, make a note in the appropriate place on the schedule face sheet of the date and time of *each* attempt. Determine, if you can (from neighbors or other clues), when there will be somebody home. Make a note of that on the Assignment Sheet and return at that time if possible.

7. If the address is vacant, demolished, moved, or nonexistent, make a note to that effect on the Assignment Sheet.

8. If the address turns out to be a business address and nobody lives there, make a note to that effect on the Assignment Sheet and do not conduct an interview.

9. If the person at the address is uncooperative and refuses to answer the door and/or to grant an interview, *try* to obtain the interview. Be as persuasive as possible, try to allay his fears and convince him, BUT, do not be obnoxious or abusive, and do not become angry. Perhaps another interviewer later will have better luck. Especially, do not let this hurt your feelings, since you can *expect* some refusals. *No* survey is without them.

10. SAMPLE:
    a. At *odd-numbered* interviews you are to interview a *woman.* Even if a man is at home and the woman is not, you are to call back later and interview the woman. If no woman lives at the address, then go ahead and interview a man.
    b. Similarly, at *even-numbered* interviews you are to interview a *man.* Even if a woman is at home and the man is not, you should call back later and interview the man. If no man lives at that address, then go ahead and interview the woman.

c. Our sample includes only persons who have passed their 20th birthday. Under no circumstances should you interview anyone under 20.

d. For every six interviews you complete, it is *desired* that you obtain:

3 persons, age 20 thru 39
2 persons, age 40 thru 59
1 person, age 60 and over

Therefore, if you have a choice among several men (or women) at a given address, try to conform to this distribution. (See E. 4, below)

C. WHEN TO INTERVIEW

1. Men are seldom found at home during the day, but will more likely be available at lunch time, and in the evening, and on Saturday.

2. Do not interview too late in the evening—certainly do not run the risk of waking people if it looks as though they might have gone to bed.

3. Sunday is generally a bad day for interviewing.

D. INTERVIEWING CONDITIONS

1. If at all possible, interview the informant in private. If others must be present address yourself only to the informant and tactfully attempt to exclude others from interfering.

2. Attempt to conduct the interview without any external interruptions or disturbances.

E. THE APPROACH

1. Fill out all the information on the schedule face sheet—top and bottom—BEFORE you go to the door. But don't write in the box in the lower-right corner.

2. Avoid giving the impression of being a salesman—use a clipboard or manila envelope rather than a brief case.

3. Give a pleasant, brief greeting, introduce yourself, and make a brief statement about what you want. Words such as "survey," "statistics," "opinion poll," "research," "university research," etc., will usually satisfy people that the survey is "harmless." Attempt to convey the impression of an impersonal or research interest in the informant.

4. After your introduction, be sure that you are talking to the proper party. If the person answering the door is not of the sex you are to interview at that address, ask for the person with the characteristics you want. (See B. 10 above.) If you have any doubt as to whether the person has passed his 20th birthday, ask his age at *last* birthday. Be sure that the person is a *resident* of the housing unit, and not merely a visitor.

5. If the person is reluctant to grant an interview, sell yourself and the research as much as possible. Many techniques are possible—humor, surprise at the idea of refusal, reason, etc., etc. However, never get argumentative, belligerent, or angry, nor should you be untruthful.

6. The study is sponsored by the University—do not give any other name or even mention any other organization when introducing yourself.

7. Remember, do NOT leave the schedule for the informant to fill out at his leisure.

F. THE INTERVIEW PROPER

1. Use blue or black ink *only* in filling out the schedule.

2. *You* are to do the writing. The informant may look over your shoulder at the questions, but you read them to him and record his answers. Record them as you go along—NEVER wait till later.

3. Be neat and legible. In order to advance the frontiers of knowledge we would like to be able to read what you have written! This is very important.

4. Read the questions and the alternative answers aloud to the informant. DO NOT deviate from the *exact* wording on the schedule. Read the items and introductory statements exactly as they are printed on the schedule with no changes or omissions.

5. Follow the order of the items as they are printed on the schedule. Be sure to record a response for EVERY ITEM, WITHOUT FAIL. If an item does not apply to that informant, write "NA" for "not applicable" in the space to the *right* of the list of answers.

6. When reading the alternative answers to the informant, DO NOT read the "Don't know" and "Other." Read the alternative answers to every question, UNLESS the instructions say "DON'T READ ANSWERS."

7. Try to read the questions in a conversational manner, so as not to give the impression of a test situation. Encourage the informant to respond freely by such remarks as "Your opinion is as good as the next fellow's," etc.

8. YOU ARE TO *ENCIRCLE* THE NUMBER OR SYMBOL TO THE LEFT OF THE APPROPRIATE ANSWERS (EXCEPT AS NOTED BELOW). BE SURE TO ENCIRCLE THE NUMBERS NEATLY AND CLEARLY. DON'T ENCIRCLE THE STATEMENT—JUST THE NUMBER OR SYMBOL.

9. For most questions, the last two answers are:

   — DK
   & (Other) ______

   "DK" stands for "don't know" and you should encircle the dash (—) when the informant doesn't know, is undecided, etc. Try to avoid this answer—that is, encourage him to choose another answer, but if he still is undecided, encircle the "—".

   "Other" refers to those very rare situations where the informant gives an answer which will not fit in any of the previous categories. The most likely use of this will be when the informant refuses to answer a question. AVOID USING THIS AS MUCH AS POSSIBLE. (If you find you are using this category too often, perhaps you are misreading the question.) Whenever you use this answer you should *write something* in the blank to the right but (NOTE THIS) do NOT NOT NOT NOT encircle the "&" or anything else.

10. MAKE ABSOLUTELY NO MARKS IN THE LEFT-HAND MARGINS OF THE SCHEDULE. These will be needed later for coding.

11. For many questions the informant may give *as many* answers as he wishes, in some cases he is asked for *two* answers, and in some, just *one*. The wording of the question will always indicate how many answers you should permit.

12. There are eleven "open-end" questions—i.e., questions where you are to write the informant's answer as nearly verbatim as possible. These are items #15, 27, 29, 30, 33, 35, 36, 37, 49, 50, and 53. For these questions, write the answer in the space provided, but DO NOT encircle *any* numbers or symbols, unless the answer is "don't know" in which case encircle the "—". (People are usually flattered by comments such as, "That's a very interesting comment. Would you mind repeating it so I can write it down?")

13. If an informant makes a qualification of a structured answer, and you think it is an important statement, record it to the right of the question.

14. Do not allow the informant to go back and change an answer. If he insists, record his wishes to the right of the question, but leave the original answer as it is.

15. Pay particular attention to items #49 and 50. Occupation (#49) refers to the kind of work the individual does. For example, he drives a truck, or is an accountant, or a typist, or whatever. The industry (#50) refers to what kind of employer he works for. For example, he may be a truck driver on a *ranch*, or for *Sears*, or for the *City*. All these would be the same occupation, but different industries. Be sure you get all the information

for these two questions. Do not hesitate to ask follow-up questions until you are sure you have both answers. (If, for example, a man says he hauls cotton—what does this mean? Is he a truck driver, or does he have a fleet of trucks he rents out, or is he president of a trucking firm, or is he a farmer currently engaged in supervising cotton-harvesting, etc?)

16. In the event that the answer to item #48 is "both husband and wife" then get information on *both* for items #49 and 50.

G. CLOSING

1. Before leaving be sure that you have understood the informant.
2. Check to be certain that you have recorded answers for *all* items, and that you have recorded them in the correct spaces.
3. Especially don't overlook the last two items on the schedule. Do not ask the informant's ethnic category. Use your own judgment.
4. After the interview is completed, achieve a diplomatic, friendly exit. This is not always easy. However you do it, be sure to thank the informant for having given his time, and leave him with a feeling of pleasure at having cooperated in a worthwhile undertaking, so that he will be receptive to being revisited for possible check interviews or follow-ups.
5. Immediately at the completion of the interview, record the time of *completion* on the face sheet.

Bibliography

Abelson, Robert P. "Lectures on Computer Simulation," *Mathematics and Social Sciences,* vol. 1, ed. Saul Sternberg, et al., pp. 443–82. Paris: Mouton & Co., 1965.

———. "Simulation of Social Behavior," *The Handbook of Social Psychology,* 2d ed., vol. 2, *Research Methods,* ed. Gardner Lindzey and Elliot Aronson, chap. 12. Reading, Mass.: Addison-Wesley, 1968.

Ackermann, Robert. "Inductive Simplicity," *The Philosophy of Science,* ed. P. H. Nidditch, chap. 7. London: Oxford University Press, 1968.

Adams, Richard N., and Jack J. Preiss, eds. *Human Organization Research.* Homewood, Ill.: The Dorsey Press, Inc., 1960.

American Library Association. *A.L.A. Glossary of Library Terms.* Chicago: American Library Association, 1943.

American Psychological Association. "Ethical Principles in the Conduct of Research with Human Participants," *American Psychologist* 28:79–80 (Jan. 1973).

Anderson, R. Bruce W. "On the Comparability of Meaningful Stimuli in Cross-Cultural Research," *Sociometry* 30:124–36 (June 1967).

Aronson, Elliot, and J. Merrill Carlsmith. "Experimentation in Social Psychology," *The Handbook of Social Psychology,* 2d ed., vol. 2, *Research Methods,* ed. Gardner Lindzey and Elliot Aronson, chap. 9. Reading, Mass.: Addison-Wesley, 1968.

Asch, S. E. "Effects of Group Pressure upon the Modification and Distortion of Judgments," *Readings in Social Psychology,* ed. Eleanor E. Maccoby, Theodore M. Newcomb, and Eugene L. Hartley, pp 174–83. New York: Henry Holt & Co., 1958.

Atteslander, Peter M. "The Interactio-gram," *Human Organization* 13:28–33 (Spring 1954).

Ayer, A. J. *The Origins of Pragmatism.* London: Macmillan, 1968.

Babbie, Earl R. *Survey Research Methods.* Belmont, Calif.: Wadsworth Publishing Co., 1973.

Backman, Carl W. "Some Current blueprints for Relevance," *Pacific Sociological Review* 13:205–10 (Fall 1970).

Backstrom, Charles H., and Gerald D. Hursh. *Survey Research.* Evanston, Ill.: Northwestern University Press, 1963.

Bailey, Kenneth D. "Evaluating Axiomatic Theories," *Sociological Methodology: 1970,* ed. Edgar F. Borgatta and George W. Bohrnstedt, chap. 4. San Francisco: Jossey-Bass, Inc., 1970.

———. "Polythetic Reduction of Monothetic Property Space," *Sociological Methodology: 1972,* ed. Herbert L. Costner, chap. 3. San Francisco: Jossey-Bass, Inc., 1972.

Bales, Robert F. *Interaction Process Analysis.* Cambridge, Mass.: Addison-Wesley, 1951.

———. "Interaction Process Analysis," *International Encyclopedia of the Social Sciences,* vol. 7, ed. David L. Sills, pp. 465–71. New York: Macmillan Co. and The Free Press, 1968.

———. *Personality and Interpersonal Behavior.* New York: Holt, Rinehart and Winston, 1970.

———. "Small-Group Theory and Research," *Sociology Today,* ed. Robert K. Merton, Leonard Broom, and Leonard S. Cottrell, pp. 293–305. New York: Basic Books, Inc., 1959.

Barclay, George W. *Techniques of Population Analysis.* New York: John Wiley & Sons, 1958.

Batchelor, James P., and George R. Goethals. "Spatial Arrangements in Freely Formed Groups," *Sociometry* 35:270–79 (June 1972).

Bavelas, Alex. "Communication Patterns in Task-Oriented Groups," *Group Dynamics,* 3d ed., ed. Dorwin Cartwright and Alvin Zander, chap. 37. New York: Harper & Row, 1968.

Becker, Franklin D., Robert Sommer, Joan Bee, and Bart Oxley. "College Classroom Ecology," *Sociometry* 36:514–25 (Dec. 1973).

Becker, Howard S. "The Relevance of Life Histories," *Sociological Methods,* ed. Norman K. Denzin, chap. 26. Chicago: Aldine Publishing Co., 1970-a.

———. *Sociological Work.* Chicago: Aldine Publishing Co., 1970-b.

———**, and Blanche Geer.** "Participant Observation: The Analysis of Qualitative Field Data," *Human Organization Research,* ed. Richard N. Adams and Jack J. Preiss, chap. 21. Homewood, Ill.: The Dorsey Press, 1960.

Becker, Leonard, Jr., and Clair Gustafson, *Encounter with Sociology: The Term Paper.* Berkeley, Calif.: Glendessary Press, 1968.

Berelson, Bernard. *Content Analysis in Communication Research.* Glencoe, Ill.: The Free Press, 1952.

——— **and Gary A. Steiner.** *Human Behavior: An Inventory of Scientific Findings.* New York: Harcourt, Brace & World, 1964.

Bernstein, Ilene N., ed. "Validity Issues in Evaluative Research," *Sociological Methods & Research* 4:1–128 (Aug. 1975).

Beshers, James M. *Population Processes in Social Systems.* New York: The Free Press, 1967.

Bierstedt, Robert. "The A.S.A. and Public Policy," *American Sociological Review* 30:128–29 (Feb. 1965).

———. "Nominal and Real Definitions in Sociological Theory," *Symposium on Sociological Theory,* ed. Llewellyn Gross, chap. 4. Evanston, Ill.: Row, Peterson, 1959.

Blalock, Hubert M., Jr. *Causal Inferences in Nonexperimental Research.* Chapel Hill, N.C.: University of North Carolina Press, 1964.

———, **ed.** *Causal Models in the Social Sciences.* Chicago: Aldine-Atherton, Inc., 1971.

———. *An Introduction to Social Research.* Englewood Cliffs, N.J.: Prentice-Hall, Inc., 1970.

———. *Social Statistics.* 2d ed. New York: McGraw-Hill, 1972.

———. *Theory Construction: From Verbal to Mathematical Formulations.* Englewood Cliffs, N.J.: Prentice-Hall, Inc., 1969.

———, **and Ann M. Blalock, eds.** *Methodology in Social Research. New York: McGraw-Hill, 1968.*

Bogardus, Emory S. *A Forty Year Racial Distance Study.* Los Angeles: University of Southern California, 1967.

Bogue, Donald J. *Principles of Demography.* New York: John Wiley & Sons, Inc., 1969.

Boler, John F. *Charles Peirce and Scholastic Realism.* Seattle: University of Washington Press, 1963.

Bonjean, Charles M., Richard J. Hill, and S. Dale McLemore. *Sociological Measurement: An Inventory of Scales and Indices.* San Francisco: Chandler Publishing Co., 1967.

Borgatta, Edgar F., ed. *Sociological Methodology: 1969.* San Francisco: Jossey-Bass, 1969.

———, **and George W. Bohrnstedt, eds.** *Sociological Methodology: 1970.* San Francisco Jossey-Bass, 1970.

———, **and Leonard S. Cottrell, Jr.** "Directions for Research in Group Behavior," *American Journal of Sociology* 63:42–48 (July 1957).

Braithwaite, Richard Bevan. *Scientific Explanation.* Cambridge: Cambridge University Press, 1953.

Bridgman, P. W. *The Logic of Modern Physics.* New York: Macmillan, 1927.

Brown, Julia S., and Brian G. Gilmartin. "Sociology Today: Lacunae, Emphases, and Surfeits," *American Sociologist* 4:283–91 (Nov. 1969).

Brown, Robert. *Explanation in Social Science.* Chicago: Aldine, 1963.

Bruyn, Severyn T. *The Human Perspective in Sociology: The Methodology of Participant Observation.* Englewood Cliffs, N.J.: Prentice-Hall, 1966.

Buchler, Justus, ed. *The Philosophy of Peirce.* London: Routledge & Kegan Paul, Ltd., 1940.

Campbell, Angus, and George Katona. "The Sample Survey: a Technique for Social-Science Research," *Research Methods in the Behavioral Sciences,* ed. Leon Festinger and Daniel Katz), chap. 1. New York: Dryden Press, 1953.

Campbell, Donald T., and Julian C. Stanley. *Experimental and Quasi-Experimental Designs for Research.* Chicago: Rand McNally & Co., 1963.

Campbell, William Giles, and Stephen Vaughan Ballou. *Form and Style,* 4th ed. Boston: Houghton Mifflin, 1974.

Cannell, Charles F., and Floyd J. Fowler, Jr. "A Note on Interviewer Effect in Self-Enumerative Procedures," *American Sociological Review* 29:270 (April 1964).

Cannell, Charles F., and Robert L. Kahn. "Interviewing," *The Handbook of Social Psychology,* 2d ed., vol. 2, *Research Methods,* ed. Gardner Lindzey and Elliot Aronson, chap. 15. Reading, Mass.: Addison-Wesley, 1968.

Carnap, Rudolf. *Logical Foundations of Probability.* Chicago: University of Chicago Press, 1962.

Carney, James D., and Richard K. Scheer. *Fundamentals of Logic.* New York: Macmillan, 1964.

Caro, Francis G., ed. *Readings in Evaluation Research.* New York: Russell Sage Foundation, 1971.

Carter, Launor, William Haythorn, Beatrice Meirowitz, and John Lanzetta. "A Note on a New Technique of Interaction Recording," *Journal of Abnormal and Social Psychology* 46:258–60 (April 1951).

Cartwright, Desmond S. "Ecological Variables," *Sociological Methodology: 1969,* ed. Edgar F. Borgatta, chap. 6. San Francisco: Jossey-Bass, 1969.

Cartwright, Dorwin. "Influence, Leadership, Control," *Handbook of Organizations,* ed. James G. March, chap. 1. Chicago: Rand McNally & Co., 1965.

Catton, William R., Jr. "The Functions and Dysfunctions of Ethnocentrism: a Theory," *Social Problems,* 8:201–11 (Winter 1960–61).

———. "Intervening Opportunities: Barriers or Stepping Stones?" *Pacific Sociological Review* 8:75–81 (Fall 1965).

Chain, Sir Ernst. "Social Responsibility and the Scientist," *The Hindu* [newspaper], Madras, India, Nov. 9, 1970.

Chapple, Eliot D. "The Interaction Chronograph: Its Evolution and Present Application." *Personnel* 25:295–307 (Jan. 1949).

Chein, Isidor. "An Introduction to Sampling." *Research Methods in Social Relations,* rev. ed. (Claire Selltiz, Marie Jahoda, Morton Deutsch, and Stuart W. Cook), Appendix B. New York: Henry Holt & Co., 1959.

Chernoff, Herman, and Lincoln E. Moses. *Elementary Decision Theory.* New York: John Wiley & Sons, 1959.

Coch, Lester, and J. R. P. French, Jr. "Overcoming Resistance to Change," *Group Dynamics,* 3d ed., ed. Dorwin Cartwright and Alvin Zander, chap. 26. New York: Harper & Row, 1968.

Cohen, Kalman J., and Richard M. Cyert. "Simulation of Organizational Behavior." *Handbook of Organizations,* ed. James G. March, chap. 7. Chicago: Rand McNally & Co., 1965.

Cohen, K. J., R. M. Cyert, W. R. Dill, A. A. Kuehn, M. H. Miller, T. A. Van Wormer, and P. R. Winters. "The Carnegie Tech Management Game." *Simulation in Social Science,* ed. Harold Guetzkow, chap. 9. Englewood Cliffs, N.J.: Prentice-Hall, Inc., 1962.

Cohen, Morris R., and Ernest Nagel. *An Introduction to Logic and Scientific Method.* New York: Harcourt, Brace and Co., 1934.

Coleman, James S. "Analysis of Social Structures and Simulation of Social Processes with Electronic Computers." *Simulation in Social Science,* ed. Harold Guetzkow, chap. 5. Englewood Cliffs, N.J.: Prentice-Hall, Inc., 1962.

———. *Introduction to Mathematical Sociology.* New York: The Free Press of Glencoe, 1964-a.

———. "Mathematical Models and Computer Simulation," *Handbook of Modern Sociology,* ed. Robert E. L. Faris, chap. 27. Chicago: Rand McNally & Co., 1964-b.

———. "The Mathematical Study of Small Groups." *Mathematical Thinking in the Measurement of Behavior,* ed. Herbert Solomon, pp. 1–149. Glencoe, Ill.: The Free Press, 1960.

———. "The Methods of Sociology," *Stages of Social Research,* ed. Dennis P. Forcese and Stephen Richer, pp. 399–419. Englewood Cliffs, N.J.: Prentice-Hall, Inc., 1970-a.

———. "Relational Analysis: The Study of Social Organizations with Survey Methods." *Sociological Methods,* ed. Norman K. Denzin, chap. 7. Chicago: Aldine, 1970-b.

Cook, Mark. "Experiments on Orientation and Proxemics." *Human Relations* 23:61-76 (Feb. 1970).

Coombs, Clyde H. "Theory and Methods of Social Measurement." *Research Methods in the Behavioral Sciences,* ed. Leon Festinger and Daniel Katz, chap. 11. New York: The Dryden Press, 1953.

Cooperband, Alvin S. "The Use of a Computer in Conducting Psychological Experiments," *Behavioral Science* 11:307–11 (July 1966).

Copi, Irving M. *Symbolic Logic.* New York: Macmillan, 1954.

Costner, Herbert L., ed. *Sociological Methodology: 1971.* San Francisco: Jossey-Bass, Inc., 1971.

_______, ed. *Sociological Methodology: 1972.* San Francisco: Jossey-Bass, 1972.

_______, ed. *Sociological Methodology: 1973–1974.* San Francisco: Jossey-Bass, 1974.

_______, and Robert K. Leik. "Deductions from 'Axiomatic Theory'," *American Sociological Review* 29:819–35 (Dec. 1964).

Crider, Donald M., Fern K. Willits, and Robert C. Bealer. "Panel Studies: Some Practical Problems," *Sociological Methods and Research* 2:3–19 (Aug. 1973).

Dawson, Carl A., and Warner E. Gettys. *An Introduction to Sociology,* 3d ed. New York: The Ronald Press, 1948.

Dawson, Richard E. "Simulation in the Social Sciences." *Simulation in Social Science,* ed. Harold Guetzkow, chap. 1. Englewood Cliffs, N.J.: Prentice-Hall, Inc., 1962.

Denzin, Norman K. *The Research Act.* Chicago: Aldine Publishing Co., 1970-a.

_______, ed. *Sociological Methods: A Sourcebook.* Chicago: Aldine Publishing Co., 1970-b.

Dexter, Lewis Anthony. *Elite and Specialized Interviewing.* Evanston, Ill.: Northwestern University Press, 1970.

Dillman, Don A., James A. Christenson, Edwin H. Carpenter, and Ralph M. Brooks. "Increasing Mail Questionnaire Response: a Four State Comparison," *American Sociological Review* 39:744–56 (Oct. 1974).

DiRenzo, Gordon J., ed. *Concepts, Theory, and Explanation in the Behavioral Sciences.* New York: Random House, 1966.

Dodd, Stuart C., and Stefan C. Christopher. "A 'Quadruple' Experimental Design." Paper presented at the West Coast Conference on Small Group Research, Salt Lake City, April 1965.

Drabek, Thomas E. and Eugene Haas. "Laboratory Simulation of Organizational Stress," *American Sociological Review* 34:223–38 (April 1969).

Duncan, Otis Dudley. "Social Organization and the Ecosystem." *Handbook of Modern Sociology*, ed. Robert E. L. Faris, chap. 2. Chicago: Rand McNally & Co., 1964.

Edwards, Allen L. *Experimental Design in Psychological Research*, 3d ed. New York: Holt, Rinehart & Winston, 1968.

———. *Techniques of Attitude Scale Construction*. New York: Appleton-Century-Crofts, 1957.

Farber, Bernard. "Response Falsification and Spurious Correlation in Survey Research," *American Sociological Review* 28:123–30 (Feb. 1963).

Feigl, Herbert. "Notes on Causality." *Readings in the Philosophy of Science*, ed. Herbert Feigl and May Brodbeck, pp. 408–18. New York: Appleton-Century-Crofts, 1953-a.

———. "The Scientific Outlook: Naturalism and Humanism." *Readings in the Philosophy of Science*, ed. Herbert Feigl and May Brodbeck, pp. 8–18. New York: Appleton-Century-Crofts, 1953-b.

Felipe, Nancy Jo and Robert Sommer. "Invasions of Personal Space," *Social Problems* 14:206–14 (Fall 1966).

Festinger, Leon. "Laboratory Experiments." *Research Methods in the Behavioral Sciences*, ed. Leon Festinger and Daniel Katz, chap. 4. New York: The Dryden Press, 1953.

———, Henry W. Riecken, and Stanley Schachter. *When Prophecy Fails*. Minneapolis: University of Minnesota Press, 1956.

Finifter, Bernard M. "The Generation of Confidence: Evaluating Research Findings by Random Subsample Replication." *Sociological Methodology:1972*, ed. Herbert L. Costner, chap. 4. San Francisco: Jossey-Bass, Inc., 1972.

Flament, Claude. *Applications of Graph Theory to Group Structure*. Englewood Cliffs, N.J.: Prentice-Hall, Inc., 1963.

Freeman, Howard E. and Clarence C. Sherwood. *Social Research and Social Policy*. Englewood Cliffs, N.J.: Prentice-Hall, Inc., 1970.

French, John R. P. "Organized and Unorganized Groups under Fear and Frustration." *Authority and Frustration; Part V, University of Iowa Studies in Child Welfare* 20:229–308 (1944).

Fromkin, Howard L. "The Behavioral Science Laboratories at Purdue's Krannert School," *Administrative Science Quarterly* 14:171–77 (June 1969).

Gamson, William A. *SIMSOC: Simulated Society*. New York: The Free Press, 1969.

Garfinkel, Harold. *Studies in Ethnomethodology.* Englewood Cliffs, N.J.: Prentice-Hall, Inc., 1967.

Gibbs, Jack P., ed. *Urban Research Methods.* Princeton, N.J.: D. Van Nostrand Co., Inc., 1961.

Glaser, Barney G. and Anselm L. Strauss. *The Discovery of Grounded Theory.* Chicago: Aldine Publishing Co., 1967.

Glass, John F., and Harry H. Frankiel. "The Influence of Subjects on the Researcher: A Problem in Observing Social Interaction," *Pacific Sociological Review,* 11:75–80 (Fall 1968).

Glock, Charles Y. "Some Applications of the Panel Method to the Study of Change," *The Language of Social Research,* ed. Paul F. Lazarsfeld & Morris Rosenberg, pp. 242–50. Glencoe, Ill.: The Free Press, 1955.

Goode, William J., and Paul K. Hatt. *Methods in Social Research.* New York: McGraw-Hill, 1952.

Goodman, Nelson. "Safety, Strength, Simplicity." *The Philosophy of Science.,* ed. P. H. Nidditch, chap. 6. London: Oxford University Press, 1968.

Gordon, Raymond L. *Interviewing.* Homewood, Ill.: The Dorsey Press, 1969.

Gottschalk, Louis, Clyde Kluckhohn, and Robert Angell. *The Use of Personal Documents in History, Anthropology, and Sociology.* New York: Social Science Research Council, 1951.

Green, Bert F. "Attitude Measurement," *Handbook of Social Psychology,* vol. 1, ed. Gardner Lindzey, chap. 9. Reading, Mass.: Addison-Wesley, 1954.

Greer, Scott. *The Logic of Social Inquiry.* Chicago: Aldine Publishing Co., 1969.

Grimshaw, Allen D. "Language as Obstacle and as Data in Sociological Research," *Social Science Research Council Items* 23:17–21 (June 1969).

Gross, Edward. "Social Science Techniques: a Problem of Power and Responsibility," *The Scientific Monthly* 83:242–47 (Nov. 1956).

Gross Llewellyn. "Sociological Theory: Questions and Problems," *Sociological Theory: Inquiries and Paradigms,* ed. Llewellyn Gross, pp. 3–73. New York: Harper & Row, 1967.

Guetzkow, Harold, ed. *Simulation in Social Science.* Englewood Cliffs, N.J.: Prentice-Hall, Inc., 1962-a.

———. "A Use of Simulation in the Study of Inter-nation Relations." *Simulation in Social Science,* ed. Harold Guetzkow, chap. 7. Englewood Cliffs, N.J.: Prentice-Hall, Inc., 1962-b.

Guttentag, Marcia, and Elmer L. Struening, eds. *Handbook of Evaluation Research*, vol. 2. Beverly Hills, Calif.: Sage Publications, Inc., 1975.

Guttman, Louis. "The Principal Components of Scalable Attitudes." *Mathematical Thinking in the Social Sciences*, ed. Paul F. Lazarsfeld, chap. 5. Glencoe, Ill.: The Free Press, 1954.

Hadden, Jeffrey K. "Use of Ad Hoc Definitions." *Sociological Methodology:1969*, ed. Edgar F. Borgatta, chap. 10. San Francisco: Jossey-Bass, 1969.

Hage, Jerald. "An Axiomatic Theory of Organizations," *Administrative Science Quarterly* 10:289–320 (Dec. 1965).

Hagood, Margaret Jarman, and Daniel O. Price. *Statistics for Sociologists*, rev. ed. New York: Henry Holt and Co., 1952.

Hall, Edward T. *The Hidden Dimension.* Garden City, N.Y.: Doubleday & Co., 1966.

Hansen, Morris H., William N. Hurwitz, and William G. Madow. *Sample Survey Methods and Theory*, 2 vols. New York: John Wiley & Sons, 1953.

Hanson, Norwood Russell. *Patterns of Discovery.* Cambridge: Cambridge University Press, 1965.

Harary, Frank, and Robert Z. Norman. *Graph Theory as a Mathematical Model in Social Science.* Ann Arbor: University of Michigan Institute for Social Research, 1953.

Hare, A. Paul, Edgar F. Borgatta, and Robert F. Bales, eds. *Small Groups*, rev. ed. New York: Alfred A, Knopf, 1965.

Harper, Dean. "Observation Errors in Sociological Surveys: a Model and a Method," *Sociological Methods and Research* 2:63–83 (Aug. 1973).

Hauser, Philip M., ed. *Handbook for Social Research in Urban Areas.* New York: UNESCO Publications Center, 1965.

Hayes, Donald P. "The Cornell Datalogger." *Administrative Science Quarterly* 14:222–23 (June 1969).

Heise, David R., ed. *Sociological Methodology: 1975.* San Francisco: Jossey-Bass, 1974.

———. *Sociological Methodology: 1976.* San Francisco: Jossey-Bass, 1975.

Hempel, Carl G. *Aspects of Scientific Explanation.* New York: The Free Press, 1965.

———. "Explanation in Science and in History," *The Philosophy of Science*, ed. P. H. Nidditch, chap. 3. London: Oxford University Press, 1968.

———, **and Paul Oppenheim.** "The Logic of Explanation," *Readings in the Philosophy of Science,* ed. Herbert Feigl and May Brodbeck, pp. 319–52. New York: Appleton-Century-Crofts, 1953.

Hemphill, John K., and Charles M. Westie. "The Measurement of Group Dimensions," *Journal of Psychology* 29:325–42 (April 1950).

Heyns, Roger W., and Alvin F. Zander. "Observation of Group Behavior," *Research Methods in the Behavioral Sciences,* ed. Leon Festinger and Daniel Katz, chap. 9. New York: The Dryden Press, 1953.

Hochberg, Herbert. "Axiomatic Systems, Formalization, and Scientific Theories," *Symposium on Sociological Theory,* ed. Llewellyn Gross, chap 13. Evanston, Ill.: Row, Peterson, 1959.

Hoggatt, Austin C., Joseph Esherick, and John T. Wheeler. "A Laboratory to Facilitate Computer-controlled Behavioral Experiments," *Administrative Science Quarterly* 14:202–7 (June 1969).

Holsti, Ole R. "Content Analysis," *The Handbook of Social Psychology,* 2d ed., vol. 2, *Research Methods,* ed. Gardner Lindzey and Elliot Aronson, chap. 16. Reading, Mass.: Addison-Wesley, 1968.

———. *Content Analysis for the Social Sciences and Humanities.* Reading, Mass.: Addison-Wesley, 1969.

Holt, Robert, T., and John E. Turner, eds. *The Methodology of Comparative Research.* New York: The Free Press, 1970.

Horowitz, Irving Louis, ed. *The Rise and Fall of Project Camelot.* Cambridge, Mass.: The MIT Press, 1967.

Horwitz, Murray, and Dorwin Cartwright. "A Projective Method for the Diagnosis of Group Properties," *Human Relations* 6:397–410 (1953).

Hoult, Thomas Ford, ed. *Dictionary of Modern Sociology.* Totowa, N.J.: Littlefield, Adams & Co., 1969.

———. ". . . Who Shall Prepare Himself to the Battle?" *American Sociologist* 3:3–7 (Feb. 1968).

Hyman, Herbert H. *Secondary Analysis of Sample Surveys.* New York: John Wiley & Sons, Inc., 1972.

———. *Survey Design and Analysis.* Glencoe, Ill.: The Free Press, 1955.

Hyman, Herbert H. et al. *Interviewing in Social Research.* Chicago: University of Chicago Press, 1975.

Inkeles, Alex. *What Is Sociology?* Englewood Cliffs, N.J.: Prentice-Hall, Inc., 1964.

Jennings, Norman H., and Justin H. Dickins. "Computer Simulation of Peak Hour Operations in a Bus Terminal," *Simulation in Social Science,* ed. Harold Guetzkow, chap. 12. Englewood Cliffs, N.J.: Prentice-Hall, Inc., 1962.

Joel, Walther, and David Shapiro. "A Genotypical Approach to the Analysis of Personal Interaction," *Journal of Psychology* 28:9–17 (July 1949).

Junker, Buford H. *Field Work.* Chicago: University of Chicago Press, 1960.

Kaplan, Abraham. *The Conduct of Inquiry.* San Francisco: Chandler Publishing Co., 1964.

Kegeles, S. Stephen, Clinton F. Fink, and John P. Kirscht. "Interviewing a National Sample by Long-Distance Telephone," *Public Opinion Quarterly* 33:412–19 (Fall 1969).

Kelman, Herbert C. "Human Use of Human Subjects: The Problem of Deception in Social Psychological Experiments," *Psychological Bulletin* 67:1–11 (Jan. 1967).

———. *A Time to Speak: On Human Values and Social Research.* San Francisco: Jossey-Bass, 1968.

Kemeny, John G. *A Philosopher Looks at Science.* Princeton, N.J.: D. Van Nostrand Co., 1959.

Kershner, R. B., and L. R. Wilcox. *The Anatomy of Mathematics,* Second Edition. Copyright © 1974. The Ronald Press Company, New York.

Kinch, John W. "A Formalized Theory of the Self Concept," *American Journal of Sociology* 68:481–86 (Jan. 1963).

Kish, Leslie. *Survey Sampling.* New York: John Wiley & Sons, 1965.

Klecka, William R., Norman H. Nie, and C. Hadlai Hull. *SPSS Primer.* New York: McGraw-Hill, 1975.

Kuder, G. Frederic *Kuder Preference Record–Vocational.* Chicago: Science Research Associates, 1946.

Kuhn, Thomas S. *The Structure of Scientific Revolutions.* Chicago: University of Chicago Press, 1962.

Labovitz, Sanford. "The Assignment of Numbers to Rank Order Categories," *American Sociological Review,* 35:515–24 (June 1970-a).

———. "The Nonutility of Significance Tests: The Significance of Tests of Significance Reconsidered," *Pacific Sociological Review* 13:141–48 (Summer 1970-b).

———. "The Zone of Rejection," *Pacific Sociological Review* 14:373–81 (Oct. 1971).

Land, Kenneth C. "Formal Theory," *Sociological Methodology: 1971,* ed. Herbert L. Costner, chap. 7. San Francisco: Jossey-Bass, 1971.

Largey, Gale Peter, and David Rodney Watson. "The Sociology of Odors," *American Journal of Sociology* 77:1021–34 (May 1972).

Lastrucci, Carlo L. *The Scientific Approach.* Cambridge, Mass.: Schenkman Publishing Co., 1963.

Laumann, Edward O. "The Social Structure of Religious and Ethnoreligious Groups in a Metropolitan Community," *American Sociological Review* 34:182–97 (April 1969).

Lazarsfeld, Paul F. "The Sociology of Empirical Social Research," *American Sociological Review* 27:757–67 (Dec. 1962).

———. "Some Remarks on Typological Procedures in Social Research," *Continuities in the Language of Social Research,* ed. Paul F. Lazarsfeld, Ann K. Pasanella, and Morris Rosenberg, chap. 12. New York: The Free Press, 1972.

———, and Neil W. Henry. *Latent Structure Analysis.* Boston: Houghton Mifflin Co., 1968.

———, Ann K. Pasanella, and Morris Rosenberg, eds. *Continuities in the Language of Social Research.* New York: The Free Press, 1972.

Lazerwitz, Bernard. "Sampling Theory and Procedures," *Methodology in Social Research,* ed. Hubert M. Blalock, Jr., and Ann B. Blalock, chap. 8. New York: McGraw-Hill, 1968.

LeClair, Edward E., Jr. "Problems of Large-Scale Anthropological Research," *Human Organization Research,* ed. Richard N. Adams and Jack J. Preiss, chap. 3. Homewood, Ill.: The Dorsey Press, 1960.

Leik, Robert K. " 'Irrelevant' Aspects of Stooge Behavior: Implications for Leadership Studies and Experimental Methodology," *Sociometry* 28:259–71 (Sept. 1965).

Levine, Joel H. "The Sphere of Influence," *American Sociological Review* 37:14–27 (Feb. 1972).

Ley, David, and Roman Cybriwsky. "The Spatial Ecology of Stripped Cars," *Environment and Behavior* 6:53–68 (March 1974).

Liebow, Elliot. *Tally's Corner.* Boston: Little, Brown & Co., 1967.

Lindzey, Gardner, and Donn Byrne. "Measurement of Social Choice and Interpersonal Attractiveness," *The Handbook of Social Psychology,* 2d ed., vol. 2, *Research Methods,* ed. Gardner Lindzey and Elliot Aronson, chap. 14. Reading, Mass.: Addison-Wesley, 1968.

Lipset, Seymour Martin, Martin A. Trow, and James S. Coleman. *Union Democracy.* Glencoe, Ill.: The Free Press, 1956.

Locke, Harvey J. *Predicting Adjustment in Marriage.* New York: Henry Holt & Co., 1951.

Lockyer, K. G. *An Introduction to Critical Path Analysis.* London: Sir Isaac Pitman and Sons, 1969.

Louch, A. R. *Explanation and Human Action.* Oxford: Basil Blackwell, 1966.

Lundberg, George A. *Social Research.* New York: Longmans, Green and Co., 1942.

Lynd, Robert S., and Helen Merrell Lynd. *Middletown.* New York: Harcourt, Brace & World, Inc., 1956.

Manaster, Guy J., and Robert J. Havighurst. *Cross-National Research.* Boston: Houghton Mifflin Co., 1972.

Manheim, Henry L. "Intergroup Interaction as Related to Status and Leadership Differences between Groups," *Sociometry* 23:415–27 (Dec. 1960).

———. "Marriage Preparation Courses in Southern California Colleges," *Journal of Educational Research* 55:5–12 (Sept. 1961-a).

———. "Personality Differences of Members of Two Political Parties," *Journal of Social Psychology* 50:261–68 (Nov. 1959).

———. "A Socially Unacceptable Method of Mate Selection," *Sociology and Social Research* 45:182–87 (Jan. 1961-b)

———**, and Frederick W. Howlett.** "Evaluation of the Effectiveness of a Local Heart Council Program." American and Arizona Heart Associations, 1964. (Mimeographed)

Maris, Ronald. "The Logical Adequacy of Homans' Social Theory," *American Sociological Review* 35:1069–81 (Dec. 1970).

Markoff, John, Gilbert Shapiro, and Sasha R. Weitman. "Toward the Integration of Content Analysis and General Methodology," *Sociological Methodology: 1975,* ed. David R. Heise, chap. 1. San Francisco: Jossey-Bass, 1974.

Martel, Martin U., and George J. McCall. "Models from Limbo—Methodological Notes and Confessions." Paper presented at the American Sociological Association, Los Angeles, Aug. 1963.

Martin, Thomas L., Jr. *Malice in Blunderland.* New York: McGraw-Hill, 1973.

Mazur, Allan. "The Littlest Science," *The American Sociologist* 3:195–200 (Aug. 1968). (See also subsequent three issues of *The American Sociologist* for replies.)

McCall, George J., and J. L. Simmons, eds. *Issues in Participant Observation.* Reading, Mass.: Addison-Wesley, 1969.

McCracken, Daniel D. "The Monte Carlo Method," *Mathematical Thinking in Behavioral Sciences: Readings from Scientific American,* comp. David M. Messick, pp. 33–36. San Francisco: W. H. Freeman & Co., 1968.

McDonagh, Edward C., and A. Leon Rosenblum. "A Comparison of Mailed Questionnaires and Subsequent Structured Interviews," *Public Opinion Quarterly* 29:131–36 (Spring 1965).

McKinney, John C. *Constructive Typology and Social Theory.* New York: Appleton-Century-Crofts, 1966.

Mead, Margaret. *Sex and Temperament in Three Primitive Societies.* New York: William Morrow and Co., 1963.

Meehan, Eugene J. *Explanation in Social Science.* Homewood, Ill.: The Dorsey Press, 1968.

Melbin, Murray. "Mapping Uses and Methods," *Human Organization Research,* ed. Richard N. Adams and Jack J. Preiss, pp. 255–66. Homewood, Ill.: The Dorsey Press, 1960.

Merton, Robert K., Marjorie Fiske, and Patricia L. Kendall. *The Focused Interview.* Glencoe, Ill.: The Free Press, 1956.

Merton, Robert K., and Patricia L. Kendall. "The Focused Interview." *The Language of Social Research,* ed. Paul F. Lazarsfeld and Morris Rosenberg, pp. 476–89. New York: The Free Press, 1955.

Milgram, Stanley. "Issues in the Study of Obedience: a Reply to Baumrind," *The Social Psychology of Psychological Research,* ed. Arthur G. Miller, pp. 112–21. New York: The Free Press, 1972.

———. *Obedience to Authority.* New York: Harper & Row, 1974.

Miller, Arthur G., ed. *The Social Psychology of Psychological Research.* New York: The Free Press, 1972.

Miller, Delbert C. *Handbook of Research Design and Social Measurement,* 2d ed. New York: David McKay Co., 1970.

Miller, James G. "Living Systems: Cross-Level Hypotheses," *Behavioral Science* 10:380–411 (Oct. 1965).

Mills, C. Wright. *The Sociological Imagination.* Middlesex, England: Penguin Books, Ltd., 1959.

Moreno, J. L., ed. *The Sociometry Reader.* Glencoe, Ill.: The Free Press, 1960.

———. *Who Shall Survive?* Beacon, N.Y: Beacon House, 1953.

Morrison, Denton E., and Ramon E. Henkel, ed. *The Significance Test Controversy.* Chicago: Aldine Publishing Co., 1970.

Moser, C. A. *Survey Methods in Social Investigation.* London: Heinemann, 1958.

Mosteller, Frederick, and John W. Tukey. "Data Analysis, Including Statistics," *The Handbook of Social Psychology,* 2d ed., vol. 2, *Research Methods,* ed. Gardner Lindzey and Elliot Aronson, chap. 10. Reading, Mass.: Addison-Wesley, 1968.

Movahedi, Siamak, and Richard H. Ogles. "Axiomatic Theory, Informative Value of Propositions, and 'Derivation Rules of Ordinary Language'," *American Sociological Review* 38:416–24 (Aug. 1973).

Mueller, John H., Karl F. Schuessler, and Herbert L. Costner. *Statistical Reasoning in Sociology*, 2d ed. Boston: Houghton Mifflin Co., 1970.

Nagasawa, Richard H., and Philip von Bretzel. "The Utility of Formalization in Constructing Theories in Sociology: an Illustration." Paper presented at the Pacific Sociological Association, San Jose, California, March, 1974.

Nagel, Ernest. *The Structure of Science.* New York: Harcourt, Brace and World, 1961.

Naroll, Raoul. "Some Thoughts on Comparative Method in Cultural Anthropology," *Methodology in Social Research,* ed. Hubert M. Blalock, Jr., and Ann B. Blalock, chap. 7. New York: McGraw-Hill, 1968.

Naylor, Thomas H., Joseph L. Balintfy, Donald S. Burdick, and Kong Chu. *Computer Simulation Techniques.* New York: John Wiley & Sons, 1966.

Newman, Robert P., and Dale R. Newman. *Evidence.* Boston: Houghton Mifflin Co., 1969.

Nidditch, P. H. *Elementary Logic of Science and Mathematics.* Glencoe, Ill.: The Free Press, 1960.

———, **ed.** *The Philosophy of Science.* London: Oxford University Press, 1968.

Nie, Norman, Dale H. Bent, and C. Hadlai Hull. *SPSS: Statistical Package for the Social Sciences.* New York: McGraw-Hill Book Co., 1970.

Nie, Norman H., C. Hadlai Hull, Jean G. Jenkins, Karin Steinbrenner, and Dale H. Bent. *SPSS: Statistical Package for the Social Sciences,* 2d ed. New York: McGraw-Hill Book Co., 1975.

Noël, Robert C. "The POLIS Laboratory," *American Behavioral Scientist* 12:30–35 (July–Aug. 1969).

North, Robert C., Ole R. Holsti, M. George Zaninovich, and Dina A. Zinnes. *Content Analysis.* Evanston, Ill.: Northwestern University Press, 1963.

Nutch, Frank J., and Milton Bloombaum. "A Smallest Space Analysis of Gang Boys' Behaviors," *Pacific Sociological Review* 11:116–22 (Fall 1968).

Nygreen, G. T. "Interactive Path Analysis," *The American Sociologist* 6:37–43 (Feb. 1971).

Oppenheim, A. N. *Questionnaire Design and Attitude Measurement.* New York: Basic Books, 1966.

Pap, Arthur. "Does Science Have Metaphysical Presuppositions?" *Readings in the Philosophy of Science,* ed. Herbert Feigl and May Brodbeck, pp. 21–33. New York: Appleton-Century-Crofts, 1953.

Parker, Douglas A. "On Values and Value Judgments in Sociology," *American Sociological Review* 32:463–66 (June 1967).

Parten, Mildred. *Surveys, Polls, and Samples.* New York: Harper & Bros., 1950.

Peirce, Charles S. *Essays in the Philosophy of Science,* ed. Vincent Tomas. New York: The Liberal Arts Press, 1957.

———. *Selected Writings (Values in a Universe of Change),* ed. Philip P. Wiener. New York: Dover Publications, 1958.

Perry, Ralph Barton. *Realms of Value.* Cambridge, Mass.: Harvard University Press, 1954.

Phillips, Lawrence S. *Bayesian Statistics for Social Scientists.* New York: Thomas Y. Crowell Co., 1974.

Pool, Ithiel de Sola, ed. *Trends in Content Analysis.* Urbana, Ill.: University of Illinois Press, 1959.

Popovich, Mihailo. "What the American Sociologists Think about Their Science and Its Problems," *The American Sociologist* 1:133–35 (May 1966).

Popper, Karl R. *The Logic of Scientific Discovery.* New York: Science Editions, Inc., 1961.

Quinney, Richard. *The Social Reality of Crime.* Boston: Little, Brown & Co., 1970.

Raj, Des. *The Design of Sample Surveys.* New York: McGraw-Hill, 1972.

———. *Sampling Theory.* New York: McGraw-Hill, 1968.

Raser, John R. *Simulation and Society.* Boston: Allyn & Bacon, 1969.

Reiss, Albert J., Jr. "Systematic Observation of Natural Social Phenomena," *Sociological Methodology:1971,* ed. Herbert L. Costner, chap. 1. San Francisco: Jossey-Bass, 1971.

Reissman, Leonard, and Kalman H. Silvert, eds. "Ethics and Social Science Research," *American Behavioral Scientist* 10:1–34 (June 1967), entire issue.

Rhoades, Larry. "NSF Program Outlined: Emphasized Areas Cited," *Footnotes* 3:1 (Jan. 1975).

Richardson, M. *Fundamentals of Mathematics.* New York: Macmillan, 1941.

Riecken, Henry W. "Compliant Subjects," *Science* 184:667–69 (May 10, 1974).

———. "A Program for Research on Experiments in Social

Psychology." *Decisions, Values and Groups,* vol. 2, ed. Norman F. Washburne, pp. 25–41. New York: Macmillan, 1962.

———. "The Unidentified Interviewer," *American Journal of Sociology* 62:210–12 (Sept. 1956).

Rijsman, John. "The Leuven Laboratory for Experimental Social Psychology," *Administrative Science Quarterly* 14:254–9 (June 1969).

Robin, Stanley S. "A Procedure for Securing Returns to Mail Questionnaires," *Sociology and Social Research* 50:24–35 (Oct. 1965).

Roethlisberger, F. J., and William J. Dickson. *Management and the Worker.* Cambridge, Mass.: Harvard University Press, 1939.

Rogers, Carl R. *Counseling and Psychotherapy.* Boston: Houghton Mifflin Co., 1942.

———. "The Nondirective Method as a Technique for Social Research," *American Journal of Sociology* 50:279–83 (Jan. 1945).

Roistacher, Richard C. "A Review of Mathematical Methods in Sociometry," *Sociological Methods & Research* 3:123–71 (Nov. 1974).

Rokeach, Milton. *The Nature of Human Values.* New York: The Free Press, 1973.

Rokkan, Stein, ed. *Comparative Research Across Cultures and Nations.* Paris: Mouton, 1968.

———**, ed.** *Data Archives for the Social Sciences.* Paris: Mouton, 1966.

Rome, Sydney C., and Beatrice K. Rome. "Computer Simulation Toward a Theory of Large Organizations," *Computer Applications in the Behavioral Sciences,* ed. Harold Borko, chap. 22. Englewood Cliffs, N.J.: Prentice-Hall, 1962.

Rose, Arnold M. *Theory and Method in the Social Sciences.* Minneapolis: University of Minnesota Press, 1954.

Rosenthal, Robert. *Experimenter Effects in Behavioral Research.* New York: Appleton-Century-Crofts, 1966.

———**, and Ralph L. Rosnow, eds.** *Artifact in Behavioral Research.* New York: Academic Press, 1969.

Ross, John, and Perry Smith. "Orthodox Experimental Designs," *Methodology in Social Research,* ed. Hubert M. Blalock, Jr., and Ann B. Blalock, chap. 9. New York: McGraw-Hill, 1968.

Rossi, Peter H., and Walter Williams, eds. *Evaluating Social Programs.* New York: Seminar Press, 1972.

Roth, Julius A. "Hired Hand Research," *The American Sociologist* 1:190–96 (Aug. 1966).

Russell, Bertrand. "On the Notion of Cause, with Applications to the Free-Will Problem," *Readings in the Philosophy of Science,* ed. Herbert Feigl and May Brodbeck, pp. 387–407. New York: Appleton-Century-Crofts, 1953.

Ryan, Alan. *The Philosophy of John Stuart Mill.* London: Macmillan, 1970.

Ryder, Norman B. "The Cohort as a Concept in the Study of Social Change," *American Sociological Review* 30:843–61 (Dec. 1965).

Sales, Stephen M. "Threat as a Factor in Authoritarianism: an Analysis of Archival Data," *Journal of Personality and Social Psychology* 28:44–57 (Oct. 1973).

Savage, I. Richard. *Statistics: Uncertainty and Behavior.* Boston: Houghton Mifflin, 1968.

Sawyer, Jack, and Morris F. Friedell. "The Interaction Screen: an Operational Model for Experimentation on Interpersonal Behavior," *Behavioral Science* 10:446–60 (Oct. 1965).

Scheffler, Israel. *The Anatomy of Inquiry.* New York: Alfred A. Knopf, 1963.

———. *Science and Subjectivity.* Indianapolis, Ind.: The Bobbs-Merrill Co., 1967.

Schlesinger, Arthur, Jr. "The Humanist Looks at Empirical Social Research," *American Sociological Review* 27:768–71 (Dec. 1962).

Schmid, Calvin F. "Research Techniques in Human Ecology." *Scientific Social Surveys and Research,* 4th ed., by Pauline V. Young, chap. 14. Englewood Cliffs, N.J.: Prentice-Hall, 1966.

Schwirian, Kent P., and John W. Prehn. "An Axiomatic Theory of Urbanization," *American Sociological Review* 27:812–25 (Dec. 1962).

Scott, Frances Gillespie. "Mail Questionnaires Used in a Study of Older Women," *Sociology and Social Research* 41:281–84 (March 1957).

Scott, W. Richard. "Professionals in Bureaucracies—Areas of Conflict," *Professionalization,* ed. Howard M. Vollmer and Donald L. Mills, pp. 265–75. Englewood Cliffs, N.J.: Prentice-Hall, Inc., 1966.

Scott, William A. "Attitude Measurement," *The Handbook of Social Psychology,* 2d ed., vol. 2, *Research Methods,* ed. Gardner Lindzey and Elliot Aronson, chap. 11. Reading, Mass.: Addison-Wesley, 1968.

Sebald, Hans. "Studying National Character through Comparative Content Analysis," *Social Forces* 40:318–22 (May 1962).

Selltiz, Claire, Marie Jahoda, Morton Deutsch, and Stuart W. Cook. *Research Methods in Social Relations,* rev. ed. New York: Henry Holt and Co., 1959.

Shaw, Clifford R. *The Jack-Roller.* Chicago: University of Chicago Press, 1930.

Sherif, Muzafer. "Group Influences upon the Formation of Norms and Attitudes," *Readings in Social Psychology,* 3d ed., ed. Eleanor E. Maccoby, Theodore M. Newcomb, and Eugene L. Hartley, pp. 219–32. New York: Henry Holt and Co., 1958.

———, **and Carolyn W. Sherif.** *An Outline of Social Psychology,* rev. ed. New York: Harper & Bros., 1956.

Shils, Edward A. "Social Inquiry and the Autonomy of the Individual," *The Human Meaning of the Social Sciences,* ed. Daniel Lerner, pp. 114–157. New York: Meridian Books, 1959.

Shryock, Henry S., and Jacob S. Siegel, and Associates. *The Methods and Materials of Demography,* 2 vols. Washington, D.C.: U.S. Department of Commerce, Bureau of the Census, 1971.

———. *The Methods and Materials of Demography,* condensed edition by Edward G. Stockwell. New York: Academic Press, 1976.

Shure, Gerald H., and Robert J. Meeker. "A Computer-based Experimental Laboratory," *Administrative Science Quarterly* 14:286–93 (June 1969).

Sibley, Elbridge. *The Education of Sociologists in the United States.* New York: Russell Sage Foundation, 1963.

Sidowski, Joseph B., ed. *Experimental Methods and Instrumentation in Psychology.* New York: McGraw-Hill, 1966.

Siegel, Sidney. *Nonparametric Statistics for the Behavioral Sciences.* New York: McGraw-Hill, 1956.

Simon, Herbert A. "A Formal Theory of Interaction in Social Groups," *American Sociological Review* 17:202–11 (April 1952).

———. "On Judging the Plausibility of Theories," *Logic, Methodology and Philosophy of Science III,* ed. B. Van Rootselaar and J. F. Staal, pp. 439–59. Amsterdam: North-Holland Publishing Co., 1968.

Simon, Julian L. *Basic Research Methods in Social Science.* New York: Random House, 1969.

Sjoberg, Gideon, ed. *Ethics, Politics, and Social Research.* Cambridge, Mass.: Schenkman Publishing Co., 1967-a.

———. "Operationalism and Social Research," *Symposium on Sociological Theory,* ed. Llewellyn Gross, chap. 19. Evanston, Ill.: Row, Peterson, 1959.

———. "Project Camelot: Selected Reactions and Personal Reflections," *Ethics, Politics, and Social Research,* ed. Gideon Sjoberg, chap. 6. Cambridge, Mass.: Schenkman Publishing Co., 1967-b.

———, **and Roger Nett.** *A Methodology for Social Research.* New York: Harper & Row, 1968.

Skinner, B. F. "Is a Science of Human Behavior Possible?" *Philosophical Problems of the Social Sciences,* ed. David Braybrooke, pp. 19–26. New York: Macmillan, 1965.

Smart, J. J. C. *Between Science and Philosophy.* New York: Random House, 1968.

Social Science Research Council. "'Basic Research in the Sciences of Behavior': Abridgment of a Chapter in the Report by the Behavioral and Social Sciences Committee," *Social Science Research Council Items* 23:49–54 (Dec. 1969).

Sommer, Robert. *Personal Space.* Englewood Cliffs, N.J.: Prentice-Hall, Inc., 1969.

Sorokin, Pitirim A. *Fads and Foibles in Modern Sociology and Related Sciences.* Chicago: Henry Regnery Co., 1956.

Spiegelman, Mortimer. *Introduction to Demography,* rev. ed. Cambridge, Mass.: Harvard University Press, 1968.

Stephan, Frederick F., and Philip J. McCarthy. *Sampling Opinions.* New York: John Wiley & Sons, 1958.

Stevens, S. S. "Mathematics, Measurement, and Psychophysics," *Handbook of Experimental Psychology,* ed. S. S. Stevens, chap. 1. New York: John Wiley & Sons, 1951.

Stone, Philip J., Dexter C. Dunphy, Marshall S. Smith, and Daniel M. Ogilvia. *The General Inquirer: A Computer Approach to Content Analysis.* Cambridge, Mass.: MIT Press, 1966.

Stouffer, Samuel A. "Some Observations on Study Design," *American Journal of Sociology* 55:355–61 (Jan. 1950).

———, Louis Guttman, Edward A. Suchman, Paul F. Lazarsfeld, Shirley A. Star, and John A. Clausen. *Measurement and Prediction,* vol. 4 of *Studies in Social Psychology in World War II.* Princeton, N.J.: Princeton University Press, 1950.

Strodtbeck, Fred L. "Bales 20 Years Later: A Review Essay," *American Journal of Sociology* 79:459–65 (Sept. 1973).

Struening, Elmer L., and Marcia Guttentag, eds. *Handbook of Evaluation Research, vol. 1.* Beverly Hills, Calif.: Sage Publications, Inc., 1975.

Stycos, J. Mayone. "Sample Surveys for Social Science in Underdeveloped Areas," *Human Organization Research,* ed. Richard N. Adams and Jack J. Preiss, chap. 28. Homewood, Ill.: The Dorsey Press, 1960.

Suchman, Edward A. *Evaluative Research.* New York: Russell Sage Foundation, 1967.

Sudman, Seymour. *Reducing the Cost of Surveys.* Chicago: Aldine Publishing Co., 1967.

Sudnow, David, ed. *Studies in Social Interaction.* New York: The Free Press, 1972.

Taeuber, Irene B. "Population and Society," *Handbook of Modern Sociology,* ed. Robert E. L. Faris, chap. 3. Chicago: Rand McNally & Co., 1964.

TenHouten, Warren D., and Charles D. Kaplan. *Science and Its Mirror Image.* New York: Harper & Row, 1973.

Thomas, William I., and Florian Znaniecki. *The Polish Peasant in Europe and America,* 2 vols. New York: Dover Publications, Inc., 1958.

Thrasher, Frederic M. *The Gang.* Chicago: University of Chicago Press, 1927.

Torgerson, Warren S. "Scaling," *International Encyclopedia of the Social Sciences,* vol. 14, ed. David L. Sills, pp. 25–38. New York: Macmillan Co. and The Free Press, 1968.

———. *Theory and Methods of Scaling.* New York: John Wiley & Sons, 1958.

Upshaw, Harry S. "Attitude Measurement," *Methodology in Social Research,* ed. Hubert M. Blalock, Jr., and Ann B. Blalock, chap. 3. New York: McGraw-Hill, 1968.

Vaughan, Ted R. "Governmental Intervention in Social Research: Political and Ethical Dimensions in the Wichita Jury Recordings," *Ethics, Politics, and Social Research,* ed. Gideon Sjoberg, chap. 3. Cambridge, Mass.: Schenkman Publishing Co., 1967.

Voss, Harwin L. "Pitfalls in Social Research: a Case Study," *The American Sociologist* 1:136–40 (May 1966).

Vroom, Victor, ed. *Methods of Organizational Research.* Pittsburgh: University of Pittsburgh Press, 1967.

Walker, Marshall. *The Nature of Scientific Thought.* Englewood Cliffs, N.J.: Prentice-Hall, Inc., 1963.

Watrous, Blanche, and Francis L. K. Hsu. "An Experiment with TAT," *Psychological Anthropology,* new edition, ed. Francis L. K. Hsu, chap. 8. Cambridge, Mass.: Schenkman Publishing Co., 1972.

Webb, Eugene J., Donald T. Campbell, Richard D. Schwartz, and Lee Sechrest. *Unobtrusive Measures.* Chicago: Rand McNally & Co., 1966.

Weick, Karl E. "Systematic Observational Methods," *The Handbook of Social Psychology,* 2d ed., vol. 2, *Research Methods,* ed. Gardner Lindzey & Elliot Aronson, chap. 13. Reading, Mass.: Addison-Wesley, 1968.

Weiss, Carol H. *Evaluation Research.* Englewood Cliffs, N.J.: Prentice-Hall, Inc., 1972.

Werkmeister, W. H. "Theory Construction and the Problem of Objectivity," *Symposium on Sociological Theory,* ed. Llewellyn Gross, chap. 15. Evanston, Ill.: Row, Peterson, 1959.

Whiting, John W. M. "Methods and Problems in Cross-Cultural Research," *The Handbook of Social Psychology,* 2d ed., vol. 2, *Research Methods,* ed. Gardner Lindzey and Elliot Aronson, chap. 17. Reading, Mass.: Addison-Wesley, 1968.

Whyte, William Foote. "Interviewing in Field Research," *Human Organization Research,* ed. Richard N. Adams and Jack J. Preiss, chap. 27. Homewood, Ill.: The Dorsey Press, 1960.

———. *Street Corner Society,* [2d ed.] Chicago: University of Chicago Press, 1955.

Williams, Robin M., Jr. *American Society,* 3d ed. New York: Alfred A. Knopf, 1970.

———. *The Reduction of Intergroup Tensions.* New York: Social Science Research Council, 1947.

Winchell, Constance M. *Guide to Reference Books,* 8th ed. Chicago: American Library Association, 1967.

Wormser, Margot Haas, and Claire Selltiz. *How to Conduct a Community Self-Survey of Civil Rights.* New York: Association Press, 1951.

Yates, Frank. *Sampling Methods for Censuses and Surveys.* New York: Hafner Publishing Co., 1960.

Yinger, J. Milton, Kiyoshi Ikeda, and Frank Laycock. "Treating Matching as a Variable in a Sociological Experiment," *American Sociological Review* 32:801–12 (Oct. 1967).

Young, Pauline V. *Scientific Social Surveys and Research,* 4th ed. Englewood Cliffs, N.J.: Prentice-Hall, Inc., 1966.

Zeisel, Hans. "The Panel." *Sociological Methods,* ed. Norman K. Denzin, chap. 21. Chicago: Aldine Publishing Co., 1970.

Zelditch, Morris, Jr. "Can You Really Study an Army in the Laboratory?" *A Sociological Reader on Complex Organizations,* 2d ed., ed. Amitai Etzioni, pp. 528–39. New York: Holt, Rinehart & Winston, 1969.

———. "Some Methodological Problems of Field Studies," *American Journal of Sociology* 67:566–76 (March 1962).

———, **and William M. Evan.** "Simulated Bureaucracies: a Methodological Analysis," *Simulation in Social Science,* ed. Harold Guetzkow, chap. 4. Englewood Cliffs, N.J.: Prentice-Hall, Inc., 1962.

Zetterberg, Hans L. *On Theory and Verification in Sociology,* 3d enlarged ed. Totowa, N.J.: The Bedminster Press, 1965.

INDEX

Index

Note: Items in the Bibliography by two or more authors are indexed only by the first author's name.

T

U

V

This book has been set in 11 point and 10 point Caledonia, leaded 2 points. Part numbers are set in 20 point Helvetica Bold and part titles, chapter numbers, and chapter titles are set in 18 point Helvetica Bold. The size of the type page is 27 × 46 picas.